Getting straight "A"s doesn't have to be a mystery...

these practical, concise, and affordable study guides will tell you how!

The Harbrace Guides to

STUDENT SUCCESS

from Harcourt Brace Canada

D1364752

CHILDREN at the Centre

PRINCIPLES OF EARLY CHILDHOOD EDUCATION IN CANADA

Janet Blaxall
Fanshawe College

Kenise Murphy Kilbride
Ryerson Polytechnic University

Donna McKenna
Conestoga College

Carolyn Warberg
Centennial College

Marilynn Yeates
St. Lawrence College

HARCOURT
BRACE
CANADA

Harcourt Brace & Company, Canada
Toronto   Montreal   Fort Worth   New York   Orlando   Philadelphia
San Diego   London   Sydney   Tokyo

Canadian Cataloguing in Publication Data

Main entry under title:

Children at the centre : principles of early
   childhood education in Canada

Includes index.
ISBN 0-7747-3235-0

1. Early childhood education — Canada.
I. Blaxall, Janet

LB1139.3.C3C55 1996   372.21'0971   C95-931829-1

Publisher: Heather McWhinney
Acquisitions Editor: Joanna Cotton
Projects Manager: Liz Radojkovic
Developmental Editor: Laura Paterson Pratt
Director of Publishing Services: Jean Davies
Editorial Manager: Marcel Chiera
Supervising Editor: Semareh Al-Hillal
Production Manager: Sue-Ann Becker
Production Co-ordinator: Sheila Barry
Copy Editor: Claudia Kutchukian
Cover and Interior Design: Avril Orloff
Typesetting and Assembly: Pixel Graphics Inc.
Printing and Binding: Edwards Brothers Incorporated

Cover Art: A painting by Brittany Ber, age 4.

This book was printed in the United States of America.

1 2 3 4 5   00 99 98 97 96

PREFACE

As Canadian early childhood educators, we find our field in a state of transition. Early childhood education is evolving and expanding as more parents are involved in the work force and more children enter early childhood education programs. Schools are expanding their mandates to include younger children. The range of ages and needs of the children we work with is widening, the needs of families are becoming more diverse, and the expectations of the community are increasing. As we find our way amidst these transitions, it is essential that we understand the foundations of early childhood education, both in the traditions that we hold dear and in the framework of current philosophy, knowledge, and practice.

Children at the Centre: Principles of Early Childhood Education in Canada was written to present and clarify the principles of early childhood education from a Canadian perspective for a Canadian audience of current and beginning early childhood educators and other professionals who will work closely with young children. *Children at the Centre* is a comprehensive overview of all aspects of early childhood education, integrating theory and appropriate practice for implementing all major components of the early childhood curriculum.

Philosophy of This Book

The primary focus of early childhood education is the children. We have written this book to reflect the child's perspective and the child's experiences within early education. Throughout *Children at the Centre*, we use theories to give insight into children's perceptions and to describe the characteristics that influence how young children learn and make sense of the world. When suggesting approaches or strategies, these are presented from a perspective of what is best for the children in terms of their development and interpersonal relationships.

Children at the Centre is not a traditional methods textbook in the sense that curriculum content and teaching techniques are not the primary emphases. The focus is on understanding the process of learning and development, and on understanding the role of the educator in facilitating this process. Curriculum content and activities are presented to illustrate the process and to demonstrate the types of learning experiences that best facilitate children's learning.

When children are the focus, the role of the educator is two-fold: to build relationships with children, and to design a child-centred curriculum that enhances the natural processes of development and learning.

RELATIONSHIPS AS THE FOUNDATION

All young children depend on caring relationships with trusted adults and thrive when they experience the support of educators who are sensitive and nurturing. The importance of these early relationships cannot be overemphasized — interpersonal relationships are the foundation of early childhood education. The most important role of the educator is to become a partner in a relationship that supports the natural process of development. The absence of warm, meaningful relationships has a negative impact on all areas of children's development. Building meaningful relationships with all children means accepting and having respect for diversity of culture, family, ability, and background.

THE CURRICULUM APPROACH

A meaningful curriculum for young children is child-centred and is created from an understanding of the child's characteristics and needs. A child-centred approach begins with an awareness and understanding of each child's experience and provides what each child needs to grow and develop. Observation is crucial to understanding children's individual abilities.

Because children are active learners, the curriculum is play-based and child-directed. Educators provide a rich learning environment and play a supportive role through their interactions. The ECE curriculum is continually adapted to be responsive to the capabilities and needs of the children in the group at that particular time, using observation as a basis for planning dynamic and meaningful learning experiences.

Content and Organization

Children at the Centre begins by considering the people who are involved in an early childhood education setting (the children, their families, and the educators themselves), emphasizing the importance of respect for and understanding of others, as well as self-awareness and self-development. To better understand young children, we include an overview of developmental

processes and issues in the early years, and guide students in strategies to observe the milestones and characteristics of each area of development.

Next we consider the interpersonal relationships within an early childhood setting that are essential to creating an environment where children feel safe, secure, valued, and respected. At a time of life when young children are highly dependent on the emotional support of adults, these relationships are the foundation of quality early childhood education, and thus are the focus of a number of chapters in this book.

Recognizing emotional development as a foundation and beginning point for children's development and well-being, we consider how adults influence the child's self-concept and self-esteem. Caring relationships are seen as the key to achieving emotional milestones, positive self-concept, self-discipline, and social skills.

In Parts 3 and 4, we define principles for designing a child-centred environment and curriculum based on principles of early education, as well as an understanding of child development and individual diversity. The early childhood curriculum integrates and enhances creative, motor, sensory, language, literacy, and cognitive development through the natural, child-directed processes of exploration and play. The early childhood educator is a vital partner in supporting and facilitating learning and development.

The final chapter identifies some of the factors that place young children at risk and challenges early childhood educators to make a personal commitment to ensuring the quality and security of childhood for all children.

Features of Each Chapter

Each chapter begins with an overview of the content and a set of objectives that describe what students will learn. Throughout each chapter, anecdotes, examples, and suggestions help readers understand the educator's role in all areas of the curriculum.

Understanding why we choose certain curriculum approaches is as important as knowing what the best choices are. Thus, throughout each chapter, we discuss relevant theory and developmental issues as the basis for current and preferred practice. Guiding principles and practical strategies are covered in the text and highlighted in boxed material.

At the conclusion of each chapter, review questions assist students to assess their understanding. Discussion questions are designed to stimulate debate and exploration of personal values, beliefs, and philosophy, and to lead students to see the issues facing early childhood educators within the context of educational and social trends. A variety of learning activities, often involving observing children or implementing recommended practice, are suggested.

Further reading is encouraged through the inclusion of an annotated reading list at the end of each chapter, which provides suggestions for obtaining additional information on related theory and practice.

Instructor's Manual

An Instructor's Manual is available to help instructors make full use of *Children at the Centre*. We have compiled the overviews, objectives, review questions, discussion questions, and activities, and we have annotated the activities with suggested variations. New activities have been added, as well as audio-visual recommendations, class projects, transparency masters, and a glossary. We have also created a quiz for each chapter that can be photocopied and distributed

to students. Many of the items in the Instructor's Manual are class-tested favourites sent to us by the contributors to *Children at the Centre.*

ACKNOWLEDGEMENTS

This textbook has been made possible only through the work of a great many people, including the original authors who had a vision of a Canadian textbook for early childhood education, and many people who authored the individual chapters. The insights of several reviewers and editors enabled us to create a clearly articulated and Canadian perspective on early childhood education: Kevin Bisback, Algonquin College; Marie Goulet, George Brown College; Robin Krantz, Northern Lights College; Pat McKenzie, Vancouver Community College; Donna Morrison, Red Deer College; and Goranka Vukelich, Mohawk College.

The strong and clear image of early childhood education in this text results, to a significant degree, from the input of Marian Warwick, who consistently advocated a child-centred focus. Her view of early childhood education as a blend of sensitivity to the needs of children and an awareness of the theoretical foundations of child-centred education supported the final approach to curriculum design found in the various chapters.

Jane Lind, whose intuitive understanding of human development was invaluable, rewrote the chapters to create a consistent style and presentation from the voices of the many individual contributors. Her commitment to the completion of this project was infectious, and her encouragement kept our work on target.

We also wish to express appreciation to Connie Kenwell and Arbour Glen Day Nursery for the use of their facilities to take photographs. Also to Leah Blaxall, Julia Warwick, Trevor Warwick, Luke MacDonald, Alina Newton, Hannah Kenwell, and Blake Kenwell for participating in some of the photographed activities.

No book of this nature would be complete without acknowledging the children who have influenced our thinking and enriched our lives. Some of these children are members of our own families and dear to our hearts. Others are children we have known and cared for throughout our careers. We have been inspired and moved by the unique and special qualities of each of them. We have been humbled by and truly admire the insight, determination, and accomplishments of many children whose lives are not yet five years in length. To these and all children, we dedicate this book,

as we resolve to keep children at the centre of early childhood education.

A Note from the Publisher

Thank you for selecting *Children at the Centre: Principles of Early Childhood Education in Canada*, by Janet Blaxall, Kenise Murphy Kilbride, Donna McKenna, Carolyn Warberg, and Marilynn Yeates. The authors and publisher have devoted considerable time to the careful development of this book. We appreciate your recognition of this effort and accomplishment.

We want to hear what you think about *Children at the Centre*. Please take a few minutes to fill in the stamped reader reply card at the back of the book. Your comments and suggestions will be valuable to us as we prepare new editions and other books.

CONTRIBUTORS

Jane Edmonds Barken	St. Lawrence College
Maureen Cech	Algonquin College
Karen Chandler	George Brown College
Sylvia C. Chard	University of Alberta
Lou Dyck	Conestoga College
Debbie Frank-Macdonald	Conestoga College
Judith Gilles	Toronto Board of Education
Jennifer Hardacre	Institute of Child Study
Annette LaGrange	University of Calgary
Wendy Mitchell	St. Lawrence College
Marcia Moshé	Ryerson Polytechnic University
Barbara Park	Queen's University
June Pollard	Ryerson Polytechnic University
Lawrence Prochner	Ryerson Polytechnic University
Malcolm Read	Red Deer College
Monique Richard	Ryerson Polytechnic University
Marian Warwick	Fanshawe College
Sue Wells	Centennial College
Connie Winder	George Brown College
Gary Woodill	Ryerson Polytechnic University

Brief Contents

PART 1   The People Who Matter   1

CHAPTER 1   The Children   3
CHAPTER 2   The Families   15
CHAPTER 3   The Early Childhood Educators   36

PART 2   Focussing on Relationships   59

CHAPTER 4   Understanding Children's Development   61
CHAPTER 5   Observing the Development of Young Children   80
CHAPTER 6   Facilitating Emotional Development   111
CHAPTER 7   Supporting Children's Self-Concept   141
CHAPTER 8   Guiding Children's Behaviour   167

PART 3   Setting the Stage for Learning   191

CHAPTER 9   Designing an Environment for Children   193
CHAPTER 10   Designing a Curriculum   216

PART 4   The Learning Environment   247

CHAPTER 11   Nurturing Children's Creativity   249
CHAPTER 12   Facilitating Motor and Sensory Development   271
CHAPTER 13   Enhancing Language and Literacy Development   297
CHAPTER 14   Supporting Cognitive Development   328

PART 5   History and Visions   357

CHAPTER 15   Early Childhood Education: Heritage and Vision   359

APPENDIX   Bibliographies of High-Quality Children's Books   385

             PHOTO CREDITS   387
             NAME INDEX   388
             SUBJECT INDEX   390

Contents

PART 1 THE PEOPLE WHO MATTER   1

CHAPTER 1 THE CHILDREN   3
Overview   4
The Enchanted Years   4
Views of Childhood   4
Understanding Children   5
  The World through a Child's Eyes   6
Celebrating Diversity   6
Children at Risk   8
Making a Difference in the Lives of
  Children   9
Education in the Spotlight   10
Quality in Early Childhood Education   11
  What Is "High Quality"?   11
  The Need for Expertise   11
Supporting Children's Development:
  Shaping the World   12
  *Education in Canada: A Special
  Commitment*   12
Summary   13
Review Questions   13
Discussion Questions   13
Activities   14
Further Reading   14
References   14

CHAPTER 2 THE FAMILIES   15
Overview   16
Changing Families   16
  The Make-up of Families   16
  Cultural Diversity   18

Economic Forces   20
  Economic Status   20
  Changes in the Employment Picture   20
Influences in the Lives of Children   22
  Mothers in the Work Force   23
  The Impact of Family Breakup   25
  Child Abuse and Family Violence   26
  The Impact of Television   28
Summary   32
Review Questions   32
Discussion Questions   32
Activities   32
Further Reading   33
References   34

CHAPTER 3 THE EARLY CHILDHOOD EDUCATORS   36
Overview   37
On Becoming an Early Childhood
  Educator   38
Understanding Yourself   38
  The Influence of Your Experiences   38
  Nurturing Yourself   39
Developing a Philosophy of Early
  Childhood Education   40
  The Influence of Theories   40
  Your Educational Experiences   43
Reflective Practice   43
Understanding the Roles of Early
  Childhood Educators   44
  *The Early Childhood Educator as
  Care-Giver*   44

Caring for Children 45
Communicating with and
    Supporting Children 45
Supporting Families 46
Curriculum Design and
    Implementation 47
Responding to Your Community 49
Entering the Profession 50
Responsibilities 50
Rights 52
Managing Stress 53
Joining Others in the Profession 54
Summary 55
Review Questions 56
Discussion Questions 56
Activities 56
Further Reading 56
References 57

PART 2 FOCUSSING ON RELATIONSHIPS 59

CHAPTER 4 UNDERSTANDING
CHILDREN'S DEVELOPMENT 61
Overview 62
A Developmental Foundation 62
Why Study Development? 64
Building Supportive Relationships 64
Planning the Early Childhood
    Curriculum 65
Processes of Development 65
Temperament 65
Emotional Development 66
Social Development 69
Communication and Language
    Development 70
Cognitive Development 72

Physical Development 73
Play Patterns 73
Diversity in Development 75
Recognizing Developmental
    Diversity 75
Recognizing Diversity of Experience 76
Summary 77
Review Questions 78
Discussion Questions 78
Activities 78
Further Reading 78
References 79

CHAPTER 5 OBSERVING THE
DEVELOPMENT OF YOUNG CHILDREN 80
Overview 82
Why Observation Is Valuable 82
Understanding Patterns and Diversity
    in Development 83
Understanding Children's Behaviour 84
Recognizing the Need for
    Intervention 84
Planning the Child-Centred
    Curriculum 85
Appreciating Children 85
The Process of Observation 85
Objectivity in Observation 86
Techniques for Observation 87
Anecdotal Record 87
Running Record 89
Event Sampling 91
Time Sampling 91
Rating Scale 92
Checklist 93
Play Interview 94
Additional Techniques 95

What You Should Observe 96
Emotional Development and Coping 96
Social Development and Play Patterns 96
Communication and Language 99
Cognitive Development and Learning 99
Physical Well-Being and Motor
Development 100
Behaviour 100
Interpreting Development from
Observational Information 101
Recognizing Developmental
Achievements 101
Identifying Strengths and Needs 102
Identifying Concerns 103
Using Observational Data 103
Communicating Your Findings 104
Recording Observations 104
Confidentiality of Records 104
Discussing Assessments with
Colleagues 104
Discussing Assessments with
Family Members 105
Discussing Assessments with Children 106
Summary 107
Review Questions 108
Discussion Questions 108
Activities 108
Further Reading 109
Additional Resources 109
References 109

CHAPTER 6 FACILITATING
EMOTIONAL DEVELOPMENT **III**
Overview 113
Emotional Well-Being 113
Milestones of Emotional Development 114
A Sense of Security 115
Forming Relationships 119
Communicating Effectively 120

Developing a Sense of Self 122
Creating Emotional Ideas 123
Emotional Thinking: Fantasy,
Reality, and Self-Esteem 125
Supporting Emotional Well-Being 125
Floor Time: The Importance of
Interactive Play 127
Linking Social and Emotional
Development 128
Development of Social Skills 129
Educators as Models 130
Coaching Social Skills 130
Nurturing Socioemotional Development 131
The Self 132
Family 133
Friends 134
The Community 135
Canadian Society 136
Global Concerns 136
Summary 137
Review Questions 138
Discussion Questions 138
Activities 138
Further Reading 138
Additional Resources 139
References 139

CHAPTER 7 SUPPORTING
CHILDREN'S SELF-CONCEPT **141**
Overview 143
What Is Self-Concept? 143
Theoretical Perspectives on
Self-Concept 144
Carl Rogers 145
Erik Erikson 145
Supporting Self-Concept in the
Early Years 149
The Importance of Trust 149
The Importance of Autonomy 149

Initiative and Risk Taking   150

A Sense of Identity   151

Gender Identity   152

Race, Culture, and Identity   153

Identification with Others   154

Mastery, Competence, and Self-Concept   155

Self-Esteem   156

Acceptance and Affirmation   156

Admiration and Encouragement   157

Social Competence and Peer Acceptance   158

Observing Children's Development of

    Self-Concept   160

Play and Self-Concept   160

Signs of Positive Self-Concept   161

Signs of Negative Self-Concept   162

Changes in Behaviour   162

Summary   164

Review Questions   165

Discussion Questions   165

Activities   165

Further Reading   165

References   166

CHAPTER 8 GUIDING CHILDREN'S
BEHAVIOUR   **167**

Overview   168

The Guidance Relationship   168

Understanding Children's Behaviour   169

Personal Attitudes and Values   170

Building the Guidance Relationship   171

Goals for the Guidance Relationship   172

The Guidance Process   173

Clarifying the Terms   173

Setting Limits   174

The Language of Guidance   177

Verbal Techniques   177

Nonverbal Techniques   179

Guidance Techniques   180

Indirect Guidance Techniques   180

Direct Guidance Techniques   182

Summary   188

Review Questions   188

Discussion Questions   188

Activities   189

Further Reading   189

References   190

PART 3   SETTING THE STAGE FOR LEARNING   191

CHAPTER 9 DESIGNING AN
ENVIRONMENT FOR CHILDREN   **193**

Overview   194

The Early Childhood Environment   194

Guiding Principles   195

Developmental Considerations   195

Creating a Positive Atmosphere   196

An Environment for Play   196

Indoor Play Space   197

Open and Private Space   197

Learning Centres   197

Play Units   201

Factors Affecting Arrangement of Space   202

Outdoor Play Space   203

Arranging Outdoor Space   203

Outdoor Zones   204

Outdoor Equipment and Facilities   205

Observing and Evaluating the Early

    Childhood Environment   206

Ensuring Safety   207

Scheduling   207

Nutrition   212

Summary   213

Review Questions   214

Discussion Questions   214

Activities   214

Further Reading   214

References   215

CHAPTER 10 DESIGNING A
CURRICULUM **216**
Overview 218
A Portrait of Early Childhood
    Curriculum 219
A Curriculum for All Children 220
    Reflecting Cultural Diversity 220
    Reflecting Diversity of Individuals 223
    Reflecting Diversity in Development 224
A Curriculum for the Whole Child 225
    A Comprehensive Curriculum 225
    Safeguarding the Qualities of
    Childhood 227
A Developmentally Appropriate
    Curriculum 227
    Planning for Individual Children 228
    The Influence of Piaget 229
    The Risk of Miseducation 230
A Curriculum Based on Play 231
    Constructivist Theory 231
    What Do We Mean by Play? 231
    Developing through Play 232
    Learning through Play 233
    Characteristics of a Play-Based
    Curriculum 234
Making Decisions about the Curriculum 235
    Responding to the Community 236
    Consulting with Children and Parents 236
    Legislative Requirements 236
The Emergent Curriculum 237
Observing and Evaluating the
    Curriculum 239
    Ongoing Observation 239
    Curriculum Evaluation 240
    Personal Reflection 241

Summary 242
Review Questions 242
Discussion Questions 243
Activities 243
Further Reading 243
References 244

PART 4 THE LEARNING ENVIRONMENT 247

CHAPTER 11 NURTURING CHILDREN'S
CREATIVITY **249**
Overview 251
What Is Creativity? 252
How Creativity Develops 252
    The Senses 253
    Emotional Development 253
    Cognitive Development 254
    Physical Development 254
Culture and Creativity 255
Observing Creativity 256
Approaches for Nurturing Creativity 257
    Creativity and Play 258
    Creative Programming 258
    A Rich Environment 258
    The Process Approach 259
Creative Art 260
    The Link between Language and Art 261
    The Link between Cognition and
    Art 261
    The Creative Centre 263
    Art Experiences 263
Music 264
Creative Movement 265
    Body Awareness 265
    Creative Visualization 265

Making Space   266
Linking Art, Music, and Creative
  Movement   267
Linking Language, Creativity, and
  Discovery   267
Summary   268
Review Questions   268
Discussion Questions   268
Activities   269
Further Reading   269
References   269

CHAPTER 12 FACILITATING MOTOR
AND SENSORY DEVELOPMENT   **271**
Overview   272
Stages in Motor and Sensory
  Development   272
  Motor Development   273
  Sensory Development   274
  Special Conditions   277
Cultural Factors in Motor and Sensory
  Development   277
  Environment   278
  Sex Differences   278
Observing Motor and Sensory
  Development   278
A Learning Environment for Motor
  and Sensory Development   279
  Balancing Challenge and Mastery   282
  Encouraging Exploration   283
  Supporting Emotional Well-Being   284
Learning Centres   285
  Large-Muscle Activities   285
  Enhancing Physical Well-Being   285
  Small-Muscle Activities   290

Sensory Experiences   291
Summary   291
Review Questions   293
Discussion Questions   293
Activities   294
Further Reading   294
Additional Resources   295
References   296

CHAPTER 13 ENHANCING LANGUAGE
AND LITERACY DEVELOPMENT   **297**
Overview   299
Communication and Language   299
  Dimensions of Language   300
Development of Language   300
  *A Developmental Sequence for
    Language*   300
  Influences on Language Development   303
Supporting Language Development   305
  Conversations with Children   306
  Language in Social Interactions   308
Language throughout the Curriculum   309
  Music   309
  Finger Plays   309
  Children's Literature   309
Emerging Literacy   311
  Development of Reading   312
  Development of Writing   313
Setting the Stage for Literacy   314
  Principles and Practice   314
  Linking Literature and Literacy   316
  The Benefits of Literature   317
  Sharing Literature with Children   317
  Linking Play and Literacy   320
  Encouraging Writing   321

Summary	322
Review Questions	322
Discussion Questions	322
Activities	322
Further Reading	323
Additional Resources	324
Children's Books Cited	325
References	325

CHAPTER 14 SUPPORTING COGNITIVE
DEVELOPMENT **328**

Overview	330
What Is Cognition?	331
Theories of Cognitive Development	332
Jean Piaget	332
Lev Vygotsky	335
Educational Perspectives	335
Maria Montessori	335
Constructivist Theory	336
Influences on Cognitive Development	338
Culture	338
Experiential Diversity	339
Developmental Diversity	339
Diversity of Learning Styles	340
Gender	341
Observing Cognitive Development	343
Cognition and Play	343
Cognition and Language	343
A Curriculum for Cognitive Development	344
The Importance of Play	344
The Learning Environment	345
The Role of the Educator	345
Components in the Cognitive Curriculum	347
Natural Science	347
Mathematics	350
Computer Skills	351

Summary	353
Review Questions	353
Discussion Questions	353
Activities	353
Further Reading	354
References	355

PART 5 HISTORY AND VISIONS **357**

CHAPTER 15 EARLY CHILDHOOD
EDUCATION: HERITAGE AND VISION **359**

Overview	361
The Evolution of Child Care and Early Childhood Education	361
The European Beginnings	362
Day Care in Canada, 1850 to 1950	363
Increasing Interest in Child Development and Educational Practices	364
Early Childhood Care and Education in Canada, 1960s to 1980s	365
Early Childhood Care and Education in Canada in the 1990s	367
What Is the Legislation?	367
Who Provides Funding?	368
What Is the Administrative Structure?	368
What Are the Types of Care?	368
Who Provides the Care, and Where?	373
Current Issues	374
Into the Twenty-First Century	375
Families and Children at Risk	375
Visions for Early Childhood Education	377
Supporting Children	377
Supporting Families	378

Ensuring Quality Educational
   Experiences   *378*
Beliefs in Action   *379*
Summary   380
Discussion Questions   380
Activities   380
Notes   381
Further Reading   381
References   382

APPENDIX BIBLIOGRAPHIES OF
HIGH-QUALITY CHILDREN'S BOOKS   **385**

PHOTO CREDITS   **387**

NAME INDEX   **388**

SUBJECT INDEX   **390**

PART 1
The People who Matter

A career in early childhood education centres around children, recognizing and enjoying the special characteristics of young children, and responding to the needs and vulnerabilities that are a part of the early years of life. A career in early childhood education also focusses on families, recognizing the prime importance of the family in the lives of children, and supporting families in the important job of raising and caring for their young children.

As you begin the process of becoming an early childhood educator and prepare for your various roles with children and families, you will learn much about yourself. You will explore your own values and beliefs, and discover the shared beliefs that are the foundation of the profession of early childhood educator.

Early childhood educators develop interrelationships with children, with families, and with other educators, relationships that are mutually beneficial and that support the development of young Canadian children.

CHAPTER 1
The Children

- Overview
- The Enchanted Years
- Views of Childhood
- Understanding Children
  - The World through a Child's Eyes
- Celebrating Diversity
- Children at Risk
- Making a Difference in the Lives of Children
- Education in the Spotlight
- Quality in Early Childhood Education
  - What Is "High Quality"?
  - The Need for Expertise

- Supporting Children's Development: Shaping the World
  - Education in Canada: A Special Commitment
- Summary
- Review Questions
- Discussion Questions
- Activities
- Further Reading
- References

OVERVIEW

This book is about children and the adults who interact with them, care for them, and nurture them in the process of learning and developing. Most of the book discusses the current state of knowledge, research, and theory about the way children develop and the way adults can best support this process.

To set the stage and to start you thinking about the children with whom you will spend many years of your life, we first offer these images of childhood.

THE ENCHANTED YEARS

There are no big or little events to the two-year-old, all is breathless excitement, awe and wonder.
— *Pearce 1968, p. 116*

"The child, roughing in a world knowledge, wanders without rhyme or reason, and he plays. He has no goals other than the moment, and no other time exists" (Pearce 1980, p. 123). We often envy the spontaneity of childhood, a time that seems carefree and natural. All of us, regardless of age, benefit when there is time to wander without rhyme or reason.

"He knows only one world and that is the very real one in which and with which he plays" (Pearce 1980, p. 169). Imagine a child rolling down a hill, splashing through puddles, or running barefoot through the grass. Picture the same child stirring cookies in the sandbox, creating a castle from blocks, or rocking a favourite teddy bear. The world of play is enchanting and the adults who are invited in are fortunate indeed. "The fun, the playfulness of childhood is a legacy that reaps rich rewards forever" (LeShan 1968, p. 333).

VIEWS OF CHILDHOOD

Throughout history, children have been portrayed as angels and cherubs or viewed as exasperating parasites, nurtured or abused as societies dictated. Not so long ago, educators believed that children were born as "blank slates," open to whatever learning we chose for them. Since the beginning of the twentieth century, much study and thinking has occurred in response to questions about the nature of the child. As we have observed and studied children, we have come to realize the complexity and diversity of characteristics and influences that shape their lives. We have also become increasingly aware that the way children experience early childhood significantly affects the people they will be in later years.

Margaret Mead and Rhoda Metraux studied children across cultures in efforts to understand the experiences of children. They suggest that one of the great accomplishments of our century is the discovery of the nature of childhood, the early efforts of children to actively shape their own lives, and the many different ways we can use these discoveries to build meaningful relationships with children (1993).

Through the process of coming to recognize childhood as a distinct stage, we have also come to recognize its unique qualities. "Nature wants children to be children before they are [women and] men. ... Childhood has ways of seeing, thinking and feeling peculiar to itself. Nothing can be more foolish than to substitute our ways for them" (Jean Jacques Rousseau, in LeShan 1968, p. 326).

"The child's need is to be a child" (Pearce 1980, p. 137). Pearce reminds us to respect the children's needs and perceptions as valid, and to resist expecting them to give up their own understanding. To expect children to accept adult realities too soon is a form of psychological abandonment that creates stress for young children. The adult should join and support children in their own reality, affirming for children "the significance of childhood" (LeShan 1968).

"What is sacred about childhood is that it is the beginning, the essence of human life, the potential and the promise of individual uniqueness, which we cannot predict and which we therefore must not try to harness" (LeShan 1968, p. 325).

The message of each of these people is to ask us to respect and value childhood for the children. Rooted in the experiences of childhood are the values, attitudes, and capabilities for the human community in the future.

UNDERSTANDING CHILDREN

It was late October in Veena's first term of her college course in early childhood education.

One morning on her way to class, she happened to meet her instructor and they walked the rest of the way together. When her instructor asked Veena if she was enjoying school, Veena replied, "Yes, but I thought we'd be doing more work with the children — not so much head work. Do we really need all this stuff about child development? I mean, I went into this because I love being with kids."

Her instructor smiled. "I can understand that, but I wonder if anything has come up in class so far that 'grabbed' you?"

"Well, when we were talking about toddlers I was surprised to hear you say that it's healthy for little kids to say 'no' to their parents. When I was baby-sitting my little cousin, I thought he was just being contrary when he kicked up a big fuss and yelled 'No!' at nap time."

"So do you still think he was just being contrary?"

Veena replied, "Well, from what you said about kids' need for autonomy at that age, I guess I can see that he was just trying to — well, be more independent, not just always doing what we told him to. I guess being annoyed and trying to clamp down on him makes no sense because a kid is doing what he has to do to grow up."

Her instructor chuckled and said, "Right, so I'll take a chance — what does that say to you about studying child development?"

Veena grinned. "Okay, you got me! I guess it's saying that learning about child development means understanding behaviour that just seemed annoying before. If we get mad and yell at kids for doing those things, it's like punishing them for growing up."

"That's a good way of putting it," commented her instructor.

As Veena discovered, the danger of not knowing about how children grow and develop is that the behaviour one can expect at the various stages comes as a surprise, and often an unpleasant one, like the tantrums of a 2-year-old. Not knowing that the behaviour is normal and healthy, some adults do indeed punish the child for growing up, as Veena puts it. Punishment for natural development is hard on the child and causes a lot of confusion and resentment.

As the year progressed, Veena became more and more interested in the many facets of children's development. She began feeling happy that she would have many opportunities to share with children their unique perspective on life.

The World through a Child's Eyes

Lucia's mother, who has always picked Lucia up after nursery school, has a new job, so she made car-pooling arrangements for the days she cannot get to the school on time. Lucia likes the other parents and children with whom she will be travelling, so on the first day of the new arrangement the teacher does not anticipate that Lucia will object. She says to Lucia, "Well, this should be fun for you — you're going home in the car pool with Riccardo and Elizabeth today," and is taken aback when Lucia scowls and walks away. As the morning passes, Lucia becomes more and more agitated and irritable. Finally, when the children are preparing to go home, Lucia bursts into tears, and again the teacher is puzzled.

"Oh, Lucia," says her teacher, hugging her, "What is the matter? Elizabeth's mom is the driver for the car pool today. She will take you home to your mother."

Through her sobs, Lucia wails, "But I don't know how to swim!"

It is unfortunate that most of us, as adults, develop a kind of amnesia about how the world seemed to us as children. We forget the fear and wonder, the confusion and amazement we felt when we were little and the world was so big and strange. We forget, and assume that children understand the meaning of what we say.

Lucia's experience is only one example of how the world appears to a child. The best educators are those who not only know a lot about child development, but who also are in tune with children and who are sensitive to the way children see the world.

CELEBRATING DIVERSITY

If you were to take an average group of about 20 youngsters, all 5 years old and all born on the same day, and lined them up in a row, the first thing you would likely notice is how much they differed in height. Some might be as much as 8 or 12 cm taller than others! And that would be just the beginning of the developmental differences you would see. In every area of development, there is great variation from one child to the next. Most of that variation is well within the range of what is considered "normal."

For example, 4-year-old Joel paints recognizable human figures, houses, and trees. His best pal, Eric, spins terrific stories about his paintings which, to adults, are just blobs of colour. These boys are both normal for their age. Fifa knows that a group of seven buttons is still seven buttons even if you change their arrangement. Her best friend, Bo Lin, thinks that if you spread out the seven buttons in a longer line, you have more. These two girls are both normal for their age. Leslie can decode a few short phrases in print, like "I see Mom" and "I like you," while for Leo, reading is

BOX 1.1 THE DEVELOPING CHILD

"Let me be how *I* grow" is the protest one child shared with her parents (LeShan 1968). Children's "intrinsic possibilities are there when they are born. ... Permit the child to unfold himself" (LeShan 1968, p. 325). Recognize, respect, and care for the children as they are, without pressure to be what you think they should be. This requires trust in children's inherent qualities and faith that, with your support and encouragement, they will grow to be the best that they can be.

looking at pictures in books and making up a story to go with them. These children are also normal for their age.

Many factors influence developmental diversity. Some are inherited, like the tendency to be tall or short, big-boned or fine-boned. Some are congenital — caused by some event during pregnancy — such as low birth weight resulting from inadequate nutrition. Others are perinatal — caused by something that occurred during birth — such as some degree of learning difficulty related to a lack of oxygen to the brain at birth. Still other differences have to do with environment; if there are chemicals in the atmosphere or water, there can be health and learning consequences. Upbringing and culture have an influence, too. Children whose parents read to them and have lots of books and magazines in their home are often more advanced in reading ability than children from homes in which no one reads much. A child from a culture that values independence may be adept at dressing herself sooner than a child from a culture in which parents look after such needs for a longer time.

An error that anyone can fall into, but which can seriously interfere with our effectiveness as early childhood educators, is to assume that the way we do things is the way everyone does things. Or *should* do things.

Our assumptions about how things are or should be done are formed in our childhood by our families and our cultures. These assumptions include everything from the preferred way to eat to what it means to be an "adult." As children, we took these assumptions as unquestioned universal truths. Our first inkling that they were not perhaps occurred when we first went to a friend's home for supper and discovered that his or her family held their knives and forks differently from the way our family did, or perhaps used chopsticks.

As professional early childhood educators, we must keep in mind that the youngsters we deal with are from many very different family backgrounds and cultures whose ideas about how things are, or ought to be, done can be very different from ours. We may be surprised and puzzled by those differences.

Let's take a look at something that typically happens in early childhood programs — encouraging children and, specifically, teaching them to dress themselves. Why do we do this? Because in North American culture it is assumed that as children grow, they should become more and more independent. It is expected that in adulthood, they will leave their birth family and set up households of their own. Independence and separation from the birth family are considered the hallmarks of adulthood. Learning to dress yourself — sooner rather than later — is regarded as a natural step toward this goal.

However, in some cultures, becoming independent and leaving the family is not a prime goal of child rearing. Interdependence within the family is much more important. It is expected that adult children will stay with their birth family when married, or join their spouse's family, to form a large, extended family whose members collaborate with and depend on one another for their livelihood, perhaps in farming, small-scale manufacturing, or retailing. When a child from this culture comes to your centre, you might be surprised to see that Mother still dresses and undresses him or her, even though the child is 5, 6, or 7 years old. The mother in turn will be dismayed if you insist that the child must learn to dress and undress "independently," because this requirement is in direct contradiction to her deeply held cultural values.

This is just one example of how cultural assumptions can clash. There are others. For instance, in North America, we expect people to look each other in the eye when conversing. But in many cultures doing so is rude, especially when children talk to an adult. As another example, take assertiveness. North Americans value a certain amount of forthrightness in youngsters, but in many cultures this is not desirable, particularly in girls. And we may cause great stress for some Native Canadian children when we create learning experiences that include competing with one another to get the answer or to be "the best." In many cultures, co-operation and group consensus are more highly valued than individual striving and success, where one wins and everyone else loses.

So you can see that recognizing and respecting cultural diversity means much more than just admiring the costumes and music of different ethnic groups or sampling "exotic" foods from other countries. Respecting cultural diversity requires that all of us carefully examine our own assumptions about child rearing, family life, and what growing up means. Then we must truly open ourselves to listen to people from other cultures, and make an effort to see things from their point of view. We might not always agree, and perhaps we will not always understand, but we can try. This expanded understanding enables us to work with families to provide their children with programs and experiences that reflect sensitivity and respect for the shared humanity of all of us.

Early childhood educators expect to see a great deal of diversity, both developmental and in the children's background, and they make sure that their programs accommodate those differences. Although educators have clear goals for youngsters, they do not expect all the children to be ready for certain experiences at the same time, or to reach certain goals within the same time-frame. Educators include a wide variety of activities and experiences in their programs so that every child can experience meaning, challenge, and success. They show that they expect, accept, and value all aspects of diversity.

CHILDREN AT RISK

Our images of childhood have created a picture of a peaceful and enchanting time for children. The unhappy truth is that this is not the experience of many Canadian children. We must not lose sight of the children whose well-being is at risk. Increasingly in recent years, younger children are experiencing stress, high anxiety, depression, anger, and alienation. Those of us who work with and care about children must be aware of their

unhappiness and try to alleviate the sources of stress in their lives.

Where does this stress come from? For the most part, children react to the same sources of stress that adults do — pressures to do too much in the course of the day, to hurry from place to place, and to meet seemingly impossible demands. Adults should plan and structure the lives of children in a way that allows them to move at a comfortable pace, and to provide a sense of calm, predictability, and security.

Many of the pressures on children are a direct result of similar pressures on families. As families struggle to stay afloat economically and to juggle the endless and competing demands of work and family responsibilities, parents suffer stress. As they relate to their children, their tension is unintentionally conveyed to the children, who also end up feeling tense and rushed.

Other stresses in children's lives may come from the struggle some families face as they raise children. When marital relationships break up, resulting in one parent leaving the home, children are obviously affected and typically experience strong feelings of abandonment, grief, anger, guilt, and insecurity.

Children who are not given adequate love and affection, who receive harsh and punitive discipline, who are abused, or who witness hostility and abuse in relationships between family members suffer deeply.

Outside the family, young children can experience stress in adjusting to transitions. While parents work outside the home, children are cared for in a variety of other settings. Depending on the parents' work schedules and availability of child-care options, some young school-aged children can be involved in two or three different arrangements each day. This makes for a lot of adjustments and contributes to stress for some children. They experience difficulty fitting in, and coping with and meeting the demands of the family and the early childhood setting, particularly if there is a poor match between the children's characteristics (age, personality, abilities, and resources for coping) and the demands placed on them.

Finally, the very real problem of poverty, with all of its consequences of inadequate nutrition, substandard housing, and limited access to educational and recreational opportunities, continues to affect the life of one in every five Canadian children every day.

MAKING A DIFFERENCE IN THE LIVES OF CHILDREN

By being aware of the challenges that Canadian families face, you can make a difference in the lives of their children. Through sharing with families in caring for children, you support both families and children. The caring relationships that are part of children's experiences in early childhood settings can nurture and support those who face family stress.

When poverty is an issue, the resources of the early childhood setting supplement the families' resources and provide experiences and opportunities not otherwise available. Co-ordination of early childhood education and care reduces the need for transitions (and transportation), and quality programs reduce the worry that parents often feel about the care being provided for their children.

Early childhood educators are regularly inspired by the impact they have on young children — in the way so many children respond openly and trustingly to them, and in the tremendous changes that occur in young children in such short periods of time. Many young children will respond genuinely and enthusiastically to their relationship with you, and they have the capacity to give back a great deal. They have no need to pretend to be bored when learning is fun, and generously give adults hugs, ladybugs, and beautiful drawings. Although the work of an early childhood educator is demanding, it is also full of rewards.

As you can see, the role that you have chosen is very important for the well-being of children and families. Fortunately, you do not have to do your work alone. As an early childhood educator, you will be working alongside many other caring and committed professionals in providing quality care to families and children.

EDUCATION IN THE SPOTLIGHT

People as long ago as Plato, in ancient Greece, described the work of the educators of young children as critical for society. Plato claimed that "children are your riches; and upon their turning out well or ill depends the whole order of their father's house," and by extension, we may say the same for society as a whole. Today, we are still looking at the children themselves and where we stand in the larger picture of Canadian society when we take a child by the hand and say we are educators.

Stage centre is where we find ourselves. Children are the focus of an enormous amount of attention; in particular, their early years and their education are receiving critical examination across Canada. Royal commissions and studies are examining what is happening in the lives of children in their early years, and asking what they need from the institutions that will provide their care and education. Canada is not alone in its concern about young children and the process of education; this concern seems to be worldwide.

How do young children learn and grow? How should children be taught? What must they learn? How do we facilitate their future success through what we do with them when they are young? Are there ways that we can ensure their well-being and instil in them a sense of compassion and caring for others? The children await you, with all their hopes and trust and eagerness, so if you are among those privileged to be called Canadian early childhood educators, you must develop your craft well. Many people will question the needs and rights of children and the responsibilities of society for the quality of their lives. You will want to speak with confidence and expertise to the challenges that critics place before you as you advocate for our children.

QUALITY IN EARLY CHILDHOOD EDUCATION

Gillian Doherty-Derkowski, a Canadian educator, has compiled information about what constitutes "quality" in early childhood education. In a book called *Quality Matters* (1995), she identifies the hallmarks of good care and education and answers some of the questions in current debates about the role of a teacher in early childhood education.

What Is "High Quality"?

First, Doherty-Derkowski defines "high quality" in early childhood education as that which goes beyond minimal standards and offers a program "that supports and assists the child's physical, emotional, social, and intellectual development; and supports and complements the family in its child-rearing role" (p. 4).

Later, she reviews the studies that address different types of early childhood education

programs and shares their conclusions: the type of work with young children that is most likely to support their development is that which enables them to interact creatively with their surroundings, guided by their curiosity and imagination, under the thoughtful supervision of an educator who provides an interesting and appropriate environment and who interacts warmly and supportively with each child. What the young child does in such settings is usually called play, although it is the source of considerable personal development and the basis for even more learning in the future. The educator's role is to plan for this play in such a way as to offer children the incentive to explore, to extend their limits of knowledge, to learn, and to enjoy the process.

The Need for Expertise

Doherty-Derkowski cites studies that show that without many opportunities to explore and enjoy new experiences of their own choosing, children learn far less than their counterparts

---

BOX 1.2 THE LEARNING CHILD

The child's intent is to play with the world. We must avoid the attempt to make her conform to our goals and plans.
—Pearce 1980, p. 165

We need to help our children understand that we value risk taking more than success; we value commitment and involvement more than doing things "right" or "safely."
—LeShan 1968, p. 337

who do have such a stimulating environment. She also shows that when the learning is highly structured and directed by the educator in a restrictive way, children have more behavioural problems in their school careers and lower scores on tests of cognitive development and language skills. The opposite situation does not bring contrary results, however; when we take away the educator, the results are also poor. In this case, children do not learn from their random play experiences nearly so much as they do when they have the benefit of an adult who interacts warmly with them as special individuals and plans a curriculum full of challenging but appropriate experiences and activities from which they can choose.

A crucial difference between educators who provide those wonderful learning experiences and those who do not is their own education: those with a background in early childhood education provide the best learning experiences for children. So both your role and your work are crucial — who you are as an educator and what you do with young children will make a significant difference in their growth and development.

SUPPORTING CHILDREN'S DEVELOPMENT: SHAPING THE WORLD

When you see a toddler splashing through puddles, or discover a preschooler turning his T-shirt into a "coat of many colours" with his finger painting, you are not likely to think about these children as the future, much less the future leaders of our country. And yet they are, and so our influence upon their development has importance beyond their individual lives. This gives us all a double obligation to learn as much as possible about children's development.

A frequently quoted nineteenth-century insight claimed that whoever shapes the mind of a child to the age of 6 influences the person for life. An even stronger claim was made by Henry Brooks Adams, who stated that a teacher affects eternity.

Education in Canada: A Special Commitment

As Canadian educators, we must have a commitment to helping children acquire the skills necessary for living successfully in a society that is known around the world for its diversity, its compassion toward others, and its peacefulness.

Canadians serve in a wide assortment of aid agencies in developing countries, sharing technical and professional expertise and serving as volunteers in many areas. Some of them are early childhood educators working in partnership with child-care providers and educators on a number of different continents, among them Africa, Asia, and Latin America. Some people began this kind of work while they were still students and have continued it in their professional careers.

Educators dedicated to young children must be committed to helping them build skills in relating well and fairly to other children and adults of different cultures, races, religions, classes, and abilities. This commitment will have an impact on your professional practice. It will mean, as you will see in later chapters, that you will design your centres and plan your curriculum in ways that will

❖ enhance your children's understanding and acceptance of human diversity in its many forms;

❖ demonstrate the similarities that unite us all;

❖ provide a perspective that will enable them to celebrate and enjoy the benefits of diversity; and

❖ help them develop the courage and commitment to challenge and change discrimination or prejudice wherever they encounter it.

There is a great potential for making a real difference in the lives of children and, through them, in the life of the world. With the potential for this kind of impact on children, early childhood educators have good reason to approach their work with enthusiasm, joy, and humility.

SUMMARY

In this chapter, we have introduced the children who will be the focus of your chosen career. We urge you to cherish them and safeguard their childhood as a sacred time in which their experiences of life are meaningful and joyful.

In a general way, we have introduced you to the joys and challenges of working with young children. You will be richly rewarded for your work, and will take pride in knowing that your chosen work is among the most important of any profession.

REVIEW QUESTIONS

❶ Imagine that you are giving a talk to high-school students about the field of early childhood education. What would you tell them about the challenges of working in this field?

❷ Describe what you think "high-quality" early childhood education is.

❸ What characteristics of Canada have an impact on your approach to early childhood education?

DISCUSSION QUESTIONS

❶ Some people think that to be a good early childhood educator all you need is to be a warm and loving person. Why would they think that? How would you respond to such a claim?

❷ It has been noted that human beings have a childhood longer than that of any other creature. What is "childhood"? What is it for? When does it end?

ACTIVITIES

❶ Form a team of three or four people. Each person seeks out about five children and asks them, "Why do we have grown-ups?" Record the responses and then look at them with your team. What do the responses tell you about children's understanding of the role of adults in their lives?

❷ In the same team, make a list of misconceptions you had when you were children about the way things work, misunderstandings that were a result of explanations adults gave you. Then think of terminology and situations that are common to you as adults that may be confusing for children.

❸ Create your own images of childhood using songs, art materials, photographs, and recordings. Share them with your classmates.

FURTHER READING

Best, Raphaela. (1983). *We've All Got Scars*. Bloomington, IL: Indiana University Press.
A fascinating look at the "second curriculum" of elementary school — learning what it is to be a girl and what it is to be a boy. A must-read for early childhood education professionals who plan to work with school-age youngsters.

Katz, Lilian. (1984). *More Talks with Teachers*. Urbana, IL: ERIC.
Common-sense discussions of what it means to be a professional early childhood educator, including a valuable exploration of the distinctions between the roles of mothers and educators.

Paley, Vivian G. (1981). *Wally's Stories*. Cambridge, MA: Harvard University Press.
A sensitive and loving kindergarten teacher encourages children to tell and dramatize their personal stories. The result is a lively, funny, and touching collection of stories that present real children in all their delightful variety.

REFERENCES

Doherty-Derkowski, G. (1995). *Quality Matters*. Don Mills, ON: Addison-Wesley.

LeShan, E.J. (1968). *The Conspiracy against Children*. New York: Athenaeum.

Mead, M., and R. Metraux. (1993). A new understanding of childhood. In R.H. Wozniak, ed., *Worlds of Childhood: Reader*. New York: HarperCollins College Publishers.

Pearce, J.C. (1980). *Magical Child: Rediscovering Nature's Plan for Our Children*. Toronto: Bantam Books.

Riley, S.S. (1984). *How to Generate Values in Young Children*. Washington, DC: National Association for the Education of Young Children.

CHAPTER 2
The Families

✏ **Overview**

✏ **Changing Families**
- ◆ The Make-up of Families
- ◆ Cultural Diversity

✏ **Economic Forces**
- ◆ Economic Status
- ◆ Changes in the Employment Picture

✏ **Influences in the Lives of Children**
- ◆ Mothers in the Work Force
- ◆ The Impact of Family Breakup

- ◆ Child Abuse and Family Violence
- ◆ The Impact of Television

✏ **Summary**

✏ **Review Questions**

✏ **Discussion Questions**

✏ **Activities**

✏ **Further Reading**

✏ **References**

OVERVIEW

Perhaps you do not spend much time thinking about your family roles — child, grandchild, sibling, niece, nephew. Your life as student, friend, and part-time or full-time worker probably occupies more of your thoughts and requires all of your energy. In contrast, if you are a spouse, partner, or parent, you might spend a significant amount of time thinking about family relationships and responsibilities.

In this chapter, we introduce you to Canadian families. We begin with a look at the make-up of Canadian families and then discuss the changes that are forcing us to reexamine our traditional images of a family. We explore the changing patterns of immigration that have resulted in the cultural, racial, and language diversity of today's Canadian families. We also look at the changing world of work and its impact on families. You will learn why the changes in Canadian families and family life have important implications for early childhood educators.

We also discuss how children's lives are being transformed by changes within the family and within society as the result of several factors: mothers' employment away from home, family breakup, family violence, and television.

The partnership between you and families is one of the most important elements in children's lives, since families play such a crucial role in children's development. Nurturing and training children to become mature, competent adults takes place within families, and they can carry out these responsibilities most effectively when they have strong ties to the community. Schools and child-care centres are the young child's first experience of this community beyond the family.

If you intend to become an early childhood educator, this is a good time to learn what it means to work as a partner of the families of the children in your care. When you gain an understanding of people in their family roles, you become more comfortable and skilled in working with them.

By the end of this chapter, you will be able to

❖ describe the factors contributing to the diversity of Canadian families;

❖ understand the cultural and racial diversity of Canadian families;

❖ explain how the changes in our society affect families;

❖ understand the impact of mothers' employment, family breakup and violence, and television on children and families.

CHANGING FAMILIES

The Make-up of Families

Veena, whom you met in Chapter 1, arranged to visit the Mill Street Day-Care Centre during an open house for families. She went early and observed as clusters of adults and children arrived. First one woman came with 2-year-old twin boys, and then a man and a woman with a 3-year-old girl. One man with 2 children came, and an elderly woman along with a younger man and a baby, and 2 women also with a child too young to walk. The director of the centre introduced Veena to a number of parents as an early childhood education student, which made her feel more comfortable.

Veena wondered about these groupings of people. Who were they? Was each group a family? Just as Veena was noticing the diversity, an older man with 2 older women arrived with a girl who might have been 3 or 4. Veena guessed they were the child's grandparents, and perhaps an aunt, but she could not be sure. The more people who arrived, the more curious she became about the unpredictability of the family groupings.

Veena grew up in a traditional family with a father, a mother, and two brothers. That is what she thought of as a "family." What image first comes to your mind when you think of a family? Do you imagine a father who goes out to work and a mother who stays at home and assumes primary responsibility for housework and the raising of two or more children? As Veena discovered, these traditional images are not necessarily the reality in today's families.

Over the last several decades, declining birthrates, high rates of separation and divorce, and an increase in the number of women in the labour force have changed Canadian families. The single-wage-earner, nuclear family with the mother looking after the home is no longer the typical family portrait. The majority of Canadian families are husband–wife based and rely on two incomes for economic security. More than 7 percent of Canadian families are headed by common-law couples. In 1991, 13 percent of all families were single-parent families, most often resulting from divorce (Vanier Institute n.d.).

One-child and two-child families are now common as couples decide to have fewer children. The number of single-parent families has increased, with the majority of these headed by women. Blended (or step-parent) families have also increased in number as more partners end one marriage and go on to find a new partner and/or remarry. Finally, the majority

of parents, single and married, are now employed outside the home.

Who makes up a family? The variety of family forms and constellations continues to increase: couples who are not legally married; couples who become first-time parents in their late 30s or early 40s; unmarried teenage mothers; single-parent fathers; mature single women who choose to be unmarried mothers; same-sex couples; blended families of two parents who start a new family grouping with children from previous marriages; families that include aunts, uncles, and grandparents; or grandparents raising young children. This diversity in family composition challenges the traditional definition and expands today's image of the family.

Along with the changes in the composition of families, there are also changes in the roles of family members. Traditionally, mothers were the primary care-givers and made most of the decisions regarding children's day-to-day routines. In some families today, fathers carry out what had been thought of as the "maternal" responsibilities, while mothers take on demanding careers and full-time jobs. In other families, fathers and mothers both take responsibility for the care of the children and share the day-to-day decision-making process. In yet other families, fathers make the decisions but mothers provide the care. Some families entrust the care of their children to grandmothers or great-aunts while the parents have jobs or businesses that support the whole family.

These changes in Canadian families have implications for you as an early childhood educator. First, given the current diversity in family forms and roles, you must recognize and respect that each child's family may be defined, and may define itself, in a variety of ways. You must learn to think in terms of families rather

BOX 2.1 WHAT CAN EDUCATORS DO TO SUPPORT FAMILIES?

Early childhood educators can support people in their family roles in a number of ways. First, they can offer professional advice about effective child-rearing strategies without pretending to have the final word. Second, they can provide valuable information on child development or on other community support services for families. Third, they can boost the self-confidence of people in their family roles by listening with empathy, by affirming families' positive efforts, and by allaying doubts and fears. This kind of support reduces family stress, improves family functioning, and enhances parent–child relations.

The partnership between you and families will facilitate children's development. For example, the learning activities you design for children in your care will be even more effective if families encourage these activities at home. Children will also benefit if there is consistency at home and at school in child-rearing practices, such as discipline.

You can foster this partnership with families by welcoming their participation in your program, by sharing information with them, by arranging visits, and by doing what you can to make them feel comfortable at your centre (for example, by setting up a parents' corner in the centre). To work with families effectively, however, you must first get to know them.

---

than just certain parents who make decisions and nurture children. Second, to be able to develop a good relationship with children, you need to understand the ways in which many factors in their families' lives affect them.

Cultural Diversity

LANGUAGE AND CUSTOMS

Veena's visit to the open house at the Mill Street Day-Care Centre reminded her of something she had discovered in high school — English is not the first language in many Canadian families. In the first hour of her visit, she figured out that people spoke at least four other languages: Chinese, French, German, and Urdu. Veena wondered if these young children would not have difficulty communicating with the teachers, but she was glad to see that they seemed comfortable. Veena would come to realize that in addition to a different first language, many families have cultural values and practices that vary widely.

Veena's experience told her that this centre was probably typical. Canadian families have always been descendants of Native Canadians or immigrants, but there have been shifting percentages of people from the different groups represented in each census. Perhaps because of history books that emphasize one point of view, you might think of the French and the British as historically the two largest immigrant groups in Canada. However, a careful reading of Canadian history shows that people from many different countries were represented here from the beginning, and sometimes the first immigrants watched as succeeding generations lost their connections to their homelands.

Perhaps your great-grandparents emigrated to Canada and then saw their children abandon their original language, and now their grandchildren, your parents, may know little or nothing of the family's original way of life. Today's immigrant families, however, have great variations on that story.

In many families, the children learn the traditions of their cultural heritage — lighting candles safely before special prayers, performing the folk dances taught by their grandparents, or baking the shortbread cookies that the family has loved for generations. Unfortunately, in some families the children reject these kinds of ethnic customs; in other cases, for reasons usually having to do with hardship or persecution in their homeland, families try to make their children become "Canadian only" as quickly as possible. Still others have the best of both worlds, with Saturday heritage schools teaching their language and culture to their children, as well as the public school system's adult courses in English and Canadian history. In just one generation, these children leap to full participation in Canadian life. At the same time, they retain multilingual skills and multicultural perspectives.

Some children will, therefore, come to you speaking a variety of languages from different continents, and yet their ancestors might have been in Canada for many generations. Other children's parents might be recent immigrants, and still others might speak a form of English that is not familiar to you. Perhaps the child who seems to resemble your favourite cousin is a refugee whose history even includes the horror of witnessing the deaths of family and friends. Understanding each child and each family will be a new learning experience for you and a new challenge for your professional practice.

CHANGES IN IMMIGRATION PATTERNS

It may be useful for you to remember that across the years of immigration at least three significant characteristics of immigrants have changed. First, the percentage of foreign-born Canadians has changed. Second, the percentage of English-speaking immigrants has increased, with many being fluent in more than one language when they come to Canada. Third, immigrants of European ancestry no longer make up the vast majority of immigrants. We examine the implications of each of these facts as they affect early childhood educators.

First, the percentage of foreign-born Canadians has decreased significantly since 1920. As the number of descendants of earlier immigrants increases and the number of immigrants and refugees we allow into the country shrinks, it is easier for people to view "foreigners" as the exception rather than the rule, and to expect them to change and "blend in" with others already here. In addition, as people become more and more distant from their own immigrant ancestors, it is possible that they have never even heard the stories of their own family's difficulties of adjusting to a new country and culture. In places where new Canadians tend to live, usually because of housing and work opportunities or family contacts, longer-established Canadians might view the arrival of immigrants as a startling new phenomenon that makes them uncomfortable.

Educators have a responsibility to do what they can to ease divisions and bad feelings based on race, culture, or social class, and, if possible, to prevent them from occurring among the families of the children in their care. They also have an opportunity to do what they can in influencing young children to develop a welcoming attitude toward the diversity of a cosmopolitan, multiracial, multicultural world. For this reason, you need to acquire the understanding and skills that will help you in this part of your task. Learning the history of your own family's immigration and adjustment experience and comparing it with those of others is a good beginning.

Second, the percentage of English-speaking immigrants who have another first language has risen dramatically. In the early part of the twentieth century, Canada welcomed many people from the Ukraine and South Asia, for example, who worked hard and made splendid contributions to our country. These immigrants were successful despite not speaking English, or even with having to put forth the enormous effort of learning English informally or in night school. Today there are still many immigrants, especially family-sponsored women and children, who do not speak English. Many more, however, arrive already speaking English as well as one or more other languages.

You will likely be appreciative of the many immigrant families who are proficient in several languages. However, you will also need to be supportive of the others, particularly mothers and children, who have not learned English and perhaps feel overwhelmed and shy about trying to learn a new language. Often their needs are last on a list of priorities that includes such basics as obtaining work, food, clothing, and shelter in their new land. You can understand and respect these priorities, but at the same time, you might be the main source the women and children have for meeting the need for language training and finding out about community services for the whole family that would make them feel more at home. Learning to teach English is useful, as is learning how to organize local community resources to provide classes in English as a second language for adults.

Finally, the percentage of non-European immigrants has changed. This change has given rise to the term "visible minorities." European immigrants and their descendants remain "invisible" minorities (see Box 2.2).

It is particularly important that you model respect for all human diversity. If you show respect for other people, no matter who they are, your attitude will influence the children to appreciate human diversity and to enjoy the richness of the many cultures in our society, instead of being prejudiced against people who are "different."

ECONOMIC FORCES

Economic Status

Regardless of the cultural heritage of a family, economic status has a strong impact on parenting. Of course, economic status is linked to the jobs and income families have. Twenty percent of Canada's children live below the poverty line; their families, and those who are barely staying just above it, are increasingly insecure about their ability to care for their children effectively.

The lack of resources to care for a family creates anxiety that can affect parents' ability to nurture their children. Many children who live in poverty are disadvantaged because they miss out on experiences and opportunities that others take for granted. They may not have access to a wide variety of toys and books, or they may not go on outings to recreational and cultural events. Exposure to computers and other vehicles of technology may be limited or nonexistent. Sometimes children growing up in poverty can overcome these early disadvantages, but for many the impact is long-term and severe.

Changes in the Employment Picture

Most families have always had to work hard to support themselves. However, in the latter part of this century some fundamental changes are occurring that affect families dramatically.

BOX 2.2 WHO ARE OUR "VISIBLE MINORITY" FAMILIES?

At first this seems an easy question to answer: a "visible minority" is a group that "stands out" in a crowd, usually because of skin colour, facial features, or other physical characteristics. However, "standing out" is not just a matter of physical differences that the eye perceives. The eye must also be taught to see those differences as significant.

Here are some examples. One of the earliest books on racism in Canada is not about relations between people we may think of as visually different (between European settlers and Native Canadians, or between white and black immigrants, for instance). It is about relations between French and English immigrants and their descendants, who saw themselves as coming from two different races!

In England in the last century, much was written about the problems between the two feuding "races" in the British Isles, namely the English and the Irish. In Canada, however, all English, Irish, Scottish, and Welsh are lumped together by our census as one group.

The same group may be "visible" in one jurisdiction and "invisible" right across the border depending on such factors as social class, distribution of power, and historical relationships. For example, the Americans see Americans of Spanish descent as a visible minority *if* their Spanish ancestors came to the United States by way of Latin America, but *not* if they came directly from Spain. People from India, who until recently were relatively few in number in the United States and were often members of professional groups, were not seen as "visible" unless they wore their traditional garb. Across the border in Canada, however, the same Indians might be lumped together with all other people from South Asia (Pakistanis, Bangladeshis, Sri Lankans) and deemed highly "visible," while Latin Americans, at least in the early days of their immigration to Canada, were not.

Confusing? Yes, but with enormous repercussions for the people labelled "visible." Race may be in the eye of the beholder, but racism is real, and it hurts large numbers of our children.

For instance, during the affluent post–World War II period, families could increase their standard of living on the income of only the father. Now, however, it is increasingly difficult for families to maintain their parents' standard of living, even with two incomes. When mothers take on jobs, they are no longer working to get "the little extras" — in many families, this second income is necessary simply to meet the basic needs of family members. In the next section, we discuss the effects on children when both parents are occupied full-time away from home.

Technological change also has an impact on family income. For example, as you drive along country roads you can see evidence of what is happening to family farms — in some areas, many farms are for sale or are abandoned, and barns are being taken down. Rural communities whose lives depend on their farms have witnessed farm families being shattered and their way of life irrevocably changed as a result of agribusiness and land development.

One of the negative effects of technological change is increasing economic insecurity. Some people are experiencing the shift from well-paid, full-time, lifelong jobs with the same company to a series of jobs, some of them part-time, with a variety of employers. Still others are discovering that large companies are letting go huge numbers of their own work force and contracting out work to groups of smaller firms who pay less for that work, some of which must be done in the employee's own home. The majority of jobs that are created now tend to be lower-paid, service-sector, part-time jobs that leave families with far less financial security than before.

Some companies in the public and private sectors are becoming aware of the stress families are experiencing from these changes. It is not news that people work best when they are not preoccupied with family problems. Now, besides setting up workplace child-care centres, some employers offer extended parental leave and allow parents to decide whether the mother or the father will stay home after the birth or adoption of a child. Others are designing creative benefits packages for employees so that they may "spend" their benefits appropriately for their families' needs. For example, a young parent may choose to take a substantial chunk of those benefits in a child-care subsidy; a little later, it may be spent on summer camp; years later, it may go to university tuition; and finally, it may go into pension benefits.

These "flexible" or "cafeteria-style" benefit packages are just one way that some employers have addressed the dual responsibilities of working families. However, many employers and decision-makers in our country still believe that families should be totally responsible for taking care of their own children, and offer little support to share the load with the family. As a professional in early childhood education, you need to be alert to every possibility to make employers and decision-makers in your community aware that they can contribute creatively and significantly to the strength and well-being of families and their children.

In your courses that focus on the family, you will be offered in-depth studies of the effects of employment and poverty on children, but in this course on curricula and methods, it is enough to keep in mind this brief discussion of the family's economic security, or lack of it, and its impact on parenting.

INFLUENCES IN THE LIVES OF CHILDREN

If you were to choose a street in the town where you live, or several kilometres of country road in your county, do you think you would find a family with "typical" children? Do you know first-hand what the lives of young children are like? Do you think a 3-year-old on the street or country road you choose has a life like yours was at age 3? Perhaps you have not thought about yourself in this way, but you are a generation older than the young children you see at a child-care centre, and a generation's difference means many changes.

We discuss these changes because they are transforming the lives of Canadian children, and to work successfully with them you need to understand what is happening to them. The trend toward increased participation of mothers in the labour force has changed children's lives. More of today's mothers are not only employed, they are entering and staying in the work force when their children are preschoolers or even infants. As a result, children are cared for outside the home more often and at a younger age.

Rising divorce rates continue to make family life less stable. A child may experience a series of family transitions: moving from a two-parent family, to a single-parent, divorced family, to a blended family, and, in cases where a remarriage fails, back to a single-parent family.

Today's children live in a society that poses threats to their safety and their psychological and physical well-being. Although you might think that children are most at risk from abuse or abduction by a stranger or through exposure to harmful, illicit drugs, you will learn that the threats to some children's safety and well-being come not only from their external environment but too often from the family itself. Family violence, child abuse, and substance abuse by family members are disturbingly common and have a distressing impact on a large number of Canadian children.

Major technological innovations also exert a powerful influence on today's children. In 1994, 71 percent of Canadian children lived in a house with cable television, and 84 percent had a videocassette recorder. Thirty-three

percent of Canadian families had a computer in 1994, and 39 percent had a video game system. These media have become a significant part of children's lives.

In the following sections, we examine in greater detail the factors that have an impact on children: employed mothers, divorce, family violence, and television. You will learn that most children — with the support of parents, relatives, and teachers — are adapting well to the changing family.

Mothers in the Work Force

The mother who stays at home, welcoming her children's return from play or school with a batch of freshly baked cookies and milk, is an infrequent sight today and in many cases was only ever a fantasy. Although some families are able to choose and maintain this lifestyle effectively, it was, and is, far more rare than we are led to believe by those old TV programs. The impression that the 1950s was representative of an era of ideal family life is inaccurate; rather, it was an unusually affluent and brief period in North American history.

Most mothers today work outside the home either part-time or full-time. In 1988, 60 percent of children under age 15 in 2-parent families had employed parents, and 69 percent of children in single-parent families lived with an employed parent. In 1990, almost 60 percent of mothers with children under age 3 were employed, usually full-time (Lero 1994).

The increased number of employed mothers, especially those with infants and preschoolers, has raised concern about two issues. First, how does employment of mothers affect children? Second, what are the effects of nonparental care on children? We examine each of these questions in the following sections.

HOW DOES MOTHERS' EMPLOYMENT AFFECT CHILDREN?

Contrary to popular opinion, children suffer few negative effects from mothers being employed outside the home. In fact, this is one change that has some positive consequences for the family environment and for children's development. Mothers who want to have a career, who like their job, and who have stable child-care arrangements are happier than mothers who prefer involvement in the public sphere but work only at home. When mothers experience fulfilment and satisfaction, they are better parents. Another positive effect of mothers' employment is that, in two-parent families, fathers in varying degrees take on more responsibilities for child care and household tasks. The father's stronger presence results in increased social and academic competence in children (Hoffman 1989).

Families in which mothers are employed and fathers are active in child rearing and housework offer children less stereotypical sex-role models. Therefore, it is not surprising that children of employed mothers have more flexible views about appropriate roles and activities for males and females. They are also more likely to believe that women are competent. This positive effect is stronger for daughters than for sons and is important for girls' self-esteem. Daughters of employed mothers have better social adjustment, do better in school, and have higher career goals than daughters of nonemployed mothers (Hoffman 1989).

There are indications that employed mothers value and encourage independence in their children more than do nonemployed mothers. As a result, their children are able to care for themselves and take on household responsibilities at an earlier age. This may also explain why many children of employed mothers display such mature social behaviour.

HOW DOES SHARED CHILD CARE AFFECT CHILDREN?

Although Canadian children who have employed mothers are in many different types of child-care arrangements, the vast majority are in privately arranged unlicensed care (such as care by a baby-sitter, neighbour, friend, or relative). Only 10 percent of children are in licensed child-care centres (Vanier Institute n.d.). For young children not yet attending school, up to 90 percent receive informal and unlicensed care while their parents work. In 1988, 2.6 million children under 13 needed child care to accommodate parents' work or study.

What is the impact of child care on development? There is no evidence to suggest that child care in itself is detrimental to young children. In fact, high-quality care enhances the development of children, especially those from nonstimulating home environments (Doherty-Derkowski 1995). Children who receive good care develop enhanced communication and cognitive abilities and social skills while enjoying meaningful relationships with caring adults and peers. What can be detrimental is poor-quality care, whether provided by parents or by people outside the family. Dimensions of high-quality care include small group size, low care-giver–child ratios, and care-givers who are educated, responsive, nurturing, and stimulating.

Unfortunately, not all Canadian children are receiving the high-quality care that is essential for their optimal development. Good child care is expensive and difficult to find. Furthermore, the demand for child care is growing as the trend of mothers' involvement in the work force continues. Since we know that day care affects children's development, the need for more affordable, accessible, and high-quality facilities is urgent. This is an issue that needs to be addressed politically and at the community level.

THE TIME CRUNCH

When asked to discuss the most important issues facing Canadian families, Dr. Robert Glossop, researcher with the Vanier Institute of the Family, identified two things (Statistics Canada 1994). The first was economic security and the resulting feelings of choice and control over their lives. This concern was discussed earlier, both as a source of family stress and as the most common motivation for the participation of mothers in the work force.

The second was the "time crunch" experienced by many parents as they attempt to meet incompatible demands of family and work. Both men and women are spending more time working outside the home to make ends meet: "This necessary economic activity takes its toll in human terms" (Statistics Canada 1994, p. 28). Glossop describes the schedules of many families as "frenetic" and an obvious source of tension and stress. Lero (1994) points out a further factor, the extent to which many parents work at nontraditional times, such as on weekends and late or night shifts. Balancing work, caring for children, and keeping the home running creates an impossible time crunch for many families and all but eliminates the possibility of extended periods of quality family time.

The Impact of Family Breakup

Separation and divorce in families is an increasing trend. In 1990, 35 percent of all divorces involved children, affecting a total of 47 631 children in Canada. Most children of divorced parents (73 percent) live in the custody of their mother. A minority are in father-custody (12 percent) or joint-custody (14 percent) arrangements (Statistics Canada 1993a).

Family breakup creates stress and brings enormous change for most children in their living arrangements and family relationships. For example, if children live with their mother, they commonly experience severe financial hardship. In fact, the majority of single-parent families are poor, and most of these are headed by separated or divorced mothers (Vanier Institute n.d., p. 68). Money for new clothes, toys, books, music lessons, or camp is often unavailable. The family might need to find less expensive housing; in turn, a change of neighbourhoods could mean new schools, new child-care arrangements, and the loss of familiar friends and teachers.

A single parent who must work outside the home after the divorce to support the family invariably has less time and energy available for the children. The pressure of performing well at work often means a single parent becomes preoccupied even while she or he is with the children, which changes the nature of the relationship. The time crunch described earlier is often intensified in the single-parent family.

In addition, conflict is likely to occur between parents after the separation, and children tend to get caught in the middle of their parents' battles. As well, children often feel that the whole mess is their fault. The crisis of the separation and the demands of life as a single parent often cause custodial parents to become preoccupied, and in some cases they are unable to give the children what they need. Custodial mothers usually become more strict and inconsistent in dealing with their children, particularly with their sons. On the other hand, noncustodial fathers often become permissive and indulgent. Although noncustodial fathers generally have frequent contact with their children immediately after the divorce, many of them become less available to their children as time passes.

Given these changes, it is not surprising that children are intensely distressed by their parents' separation. It is common for them to feel depressed, lonely, angry, and rejected. They are anxious about what will happen to them. They worry about who they will live with, where they will live, and whether they'll see the noncustodial parent again. Most children wish, or even expect, that their parents will reunite.

Children vary in their initial responses to divorce depending on their age and sex. For example, in mother-custody families, boys show more aggressive, rebellious behaviour than girls. They typically become more difficult to manage, both at home and at school, and have greater difficulty getting along with peers. Preschool and early-elementary-school children are often extremely upset and frightened because they have a limited capacity to understand divorce. They often blame themselves for the divorce or fear abandonment by both parents. Young children can also regress — by lapsing in toilet training or returning to a security blanket — or they may be very anxious about leaving home to attend nursery school or kindergarten.

After two years, most children and parents have adapted to the divorce and to life in a single-parent family. However, this period of family stability is often temporary, since most divorced parents find new partners and/or eventually remarry. With a new marriage, children must again adjust to a complex set of new relationships, this time with step-parents, step-siblings, and step-grandparents.

Children suffer less from a divorce when parents put aside their conflict and co-operate with and support each other in their parenting roles. Of course, if both parents maintain a warm, caring relationship with the children, the children experience less trauma. Good financial resources and social supports facilitate parents' as well as children's adjustment. Schools and child-care centres play an important role in children's adjustment to divorce and remarriage. They can provide a warm, secure, predictable, and structured environment for children whose home lives are chaotic and unstable.

The long-term outcomes of divorce and remarriage are diverse. Many children adjust well, while others show delayed effects: they appear to adjust well initially, but have problems that emerge at a later time. Finally, a minority experience the divorce as extremely traumatic, resulting in emotional and behavioural problems for years after the divorce or remarriage.

Child Abuse and Family Violence

No discussion of the child and the family would be complete without addressing the serious and devastating issues of violence within family relationships. Accounts of abuse continue to be alarming. Although accurate statistics are difficult to compile, estimates and available figures tell us that thousands of children in Canada experience physical, emotional, or sexual abuse within their own homes.

Child abuse is such an unacceptable act that we become angry and are tempted to blame and reject the abusive parents. Although this reaction is understandable, it is not helpful to either abused children or their families. Child abuse occurs in our society for many complex and interrelated reasons.

Perhaps the most fundamental reason that child abuse continues is that our society fails to really cherish children. In recent years, at international conferences, world leaders (Canada's among them) have formulated statements on improving conditions for children.

But the reality is that these statements have not changed the conditions that often give rise to abuse.

Partly to blame for the abuse is society's expectation that children must be controlled and that parents who do not control their children are somehow inadequate. Parents with little understanding of children's behaviour and limited skills in child guidance are nonetheless expected to ensure appropriate behaviour from their children. When children misbehave, parents feel inadequate and frustrated, and resort to excessive means to demonstrate their authority. Most cases of child abuse fall in the mild to moderate range, when the abuse is the result of loss of control during discipline rather than an intentional act of violence. When excessive harsh and punitive methods are a regular occurrence, the child experiences negative effects on self-esteem, the ability to trust, and

overall development. The abused child is a victim and needs society's intervention and protection.

Also to blame is our collective tolerance of aggression in many contexts. The media overwhelm us with violent images in programming for children, adolescents, and adults. Aggressiveness is accepted and even encouraged in many sports. Historically and currently, our cultural heroes (real and fantasy) are often characterized by their power and their control over others. Child abuse exists in society because it is still acceptable to influence or control others through expressions of power and physical strength.

The true cost of family violence is that it teaches children that violence is an acceptable part of relationships and a justifiable way to resolve conflicts. Victims and witnesses of abuse often grow up to abuse their own children or re-create the pattern by taking the role of victim in future relationships. Thus, the cycle continues.

Here is another area of children's lives where you can make a difference. Early childhood educators can begin to break the cycle of abuse in four main ways:

1. Try to understand and support family members in their struggle to care for and raise their children. Help parents to understand what children need, and teach positive methods of child guidance.

2. Help parents to find sources of support and assistance in the community to deal with any personal or family problems.

3. Relate to children in ways that demonstrate that violence is not an acceptable or normal part of human interaction. Teach children verbal and nonaggressive ways to resolve conflicts.

4. Report children who need protection from family members to the proper authorities, so that the family can be helped and the child's safety can be assured.

The Impact of Television

It is 7:40 on Wednesday morning and Michael, age 6, and Jennifer, age 5, have eaten breakfast and dressed themselves and are ready for school. They ask their mother if they can watch television until she is ready to drive them to school. She agrees, simply to give herself some time to dress and quietly feed her 18-month-old. As the children get older, it seems they spend more and more time in front of the TV set, and she wonders from time to time if watching a lot of television hurts kids, even if the programs are good.

This scenario is likely repeated thousands of times across the country. Given the pressures of too much to do and too little time, parents often make television available to children at nearly any time of the day. Given its availability, the television set can, in a certain sense, be viewed as "a member of the family" (Singer, Singer, & Zuckerman 1990, p. 12). In many cases it almost becomes a parent, or at least a baby-sitter.

Canadian children between the ages of 2 and 11 watch television an average of about 20 hours a week. Some of this time is spent watching children's programming (Statistics Canada 1993b). However, most of the programs children watch are designed for adult audiences. Aside from the impact of programming, long periods of television viewing have a negative effect on children's ability to concentrate and on their creativity.

Television has dramatically changed children's experiences within the family. It has become the background for many activities — many children even do their homework while watching television. Some families routinely watch television during mealtimes, a practice that not only disrupts, but even precludes, parents and children talking to each other while they eat. Watching television has become a family-time activity, but critics argue that family members may simply watch the set passively rather than communicating with one another. Other activities, such as family games, playing with friends outdoors, or reading are frequently displaced by television. This means that the impact of television is greater than simply the program itself, and becomes especially problematic for children who are heavy TV viewers.

The impact of television goes beyond its effects on children's family life and activities. Because of its availability, popularity, and appeal, television plays a powerful role in socializing today's children. Television conveys, through both its shows and its advertising, attitudes and values not of the family's choosing. These attitudes and values are determined by people who do not necessarily have children's best interests at heart. In fact, the values are usually determined by companies intent on selling something. Many families are concerned because television often teaches children undesirable behaviours, beliefs, values, and attitudes. Research indicates that there is legitimate cause for concern. The results of one such study are discussed in Box 2.3.

Most experts agree, based on evidence from literally hundreds of research studies, that TV violence promotes aggressive behaviour in children (Heusman, et al. 1983; Liebert & Sprafkin 1988). This finding is especially disturbing given that the most violent TV programs are those designed for children. Saturday morning cartoons contain between 20 to 25 violent acts per hour — a number 4 times greater than the acts of violence on prime-time television!

Television violence has other undesirable effects. It can harden children to violence, causing them to tolerate real-life aggression. In addition, children who are heavy viewers of TV violence are more likely to believe that the world of television accurately reflects the real world. They are thus more likely to perceive their world as a mean, scary place in which conflicts are commonly resolved through aggression.

Television reinforces the gender, racial, and ethnic stereotypes that are common in our society. Racial and ethnic minorities in Canada are either underrepresented or virtually absent on television programs. When minorities are assigned roles, they are usually portrayed as villains or as victims of violence. Women are also underrepresented, and when

they do appear, their roles and personalities conform to gender stereotypes. They appear mainly in marital, romantic, or family roles and are portrayed as passive, deferential, weak, and emotional. In contrast, men are typically portrayed as active, dominant, logical, and powerful. As the study described in Box 2.2 revealed, children's sex-role attitudes are influenced by these stereotyped portrayals on television.

Finally, television advertising teaches children poor nutritional habits and promotes indiscriminate consumerism. Eighty percent of children's television advertising is for such highly sugared food products as cereals, snacks, candy, and soft drinks. Advertisements for these and other products — toys, games, and clothes — often convey the message that ownership of the products brings happiness, fun, and popularity. Children, especially the youngest ones, are particularly vulnerable to these persuasive messages. As a result, they beg their parents for toys or other products they have seen advertised. When parents deny these requests, an argument or temper tantrum typically ensues, often in the department store or supermarket.

Television commercials manipulate children's beliefs and preferences. Studies find that children who are frequently exposed to food ads think that sugared products are highly nutritious and they prefer these foods. Furthermore, ads that include information on good nutrition, although readily understood by children, are not effective in increasing the number of times children select unsugared snacks.

In summary, television teaches aggressive behaviour, stereotypes of minorities and women, and indiscriminate consumerism — all of these disturbing findings of research. So far, North American television is more about selling products than anything else.

BOX 2.3 THE IMPACT OF TELEVISION: A NATURAL EXPERIMENT

How does TV viewing affect children's creativity, reading skills, sex-role attitudes, and aggressive behaviour? These and other questions were addressed in a unique study of a non-isolated Canadian community that had no television reception until 1973. Tannis MacBeth Williams, a psychologist from the University of British Columbia, and a team of colleagues tested and observed the children of this anonymous town, referred to as "Notel," and compared them with children from two other Canadian communities that had television. Children from all three communities were studied both before and two years after the arrival of TV reception in Notel.

The results of this natural experiment revealed that television negatively affected the children in a variety of areas. For example, before TV, the children in Notel had higher creativity scores than the children in the other two communities. Their creativity scores were similar, however, after two years of exposure to television. The before-and-after TV comparisons also indicated that TV may slow the acquisition of reading skills. Why does TV interfere with the acquisition of reading skills and creative thinking by children? Dr. MacBeth Williams and her colleagues believe that children may choose to watch television rather than practise reading or engage in other activities that facilitate creativity.

Notel children were also less aggressive before TV than the children who grew up with TV. The Notel children showed a significant increase in both physical and verbal aggression, however, after television became available in their community. The increase in aggression was observed in both boys and girls and for children at all age levels. The effect was apparent even in children who were initially low in aggression, not just among a small group of highly aggressive children.

Finally, Notel children's beliefs about appropriate and typical behaviour for boys and girls became more strongly sex-typed after two years of television viewing. Dr. MacBeth Williams and her colleagues were surprised that the influence of television on sex-role stereotyping was strong enough to be noticeable at all given the prevalence of traditional sex-role models and messages in our society, but it was clear that it had been strengthened by television.

The researchers' conclusions support the concerns of families and educators as to the impact of television on children:

We designed our research with the expectation that television has the potential to affect its viewers in a variety of ways, some positive and some negative. This summary of the results points to the conclusion that for the topics we studied, the net effects of North American television on regular viewers, especially children, are negative.
— Williams 1986, p. 426

However, television has as much potential to benefit children as it does to harm them. On the positive side, nonviolent television programs with such themes as sharing, co-operating, helping one another, and settling disputes in a peaceful manner foster healthy behaviour in children. Such educational programs as "Sesame Street" facilitate school readiness skills. The creative and prosocial potential of television has yet to be fully explored and utilized.

IMPLICATIONS FOR EARLY CHILDHOOD EDUCATORS

In Veena's visit to the day-care centre, she noticed several children acting strangely. Then she realized they were blocking and kicking in imitation of their favourite television heroes. Immediately, the teacher reminded them that this game was not allowed at school.

Like Veena, you will discover that some of children's negative behaviours in child-care centres and schools have been learned from television. You will likely see that as children play and relate to their peers they imitate the aggressive words and actions of such superheroes as Power Rangers, Ninja Turtles, GI Joe, the Terminator, and Batman.

There are many things you can do to minimize the negative effects of television on children. First, become aware of what is on television and what the children in your care are watching. By increasing your awareness of the form and content of television, you will be able to give more accurate interpretations and responses to what the children say and do with the messages they are given.

Second, you can advocate for more high-quality children's programming. Write to major commercial networks and your local stations to protest television content that is highly violent or that portrays women and other groups in derogatory or stereotypical ways.

Third, educate families about the potential harmful effects of television on their children. Advise families not to use television as an electronic baby-sitter, and recommend that they monitor not only how much but also what their children watch. Explain to families of children who are heavy TV viewers how excessive viewing time and inappropriate television content harms the children, and encourage them to cut back on the amount of time the television is on. Suggest alternate activities for children that help their development. In addition, advise families to interest their children in nonviolent, entertaining, and educational children's programming.

Fourth, design curricula to help children critically evaluate what they see on television. Research indicates that teaching children television literacy skills helps them understand the medium better and can counter some of its harmful effects. Even children as young as 3 can be taught critical viewing skills. One 5-year-old Ontario boy, upon hearing about 2 boys having killed another boy, which some people attributed to TV violence, became so frightened by this news that he decided to stop watching the show "Mighty Morphin Power Rangers"!

Your curricula will be even more effective if you teach families how they can help their children understand television. Encourage parents and other adult family members to watch television with their children and discuss program content both during and after viewing. The adults should voice disapproval of aggressive on-screen behaviour; propose alternative, nonviolent methods of conflict resolution; and discuss with children the real-life consequences of violence for both the aggressor and the victim. Discussing television shows in this way reduces the children's tendency to imitate violence.

Finally, remember that television is a powerful, appealing medium. Think of creative ways in which to capitalize on its positive potential. Most families will not ban television altogether, so think of ways to use it as an educational tool in your centre or school.

SUMMARY

The people who bring their children to you for care represent an enormous variety of cultural histories and family experiences that preceded their arrival at your door. These families are usually alike, however, in bringing with them high hopes for their children's happiness and success. They need you, as their principal partner in this important enterprise, to understand and respect them and their children.

Many aspects in the lives of families present enormous challenges: their economic situation, pressures from their jobs, their marital status, the possible absence of supportive extended-family members, and competition from conflicting values, such as those represented on television. Helping families find the resources in the community to work through difficult situations will be one of your greatest contributions to the well-being of the children in your care.

REVIEW QUESTIONS

❶ Describe the make-up of Canadian families today.

❷ How do the changes in families affect children?

❸ What are the implications of these changes for early childhood educators?

❹ Give a reason why child abuse continues in our society.

❺ What can early childhood educators do about abuse?

❻ What are the responsibilities of early childhood educators regarding television?

DISCUSSION QUESTIONS

❶ What are the many family forms represented in our classrooms today? How do you think they are the same as or different from the forms in classrooms 50 years ago, and why?

❷ What are the stereotypes we hold of men? Of women? How are these helpful or harmful in our dealings with families and their children?

❸ What are the stereotypes we hold of some of the ethnic or racial communities in Canada? Where did we get these stereotypes? How might they stand in the way of our becoming successful partners with the families of our children?

❹ What specific examples can you give of the influence television has had on someone you know? Of someone you have heard about?

ACTIVITIES

❶ One of the most important activities having to do with families is that of getting to know your own family's history and its pattern of family dynamics. In this course, it will be sufficient for you to begin an oral history of your family, particularly the story of how various members of your family came to Canada, or, if they include members of First Nations, how they came to meet and interact with those who came as immigrants. If you begin this with your grandparents, great-aunts, or great-uncles and ask about the stories told them by their grandparents, you will become familiar with five generations of your family's history, including your own.

Ask them about what made your ancestors leave their countries of origin, what they know of the journey, and how those ancestors were received here in Canada. What helped them integrate into Canadian society? Did it take very long? Were there people who made integration difficult, as well as those who helped?

❷ After you have completed Activity 1, choose a family that has come to Canada fairly recently, and ask them the same questions you have put to your own relatives. Find the similarities (often about wanting a better life for one's children), and any differences. This can give you a better insight into that major fact of Canadian family history, the immigration experience.

❸ Discover what television programs are being watched by the children in your community. They will usually tell you in great detail when you ask! Watch these programs yourself from the standpoint of a professional dealing with young children. Identify what the children are learning, and then make a list of ideas about how you would like your own child-care program to address any problems with what the children are learning.

FURTHER READING

Carlsson-Paige, N., and D.E. Levin. (1987). *The War Play Dilemma: Balancing Needs and Values in the Early Childhood Classroom.* New York: Teachers College Press.
Aimed at the professional reader, this book addresses the thorny issue of children's (and some parents') desires for toy guns and other weapons. The authors' thorough research on the topic provides early childhood educators with sound bases for their decisions in this matter.

Carlsson-Paige, N., and D.E. Levin. (1990). *Who's Calling the Shots? How to Respond Effectively to Children's Fascination with War Play and War Toys.* Philadelphia: New Society.
A very readable version of the authors' earlier work, this book is aimed at parents.

Luke, Carmen. (1988). *Television and Your Child: A Guide for Concerned Parents.* Toronto: Kagan & Woo.
This book, which is addressed to Canadian parents but will appeal to teachers as well, is a practical guide on how to use television. Luke discusses the impact of television on children and offers excellent suggestions for introducing media literacy programs in both the school and the home.

Nelson, Joyce. (1987). *The Perfect Machine.* Toronto: Between the Lines.
Nelson is a cultural critic who writes with insight into not only the content of television, but how the medium itself affects people.

Nett, Emily. (1993). *Canadian Families Past and Present* (2nd ed.). Toronto: Butterworths.
Nett gives great satisfaction to professional and casual readers alike as she describes the various approaches people take toward studying the family, and describes the family itself in its changing and unchanging elements. What emerges is a fascinating picture of the social institution that is closest to us, and considerable insight for early childhood educators who deal with Canada's great variety of families and their children.

Singer, D.G., J.L. Singer, and D.M. Zuckerman. (1990). *The Parent's Guide: Use TV to Your Child's*

***Advantage*. Reston, VA: Acropolis Books.**
These highly respected experts answer parents' questions about the potentially harmful effects of TV on children and suggest many excellent parent–child activities that will help children become more discriminate television viewers.

REFERENCES

Ambert, A.-M. (1992). *The Effect of Children on Parents.* New York: Haworth Press.

Belsky, J. (1988). The "effects" of infant day care reconsidered. *Early Childhood Research Quarterly* 3, 235–72.

Burke, M.A., S. Crompton, A. Jones, and K. Nessner. (1991). Caring for children. *Canadian Social Trends* 22 (Autumn): 12–15.

Burnet, J.R., with H. Palmer. (1988) *"Coming Canadians": An Introduction to a History of Canada's Peoples.* Toronto: McClelland and Stewart.

Clarke-Stewart, K.A. (1989). Infant day care: Maligned or malignant? *American Psychologist* 44, 266–73.

Conway, J.F. (1990). *The Canadian Family Crisis.* Toronto: James Lorimer.

Cregheur, A., and M.S. Devereau. (1991). Canada's children. *Canadian Social Trends* 21 (Summer): 2–5.

Crysdale, S. (1991). *Families Under Stress: Community, Work, and Economic Change.* Toronto: Thompson Education Publishing.

Doherty-Derkowski, G. (1995). *Quality Matters: Excellence in Early Childhood Programs.* Don Mills, ON: Addison-Wesley.

Dorr, A., S.B. Graves, and E. Phelps. (1980). Television literacy for young children. *Journal of Communication* 30 (3): 71–83.

Gerbner, G., L. Gross, M. Morgan, and N. Signorielli. (1986). Living with television: The dynamics of the cultivation process. In J. Bryant and D. Zillman, eds., *Perspectives on Media Effects*, pp. 17–40. Hillsdale, NJ: Erlbaum.

Hardey, M., and G. Crow, eds. (1991). *Lone Parenthood.* Toronto: University of Toronto Press.

Hetherington, E.M. (1989). Coping with family transitions: Winners, losers, and survivors. *Child Development* 60: 1–14.

Hetherington, E.M., M. Stanley-Hagan, and E.R. Anderson. (1989). Marital transitions: A child's perspective. *American Psychologist* 44: 303–12.

Heusman, L.R., L.D. Eron, R. Klein, P. Brice, and P. Fischer. (1983). Mitigating the imitation of aggressive behaviours by changing children's attitudes about media violence. *Journal of Personality and Social Psychology* 44 (5): 899–910.

Hoffman, L.W. (1989). Effects of maternal employment in the two-parent family. *American Psychologist* 44: 283–92.

Kilbride, K.M. (1990). *Multicultural Early Childhood Education: A Discovery Approach.* Toronto: Ryerson Polytechnic University.

Kline, M., J.R. Johnston, and J.M. Tschann. (1991). The long shadow of marital conflict: A model of children's postdivorce adjustment. *Journal of Marriage and the Family* 53 (May): 297–309.

Lero, D.S. (1994). In transition: Changing patterns of work, family life and child care. *Ideas: The Journal of Emotional Well-Being in Child Care* 1 (3): 11–14.

Liebert, R.M., and J. Sprafkin. (1988). *The Early Window: Effects of Television on Children and Youth* (3rd ed.). New York: Pergamon Press.

Luke, C. (1988). *Television and Your Child: A Guide for Concerned Parents.* Toronto: Kagan & Woo.

Ramu, G.N., ed. (1989). *Marriage and the Family in Canada Today.* Scarborough, ON: Prentice-Hall.

Singer, D.G., J.L. Singer, and D.M. Zuckerman. (1990). *The Parent's Guide: Use TV to Your Child's Advantage.* Reston, VA: Acropolis Books.

Singer, D.G., D.M. Zuckerman, and J.L. Singer. (1980). Helping elementary school children learn about TV. *Journal of Communication* 30 (3): 84–93.

Singer, J.L., D.G. Singer, and D.M. Zuckerman. (1982). *Teaching Television.* New York: Dial Press.

Statistics Canada. (1991). *Health Report. Divorce 1990.* Catalogue No. 82-003S17, Supplement No. 17, Vols. 3 & 4. Ottawa: Supply and Services Canada.

Statistics Canada, 1991 Census of Canada. (1992). *Fami-

lies: Number, Type and Structure. Catalogue No. 93-312. Ottawa: Supply and Services Canada.

Statistics Canada. (1993a). *Basic Facts on Families in Canada, Past and Present.* Catalogue No. 89-516. Ottawa: Supply and Services Canada.

Statistics Canada. (1993b). *Television Viewing (Culture Statistics).* Catalogue No. 87-208. Ottawa: Supply and Services Canada.

Statistics Canada. (1994). Robert Glossop on the Canadian family. Interview in *Canadian Social Trends*,

Catalogue No. 11-008E. Ottawa: Supply and Services Canada.

Vanier Institute of the Family. (n.d.). *Canadian Families in Transition: The Implications and Challenges of Change.* (Booklet). Ottawa: Vanier Institute of the Family.

Wallerstein, J.S., and J.B. Kelly. (1980). *Surviving the Breakup: How Children and Parents Cope with Divorce.* New York: Basic Books.

Williams, T.M., ed. (1986). *The Impact of Television.* Orlando, FL: Academic Press.

CHAPTER 3
The Early Childhood Educators

✐ **Overview**

✐ **On Becoming an Early Childhood Educator**

✐ **Understanding Yourself**
- ◆ The Influence of Your Experiences
- ◆ Nurturing Yourself

✐ **Developing a Philosophy of Early Childhood Education**
- ◆ The Influence of Theories
- ◆ Your Educational Experiences

✐ **Reflective Practice**

✐ **Understanding the Roles of Early Childhood Educators**
- ◆ The Early Childhood Educator as Care-Giver
- ◆ Caring for Children

- ◆ Communicating with and Supporting Children
- ◆ Supporting Families
- ◆ Curriculum Design and Implementation
- ◆ Responding to Your Community

✐ **Entering the Profession**
- ◆ Responsibilities
- ◆ Rights
- ◆ Managing Stress
- ◆ Joining Others in the Profession

✐ **Summary**

✐ **Review Questions**

✐ **Discussion Questions**

✐ **Activities**

✐ **Further Reading**

✐ **References**

OVERVIEW

Now that you have read a chapter on children and one on their families, obviously the other key figure in the triangle is the educator — you. Perhaps you are approaching this chapter wondering what we have to say about educators. What do *you* have to say about educators and teachers? You have had a great deal of experience with teachers since you have spent at least a dozen years in school, so you will have your own unique insights to bring to this chapter. Which teachers stand out for you? Why? What were they like? Do you think they liked themselves? Did they like you? How did they relate to you? How did these teachers go about building an atmosphere that was conducive to good communication?

People who work in early childhood education have a unique opportunity to build strong relationships with young children. For this task they need an understanding of themselves and others, and an understanding of how to communicate effectively. Relationships with children and families will form the foundation for all of your work.

These qualities are all part of the main topic of this chapter — caring. Caring implies knowing — knowing in an authentic and meaningful way. If you care for another person, you feel motivated to learn all you can that will help you relate to him or her.

In this chapter, we present ways in which you can think about yourself as a caring early childhood education professional, with a focus on developing self-awareness and a personal philosophy of early childhood education. We suggest ways in which you can increase your understanding of what it means to care for other people's children and how you can understand and nurture yourself — a necessary part of your professional "upkeep."

We discuss what caring means as you engage in a special relationship with other people's children; as you care about children, their families, and the communities alongside whom you work and on whom you depend; and as you care about the profession of early childhood education. We also include a section about your rights and responsibilities in your chosen profession.

By the end of this chapter, you will be able to

❖ explain how an understanding of yourself will affect your work in early childhood education;

❖ explain how an understanding of theories and an early childhood education perspective can influence you;

❖ describe the elements that make up the work of an early childhood educator;

BOX 3.1 ONE-CARING: THE EARLY CHILDHOOD EDUCATOR

Whatever I do in life, whomever I meet, I am first and always one-caring or one cared-for. I do not "assume roles" unless I become an actor. "Mother" is not a role; "teacher" is not a role. When I became a mother I entered a very special relation — possibly the prototypical caring relation. When I became a teacher, I also entered a very special — and more specialized — caring relation. No enterprise or special function I am called upon to serve can relieve me of my responsibilities as one-caring.

— Noddings 1984, p. 175

❖ describe an educator's relationships with the children, their families, and the community;

❖ discuss the ways in which you can maintain good physical and emotional health in a stressful career;

❖ discuss issues related to professionalism in practice.

ON BECOMING AN EARLY CHILDHOOD EDUCATOR

Preparing to become an early childhood educator, like preparing for other areas of professional education, is a learning process made up of at least three different parts. The first part is development of self-knowledge and awareness. Self-knowledge requires an understanding of childhood experiences, the influence of family and culture, and the ways in which you have grown to become the person that you are now. Self-knowledge also means understanding how the field you have chosen confirms personal beliefs and how it suits your own qualities and goals.

Acquiring knowledge and understanding that will support you in the work that you have chosen is the second part of the process. You will study theories and practical strategies that are part of the profession of early childhood education and incorporate this knowledge into your own skills and expertise.

The last part is a reflective practice, which means that you will think about, analyze, and evaluate yourself, your learning, and your values throughout your career.

When you reach the end of this learning process and enter the profession, you will need to evaluate yourself so that you can carry out your responsibilities, rights, and strategies in a way that ensures you can offer a high quality of care to children. We discuss these aspects and processes of early childhood education in this chapter.

UNDERSTANDING YOURSELF

The Influence of Your Experiences

As you look around your classroom, you see a group of people who share the desire to participate first-hand in the development of young children. Like your classmates, you are probably fascinated by the characteristics of young children and eager to learn more about them. Although you may not have thought about it, being effective with young children depends to some extent on your self-awareness and personal values and attitudes.

You have a responsibility to be as clear as possible in understanding yourself so that you can interact with children and parents honestly and with integrity. How can you gain insight into your biases, beliefs, and practices? First of all, you can learn to reflect on your own childhood and other personal experiences. This is a process that could be called life-histories, life-stories, or autobiography, which can help you understand the person you are, including yourself as an early childhood educator. Autobiography requires quiet time for reflecting on formative events, experiences, and people in your childhood. What memories stand out for you? What holidays, birthdays, and childhood illnesses do you remember? Why do you still remember those particular events and people, and how do they affect you? Perhaps reconstructing a life-history requires that you talk about childhood events with your siblings, parents, or grandparents. The purpose of this process is twofold: to help you understand the formation of your belief system and your responses to children, and to increase your sensitivity to how children in your care experience the world.

You will come to recognize values, attitudes, and beliefs that are part of your family and cultural background. Perhaps you have well-established family traditions that you value but that are not familiar to your classmates, nor do they understand them. You may be aware that your ways of thinking and doing things are different from your own family's or from your peers'.

Your values, attitudes, and beliefs develop throughout life, often from taking bits and pieces from many sources to create your own way of thinking and doing. Friends, teachers, classmates, and colleagues have influenced you and continue to contribute to the foundation of your belief system. Throughout this process, you may decide to forego some assumptions or perceptions from your past, and emphasize and highlight others. This is an important part of coming to know yourself better and to choose for yourself the direction of your future growth.

Nurturing Yourself

To provide a nurturing environment for young children all day, adults must also receive some nurturing — they cannot always be dispensing love and attention without receiving some love and attention back.

Most people think of caring for young children as having a selfless quality because the children are the primary focus. You are constantly aware of where they are, what they are doing, and how they are doing it so that they will be safe and so that you can meet their needs and provide them with opportunities and encouragement for optimal growth and development. The rewarding part, in addition to the children's progress, is that you also benefit from the relationships you develop and you grow in the process. In trusting, understanding, responding honestly to, and taking responsibility for children, you enter into experiences that make you a better person. The result is that you come to value the children for who they are and for your mutual relationship.

At the same time, caring for children demands a great deal of energy and inner strength. Many early childhood educators overlook their own need for nurturing. Adults have needs, too, and because they are adults and not children, they must take responsibility for filling their own needs. How? This is where knowing yourself comes in. When you care for children, you make an effort to get to know them (their likes, dislikes, moods, fears, and limitations), to accept them, and to be patient and honest in your relations with them. This is how you should respond to yourself as well.

It is easy to overlook the simple, obvious parts of caring for yourself — getting enough rest, eating properly, and exercising. In addition to meeting your physical needs, what gives you pleasure and makes you feel whole and adequate for your work? For some people, reading or spending time with friends fills their needs; for others, it may be listening to music or going dancing.

Some people feel that paying attention to oneself is selfish and egocentric. It is not. Recognizing and giving attention to your needs ensures your own physical and emotional well-being, and means that you will also be able to continue to meet the needs of the children in your care.

DEVELOPING A PHILOSOPHY OF EARLY CHILDHOOD EDUCATION

The Influence of Theories

Mark is 4 years old. Like all children, sometimes he is fearful and insecure because there are many things around him he does not understand. Since his baby sister was born, he says his parents do not like him as much as they used to. He tries to do nice things for the other children, but then he interferes with their play, argues, and, most recently, has begun shoving and hitting other children for the kind of minor irritations that did not bother him six months earlier.

Some of the teachers at the day-care centre have become concerned about Mark, and they have differing opinions on how to support him and deal with his behaviour. Judy thinks the children need more structure in the room. She suggests that clarifying the rules, reminding the children what the rules are, and consistently enforcing them with predetermined consequences will help not only Mark, but all the children. She favours withdrawing him from the activities in the room as a way of coping with him, especially when he behaves "inappropriately."

Damion objects, stating that he thinks this solution is too extreme. He feels sure that Mark's disruptive behaviour is temporary and that as he matures he will grow out of it. Damion suggests that they continue to provide safe and nurturing relationships for Mark and that, over time, he will relate to his peers in a more acceptable way.

Brenda's focus is different. She says it is important that everyone — Mark and the adults at the centre — understand his experiences and how they may have contributed to changes in his behaviour. She thinks the adults need to be responsive to Mark, discuss his behaviour with him, and continue to meet his needs without conditions. It is also important, she states, that everyone give Mark honest messages in their interactions.

Mark's behaviour is a common occurrence. The points of view of the three early childhood educators are typical of adults' responses to Mark's behaviour. These responses are determined in part by their particular belief systems, values, and biases, some of which may be shared by other colleagues or by parents. An exploration of your personal and professional qualities and attitudes may help you understand how these differences came to be and to assess how they will affect your style and approach to children. If you could speak to Judy, Damion, and Brenda, you might ask each of them how they arrived at their conclusion about how to respond to Mark. You would want to know if they based their opinions on a particular theory or on their knowledge about Mark and their feelings for him.

Perhaps they would say they were responding simply in a way that draws on both theory and their feelings about Mark's needs.

As you enter the field of early childhood education, you can benefit from exploring the theories that influence the views of many people in the profession. These theories, which result from both research and practice, attempt to explain children's behaviour, to predict how they might behave in the future, and to indicate what they need for healthy development. Early childhood education philosophy and practices are eclectic, which means that they incorporate and blend perspective, research, and practice from other disciplines, such as psychology, mental health, and education.

Child development theories are either maturationist or interactionist. Theories emphasizing **maturation** describe common patterns, sequences, and stages of development and behaviour and consider these to be universal and determined by genetic make-up. Damion's interpretation of Mark's behaviour would fall into this category. For many years, these concepts have helped parents and educators determine whether the development or behaviour of a child is typical.

Interactionist theories, such as constructivist theory, emphasize the interaction between genetic predisposition and experience. Constructivism holds that both environment and genetic inheritance are important and that a child gains knowledge and understanding from all experience. This means that opportunities to interact actively and autonomously with people and materials lead to healthier development in children. Brenda's point of view on Mark's behaviour is in line with this type of theory (based on the works of John Dewey, Jean Piaget, Lawrence Kohlberg, and Constance Kamii). Constructivist theory, which forms a foundation for early childhood

education based on the whole child, is discussed in greater detail in Chapter 10.

Learning and behaviourist theories emphasize the role of the environment and reactions of others as influences on behaviour. They provide understanding of the factors within the environment and in your own responses to children that influence behaviour, and over time can affect learning. Judy's perspective reflects a behaviourist viewpoint. Although these theories alone provide a limited perspective on development, they can expand our understanding of ways to change the environment and our own behaviours to facilitate development.

Urie Bronfenbrenner (1979) introduced another framework for understanding many facets of our lives with children called the **ecological system** (see Figure 3.1). Ecological theory informs and reminds us of the complexity of our world and the various influences of family, community, society, and cultural values. Each aspect has a role to play and influences the experiences of children. Early childhood educators, in turn, have a role to play in each of the layers of the ecological system. In this chapter, this theory can help us to think about who we are with children, and the complex influences that affect our relationships and work.

Ecological theory claims that there are three layers of interconnected influence. At the most central layer, which is called the microsystem, children live in their most immediate worlds, the family and child care. This is where children experience the most direct influence and interaction with other people. Other members of the child's microsystem normally include parents, siblings, educators, and peers. The extent of positive influence of the child's microsystem is often determined by the strength of relationships among its various parts, called the mesosystem. The relationships

FIGURE 3.1 ECOLOGICAL SYSTEM

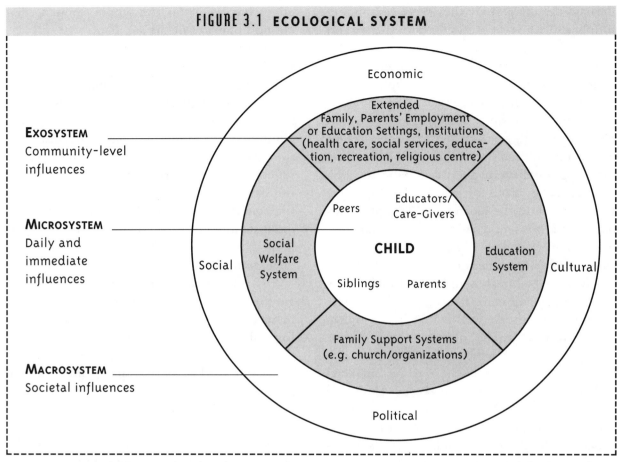

Source: Based on U. Bronfenbrenner. (1979). *The Ecology of Human Development: Experiments by Nature and Design.* Cambridge, MA: Harvard University Press; and D. Peters and S. Kontos. (1987). *Continuity and Discontinuity of Experience in Child Care.* Norwood, NJ: Ablex Publishing.

among members of the microsystem include meetings between parents and teachers, their contact with the children's siblings, and the extent to which parents know the children's peers.

The second layer of the ecological system is known as the exosystem. This layer consists of those institutions or people who might influence children's development, but with whom they have less direct contact. Extended family, parents' work or study environment, and such institutions as health care, social services

education, recreation, and church are all part of the exosystem. They affect children in powerful, but less direct, ways. For instance, if you are familiar with the pressures that a parent is facing in the work environment, such as the threat of being laid off, you can understand better the interactions that occur at drop-off and pick-up times. This, in turn, may help you provide supportive responses to the parent and the child.

The third, or outer, layer is called the macrosystem, which refers to societal values that influence the child and child care. For instance, there may be a strong belief in society that mothers should stay at home and care for their children and not enter the work force. This belief may influence whether parents choose to use child care, whether politicians support child-care services, and whether people decide to enter the field of early childhood education.

As you read this text and consider your own ideas about children and what you think is important for their development, you may find that your beliefs fit all or some of the theories discussed here. We encourage you to become familiar with all of the theories so that you can gain a deeper understanding of children in your work.

Your Educational Experiences

You may be enrolled in a postsecondary education program in preparation for work in early childhood education. In Canada, the programs vary from region to region. Some are intended simply to introduce a novice to the field and may be as brief as a few months, while others provide the opportunity for students to obtain a diploma or degree. Your decision to enter such a program affirms a commitment to a career with young children and their families.

Whatever the length of your early childhood education program, you will have many opportunities to think, read, write, and talk about children, families, and yourself within the profession of early childhood education. You will have the opportunity to experience and practise being with children in child-care or early education environments. You have an opportunity to learn — through doing and thinking — the particular bodies of knowledge, skills, and attitudes required to work effectively with young children and their families.

Opportunities to examine and change your understanding of yourself and children can lead you to knowledge, skills, and attitudes that are different from the ones you had when you entered the program. You could experience conflicts between your "established" views and those presented as a part of your formal education. It is important to examine new ideas, whether they are the result of information given in lectures or books, through peer discussion, or from direct experience. You are beginning a journey of personal discovery and development that will benefit you long after you have graduated from the program. There are risks to opening yourself sufficiently to consider change, but these are part of the challenge and excitement of this period of formal education.

REFLECTIVE PRACTICE

One valuable component of your education is your practicum, which gives you the opportunity to relate theory and practice. Developing new skills and methods requires that you think about and analyze their effectiveness and compatibility with your own philosophy. This process is called **reflective practice**, a process that is vital to your continuing development as a professional. During your formal education, you will learn about current theory and preferred methods of enhancing development and learning. However, the field is constantly growing with new research and information. Methods and techniques change and must be adapted to meet the unique needs of individuals, groups, families, and communities. For these reasons, you need to develop the habit of evaluating your own level of knowledge and skills. Are you aware of current literature? Do you know what issues are being debated in your region or community? Are you applying current methods and practices? In what areas are you effective? In what areas would you like to gain new knowledge and skills?

The profession of early childhood education is evolving — the learning process never ends. As a professional, you can continue to explore ways to improve your practice throughout your career. From time to time, you can attend workshops and seminars, take courses, and discuss your work with others, along with doing personal reading and writing. The limits on learning come only from the limits of one's own curiosity and imagination, and whether one is able to follow the childhood desire to explore. Wise teachers learn this from the children in their care.

UNDERSTANDING THE ROLES OF EARLY CHILDHOOD EDUCATORS

The Early Childhood Educator as Care-Giver

Adults who take care of children need to know, understand, and care about themselves; care about the children, their families, and their communities; and carefully prepare spaces and relationships so that children can develop. There are at least three ways in which to understand the word "care" in the context of early childhood education.

The first sense is care as compassion or empathy: being concerned for the children and their parents; feeling and sharing something of the experience of separation and of the transition from the private world of home and family to the more public world of child care and other

care-giver. To care in this way is to see the child as a person — not as an object for your curriculum plan, or the focus of your daily goals, or the way to make a name for yourself in your career. This kind of caring means seeing the child as a person whose experiences and attempts to make sense of the world you cannot fully understand but by which you can be touched, and to whom you can respond.

A second sense of caring is doing for, or with, children what they cannot do for themselves. This "nitty-gritty" kind of care-giving entails helping them with all the activity of daily living: eating, washing, dressing, going to the toilet, and meeting all manner of personal needs. It may also include helping children with their decision making so that they understand the possible consequences of their actions. Caring in this way is intended to assist children to attain a sense of security and well-being and to help them predict and understand their world, with the intent to encourage them to develop as much independence as they can handle. At the same time, they also need to experience the pleasure of interdependence and doing many things to please and assist others.

A third sense of caring is in providing opportunities for children to increase and value both their self-knowledge and understanding, and their knowledge of their world and of how they fit into it. Understanding how children develop can guide you in creating an environment in which they can expand these qualities in their play. They depend on you to provide materials, spaces, and worthwhile experiences that are appropriate for them, and to encourage and facilitate positive and strong relationships among the children and their families.

These types of caring are not mutually exclusive, nor are they separable in good early childhood education practice. To meet the needs of the child, you must address and provide for all aspects of development (cognitive, physical, emotional, and social) to ensure healthy development. It is a challenge for the early childhood education field, and for you as a professional working directly with children, to attend to each type of caring and to work from the whole concept for the good of every child and family.

Caring for Children

Being in charge of a group of children means having an awareness of many children at the same time, which is what Mina discovered in her first year in the profession. Every day when she was with the children, she entered into a state of watchfulness, something that soon felt natural to her.

Typically, on her way to the door to welcome a late parent with a child, she helped Emma open a stubborn lid on a paint pot, checked on Pedro, who was watering plants, and noted that Pascale and Norma had spilled all the Lego when they took it down from the shelf. The latecomer was Nadia, who immediately showed Mina the bandage on her knee and insisted that Mina listen to her story about falling off her bicycle before she allowed her grandmother to leave. Meanwhile, Mina had to show the janitor which shelving unit needed repair as a group of children gathered around her for a spontaneous story in the library corner. As she read aloud, she frequently glanced around the room to be sure she knew what each child was doing while she tried to observe how the new parent volunteer got along with the children. She made a mental note that at the end of the day she wanted to record how well Jules and Sarah progressed in working on the new puzzles that were usually difficult for 3-year-olds. As you can see from this portrait of only a few minutes of Mina's morning, "a state of watchfulness" describes well her demeanour, a way of being that is essential for all early childhood educators.

Mina's day was not over after the children were all gone. Once the room was quiet, while the day was fresh in her mind, she recorded her observations of the day. She had jotted down a few notes on a small notepad throughout the day to help her remember some of the most important things.

Communicating with and Supporting Children

Children experience adults in a variety of ways. For example, the way you say hello in the morning, how you respond when they show you their new boots, whether you listen to their story about their kitten that got chased by a big dog — all these "small" events have significance to young children. Their perception of whether you think their experience is valuable depends on your response.

You as an educator communicate through seeing and listening to children, and whether you are totally involved has a profound effect on your relationship with them. Every child needs to be seen and heard. But seeing means more than just using your eyes, and listening is more than just using your ears. When you actively attend and listen to children, you understand them. Your body responds to what they say or do in such a way that it shows your caring. Children know if your questions are purely rhetorical or if you are genuinely interested in their opinion or decision.

Children communicate in various ways. Younger children use crying, gesture, and body movement, while older children learn and refine spoken language. Listening therefore encompasses paying attention to all that the children "say," even if it is not always communicated in words. Adults who work with children need good communication skills. These include the ability to listen to the ideas of others, to pay attention, to ensure that nonverbal messages are congruent with spoken messages, and to be able to express themselves clearly. Adults need good conversation skills, including taking turns in sharing information and in not dominating conversations.

The nature of conversations with children can be different from those with other adults. Remember to wait for a response from children without continuing to talk just because the child does not respond immediately. Children need time to respond, although sometimes you can remind a child that it is his turn with a statement like, "What do you think?" Paraphrasing is an excellent way to introduce new concepts or words to children as well as to ensure that you fully understand their message. Paraphrasing means reflecting back to the child your understanding of what she said. For instance, when a toddler is gesturing at the end of nap time, a paraphrased response might be: "You want to get up?"

Your conversations throughout the day need to be authentic and not simply ways to develop speech and language in the children. The focus of your communication with the children will determine the levels of trust and security they experience. When they feel safe, secure, and cared-for, they develop new skills and understandings and explore their world with confidence. In addition, how you communicate with children directly influences how they relate to others.

To have a "real talk" with children, it is important that the relationship be one of mutual trust and that you are attentive, honest, and reassuring. It is only when children feel that they are really heard and accepted that meaningful dialogue can take place. Meaningful conversations allow children to increase their understanding of themselves and their world. Such conversations permit exchanges of real ideas and values and build relationships and connections.

Supporting Families

For many early childhood professionals, establishing and maintaining a good relationship with parents is the most challenging aspect of their work. Developing relationships between the home and the early childhood setting, fostering a sense of caring and understanding with families, and creating an atmosphere of belonging can become a most rewarding part of the job.

There are many reasons why open and positive relationships are essential for the children, the family, and the early childhood professional. Two of the most apparent are also two of the most important:

1. Parents must be recognized and respected as the most significant people in their children's lives. Your role as care-giver and educator is to support, reinforce, and complement this relationship.

2. Meaningful involvement of the families enables early childhood programs to have a positive and lasting influence on children.

A meaningful relationship with families is one of mutual support and shared power and decision making, which means sharing information and inviting parents to participate in the centre's activities. The aim is to enhance the parents' understanding of and pleasure in their child and to increase their confidence as parents. While formal, scheduled contacts such as meetings or projects may help, the most important opportunity to build relationships is the daily exchange between parents and early childhood professionals. Implicit in an approach that stresses mutual support is working with parents to provide care for the child, rather than working for or substituting for parents. Both sides can learn from and contribute to the other.

Early childhood educators have an influence on parents even when communication is limited or when parents' involvement is not solicited. Professionals may sometimes make parents feel less than competent or decrease their self-confidence by giving unsolicited advice or telling them what to do. Often parents view even the least experienced early childhood professional as an authority on children, and so it is easy for them to believe that you know more than they do, even about their child, and that you do a better job than they do. This kind of interaction does not benefit the children or their families.

You may attempt to relate to parents by involving them in the program. Although this

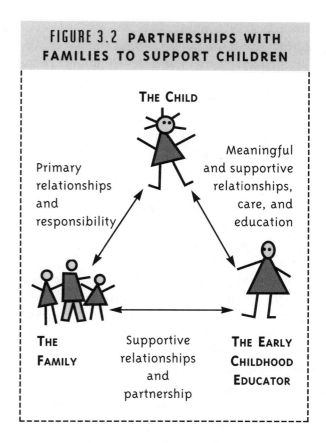

FIGURE 3.2 PARTNERSHIPS WITH FAMILIES TO SUPPORT CHILDREN

THE CHILD

Primary relationships and responsibility

Meaningful and supportive relationships, care, and education

THE FAMILY

Supportive relationships and partnership

THE EARLY CHILDHOOD EDUCATOR

is an excellent goal, you need to be careful about the message you send. If you invite their participation as a way of enlisting "help" that you control, through invitations such as, "We need help with this project and would like you to help us with it," you are likely to maintain only limited parental involvement in the program. There is a real difference between letting parents help out and working in partnership with them.

Curriculum Design and Implementation

The purpose of early childhood programs extends beyond notions of providing a safe place for children while their parents are at work or school. The range of needs moves from that of providing shelter and safe surroundings to that of supporting and encouraging personal growth and development. In an early childhood setting, you have a fundamental responsibility to ensure that children are safe and receive adequate nutrition and opportunities for physical fitness and good health. When parents leave their children in your care, they implicitly trust that you will ensure that these basic needs are met. Only when children and their parents are confident in these essentials can other goals be pursued. What are the goals that families might have for the care of their children? How are these goals to be incorporated into life in the child-care setting? You can find the answers to these questions through communication with the children's families. Among these is teaching children to care for themselves and for their possessions, to act in ways that will avoid harm to themselves and others, and to understand relationships with others and the boundaries of those relationships.

Beyond this, parents need an understanding that their children will receive the quality of attention and care that will benefit their children. Parents are usually intensely interested in and concerned about their children, and although they may not expect you to share the extent of their enthralment, they do need to know that you enjoy their children and think they are special. This means communicating with parents about the children's experiences and keeping them informed about the children's progress, accomplishments, and relationships.

In addition to quality care and meaningful relationships, parents expect that their children will be given opportunities to develop in creative, social, cognitive, and emotional areas.

Therefore, they expect early childhood settings to provide opportunities for play that is facilitated by attuned adults. Through curriculum that is based in the natural processes of play, educators carefully plan to ensure that learning opportunities are at a level that will challenge, but not overwhelm, the children. Although this planning may appear simple, a blend of theoretical expertise and practical methods is required to create a curriculum that is suitable for nurturing young children's learning. Through play, the children can learn about themselves and their relationships with others, including developing an understanding of socially acceptable behaviour. As children learn from these situations, you can also help them to identify feelings and emotions, express these appropriately, and respond to the expressions of others. Parents want their children to develop social and cognitive competence, learn to solve problems, and attempt new experiences.

During their first few years, children experience growth and development at a faster rate than at any other time in life. As a result, they spend a lot of time learning new skills and in transition from one developmental level to another. Preschool settings provide one of the earliest opportunities to identify difficulties or problems in a child's growth or development. Families expect early childhood professionals to work with them in helping children with the transitions in the maturation process as well as helping with problems that develop along the way.

Whether you work with families as a day-home provider, caring for four or five children in your home, or as an educator in a child-care centre or a kindergarten program, your work will include these elements:

❖ making observations and keeping written records;

❖ planning and preparing appropriate learning experiences for children that are based primarily on their needs and interests;

❖ playing with children and guiding their behaviour;

❖ entering into meaningful conversations with each child and his or her parents;

❖ meeting with other educators to discuss the program and to exchange ideas and recommendations;

❖ meeting with people from other social agencies or institutions, such as health, education, recreation, and social services.

Underlying your routine responsibilities, you will need an understanding and knowledge of each individual child. An early childhood educator does not respond in particular ways simply because a child is 3 years old, but because this is Jennifer, who happens to be 3

years old, but who has all sorts of other individual characteristics. In other words, you need to know what is appropriate for individual children and the group based not just on theory, but on your accumulated experience with children. In this way, you will begin to respond to them spontaneously at a given moment without stopping to think it over. The need for an immediate response to a child does not permit time to stop and think for very long. You might find that you respond before you are conscious of what you are doing. For instance, you would spontaneously hold and comfort a child who has fallen and bumped her head, and you would not stop to think about what the right approach is. It is only after the act that you reflect on the appropriateness and adequacy of your response. Given this characteristic of working with children in this profession, our caring means that we need to be alert so that we can be totally involved with the children in both mind and body.

Responding to Your Community

Your work in child care is affected by the community in which you live and work, and by the communities in which the families live and work. The institutions, work environments, and cultural beliefs also shape the world in which you and the families live. Familiarity with the community assists you in many facets of your work: insight into the experiences of the children, understanding of particular beliefs and child-rearing practices of parents, and facilitation of communication and support for families. Communities vary in many ways. Following are some of the environmental, social, and personal factors that make up communities or neighbourhoods.

❖ Population density: Neighbourhoods range from those comprised mostly of highrise apartments to those in which children live in sparsely populated rural regions.

❖ Noise levels: Often areas of high density are also areas of high noise levels.

❖ Physical characteristics: These characteristics include arrangement of streets and access to parks or open spaces, recreational facilities, and libraries.

❖ Population characteristics: These include income levels, ages, and racial, ethnic, and educational backgrounds.

Communities that are populated by people of similar backgrounds are described as *homogeneous*; those that include people of different backgrounds are *heterogeneous*. The make-up of the community affects the ways in which families and children live together, the experiences that children have, and beliefs and values about what is important in life.

Social and personal differences include the patterns of interactions among community members, the ways in which people living there perceive their environment, the services available in the community, and the ways in which families use these services.

The ways in which people interact with one another in a community may be associated with its size and the stability of its population. For example, people in small, rural towns where the same families have lived, worked, received their formal education, and raised children for two or three generations have different patterns and methods of interaction than people in an inner-city community, where a resident might not see a familiar face for several days. The experiences of families and children are different in these two settings — different in their experiences of support available for child rearing, and in the experiences of relationship, trust, concern, and co-operation.

How adults perceive their community affects children. Parents who think the community is safe and other families are trustworthy encourage more freedom, discovery, and independence in their children than those who think their community is unsafe.

Community services vary from those provided by an agency or government department situated in the community to those provided for the community but located elsewhere. These services provide support in education and health, recreational programs, and compensation in social-service welfare programs and food banks. Within each of these there may be any number of services provided by public or private agencies and by paid professionals and volunteers. Early childhood educators need to become familiar with these services and know how to use them. Child care is part of the network of community services, and it is helpful to understand how you fit into this network.

ENTERING THE PROFESSION

When you complete your education, you will make the final steps of entry into the profession. At this point, you will come to recognize the responsibilities you have accepted, the rights you have as a professional, the potential sources of stress, and the support available to you through your colleagues and a variety of organizations.

Responsibilities

When you make yourself available and offer to assist children and families, you implicitly engage in a professional act. Your responsibilities as an early childhood educator contain three commitments. First, you promise that you have recognized the need for a caring relationship based on trust; second, that you are competent and have the knowledge needed to care for and educate children; and third, that you will use that competence and knowledge in the best interest of the children and their families.

By offering your professional services, you gain access into children's lives. You learn their weaknesses and vulnerabilities as well as their strengths and abilities. You become important and close to the children and to their families. In accepting your responsibilities, you are making a commitment not to abuse the children's trust, to make their interests your priority, and to support them and their families in any areas of vulnerability or need.

As an early childhood professional, your overriding responsibility is to the children in your care. When we use the term "responsibility," we mean your legal, or regulatory, obligation and your ethical obligation. Although you also have responsibilities to parents, co-workers, yourself, and the professional field, in cases in which a decision requires you to make a choice, your responsibility to the child always takes priority.

Regulatory or legal responsibilities are normally spelled out in provincial or regional

---

BOX 3.2 THE MEANING OF "PROFESSIONAL"

There has been increasing debate about the need to professionalize the field of early childhood education and care in an attempt to improve early childhood practice and to improve the status and working conditions of its practitioners. The terms "profession" and "professional" carry several meanings and images, so that although we continue to use these terms in early childhood education, we are not always sure about what we mean. The terms are used to describe the fields of law and medicine and also to describe people who make a living at a particular activity rather than engaging in it as a hobby. For instance, carpenters and cooks are called professionals if they engage in their crafts for money rather than as hobbies or as amateurs. Characteristics of professions typically include

◆ a code of ethics that provides direction and boundaries for the conduct of all members;

◆ autonomy with regard to the establishment of standards of practice and to the qualifications of members;

◆ altruism, that is, professionals provide services to others that might involve self-sacrifice;

◆ an optimum distance in relating to clients, sometimes called "detached concern";

◆ a long period of specialized formal training;

◆ practice based on specialized knowledge and skills that are known only to members of the profession;

◆ membership in a professional association.

The early childhood community is still struggling with the desirability of meeting these conditions and considering alternative ways of thinking about professionalism. In this text, we offer another way to think about what it means to be "professional."

legislation, which can then be interpreted in the form of a procedures, or licensing, manual. Other regulatory requirements can be particular to specific agencies or municipalities. Although these responsibilities vary, they usually deal with similar areas. Individual responsibilities for early childhood professionals are in areas of providing safe and healthy environments for children, including reporting particular "reportable" illnesses; providing appropriate materials and experiences for children in care, including such routine activities as naps, snacks, lunches, and toileting; and working with parents to keep them informed about their children's progress.

Other regulations have to do with the administration of the program and include descriptions of group size, staff-to-child ratios, written records, indoor and outdoor space requirements, and staff qualifications.

Ethical responsibilities include those aspects of work that are not determined through regulation, or cases in which conflict arises between a legal requirement and what you believe to be in the best interests of the children. Working with young children implies that caring is authentic and also ethical. In caring, you want the children to develop and grow, and your energy is directed toward that purpose. You also have a responsibility to keep informed on new theories and recommended educational practices that will enhance the learning process. The curriculum you provide will need to incorporate increasing understanding about children, their development, and the learning process.

Your decisions, then, will always be for the good of the children, and to that end you strive to use the best of your knowledge and skills to advance their growth and development.

Rights

The rights of an early childhood professional are more difficult to describe than the responsibilities. However, being treated fairly and with respect is certainly at the top of the list. These rights mean that you can expect to be employed on the basis of a written contract that describes the rights that you and the employer have. In effect, you agree to provide child-care and/or educational services, and the employer agrees to pay you a given rate for a specific length of time.

Although they are not always included in a written contract, there are several personnel matters that you can consider as "rights." The job description, which should be in writing, outlines what is expected of you in the job you accept. A salary scale indicates the remuneration you may expect to receive, and any increases based on experience and education qualifications. This scale usually includes details of exceptional situations: holiday pay, sick leave, professional development, and overtime pay. Benefits should be stated clearly and include detailed statements regarding retirement plans, liability insurance, health insurance, and workers' compensation. Any particular conditions that are required, such as immunization records or police checks, should be given in writing with an assurance of confidentiality. Other conditions about which you should be informed are vacations: how much vacation time you are entitled to and how you book it; the schedule of meetings, especially if they fall outside regular work hours; if there is a probationary period, how long it lasts and how this will be changed to permanent employment; and how evaluation and grievance procedures work.

Less tangible, but equally important, are the right to feel free to express your opinions, to question, and to suggest; the right to be given advance notice of decisions that affect your life; and the right to be given an opportunity to have a voice in any prospective changes.

These rights are basic to your well-being as you work with children and address potential sources of workplace stress.

Managing Stress

To say that caring for young children is demanding is stating the obvious — ask any parent or educator! At the same time, educating young children is the most stimulating kind of work imaginable. Providing learning experiences appropriate to each child in your program is a challenge — time and energy are required to evaluate and adapt activities to ensure that each child is benefiting from your curriculum. Providing appropriate experiences means ongoing planning and research to obtain resources. Children's eagerness to learn and their liveliness, along with the rewards and satisfactions of seeing them learn and grow, generate energy and enthusiasm in adults. The "internal" aspects of child care — being with the children and like-minded colleagues — provide drive and motivation for professionals in the field.

Early childhood educators also experience a degree of stress that is inherent in our profession — it has to do simply with children's needs. Children's needs sometimes seem of enormous proportions, greater than the capacity of adults to fill those needs. Some of the stress inherent in being with children every day is a result of aspects of caring, that is, stress having to do with the difference between the terms "caring for" and "caring about" (Noddings 1984; Baines, Evans, & Neysmith 1991; Abel & Nelson 1990). When you care for

children, you interact with them and develop feeling for them. The tension between "caring for" and "caring about" arises in situations in which you feel unable to adequately provide for children whom you "care about." Although you do the best you can, you will not always be able to provide for all the needs of every child. Recognizing this reality can go a long way to reducing the stress and relieving the feeling of inadequacy.

Stress from simply being with the children can be compounded by additional relationships and communication with parents, co-workers, supervisors, and administrators, each of whom might have different ideas, expectations, and ways of communicating. Differences in opinion about relating to children can give rise to conflicts between what you wish to do, or think is appropriate, and the practices, regulations, or policies that govern your practice.

Being aware of inherent sources of stress in your profession can help you avoid becoming worn down. You will need to find ways to counteract stress to ensure continued job satisfaction and a sense that you have control over your own life. Maintaining involvement and enthusiasm at work is essential. The quality of your life and the quality of the lives of people who share your microsystem (children in your care, their families, and your colleagues) may be directly affected by the state of your well-being.

This acknowledgement of the stress that can potentially affect professionals in early childhood education might seem discouraging. However, recognizing the possibility and working to prevent stress helps to reduce its occurrence and impact. As we suggested earlier in the chapter, it is possible to learn how to care for yourself in ways that keep you

Among the many professional associations in Canada with a focus on the well-being of children and families, three national associations are briefly described below. We encourage you to gather more information on these and other national, international, and local associations.

The Canadian Association for Young Children (CAYC) is made up of members from across North America, including parents, teachers, care-givers, administrators, and students. It is specifically concerned with the well-being of children from birth through age 9. The aims of the association include

- working for the development and well-being of children;
- fostering desirable conditions, programs, and practices for children;
- encouraging continual professional growth;
- bringing into active co-operation all groups concerned with children;
- disseminating information on child development.

CAYC also publishes *Canadian Children*.

The Canadian Child Care Federation (CCCF) is committed to improving the quality of child-care services by providing information and support services to the Canadian child-care community. It aims to

- support the development and activities of the child-care community;
- provide information, facilitate communication, and develop resources;
- develop models, standards, and guidelines for quality care, professional development, and organizational design;
- promote research and link research to practice.

CCCF also publishes *Interaction*.

The Child Care Advocacy Association of Canada (CCAAC) is committed to accessible, affordable, high-quality, nonprofit child care. Its aims include

- expanding the child-care system so that it is affordable, comprehensive, and accessible to all Canadians;
- improving child care in Canada, so that high-quality, not-for-profit child care is available to all Canadians.

CCAAC also publishes *Vision*.

healthy. Many people manage stress by using such relaxation techniques as yoga and tai chi, or exercising by swimming, stretching, or doing aerobics. Frequent, open discussion with colleagues and friends also helps to dissipate stress.

How you handle your day can also make a difference. Taking breaks, including a full lunch break, is a necessity, even if you think you do not need them. The cumulative result of working without breaks can intensify your stress and lead you to be less effective in your work. Planning each day well also helps you feel relaxed.

Developing an awareness of your stress levels and understanding and responding to your own needs are steps you can take to remain physically and mentally healthy and alert.

Joining Others in the Profession

In early childhood education, you will almost inevitably encounter experiences for which you need professional support: advice on handling a particular working condition issue with your employer, information that might help a particular situation with a child, or someone to talk with who understands the nature of your work. For these reasons and others, you may wish to consider joining a professional organization.

Professional associations provide members with information, advocate for improvements in the standards of care for children and in the working conditions of their members, and determine or describe standards for practice. These recognized purposes of professional organizations are not the only benefits for early childhood professionals. Other, less tangible, personal and professional benefits to membership include

❖ opportunities to meet and share ideas with colleagues who work in similar situations or with similar groups of children;

❖ opportunities for formal and informal professional growth through reading and contributing to professional journals and through participation in workshops, seminars, and conferences;

❖ opportunities for you to stay up-to-date with what is happening elsewhere in child care;

❖ opportunities to find out what governments are doing in the area of child care;

❖ a collective voice for important issues that may help create change.

As in many professional fields, there are local, regional, national, and international organizations that provide various services to their members.

SUMMARY

Working effectively with young children requires that we be knowledgeable, well-prepared, caring adults. We have presented views on what is entailed in both attaining and recognizing the knowledge we have from our experience, theoretical study, and practice.

Early childhood professionals need to continue to search for greater insight into and understanding of themselves and the various experiences that influence who they are and how they view their work with children. They need to develop an awareness of their biases and prejudices and of the forces in their lives that might cause stress, and to find ways to excel by being thoughtful about children and in association with other professionals.

As professionals, we need to search for ways to improve our practice with children and families by increasing our awareness and sensitivity to the influences that affect them and by understanding the communities within which we live and work.

Finally, we must take seriously our professional commitment to provide for children in ways that enhance their opportunities to grow, develop, and understand themselves and their world.

REVIEW QUESTIONS

❶ Why do early childhood educators need to understand themselves?

❷ Explain two types of theories that influence how educators respond to children's behaviour.

❸ What is the meaning of "care" in the context of early childhood education?

❹ Describe the characteristics of a meaningful relationship with families.

❺ List at least five responsibilities of the early childhood educator.

❻ Why do you need to be familiar with the community in which you work?

❼ What are the rights and responsibilities of the early childhood educator?

❽ What are the sources of stress in the profession of early childhood education?

❾ What are some of the benefits of belonging to a professional association?

DISCUSSION QUESTIONS

❶ How are education and caring the same when you work with young children?

❷ How can a person be self-nurturing and still respond to the demands and responsibilities of the profession of early childhood education?

❸ What are the roles of the educator, the families, and the community in early childhood education?

❹ Describe the kind of relationship you want with your employer when you take a contract in early childhood education.

ACTIVITIES

❶ Write an autobiography of your childhood, including people, events, and experiences that you recall well. Compare your memories of your childhood with those of siblings or parents who shared this time with you.

❷ Outline what you think are the qualifications for someone caring for young children. Ask five parents whose children are in professional care to make a similar list, and compare the lists. What do you learn from the comparison?

❸ Survey ten to twenty early childhood professionals and ask them to describe their experiences of work-related stress and how they deal with it.

❹ Make a list of the community organizations that might influence the children or families with whom you work. Find out how they operate, how they are funded, and who uses them.

FURTHER READING

Bredekamp, Sue, ed. (1987). *Developmentally Appropriate Practice in Early Childhood Programs Serving Children from Birth through Age 8* **(expanded ed.). Washington, DC: National Association for the Education of Young Children.**
A comprehensive description of current practice in providing care and education for young children, including many examples of appropriate and inappropriate practices.

Dickinson, P. (1990). The early childhood professional. In I. Doxey, ed., *Child Care and Education: Canadian Dimensions***, pp. 156–70. Scarborough, ON: Nelson Canada.**
This chapter describes the history of the ECE profession and the differences in background and orientation of professionals working with young

children. Dickinson advocates for increased collaboration based on the areas of commonality.

Doherty-Derkowski, Gillian. (1995). *Quality Matters: Excellence in Early Childhood Programs.* Don Mills, ON: Addison-Wesley.
This book provides a detailed discussion of the nature and determinants of quality in early childhood programs, including interpersonal relationships, parental involvement, staff consistency, programming, and physical environment.

Goffin, S.G. (1994). *Curriculum Models and Early Childhood Education: Appraising the Relationship.* New York: Merrill.
This book provides an excellent and detailed review of a number of models of ECE curricula, including models based on the thinking of John Dewey, Jean Piaget, Lawrence Kohlberg, Constance Kamii, and Rheta DeVries.

REFERENCES

Abel, P., and M. Nelson. (1990). *Circles of Care: Work and Identity in Women's Lives.* New York: SUNY Press.

Arnett, J. (1989). Caregivers in day care centres: Does training matter? *Journal of Applied Developmental Psychology* 10: 541–52.

Ayers, W. (1989). *The Good Preschool Teacher.* New York: Teachers College Press.

Baines, C., P. Evans, and S. Neysmith, eds. (1991). *Women's Caring.* Toronto: McClelland and Stewart.

Belenky, M., B. Clinchy, N. Goldberger, and J. Tarule. (1986). *Women's Ways of Knowing: The Development of Self, Voice, and Mind.* New York: Basic Books.

Bronfenbrenner, U. (1979). *The Ecology of Human Development: Experiments by Nature and Design.* Cambridge, MA: Harvard University Press.

Bullough, R. (1989). *First Year Teacher: A Case Study.* New York: Teachers College Press.

Feeney, S., and R. Chun. (1985). Effective teachers of young children. *Young Children* 4: 47–52.

Gilligan, C. (1982). *In a Different Voice.* Cambridge, MA: Harvard University Press.

Griffin, S. (1993). Defining professionalism in a different voice: Caring for a living in a world that just doesn't understand. *Interaction* 6 (4): 25–28.

Katz, L. (1984). Mothering and teaching: Some significant distinctions. In L. Katz, ed., *Current Topics in Early Childhood Education*, Vol. 3, pp. 47–64. Norwood, NJ: Ablex.

Katz, L. (1990). Dispositions in early childhood education. *Canadian Children* 15 (1): 39–52.

LaGrange, A., and M. Read. (1990). *Those Who Care: A Report on Child Caregivers in Alberta Day Care Centres.* Ottawa: Health and Welfare Canada.

Mayeroff, M. (1972). *On Caring.* New York: Harper & Row.

McLean, S. (1991). *The Human Encounter: Teachers and Children Living Together in Preschools.* London: Falmer Press.

Noddings, N. (1984). *Caring: A Feminine Approach to Ethics and Moral Education.* Los Angeles: University of California Press.

Pence, A., ed. (1988). *Ecological Research with Children and Families.* New York: Teachers College Press.

Pence, A. (1989). In the shadow of mother care: Contexts for an understanding of child day care in North America. *Canadian Psychology* 30 (2): 140–47.

Pence, A. (1990). The child-care profession in Canada. In I. Doxey, ed., *Child Care and Education: Canadian Dimensions*, pp. 87–97. Scarborough, ON: Nelson Canada.

Pence, A., and H. Goelman. (1987). Who cares for the child in day care? An examination of caregivers from three types of care. *Early Childhood Research Quarterly* 2 (4): 315–22.

Powell, D., and A. Stremmel. (1989). The relation of early childhood training and experience to the professional development of child care workers. *Early Childhood Research Quarterly* 4 (1): 339–55.

Read, M., and A. LaGrange. (1990). *Those Who Care: A Report on Approved Family Day Home Providers in Alberta.* Ottawa: Health and Welfare Canada.

Schom-Moffatt, P. (1992). *Caring for a Living.* Ottawa: Canadian Day Care Advocacy Association and Canadian Child Day Care Federation.

Spodek, B., O. Saracho, and D. Peters, eds. (1988). *Professionalism and the Early Childhood Practitioner.* New York: Teachers College Press.

Van Manen, M. (1986). *The Tone of Teaching.* Richmond Hill, ON: Scholastic Books.

Yonemura, M. (1986). *A Teacher at Work: Professional Development and the Early Childhood Educator.* New York: Teachers College Press.

PART 2
FOCUSSing On
Relationships

Young children depend on the support of caring adults to survive and to develop optimally. The human environment is the most important aspect of the early childhood curriculum. Caring relationships form the foundation of your work with young children. Through the bond that develops between children and caring adults, children experience the security and confidence to explore the world, knowing that your support is always dependable. Within respectful relationships, self-esteem is nurtured and children master the skills and competence to meet the challenges of each day

Relationships with children grow out of an understanding and appreciation of the common behaviours and ways of learning typical of the first few years of life. Meaningful personal relationships develop as you come to recognize the characteristics that contribute to the uniqueness and worth of each child as a special individual.

CHAPTER 4
Understanding Children's Development

✎ **Overview**

✎ **A Developmental Foundation**

✎ **Why Study Development?**

◆ Building Supportive Relationships

◆ Planning the Early Childhood
   Curriculum

✎ **Processes of Development**

◆ Temperament

◆ Emotional Development

◆ Social Development

◆ Communication and Language
   Development

◆ Cognitive Development

◆ Physical Development

◆ Play Patterns

✎ **Diversity in Development**

◆ Recognizing Developmental
   Diversity

◆ Recognizing Diversity of Experience

✎ **Summary**

✎ **Review Questions**

✎ **Discussion Questions**

✎ **Activities**

✎ **Further Reading**

✎ **References**

OVERVIEW

Children's development is a complex process that is made up of many aspects — temperament, emotional development, social development, communication and language development, cognitive development, physical development, and play patterns. Within each of these areas you can find common patterns among children, as well as specific milestones indicating that children are developing successfully.

As an early childhood educator, you need to understand the development of each of the children in your program. Identifying their unique characteristics and developmental levels helps you to interact effectively with them and plan ways to meet their needs. Coming to know each of the children well requires ongoing awareness of temperament, abilities, needs, and patterns of behaviour. You gain this awareness in bits and pieces as you interact with the children. This chapter describes the main processes and milestones in each area of development. By understanding these areas, you gain a framework for understanding the children in your care.

By the end of this chapter, you will be able to

❖ explain the theory of child development and norms in understanding individual children's behaviour and patterns of development;

❖ describe characteristics and milestones of each area of development;

❖ describe factors that result in diversity in patterns of development.

A DEVELOPMENTAL FOUNDATION

Jennie is an early childhood education student on her first day of practicum at a child-care centre. Arriving at 8:15, she is just in time to watch the staff, Alexa and Chris, greet several children.

David bursts into the room, eyes bright and cheeks rosy. He yells, "Hey, Russ," and races to the water table. "Hey, can I try that?" he says as he takes the funnel from Russ. Russ hands it over, seeming perplexed but not distressed. David's father calls, "See you later, David. Have a good day. I love you." David looks up, but does not reply. David's father shrugs, smiles, and says to Alexa, "He's all yours. See you tonight."

Catherine enters the room holding her father's hand. She appears apprehensive and clutches a small toy clown under her arm. She is holding back, looking around the room. Chris approaches the pair and greets them. "Hi, Catherine, I see you've brought Opie with you today. Did you have fun at your grandma's yesterday?" Catherine nods slightly and moves closer to her dad, who squats down and holds her on his knee: "You can tell Chris about the cookies you and grandma made. They were delicious." Chris says, "I hope you made peanut butter. They're my favourite. Today we're going to make pancakes for our snack. That should be fun, don't you think?" Neither Chris nor Catherine's father rush her, knowing that she needs a slow transition time. After several more minutes of conversation, Catherine's dad gives her a kiss and moves her gently toward Chris, who scoops her onto his knee and asks her if Opie would like to read a book. Catherine waves goodbye to her father and takes Chris's hand as they cross the room.

Alexa has been talking to Lisa and Jordie at their cubbies. Lisa's clothes are scattered all over the floor and she needs a reminder to put her hat, coat, mitts, and boots in her cubbie. Jordie has hung everything up carefully on his own. Lisa is enthusiastically telling Alexa that their dog chewed up one of her shoes last night. She laughs and tells the story with great expression, especially as she describes how upset her mother was and demonstrates the way the dog slunk away under the table.

Jordie watches the interaction, but says nothing. Alexa tries to include Jordie in the conversation: "How's your new baby today?" Jordie says, "He cry, he cry too much." Alexa gives Jordie a gentle hug and says, "It's hard when babies cry." Jordie nods. Alexa takes his hand and they follow Lisa into the room.

As Jennie continues to observe the children in the group, she has already noticed how different they all seem. Two children in the creative centre seem to be about the same age, but one of them is drawing simple circles and lines, and the other has created a detailed picture of a person, complete with fingers and toes. In the block area, Joy is working persistently on creating a car from Lego pieces, while Brandon has given up on his Lego tower after its third collapse. Bruce has set up an elaborate farm with fencing and blocks for bales of hay for his horses. Near him, Ellie is becoming increasingly frustrated as she fails several times in trying to jam a large car into a small garage opening.

Jennie has also noticed that Alexa and Chris seem to respond to and interact differently with each child. They meet David and Lisa's exuberance with a more intense response, but they approach Catherine and Jordie more subtly.

The children also interact with one another in a variety of ways. Bruce and Joy are talking in great detail about what they are doing, but the language that Jordie and Ellie use is more simple. Jennie is already recognizing that the role of an early childhood educator is not as simple as she had thought. She comments to Chris that the children all seem so different. Chris replies, "You're right. They are each their own person. That's what I love about this work. You can learn so much from the kids." Jennie understands what he means. "I can hardly wait to get to know them all," she says.

For those who enjoy working with young children, the study of child development is indeed fascinating. The way preschoolers experience and interpret the world is special and unique to their age group. Early childhood education literature is full of theories and explanations of the ways in which children develop and the behaviours that can be expected at any given age. The work of Piaget, Erikson, and Greenspan (cited throughout the text), as well as many others, provides the basis for understanding how young children think, feel, and learn. In interacting with children, you will frequently see them demonstrating the characteristics and behaviours described in the literature, which means that you become increasingly familiar with these patterns of development. This understanding and expertise in child development is what makes the role of the early childhood educator so specialized.

Good early childhood educators have sensitivity and perceptive insight into the development and needs of young children. This insight comes through a combination of knowledge of general developmental processes and milestones, and an awareness of how the individual child is developing in relation to this general framework. Sensitive and in-tune interactions with each individual child provide much information about how the child is feeling, thinking, and developing.

WHY STUDY DEVELOPMENT?

Developmental theories attempt to explain patterns in children's development. Several important principles of developmental theories help to explain the developmental process. Box 4.1 shows the underlying principles of the theories presented in this chapter. Understanding these can help you discover why children behave in certain ways; for example, why one child is outgoing while another seems overly dependent. When you review the theories, you can look for similar patterns in children's daily experiences. You might see that a child is acting aggressively as a means to an end (getting toys) or as an expression of anger and frustration. A high degree of dependency

might indicate a reaction to separation distress or even underlying emotional problems.

Early childhood educators need to recognize and document the developmental progress of each child. Your understanding enables you to become a trusted and secure base for each child. Your knowledge of children also helps you meet their needs through your approach and your curriculum.

Building Supportive Relationships

In early childhood settings, the relationships between children and adults are the foundation for beneficial, meaningful, and satisfying experiences for young children. A mutually satisfying and supportive relationship depends on awareness, understanding, and acceptance of the other person.

The effective early childhood educator will get to know the children individually: accepting the children, along with whatever they

BOX 4.1 PRINCIPLES OF DEVELOPMENT

There are several principles that should be kept in mind when studying the development of young children:

◆ Development of children is continual. Children, including the majority of those who are challenged by disabilities or delays, learn and progress toward a higher level of development unless there is something seriously wrong.

◆ Development progresses in a predictable and recognizable sequence that is generally the same for all children, again unless there are particularly serious problems.

◆ Indicators of development, commonly called milestones, can help us to identify the level of development reached by the child.

◆ Developmental norms tell us the average age range within which the normally developing child will reach these developmental milestones.

◆ Each individual develops at a different pace, even though the sequence is the same. Children achieve developmental milestones at somewhat different ages. The sequence of development is more important than the exact age at which a skill is developed.

bring to the relationship; understanding that children do their best to relate, cope, and develop, and that their progress is most successful with sensitive support and encouragement; and supporting the children when they have problems dealing with developmental processes. With support, children can eventually experience success, maintain their self-respect, and develop a positive self-concept.

Planning the Early Childhood Curriculum

Understanding patterns of development is a key prerequisite to the successful planning of an early childhood curriculum. To provide experiences that are developmentally appropriate, beneficial, and sufficiently challenging and interesting requires an in-depth knowledge of the characteristics of young children and the developmental sequences of the early years (Bredekamp 1987). Experiences that are too simple do not challenge children or stimulate development; experiences beyond their developmental level have minimal benefit and can cause stress (Elkind 1988).

Although the early childhood curriculum has elements that are common for all preschool children, providing experiences that meet the individual developmental needs of all children in the program is also part of the planning process. It is this that is at the heart of your profession.

PROCESSES OF DEVELOPMENT

Temperament

Temperament is an area in which children reveal their differences early in their development. Differences in temperament make them react differently to stimuli and behave differently in eating, sleeping, and other daily routines (Chess & Thomas 1987). Temperamental differences seem to be built-in aspects of children's personality that affect their behaviour and the reactions of people around them. Knowing and understanding the temperament of children can help you to respond to them appropriately. Chess and Thomas (1987) identify nine different categories of behaviour that they believe are indicative of temperamental differences among children (see Box 4.2). A high or low rating on each of these characteristics is normal, but making the analysis helps to identify the unique temperamental pattern of a child. Particular combinations of these characteristics seem to indicate three major temperamental styles: flexible, slow-to-warm-up, and intense.

The **flexible**, or easy, child has regular sleeping and eating patterns, approaches people and new situations readily, adapts easily to change, and is usually cheerful. The **slow-to-warm-up**, or cautious, child has fairly regular sleeping and eating patterns, is less responsive to new people and situations, and adapts slowly. This child's reactions to situations tend to be mild or moderate. The **intense** child is characterized by intense emotions and sensitivity. This child's reactions range from enthusiasm and exuberance to a high degree of distress and upset. Other characteristics might include irregularity in sleeping and eating patterns, resistant or withdrawn behaviours in response to new people and situations, slowness in adapting to change, and intense persistence. These children are sometimes a challenge for adults, and each of these characteristics can contribute to difficulty in coping and interacting with others. On the other hand, the enthusiasm and joyful intensity of these

BOX 4.2 CHARACTERISTICS OF TEMPERAMENT

The following are nine categories of behaviour Chess and Thomas identified as contributing to differences in temperament.

1. ACTIVITY LEVEL	Level of motor activity. Proportion of active and inactive periods.
2. RHYTHMICITY	Predictability of the timing of biological functions such as hunger, sleep, and toileting needs.
3. APPROACH OR WITHDRAWAL	The nature of the initial response to a new situation or stimulus. Approach responses are positive and withdrawal responses are negative.
4. ADAPTABILITY	Long-term responses to new or changed situations after the initial response. How easily is the initial response modified to become more desirable?
5. SENSORY THRESHOLD	The intensity of stimulation that evokes a reaction.
6. QUALITY OF MOOD	The extent of pleasant, friendly mood and behaviour as contrasted with unfriendly mood and behaviour and crying.
7. INTENSITY OF REACTIONS	The energy level of the response, either positive or negative.
8. DISTRACTIBILITY	The effectiveness of a new stimulus in interfering with or changing the direction of the child's ongoing behaviour.
9. PERSISTENCE AND ATTENTION SPAN	Continuation of an activity in the face of obstacles, and length of time an activity is pursued without interruption.

Source: Stella Chess and Alexander Thomas. (1987). *Know Your Child: An Authoritative Guide for Today's Parents.* New York: Basic Books, pp. 28–31. Copyright © 1987 by Basic Books, Inc. Reprinted by permission of Basic Books, a division of HarperCollins Publishers Inc.

children create a contagious sense of excitement and delight as they experience a wide range of emotions — they are often affectionate, sensitive, and enthusiastic as well as unpredictable. Educators appreciate and marvel at the unique qualities of intense children who approach life with such energy and determination.

These are the three most common patterns of temperament. However, many children have different combinations of behaviours and moods that can vary from day to day. Each of these patterns is normal, and good early childhood educators soon learn to adapt their expectations to match each child's unique temperament.

Emotional Development

The emotional area is one of the most complex aspects of early development. It encompasses children's sense of who they are, how they relate to other people, and how they deal with their own emotions.

When you observe children's emotional development, what you see are the outward behaviours that result from the inner feelings. This is why you need to be familiar with child development theory and research, so you can understand what the children's behaviour is telling you about these feelings. Immature behaviour or extremes of behaviour are often indicators that a young child is struggling with the challenges of emotional development.

Young children face a number of tasks as they deal with the world and the people in it (Greenspan & Greenspan 1986):

❖ Children need to feel secure in their world, safe, and in control of their emotions and behaviour.

❖ Children need to be successful in forming attachments to people who are close to them as a basis for developing in other emotional areas.

❖ Children need to develop a positive self-concept and a sense of worth through relationships in which they are valued by others.

❖ Children develop intentional communication strategies as they experience predictable and trustworthy responses to their expressions of need and desire.

❖ Children form an organized sense of the self, recognizing and taking pride in their capabilities and accomplishments and coming to terms with their own limitations.

❖ Children begin to integrate emotional thinking with their sense of self, becoming increasingly aware of their own and others' feelings, intentions, and behavioural expressions.

Whether or not children are successful in these tasks is reflected in how they handle the challenges of daily life. Table 4.1 shows the implications of these tasks for children in an early childhood education setting. In coming to understand children better, look for evidence that they have successfully mastered these emotional tasks. Children who misbehave or who indicate distress may need help in resolving one or more of these tasks.

The sense of self, or self-concept, is perhaps one of the most important indicators of emotional well-being. Because the ability to accept oneself is so dependent on the reactions and responses of others, it is essential that early childhood educators convey acceptance and respect for every child. At the same time, educators must also show consideration for the child's family and cultural background as an essential aspect of the sense of self. Young children experience acceptance and pride in their own family and culture when they experience acceptance and respect from others. Children need to feel comfortable within the expectations of early childhood programs without experiencing conflict between family and outside values. If they are pressured to avoid using their own language or to give up their habits to become more like the majority group, they will begin to question their personal worth and experience diminished self-esteem, or even shame, in who they and their families are. This feeling can have devastating and long-lasting effects for the child and the family. Accepting each child's family and cultural values is essential to nurturing their positive self-identity.

The quality of children's relationships with adults gives you information about another milestone. Young children show that they trust adults and believe that adults will support

TABLE 4.1 **RESOLVING EMOTIONAL TASKS: IMPLICATIONS FOR COPING**

TASK	IF CHILD IS SUCCESSFUL	IF CHILD HAS NOT RESOLVED TASK
Feeling secure in world	Willingly participates in a range of activities. Can usually regulate emotional expression.	Appears overly anxious. May avoid or withdraw from participation. May demonstrate outbursts of uncontrolled emotion. May be overly active.
Forming mutually satisfying relationships	Seeks and enjoys relationships with others. Usually accepts comfort and guidance.	Withdraws from or resists interactions, support, and guidance. Appears angry, aggressive, insecure, and mistrustful.
Perceiving self as worthy and likable	Shows pleasure in activities and relationships. Appears happy and confident.	Demonstrates self-doubt and lack of confidence. Seeks approval. Avoids participation.
Having intentional communication	Expresses needs and rights assertively. Expects and accepts a helpful response.	Expresses needs inappropriately or excessively (e.g., loss of control). Does not seem to expect or accept assistance. Takes what is wanted for himself/herself. Describes self or achievements in negative terms. Unwilling to try, or expects to fail. Does not understand own role in situations.
Integrating emotional thinking	Beginning to understand complex relationship among feelings, behaviours, consequences, and reactions of others. Beginning to express and work through complex emotional issues and conflicts through words and play.	Misinterprets own and others' actions. Expresses feelings through direct and excessive behaviour. Often feels victimized. Has difficulty understanding and dealing with complex interactions or conflict.

them by accepting affection and comfort and by asking for an adult's help when they need it. Young children usually co-operate with reasonable requests adults make unless they feel their own control is threatened. They normally become increasingly independent as they master the skills and knowledge needed for daily tasks. This autonomy, along with the confidence to try new challenges and take risks, is essential for optimal development. Children cannot learn and develop if they are overburdened with anxiety or guilt regarding their behaviour and choices, or the fear of negative consequences for mistakes (Erikson 1963). Being aware of how well children manage in the program provides clues about their level of independence and self-confidence. Once familiar with the program, young children should go about quite independently with confidence in their choices and pride and pleasure in their achievements. They are able to take the initiative in beginning and completing a wide range of activities. Although it might seem easier — and tempting — to organize and direct young children in what to do, too much direction can jeopardize their opportunity to resolve important challenges that lead to a sense of self-direction and willingness to take initiative.

Finally, the ways in which children express emotions tells you something about their development. All young children experience sadness, frustration, anger, and anxiety as a result of trying to participate in the daily experiences of life. Children need to express a range of emotions in appropriate ways without fear of consequences. Part of your task is to accept and validate children's feelings: "I know you are upset, Trisha. I would be upset too if someone grabbed my book from me. Tell B.J. that you want it back and that he needs to ask next time." Most children accept help from an adult when they are distressed, and use the strategies they learn in the future.

Sometimes it seems that a child displays negative emotions and other signs of stress most of the time or expresses these emotions in a way that is destructive. Destructive or immature behaviour often indicates that a child's level of distress is beyond her or his ability to cope, or that she or he has persistent needs that are not being met. Often the children who present the greatest challenge to early childhood educators and who require the most extensive intervention are those who have problems in emotional development. Children who are *consistently* withdrawn, depressed, or excessively aggressive need special attention and compassion. If children do not have a positive sense of self and are not learning control over their emotions, establishing trusting, satisfying relationships with others will be difficult.

Social Development

"The ability of young children to engage in meaningful and interesting interactions with their peers is one of the most important developmental tasks of early childhood. Successful relationships with one's peers foster communication and cognitive development, promote prosocial behaviour in general and help socialize aggression," says Michael Guralnick in the guide to the *Making Friends* video series (Littman n.d.).

In the area of social development, we look at the quality of social relationships that each child experiences. Children need to be accepted by the group and feel that they have friends who like them and want to play with them. Being aware of the nature of interactions among children helps you determine whether their needs for belonging and acceptance are being met. Does each child experience positive reactions from other children? If not, is a particular child's behaviour discouraging positive social interactions? As you gain an understanding of children's styles of interaction, you can assist them in developing more successful strategies and skills.

Many 3- to 5-year-olds are still focussed mainly on their own needs and interests (Beaty 1994). Children at this age are just beginning to develop the skills required for initiating contact and joining in play, and for getting along with others through sharing and co-operating. They are learning how to take leadership and resolve conflicts in ways that are not overly aggressive, how to handle their own feelings of anger, and how to respond to the aggressiveness of others. Awareness of the feelings, needs, and rights of other children is just beginning and needs constant interpretation by adults. It is still quite a challenge for young children to deal with others in a group, and you will observe conflicts and upsets frequently, especially during play.

The pace of development of preschool children in the social area makes working with them exciting and gratifying, especially seeing their social skills develop: concern and empathy for the feelings of others, respect for the rights of others, and a willingness to show generosity and offer care to their peers. In your interactions with children, you will see many instances of the positive relationships among young children, relationships that need to be acknowledged and encouraged.

Communication and Language Development

Children's ability to communicate effectively underlies success in social and cognitive areas. At the most basic level, children need to communicate needs and wishes such as needing a drink or wanting to play with a certain toy. The way in which children communicate these needs is of obvious importance. Most children use verbal means, and most children of 3 years and older use full sentences. However, some children might still use gestures and single words because that is the level of language development they have reached or because of such emotional factors as anxiety or discomfort in the social setting.

In interpersonal communication, a child is expected to be able to follow the conversation and take turns with the other person. This area of communication is known as **pragmatics** (Santrock 1994). Pragmatics includes such things as the ability to follow rules for effective communication: being close to the person to whom you are talking, using that person's name to get his or her attention, making eye contact, and knowing whose turn it is to talk. Most children develop this knowledge through interactions with, and imitation of, others. Learning this skill begins even before children have spoken language, through such simple games as peek-a-boo and other social interactions, and becomes incorporated into spoken language. For example, Leah, at age 2½, wanted an adult to speak to her bear. She was unhappy when the adult spoke without paying close attention to the bear, and she insisted, "Turn your head to talk to my bear. He's over here."

Keep in mind that some of the nonverbal communication behaviours common to Western cultures might not be part of other cultures. Differences in reaction to personal space, eye contact, smiling, and touch can reflect cultural diversity (Gonzalez-Mena 1993; Santrock 1994). Similarly, one or more of these skills of pragmatics may be difficult for some young children, even though their vocabulary and sentence structure seem to be developing.

You also need to be aware of the **semantic** aspects of children's language (Santrock 1994) — children's ability to communicate and understand meaning. Young children use language in a highly personal way and gradually come to understand conventional meanings of words and concepts. Kathleen, age 2, refers to all objects as being "blue," including her white blanket and her pink bear. Although she has some understanding of colour, her way of using the concept of blue is entirely her own.

In the area of semantics, there is a distinction between receptive language (how well children understand what is said) and expressive language (how well children can get their own message across to others). Vocabulary level and ability to sequence words and sentences indicate children's expressive language. Observing how children respond to directions, questions, and general conversation tells you about their receptive language abilities.

Another aspect of language is **phonology** (Santrock 1994). This concept refers to the use of sound patterns to create spoken words. The ability to produce speech sounds correctly develops as children mature physically and gain control over the many small muscles of the mouth and throat. Most 4-year-olds can produce most speech sounds and most 3- and 4-year-olds have sufficient speech sounds to make themselves understood.

Articulation, or the ability to clearly produce these sounds increases with age, although children may not be able to produce a few sounds, such as "r" and "v," until age 6 or 7. In the preschool years, most articulation problems are developmental in nature, which means that children will outgrow them. However, children who are having serious difficulty making themselves understood should be observed carefully to determine whether they need additional help.

The last aspect of language is **syntax**, or grammatical structures of language. Young children make progress in language through a sequence of grammatical structures, from single words and two-word sentences to full sentences (Santrock 1994). Preschoolers' language often reflects knowledge of grammatical rules — "I falled down" or "two fishes" — and they gradually incorporate the exceptions to the rules of syntax.

Exposure to concepts, vocabulary, syntax, and communication skills begins long before children speak their first word. Children build on this knowledge when they begin to communicate in their family's first language (Garcia 1992). Children's first language also has a role to play in reflecting the cultural heritage of the family and contributing to a positive self-concept (Garcia 1992). Children's language and communication opportunities should reflect the first language as much as possible, while gradually exposing them to a second language. Early childhood educators should attempt to learn key phrases in each child's language. Remember that much communication occurs nonverbally and can be used when the educator is not fluent in the child's language. Children who are fluent in their first language are usually quick to pick up a second language if they are sufficiently comfortable in the early childhood environment and have the opportunity to practise the new language.

Cognitive Development

Cognitive development involves the processes of thinking and learning. It is a complex, wide-reaching area of development. Much of our thinking about cognition comes from the work of Jean Piaget, who observed and studied the development of intellect (Santrock 1994; Ginsburg & Opper 1969). Piaget's theory gives us the view of children as active learners working to make sense of their experiences and connecting new experiences with existing knowledge. Children come to understand concepts of number, space, and causality through actively manipulating materials and exploring the world.

Piaget's theory also gives us the perspective that the ways in which children understand the world change as they mature and develop increasingly sophisticated ways of making sense of experiences. Preschool children are described as **preoperational**, which means that their form of thinking and logic for understanding the world follows different rules than the more conventional logic of older children. Preschoolers base their judgements primarily on sensory perceptions and egocentric interpretations. For example, Martha, age 2, dropped the telephone receiver so that it was hanging upside down when she was talking to her aunt. She asked her aunt if she was also upside down.

Cognition also consists of knowledge of concepts about objects, shapes, size, spatial location, time, and number, and understanding these concepts is an indicator of cognitive abilities. The preoperational child is developing an understanding of such relationships as "same and different" and the ability to group and sequence objects in a logical manner. Cognition also encompasses children's ability to understand cause and effect and to solve problems.

As you try to understand children's cognitive development, take into account their life experience, because cognition develops in interaction with the environment and opportunities to learn and develop are essential to the achievement of many cognitive skills. Children from varied backgrounds may show differences in general knowledge and skill development as a result of exposure to different experiences. You would not be surprised if Jared, who is frequently exposed to his mother's work as a research scientist, had an inquiring mind and a high level of problem solving. In contrast, Tessa, whose family came from a village in a developing country, seems "delayed" in some language and cognitive concepts, and has very little idea of how to solve an abstract problem such as a pre-drawn maze. However, on the playground, you observe that Tessa has advanced motor skills and practical problem-solving skills, and can open the "child-proof" gate. Differences in cognitive skills are not necessarily delays in cognitive development but may reflect diversity resulting from varied experiences.

Other areas that affect cognitive functioning are attention, memory, cognitive monitoring, information processing, and learning style (Santrock 1994). Because young children are just beginning to develop and use many of these skills, there is tremendous variability in their level of development. Although most young children learn best through active, hands-on manipulation, there are differences in the ways in which they process visual and auditory information, with some seeming to learn more easily with one approach than the other. It is valuable to note differences in the way children learn, such as a preference for hands-on learning, a reflective versus impulsive style, or an ability to think creatively when solving problems.

Physical Development

Physical development includes indicators of children's overall health and well-being, such as size, weight, appearance, colouring, and general level of activity. Preschool children generally have an abundance of energy, so that you should be concerned about continual lethargy and tiredness, frequent illness, congestion or ear infections, and serious allergies

or other health problems. Children's basic needs must be met in their eating, sleeping, and toileting habits. Many preschool children are irregular in these habits and have difficulty adapting their needs and schedules to the routines of an early childhood setting. As much as possible, try to go with the children's individual rhythms rather than imposing a fixed schedule for these activities.

Large-motor, or gross, development proceeds in a sequence that is similar for most children. Most 3-year-olds can walk up and down stairs alternating feet, balance momentarily on one foot, hop on one foot, kick a large ball, and pedal a tricycle (Allen & Marotz 1994). Wide differences in these motor skills are noticeable on the playground or during active play. The important thing is that the children are active and are using their body comfortably and effectively. Specific skills develop according to an individual timetable and the opportunity to practise and master complex and co-ordinated movements.

Fine-, or small-, motor skills include the ability to manipulate such small materials as blocks, pegboards, and Lego; to control crayons to make deliberate markings; and to fasten buttons or zippers. Again, there is much diversity in the level of co-ordination and fine-motor control in young children, and they need many varied opportunities for practising these skills in play as well as in such basic routines as eating and dressing.

Play Patterns

Children express their unique characteristics most clearly through their free-play activities. Play serves many functions for children. In play, children develop and practise cognitive and motor skills. They take on new challenges and work to master new skills and achievements. For most children, this type of play provides tremendous satisfaction and pleasure, even though at times they experience frustration and failure. Mastery through play allows children to feel competent and capable in learning and in solving manageable problems. This process is essential for the development of a positive self-concept and awareness of their abilities and limitations, all through experiences that can be planned, carried out, and controlled by the children themselves.

Children use play to express such emotions as anxiety, fear of monsters, or anger at other family members. In a play situation, children can take control over an experience that is threatening or upsetting, such as a hospital stay, a new sibling, or an angry parent. They can come to understand and feel comfortable with whatever is upsetting by replaying the scene many times.

Loretta had been in hospital for tests and was scheduled for surgery. A hospital centre was set up in the dramatic play area to give her an opportunity to express and work through her feelings. At first, she watched other children playing there, but did not join in. When one of the other children asked her to play the role of the patient, she refused loudly and left. Later, when no children were in the centre, she returned and emphatically stated to the doll, "I am the doctor. You are sick." She placed the doll in a bed and treated her with needles and medicine, saying "Don't cry. You can't have your mother. You are sick. This will hurt."

Loretta continued this type of play throughout the day, appearing oblivious to the rest of the activities in the room. The doll frequently cried for her mother, and each time Loretta told her to stop crying. Then she switched roles and scooped the doll up with much hugging. "Mommy's here now. Don't cry. It's OK." The play continued for several days, with Loretta switching roles between doctor and mother. Each day there seemed to be less emphasis on the "doctor's" abrupt handling of the doll, and more cuddling and singing by the "mother." When an adult commented on Loretta's play, she said, "The doctor hurts, but the mommy is there to take care of the baby." The role-playing had enabled Loretta to express her anxieties and to work out a strategy for coping with her fears with the help of her mother.

Sensory and motor play are excellent outlets for the release of emotions, calming and soothing the child. You frequently see children choosing such sensory types of play as water, sand, and play dough, and many children spend extensive periods of time enjoying the feel of the materials as they manipulate them. Sensory play is extremely valuable for children who lack confidence or have low self-esteem, because it offers great opportunity for success and mastery. Similarly, the active room and playground offer ideal opportunities for children to release pent-up emotions and energy and come away feeling refreshed, relaxed, and renewed.

Play also varies in purpose (Smilansky 1968). It can be **functional** — children repeat simple, manipulative actions, with or without objects, for example, filling and dumping containers or going down a slide. Play can also be **constructive** — building or creating something, such as building with blocks or making a collage. Pretence and role-playing are types of **sociodramatic** play. Children re-enact situations in which they pretend to be something or someone other than themselves, such as the mommy or the truck driver. Each of these types of play serves a different, but equally important, function.

Observing and interacting with children in their freely chosen play activities provide the most intimate and rewarding glimpses into their unique personalities. Through play, children reveal how they feel about themselves and the world, and how they attempt to deal with the many challenges of life.

SOCIAL PLAY

As you know, children play alone, alongside other children, or co-operatively within a small group. Younger children are more likely to engage in **solitary play**. Two or more children are often seen playing close by but independently of each other in **parallel play**. The capacity for **co-operative play** increases with age, so that older children are more able to participate in games that involve socialization, negotiation, and shared control (Parten 1932).

We suggested that the amount of co-operative play increases as children mature and develop the communication and social skills needed to participate successfully in such play (Parten 1932). However, this does not mean that solitary and parallel play patterns are less mature or less desirable. Although children's level of development may be one influence on the type of play they choose, their preferences and needs of the moment also determine the type of play.

Sometimes a child who is concentrating on trying to construct or create something or master an activity prefers to play alone, so that he can focus all of his energy and attention on his chosen challenge. Other times, children are more interested in the social experience, so the process of communicating and co-operating with others becomes the goal of the play.

An older child may choose solitary play when trying to master a new toy or activity or to meet emotional or physical needs. Children vary their activities just as adults do. Sometimes a child might swing or just pour water through a funnel; another time she might choose sophisticated, sociodramatic play. Children benefit from success within each of the categories of play as each provides opportunities for different developmental experiences.

DIVERSITY IN DEVELOPMENT

Recognizing Developmental Diversity

As you become familiar with the children in your own setting, you will become aware of the remarkable differences in development between them. No two children are exactly the same in their overall pattern of development or in their unique abilities and characteristics. Development is influenced by hereditary and prenatal factors, so that each child is already a unique entity at birth. Children have widely different experiences and environments ranging from rural to urban, small town to inner city, and isolated to overflowing with options, and representing lifestyles from all over the world. No one environment offers the best of everything; children's growth and development reflects the diversity of their experiences and day-to-day lives.

Although we frequently talk about "normal" development, your increasing understanding of development will show that it is not the same for every child. Even within the "normal" range of development, children develop skills at different paces, with some children appearing advanced in one or more areas and other children experiencing difficulties in mastering certain milestones. Differences in communication, thinking, and motor skills will also be evident. Some children develop communication or cognitive skills significantly more slowly or more quickly than their peers; others may have specific learning disabilities that make their learning and performance inconsistent and unpredictable.

Differences in development can be especially marked in children with physical, cognitive, sensory, or neurological disabilities. When any child experiences a dysfunction that involves the central nervous system or the sensorimotor processes (such as damage to the brain, vision, or hearing), the normal patterns and sequences of development may not occur (Neisworth & Bagnoto 1987). Some of these children still follow the sequences of development, but over a longer period of time. For others, the sequence of development may be quite different, because they are acquiring special skills to compensate for those that cannot be achieved, such as sign language rather than spoken language.

Developmental diversity is evident in emotional and behavioural areas as well. Children have different temperaments, personality, and behavioural characteristics. Some of the children you see show their upset, anxiety, and distress through difficult, withdrawn, or aggressive behaviour; others have difficulty in relationships with peers and adults. Many children will come to you from stable, nurturing homes, but you will also work with some who may be experiencing a transition into a new culture or may be affected by a stressful family breakdown, family violence, poverty, or isolation.

The individual characteristics and differences of young children will make your work challenging and rewarding. Through your interactions and observations, you will recognize the qualities that make each child her or his own person. Your ability to plan and provide for them as individuals depends on this recognition of individual needs. You will come to appreciate the ways in which children express their uniqueness. Your respect for them as individuals will grow as you recognize the diversity in their behaviour and development.

Recognizing Diversity of Experience

Families come to Canada from all parts of the world, and each family brings its own heritage of experiences, cultural values, expectations, and behaviour patterns. In a country that celebrates a multicultural composition as Canada does, the early childhood educator must be open to similarities and differences among and within diverse backgrounds and cultures.

Children, no matter what culture they come from, have different life experiences. There is no doubt that these experiences lead to diversity in lifestyle, behaviour, and, to some extent, learning and development. Traditional Western practices and customs, and even food, toys, and games, might be unfamiliar and seem quite strange to children from other parts of the world. The Western way of doing things and our daily routines can be confusing to a child who has recently come to Canada. Even the Western style of relating to others could be quite different from what is familiar to a child. Sometimes the assumptions about childhood, based on Western traditions, are not valid for many children from other parts of the world.

When you work with children, you notice differences in their patterns of behaviour. What you observe reflects their family and cultural traditions to some extent. Expectations for children in the areas of attachment, independence, obedience, and desirable behaviour vary widely. Not all cultures encourage children to be as independent and competitive as Western culture does. Such social customs as touching and eye contact might vary, as could roles and expectations. Child-rearing and discipline practices also vary from one culture to another, and can be different from those in the early childhood education setting (Gonzalez-Mena 1993).

Do not expect all members of the same race, culture, or background to have the same patterns or expectations — people in each group are not all the same. Many influences come from the experiences the family had within their original homeland, the length of time a family has been in Canada, and the lifestyle adopted. By becoming familiar with various cultural backgrounds of children in your care, especially the individual families with whom you work, you can accept and come to understand them. No one culture has the one best way, and you will need to be aware, receptive, and flexible in relating to families whose expectations and practices are different from your own.

Even when there are familial or cultural differences, remember that all children have similar needs. They share the same physical needs for rest, food, and activity, and the same emotional needs for affection, acceptance, and respect. Children from all backgrounds and cultures follow the same general patterns of development, so that we see many similarities in skills such as walking, talking, and manual dexterity. Children from all backgrounds and cultures form trusting relationships with adults and friendships with peers. All children play and learn, laugh and cry, and involve themselves in life in their own unique ways. The joys and sorrows of childhood can be seen in the faces of children from all parts of the world.

SUMMARY

Each child comes into the early childhood setting with a particular set of experiences, an individual temperament, a concept of him- or herself, a style of learning, a level of knowledge, and a level of ability to communicate and interact with others. Through play and behaviour that are personal and individual, children express the qualities and characteristics that make them who they are.

Through sensitive and perceptive interactions with children, you will come to recognize the unique way in which each child progresses through the sequences of development. The early childhood educator is influenced by knowledge of child development milestones, patterns, and issues. You develop a relationship that is supportive of the child based on your understanding of what makes the child special and secure. You develop a child-centred curriculum based on developmental theory that encourages and enhances development in all areas, challenging areas of need and celebrating areas of strength.

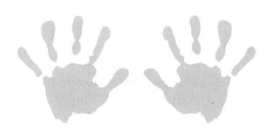

REVIEW QUESTIONS

❶ List the three most common types of temperament and describe the characteristics of each.

❷ List and describe the six milestones of emotional development in Greenspan and Greenspan's theory.

❸ In the area of communication and language, what is meant by the terms "pragmatics," "semantics," "articulation," and "syntax"?

❹ Describe several ways in which play benefits the development of the young child.

❺ Describe factors that contribute to diversity in development, and give an example for each.

DISCUSSION QUESTIONS

❶ Can we legitimately use the concept of "normal development" as a basis for assessing the development of an individual child? Why or why not?

❷ To what extent is diversity a positive or a negative aspect of development?

❸ In what ways do the early life experiences determined by one's place of birth have a lasting effect on development?

ACTIVITIES

❶ Rate yourself and someone you know well on the temperament characteristics. Consider how each style influences the way you handle new or difficult situations.

❷ Watch several children playing, and attempt to determine the function and benefit of each one's play experience.

❸ Identify factors that have contributed to your personal and unique developmental patterns.

❹ Create a glossary by listing and defining the significant developmental concepts and terms highlighted in bold throughout this chapter.

FURTHER READING

Allen, K.E., and L. Marotz. (1994). *Developmental Profiles: Pre-Birth through Eight*. Albany, NY: Delmar.

This book is a good source of developmental sequences and norms. The authors emphasize developmental principles as a foundation for observing children. Each chapter outlines what to expect at a given age in the areas of physical, motor, perceptual-cognitive, language, and personal-social development.

Crain, W. (1992). *Theories of Development: Concepts and Applications.* **Englewood Cliffs, NJ: Prentice-Hall.**

Crain summarizes the work of a wide range of theorists, such as Erikson, Piaget, Kohlberg, and Montessori, who have attempted to explain development in many areas.

REFERENCES

Allen, K.E., and L. Marotz. (1994). *Developmental Profiles: Pre-Birth through Eight.* Albany, NY: Delmar.

Anderson, Z. (1978). *Getting a Headstart on Social Emotional Growth.* Omaha, NE: University of Nebraska Medical Center.

Beaty, J.J. (1994). *Observing the Development of the Young Child* (3rd ed.). New York: Macmillan.

Black, J.K., M.B. Puckett, and M.J. Bell. (1992). *The Young Child: Development from Prebirth through Age Eight.* Toronto: Maxwell Macmillan.

Bredekamp, S., ed. (1987). *Developmentally Appropriate Practice in Early Childhood Programs Serving Children from Birth through Age 8* (expanded ed.). Washington, DC: National Association for the Education of Young Children.

Chess, S., and A. Thomas. (1987) *Know Your Child: An Authoritative Guide for Today's Parents.* New York: Basic Books.

Crain, W. (1992). *Theories of Development: Concepts and Applications.* Englewood Cliffs, NJ: Prentice-Hall.

Elkind, D. (1988). *Miseducation: Preschoolers at Risk.* New York: Alfred A. Knopf.

Erikson, E.H. (1963). *Childhood and Society* (2nd ed.). New York: W.W. Norton.

Garcia, E.E. (1992). Caring for infants in a bilingual child care setting. In J.R. Lally, P.L. Mangione, and C.L. Young-Holt, eds., *Infant/Toddler Caregiving: A Guide to Language Development and Communication*, pp. 43–53. Sacramento, CA: California Department of Education.

Ginsburg, H., and S. Opper. (1969). *Piaget's Theory of Intellectual Development: An Introduction.* Englewood Cliffs, NJ: Prentice-Hall.

Gonzalez-Mena, J. (1993). *Multicultural Issues in Child Care.* Mountain View, CA: Mayfield.

Greenspan, S., and N.T. Greenspan. (1986). *First Feelings: Milestones in the Emotional Development of Your Baby and Child.* New York: Penguin Books.

Lally, J.R., ed. (1990). *Infant/Toddler Caregiving: A Guide to Social-Emotional Growth and Socialization.* Sacramento, CA: California Department of Education.

Lally, J.R., P.L. Mangione, and C.L. Young-Holt, eds. (1992). *Infant/Toddler Caregiving: A Guide to Language Development and Communication.* Sacramento, CA: California Department of Education.

Lieberman, A.F. (1993). *The Emotional Life of the Toddler.* New York: The Free Press.

Littman, E. (n.d.). *Making Friends Guide.* (Guide to video *Making Friends*). Vancouver: Making Friends.

Neisworth, J.T., and S.J. Bagnoto. (1987). *The Young Exceptional Child: Early Development and Education.* New York: Macmillan.

Parten, M.B. (1932). Social participation among preschool children. *Journal of Abnormal and Social Psychology* 27: 243–69.

Santrock, J.W. (1994). *Child Development* (6th ed.). Dubuque, IA: W.C.B. Brown & Benchmark.

Smilansky, S. (1968). *The Effects of Sociodramatic Play on Disadvantaged Pre-School Children.* New York: John Wiley & Sons.

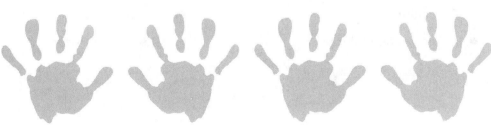

CHAPTER 5
Observing the Development of Young Children

✐ **Overview**

✐ **Why Observation Is Valuable**

◆ Understanding Patterns and
Diversity in Development

◆ Understanding Children's
Behaviour

◆ Recognizing the Need for
Intervention

◆ Planning the Child-Centred
Curriculum

◆ Appreciating Children

✐ **The Process of Observation**

◆ Objectivity in Observation

✐ **Techniques for Observation**

◆ Anecdotal Record

◆ Running Record

◆ Event Sampling

◆ Time Sampling

◆ Rating Scale

◆ Checklist

◆ Play Interview

◆ Additional Techniques

What You Should Observe

- ◆ Emotional Development and Coping
- ◆ Social Development and Play Patterns
- ◆ Communication and Language
- ◆ Cognitive Development and Learning
- ◆ Physical Well-Being and Motor Development
- ◆ Behaviour

Interpreting Development from Observational Information

- ◆ Recognizing Developmental Achievements
- ◆ Identifying Strengths and Needs
- ◆ Identifying Concerns
- ◆ Using Observational Data

Communicating Your Findings

- ◆ Recording Observations
- ◆ Confidentiality of Records
- ◆ Discussing Assessments with Colleagues
- ◆ Discussing Assessments with Family Members
- ◆ Discussing Assessments with Children

Summary

Review Questions

Discussion Questions

Activities

Further Reading

Additional Resources

References

OVERVIEW

The early childhood curriculum is designed by educators who have expertise in child development. Awareness of typical sequences of development, as well as unique individual patterns and characteristics, guide educators in relationships and in curriculum design. By observing young children during play and their interactions with adults and peers, you can learn about the development of the children in your care.

The techniques of observation that are discussed in this chapter can help you gather comprehensive and relevant information about the development of each child. We explain ways of recording, interpreting, and communicating your observations. We also describe the role of observation in planning a child-centred curriculum.

By the end of this chapter, you will be able to

❖ explain why observation is useful in supporting relationships with and development of young children;

❖ describe what you can learn through observation;

❖ identify different types of observation methods suitable for use in early childhood settings;

❖ explain the value of objective recording of observational data;

❖ describe appropriate record-keeping and reporting formats;

❖ describe appropriate ways of communicating the results of observations and evaluations to colleagues, parents, and children.

WHY OBSERVATION IS VALUABLE

Maggie, a teacher of the senior group, was concerned about the level of participation of 4-year-old Richie. She noticed that he played alone a great deal and rarely used the active or dramatic play areas of the centre. She completed several running records over the week, and her suspicions were confirmed. Richie played alone about 70 percent of the time she observed, choosing the puzzles and cognitive games most often. In that week, he never played in the housekeeping centre or block area.

Maggie was also surprised at the number of times that Richie had approached adults to tell them about the size, weight, or number of things, such as "Did you know that there are 3 million people living in Toronto?" or "There are 1000 pennies in $10," or "My baby sister is 67 cm long." Maggie had not previously noticed his interest in mathematics and his unusual comprehension. She decided to incorporate more math activities in the dramatic and constructive play centres.

The housekeeping area became a design office with calculators, drafting paper and instruments, and a variety of measuring tools. The block centre was equipped with metre sticks and tape measures. At first, Richie ventured into the dramatic play centre only when there were no other children there. Maggie joined him and supported his play. By the end of the second week, an ongoing observation confirmed that Richie had spent a total of fourteen of twenty hours of free play in either the design office or the block area. His keen sense of numbers generated interest in measuring and number concepts in several of the other children, and Richie seemed to be enjoying the social play immensely.

Maggie's experience with Richie illustrates the value that observation offers to an early childhood educator. Not only did Richie gain a great deal, but the other children benefited from Richie's interest in numbers. You can imagine how different the outcome might have been for Richie if Maggie had not recorded carefully what she had observed.

Understanding Patterns and Diversity in Development

As an early childhood educator, one of the challenges of your profession is to apply your theoretical knowledge of child development to the unique patterns of learning and behaviour of the children in your care. Taking a cue from Maggie, you can apply what you learn from continuous and objective observation of the children. You need sensitive and perceptive insight into the development and needs of young children, insight that you gain through the highly valuable process of observing and interpreting the behaviour of the children. The expertise to evaluate development comes from your experience of observing many children and the thoughtful consideration of what these observations can tell you about individual children.

The previous chapter described some of the key issues, milestones, and challenges of development. You have read that each child's development is in some ways similar to that of other children and in some ways unique. Understanding the common developmental sequences and milestones enables you to begin to understand each child's learning. However, the unique way in which each child develops cannot be found in theories or milestones. Knowledge of individual processes of development is gained through careful observation

of individual children as they play, interact, and carry out the daily routines of life.

If you had visited Maggie's centre, you would have seen the children's activities. While playing, Melanie painted intently, deliberately selecting colours and standing back frequently to look at her painting thoughtfully. Ashley dashed to the easel, produced a few quick brush strokes, called to Maggie that she was finished, and raced off. Emile worked in the block area for nearly half an hour, using cars and people as props in the town he created. Natalie built a tower of blocks, which she gleefully and loudly knocked over. At the puzzle table, Daniel quickly completed several puzzles in fifteen minutes; beside him, Lisa chewed on a piece of a puzzle and ran her fingers around the shape of the hole in the puzzle board. She explored the puzzle in a tactile way that did not interest Daniel. These children each expressed their own unique pattern of development, style, and interests.

As we mentioned in Chapter 4, children are very different in temperament, in styles of relating to others, in their view of the world, and in the way they deal with new experiences. Communication and learning styles vary, as does the timing of the achievement of physical and motor skills. Observation is an excellent way of determining where children stand in each area of development, including emotional, communicative, cognitive, physical, and social development. You can use your observations to identify when the children have accomplished significant developmental milestones and to describe each child's current developmental level. You should also be able to identify the strengths and needs of each child so that you can provide activities that allow the children to be successful and to build on strengths, as well as to encourage development in areas that need additional experience and practice.

It will be up to you to keep these individual differences in mind as you interact with the children and plan for them. A program well-suited to the children's characteristics contributes to optimal levels of development and learning.

Understanding Children's Behaviour

Young children's behaviour is complex and reflects the wide range of emotions they experience. Because young children have not had much experience in using language to explain how they feel, they express themselves through their bodies, their actions, and their overall behaviour. Clinging and whining may indicate that a child is tired, ill, or discouraged by the pressures of high expectations. Angry, aggressive behaviour may indicate that a child is frustrated or is feeling vulnerable and trying to protect him- or herself. Some children fluctuate between these extremes, behaving unpredictably from hour to hour or day to day.

Careful and frequent observations help you to sort out the reason behind troubling or unusual behaviour. Children's facial expressions and other nonverbal cues can give you information, and noticing the context of the behaviour and the factors or situations that provoke particular behaviours increases your understanding. By observing, you will become expert at understanding and interpreting the behaviour of children. When you share your observations of behaviour with the children, you can help them to understand themselves better and to learn the difficult task of self-control.

Recognizing the Need for Intervention

Early childhood educators need to recognize the extent to which the characteristics and patterns of development of individual children are problematic or are preventing them from participating fully in the program. You might be the first to recognize that a child is experiencing problems in vision or hearing, or the first to notice that a child is developing at a slower pace. You might recognize some of the early indicators of language or learning differences. You might observe behaviours that are signalling emotional distress or unhappy relationships. Identifying and acting on these concerns can benefit both the child and the family.

Child abuse, an insidious and ugly social problem, warrants special consideration. For many children, abuse goes undetected because it occurs in situations and relationships that are considered private and protected from outside interference. The victims of child abuse often have no recourse except a trusted outsider who notices the signs that child abuse may be occurring. As a professional working with children, you have a legal responsibility to know the signs of child abuse and to observe the children for these signs (Rimer 1990).

Planning the Child-Centred Curriculum

Observation is a key aspect of planning a child-centred curriculum. Throughout this textbook, we emphasize building a curriculum that is responsive to the interests and needs of the particular children in your group. To provide experiences that are developmentally appropriate, beneficial, and sufficiently challenging and interesting requires detailed knowledge of all children. As you observe Azim's interest in and fondness for animals or Michelle's advanced skills in mathematical reasoning, you can enhance your program to provide experiences that encourage and strengthen these areas. When you notice that James is unlikely to attempt any creative activity but eagerly plays in the block area, use his favourite blocks and cars as tools for a unique type of painting.

Ongoing observation and the individualized curriculum experiences that result are the most important ingredients of the child-centred curriculum. This application of observational techniques will be elaborated on in Parts 3 and 4.

Appreciating Children

In the demanding role of an early childhood educator, there can be a tendency to see children solely as members of the group rather than as individuals. Sometimes you might become more focussed on the children who present a challenge or who have difficulty handling the demands of the program. You might not always be aware that Josh is helpful and sensitive with the younger children, that Katya has a strong sense of what is fair and right, that Mariko is exceptionally creative, and that Heather is skilful at negotiating and solving conflicts among her peers.

Observational techniques offer you the opportunity to see and appreciate the whole child, not just as a participant in a routine or activity, but also in being his or her own person. Spontaneous actions and conversations are delightful and revealing. It is rewarding, and often humbling, to sit back and watch the children as they go about the day — making choices, relating to others, playing, and just being themselves. You will be pleased and proud of the caring and concern demonstrated by children. You will be thrilled to see the accomplishments that follow persistent efforts. You will be moved by the emotions children express in their play. You will be excited and appreciative of the way in which the whole child encompasses all the parts you have been thinking about. Observation provides you with the privilege of seeing the whole child.

THE PROCESS OF OBSERVATION

Observing children is more than just watching them. Systematic observation is a process that uses spontaneous or planned observations to increase understanding of an individual child or all the children. Observation means looking at different situations over time to see and record the development of children in both structured and free-play contexts. Systematic observation begins with a specific purpose: determine what you are looking for, and why, before you start. The type of observation you do varies depending on your purpose. Indicate the purpose of your observation on your written record. There are many different reasons why you might want to do ongoing observations:

❖ to obtain a complete picture of a child in a variety of situations throughout the day;

❖ to observe specific behaviours, such as social interactions;

❖ to determine whether children have achieved particular developmental milestones or specific skills;

❖ to increase your understanding of why a child is behaving a certain way;

❖ to obtain detailed information on all the children in your program to create a child-centred curriculum that responds to the strengths and needs of your group.

Having determined both your purpose and what you will be looking for, the next step is to select a method of observing that meets your purpose. There are several methods to choose from, which are described in this chapter. Each method is carried out in a way appropriate to its purpose, and each one has particular advantages and disadvantages. If you understand the characteristics of each method, you can choose the one best suited to your purpose and situation.

Objectivity in Observation

Most people, when they make observations, form their own interpretations at the same time. For example, if you see someone crying, you likely assume that person is sad. If you see someone yelling and stomping around the room, you assume the person is angry. Your assumptions mean that you have jumped very quickly from what you have seen to how you interpreted that behaviour. This type of observation is subjective, because you moved away from the factual description of the event to a personal inference about what is happening.

To record your observations objectively, choose your words carefully. In the initial recording of an event or behaviour, include the descriptive facts as you see them. Describe accurately and with words that are precise ("She screamed and cried for five minutes" rather than "She had a severe temper tantrum"). Include all relevant details, and do not ignore details that help to set the stage or explain the incident.

Stand back from the incident and record what you see, not what you think the child is thinking or feeling. Facial expressions and gestures should be described, but the emotion or motive behind the expression or gesture should not be inferred. For example: "Kelly put her hands over her face and sobbed. She pulled her shoulders tightly together and moved away when the adult put her arm around her." This account is more descriptive and objective than the following one: "Kelly was devastated and rejected the adult's comfort." In the first example, the reader can visualize more easily and accurately what has happened. In the second example, the reader does not know how Kelly expressed her "devastation" or her "rejection" and might imagine a far different incident than the one that occurred.

Although objectivity is critical in the initial recording of the observation, there is also value in recording impressions and inferences. If you know Kelly well and know that this is an extreme example of the way she expresses her emotions, an inference that she "appeared devastated" might be useful. You must ensure that you record this observation as your interpretation by using such words as "it seems," "it appears," or "I wonder." It is common practice to indicate on your records which notes describe what occurred and which notes are your interpretations. You can include your interpretations in a separate area of the page or write them in parentheses.

BOX 5.1 GUIDELINES FOR OBSERVING

- ◆ Be prepared to jot down observations at all times. Keep a pad of paper or a notebook with pages for each child available in the room.

- ◆ Use planned and spontaneous activities as opportunities to observe and gather data.

- ◆ Observe each child in a variety of situations and over a number of days to get the most complete picture possible.

- ◆ Whenever you are observing, do not draw attention to yourself. Be unobtrusive and avoid looking directly at one child.

- ◆ Record only the facts. Do not interpret as you observe.

- ◆ Choose words that describe rather than judge or interpret.

- ◆ Record as much detail as possible.

- ◆ Include notes on nonverbal cues such as body language and facial and voice expression.

- ◆ Review observations and rewrite or file notes as soon as possible.

TECHNIQUES FOR OBSERVATION

There are several different methods of observing children. The choice of method depends on your purpose. If you want to find out how often or when certain behaviours are occurring, you will choose a different method than if you are trying to determine why certain behaviours occur. If you want to assess whether a child has achieved certain developmental tasks, you need to choose a method that provides some specific items to look for. Observation of specific activities and/or routines requires yet another method. This section includes descriptions and examples of various methods of observing found to be useful in the early childhood setting.

Anecdotal Record

The anecdotal record is a brief narrative description of a particular behaviour or inci-
dent, usually written after it occurs. It includes such factual information as what happened, when, where, and what was said and done. An anecdotal record is limited to one specific incident that is important to the early childhood educator. To be useful, the record should include the context in which the incident occurred. It can focus on behaviour that is either typical or unusual for a given child.

A recommended format for recording an anecdotal record is to divide the page in two, either vertically or horizontally, with one section for the objective observations and the other section for comments. Box 5.2 is an example of a useful format.

The value of the anecdotal record is that it is brief and can be completed after the fact. For an educator absorbed with a group of children, this kind of record has advantages. You can wait until a brief lull in activities or until you are on a break to write down what has occurred. You can limit your record to what is significant to you, leaving out irrelevant

BOX 5.2 EXAMPLE OF AN ANECDOTAL RECORD

ANECDOTAL RECORD

Child's Name Kathleen   Age 3   Date November 5, 19XX

Observer Myself   Time 10:25   Place Our centre

Purpose To assess Kathleen's emotional development

Kathleen is building a block building. Beside her, Bruce is putting a block on top of his tower. As he does, the whole tower falls. Bruce starts to cry loudly. Kathleen looks at Bruce with a concerned expression. Kathleen looks at the nearest teacher, and then goes over to Bruce and squats down close to him, looking right into his face. Kathleen pats his arm and says, "That's all right, I'll help you make another one." Bruce sniffs and his crying decreases. Kathleen starts piling up the blocks.

Comments

Kathleen appears to be able to empathize with the feelings of others. She has a desire to help another child in distress and seems to have a good sense of what to do.

Child's Name Kathleen   Age 3   Date November 6, 19XX

Observer Myself   Time 3:15   Place Our centre

Purpose To assess Kathleen's problem-solving skills

Kathleen is working with a shape sorter. She picks up a piece and tries to put it into one hole, then another, without success. She tries another piece in two different holes, also without success. She picks up the first piece again and tries it where she tried it before. She looks around the room and then tries the first piece in the same hole again. She sits and stares in front of her. Then she kicks the toy with her foot until it is a few feet away from her. She moves to the paint

(continued)

BOX 5.2 (continued)

area where she says loudly, "I'm going to paint now." She picks up the brush and makes several quick strokes of blue. "I'm finished," she calls to the teacher.

Comments

Toy too difficult? K. doesn't seem to have an effective strategy, and just repeats the unsuccessful moves rather than trying other holes. (Need to observe her with other puzzles.) Seems like she was aware that it was too hard and she pushed it away before moving to an activity where she could be successful (painting). I have noticed that she usually enjoys painting, but I don't remember her trying that toy before.

Source: Adapted from J.J. Beaty. (1994). *Observing the Development of the Young Child* (3rd ed..). New York: Macmillan, p. 19. © 1994. Adapted by permission of Prentice Hall, Upper Saddle River, NJ.

details. The biggest disadvantage of this method is that it relies on your memory of the incident. We all know that memory can change or fade over time, so that the record may be less accurate if you delay writing for very long. Relying on memory can also cause you to miss important details of the behaviour or the context. There is also a danger of reading too much into a single anecdotal record. This is the reason why you need to collect a series of these records over a period of time to verify your impressions and interpretations.

Running Record

A running record is a detailed narrative of a child's behaviour in sequence, written down as the behaviour is happening. The running record includes everything that occurs over a given period of time. This method is used when you want to obtain a general sense of the child without focussing on any predetermined behaviours.

The running record contains descriptions of appearance, incidents of behaviour, any conversation that takes place, and the context. It also includes such details as the description of the setting, other children involved, and any teacher interactions. The running record paints a complete picture of the setting and the child so that the reader can visualize the situation. A running record includes an indication of the amount of time that has passed, particularly if it is longer than a few minutes.

Again, it is helpful to divide the page in two; one side can be used for observations, with the other side reserved for comments, questions, and interpretations (see Box 5.3).

The running record is an effective tool if you are interested in observing and evaluating a particular learning centre or activity. Rather than following one child, your attention is

BOX 5.3 EXAMPLE OF A RUNNING RECORD

RUNNING RECORD

Child's Name Maria   Age 2½   Date March 4, 19XX
Observer   Myself   Time 7:45   Place Our centre
Purpose   To observe how Maria enters the playroom and participates
              in free play

TIME	OBSERVATIONS	COMMENTS
7:47 AM	M runs a few feet into the room, stops, and looks around. Twists her hair and looks at B (teacher). M's hair is tousled, but otherwise clean, and she's neatly dressed. Cheeks flushed.	Seems hesitant. Is this typical?
	Smiles when B greets her. Moves few feet closer to B. Stops again. B invites her to the table. M moves to beside B and wiggles onto his lap. Hugs B. B asks her how she is. Smiles and tucks her head down. No verbal response.	Needs help to get involved? Accepts physical affection.
7:51 AM	Takes a piece of play dough and begins to roll it with her hands. Still hasn't said anything. Laughs when B shows her his creation.	Seems comfortable with B.
7:55 AM	Looks over things on table. Points to rolling pin. B asks if she wants it. She nods. B asks another child to pass it. M takes it without saying anything. B says thanks. M begins to roll her play dough.	Still hasn't talked. Does she need time to get warmed up?
8:01 AM	B gets up to leave. M frowns, sits on chair herself. Rolls play dough briefly. Looks around room. Twists hair. Stands up. Takes seven steps toward doll centre. Stops. Watches children there. Twists hair.	Is she anxious? Is it hard for her to approach children?
8:04 AM	Looks around room. Walks to where B is helping a child with her leg brace. Leans against B's back. B. tickles her. M giggles. Watches B finish with brace. B asks if M wants to do puzzles with them. M nods and takes B's hand.	Seeks teacher contact. Responds to adult suggestion.

Source: Adapted from J.J. Beaty. (1994). *Observing the Development of the Young Child* (3rd ed.). New York: Macmillan, p. 22. © 1994. Adapted by permission of Prentice Hall, Upper Saddle River, NJ.

focussed on a particular area of the room, and records are kept of each child's reactions to, and play within, the centre. If this is done for even a short period (20 to 30 minutes) on 2 or 3 occasions, you will have a good sense of whether the set-up and materials of the centre are enhancing the play, interactions, and learning that are occurring there.

The main advantage of the running record is the richness of detail it provides. A series of running records is beneficial for describing and documenting behaviour and development and for providing examples for completing an assessment of progress. The biggest disadvantage of the running record is that it requires that the observer sit back and remain uninvolved in the activities of the group. As you can imagine, this is not easy in an early childhood setting. As well, this kind of record is time-consuming. Only one child or centre can be observed at a time to avoid missing details. The running record may also present a problem if it is not used regularly, in that the child being observed may be aware that you are watching and may become self-conscious, so that you do not see typical behaviour patterns.

Event Sampling

Event sampling is a method used to record the occurrence of specific behaviours on which you decide to focus, similar to the anecdotal record. Unlike the anecdotal record, this method is carried out by continuous observation and immediate recording of incidents.

You would choose event sampling if you were concerned about what seems to trigger certain behaviours, for example, why Hira always sulks and leaves the water table if Pedro wants to play there. Event sampling allows you to include the setting and the context as well as the behaviour. When appropriately done,

event sampling keeps the entire incident intact for better understanding.

Beaty (1994) describes a format called the ABC analysis that can facilitate your understanding of what might be causing certain behaviours. The event is broken down into three parts: A = Antecedent event, B = Behaviour, C = Consequent event. Each time the behaviour is recorded, all three components should be included (see Box 5.4).

Because understanding the reasons for certain behaviours is so important to early childhood educators, we recommend this technique. Once you have a general sense of the child from the less focussed running and anecdotal records, you will find it useful to concentrate your observations on specific patterns of behaviour.

Time Sampling

Time sampling is a technique used to record how frequently behaviours occur over time. It is useful when you want to count and document the occurrence of a particular behaviour that is obvious and occurs quite frequently. This method can be helpful in recording such behaviours as sharing or changing activities. You can prepare ahead of time, defining which behaviours you will record. Decide when to sample, usually at a time when the behaviour is most likely to occur. It is often helpful to sample in more than one situation for comparison.

Time sampling is limited to providing data on the number of times a behaviour occurs. This method does not record the context or descriptions of behaviour, so that it will often need to be followed up by one of the other descriptive methods. Otherwise, the lack of information about the context in which the behaviour occurs could lead to a serious misinterpretation of behaviour.

BOX 5.4 EXAMPLE OF EVENT SAMPLING

EVENT SAMPLING

Child's Name __Manny__   Age __3½__   Date __April 17, 19XX__

Observer __Myself__   Time __3:25__   Place __Our centre__

Behaviour __Physical aggression (hitting, pushing, kicking) directed__

__toward another person__

TIME	ANTECEDENT EVENT	BEHAVIOUR	CONSEQUENT EVENT
3:30 PM	Manny approaches water play, tries to take funnel that Leah is using. Leah says, "No, I'm using it."	Manny pushes Leah	Leah cries and looks for teacher. Teacher does not intervene. Manny gets funnel. Leah leaves.
3:40 PM	Ryan approaches Manny and tries to pour water through Manny's funnel.	Manny hits Ryan on the arm.	Teacher sees and intervenes. Takes Manny aside and says firmly, "No hitting."

Source: Adapted from J.J. Beaty. (1994). *Observing the Development of the Young Child* (3rd ed.). New York: Macmillan, p. 27. © 1994. Adapted by permission of Prentice Hall, Upper Saddle River, NJ.

Rating Scale

A rating scale is an observational tool that assesses the degree to which a person possesses a certain characteristic (Beaty 1994). The scale consists of a list of characteristics, or behaviours, and a choice of ratings that indicate the extent to which each characteristic applies to a given child. Rating scales tend to use similar types of descriptors to provide the points of choice, for example: usually, frequently, sometimes, rarely, and never.

Rating scales are often used to help you decide how concerned you should be about a child's behaviour. This is a decision that you should take seriously. Some behaviours, when seen frequently or in extreme forms, can be indicators of developmental problems (see Box 5.5). You will notice that these same behaviours are quite common for all children at some point in time. The rating scale is used as a tool to help you decide whether a behaviour is frequent or severe enough to be of concern. Often it is the pattern or the number of behaviours judged to be extreme that is important when interpreting the rating scale.

The advantages of the rating scale are that it is simple to use and can be completed after the fact. Its value is determined by the way you judge and interpret significant behaviours. The

BOX 5.5 EXAMPLE OF A RATING SCALE

RATING SCALE: INTERACTIONS WITH ADULTS

Child's Name _____ Age _____ Date _____

Observer _____ Time _____ Place _____

	RARELY	SOMETIMES	USUALLY
1. Finds separating from parents difficult.	_____	_____	_____
2. Clings to certain adults.	_____	_____	_____
3. Shies away from new adults.	_____	_____	_____
4. Shows excessive number of attention-getting behaviours.	_____	_____	_____
5. Resists routines by becoming tearful, whiny, or noncompliant.	_____	_____	_____
6. Refuses help even though it is needed.	_____	_____	_____
7. Pulls away from adults when physical contact is initiated.	_____	_____	_____

Source: Adapted from Zola Anderson. (1976). *Getting a Headstart on Social Emotional Growth.* Omaha, NE: University of Nebraska Medical Center, pp. 72–73.

need to judge the child's behaviour makes the method very subjective, so you must be careful to be fair in your ratings — you may be influenced by any bias you already have concerning the child. Timing is important — be sure you are in a position to reflect carefully about the items, when your own feelings and reactions are not an issue. Have a second person complete the rating scale as well, and compare and discuss any differences in opinion.

Checklist

The checklist is one of the most valuable tools of observation because it can be used in a number of ways. Checklists are helpful in identify-ing children with developmental delays, in evaluating and recording progress, and in identifying areas for curriculum planning. If a checklist covers all areas of development, it can provide a profile of the whole child.

A checklist provides a series of behaviours or skills arranged in a logical order (Beaty 1994). It can be created from a collection of learning objectives or a sequence of developmental indicators, and it is useful for observing and recording behaviours that can be easily and clearly described.

Checklists are easily completed, usually by placing a check mark beside each item that you have observed the child performing. They are often intended to include descriptive comments in addition to the check marks. Sometimes a date is included, and the checklist is added to throughout the year so that the child's progress can be tracked. Observations can be made during play periods or by setting out specific materials and watching how the children use these. One or more persons can complete the checklist. Box 5.6 provides an example.

Play Interview

Sometimes observing a child in a group does not provide the information that you need to understand her or him. You might feel that you could find out more by spending some time alone with that child. Many children are very open and happy to sit down with a trusted and familiar adult to discuss a variety of topics. Skilful educators can gain insight into a child even within a brief time.

One method that we highly recommend is the play interview, which combines play with supportive discussion. To carry out the play interview, you should choose a time when you can spend at least half an hour alone with the

---

BOX 5.6 EXAMPLE OF A CHECKLIST

CHECKLIST OF VISION AND HEARING ABILITIES

Child's Name _____ Age _____ Date _____
Observer _____ Time _____ Place _____

Does the child seem to (YES)
... have difficulty seeing objects? ❑
... tilt his or her head to look at things? ❑
... hold objects close to his or her eyes? ❑
... squint? ❑
... show sensitivity to bright lights? ❑
... have uncontrolled eye rolling? ❑
... complain that his or her eyes hurt? ❑
... bump into things constantly? ❑
... have jerky or uncoordinated eye movements? ❑
... appear awkward in tasks that require eye–hand coordination (e.g. pegs, puzzles, colouring)? ❑

Does the child seem to (YES)
... have difficulty hearing? ❑
... consistently favour one ear by turning the same side of his or her head in the direction of the sound? ❑
... ignore, confuse or not follow directions? ❑
... rub or pull on his or her ear frequently or complain of earache? ❑
... complain of head noises or dizziness? ❑
... have a high, low or monotonous tone of voice? ❑
... not respond to your voice unless he or she is looking at you? ❑
... ask "What?" excessively? ❑
... have speech that is very difficult for you to understand? ❑

Source: A.H. Hayden, R.K. Smith, C.S. von Hippel, and S.A. Bear. (1978). *Mainstreaming Preschoolers: Children with Learning Disabilities.* Washington, DC: U.S. Government Printing Office, p. 26.

child. Choose a comfortable and familiar setting, such as the child's normal playroom, that is empty while the others are outside. Make the time very informal by providing a variety of materials such as play dough, crayons, blocks, or make-believe toys such as miniature figures and doll house furniture. The choice of materials depends on your purpose and the individual child. Any materials that make the child comfortable are suitable. If you want to discuss interpersonal relationships, either drawing or playing with miniature figures may facilitate the experience. If you are looking for indicators of cognitive or motor skills, use puzzles, games, and manipulative toys. If the child is reluctant or defensive, use more neutral materials such as Lego or play dough. In all cases, do not pressure the child into any one activity. Let the child lead the play while you follow.

If the child is comfortable with you, he or she will most likely enjoy this time and will be chatty. You should allow him or her to direct the conversation — limit your involvement mostly to supportive and interested comments that will encourage the child to continue talking. Questions should generally be used to get the child to clarify or expand: "What do you mean?" or "What happened next?" or "How did you feel about that?" Try not to change the direction of the conversation too much unless there is something specific that you want to learn.

The play interview is particularly valuable if you are concerned about unusual moodiness or extremes of behaviour or if you have suspicions about child abuse. In this situation, children may give you many clues about how they are feeling and why. The play interview can also be helpful in observing specific cognitive and communication abilities such as completing puzzles, solving problems, creating and telling stories, and describing events in sequence. An additional benefit of the individual play interview is that it provides an excellent opportunity to build on your relationship with the child and show your faith and support.

Additional Techniques

The techniques described so far represent the main options that are traditionally used in observing children. Usually your purpose in observing is to gain a better understanding of children. However, there are several other sources of information that you can use.

One excellent source of information and documentation is a sampling of children's drawing and writing. Over a period of months, these will show the children's progress in fine-motor control, awareness of detail, and conceptual knowledge. These samples are also useful for learning of children's special interests and common themes. Children's drawings and stories tell us much about how they see their environment and their place within it, and often indicate their emotional concerns. As with any observation, do not place too much emphasis on any one drawing or story, but be on the lookout for ongoing themes that might indicate when a child is struggling or in need of sensitive support.

Another important source of information is the parent interview. Sensitive and skilful discussions with family members can provide a wealth of information about and understanding of children. Early childhood educators might find that a child at home is very different from the one you see in your program. Sharing your observations with parents and asking them to observe at home may provide increased understanding for you and for them. Family members can also be helpful in completing checklists, or in providing examples of drawing or play interests.

Lastly, consider the use of audio- and video-tapes to facilitate your observations. When it is difficult for you to actually carry out or record an observation, the use of a tape recorder or video camera can provide information. Once children are accustomed to the equipment, they will behave naturally with it. Videotapes can be especially helpful in following an individual child throughout the day, or in taping specific activities such as group times. Audiotapes are helpful in collecting language samples and in taping play interviews. Because the audio- or videotape is a record of the child, do not use or show it without parents' knowledge and consent.

WHAT YOU SHOULD OBSERVE

Knowing the techniques available to you is only part of the process of successful, systematic observation. You must also know what to look for. Good observation depends on in-depth knowledge of child development: the ability to recognize indicators of development, and the ability to interpret the behaviour of individual children in terms of child development theories. Your observations will focus on

the developmental milestones and processes we discussed in Chapter 4. This theoretical perspective guides and gives meaning to your observations. The following sections provide some practical suggestions for observing in each area of development.

Emotional Development and Coping

As you begin observing, you will likely notice that children respond in different ways to the routines and expectations of the group setting. There are several reasons for these differences. The first is children's temperament. Remember that there are three common types of temperament, as described in Chapter 4. Observe each of the nine characteristics to identify any temperamental influences (Box 4.2).

Other factors that influence children's ability to cope with the program are a result of the achievement of the important milestones of emotional development, also discussed in the previous chapter. Children who are relaxed and active have high self-esteem, experience satisfying relationships with trusted and caring adults, and can handle most of the situations they encounter throughout the day. On the other hand, children who are struggling to achieve one or more of these milestones might have difficulty when they are confronted with similar challenges in your program. Use the checklist for emotional development (Box 5.7) to see how effectively you are adapting your approach to meet the child's temperamental style and emotional needs.

Social Development and Play Patterns

Through social interaction and play, children expand their communication ability and cognitive, physical, and emotional development. Yet the challenges of interacting with peers can have

BOX 5.7 EXAMPLE OF A CHECKLIST FOR EMOTIONAL DEVELOPMENT

CHECKLIST FOR EMOTIONAL DEVELOPMENT

Child's Name _____ Age _____ Date _____

Observer _____ Time _____ Place _____

Sense of Security in Program

❑ Appears comfortable, relaxed in setting.

❑ Smiles, laughs, seems happy most of the time.

❑ Does not cling to classroom staff excessively.

❑ Shows interest or engages in most activities.

❑ Eats, sleeps, and uses washroom without upset.

❑ Copes with sudden changes with minimum of upset.

Forms Satisfying Relationships

❑ Does not withdraw from others excessively.

❑ Accepts comfort from staff when distressed.

❑ Separates from parents without difficulty once comfortable with setting and staff.

❑ Enjoys contact with adults.

❑ Seeks support from adults when distressed.

Communicates with Intention and Effectiveness

❑ Expresses needs and wants effectively.

❑ Stands up for own rights.

❑ Seeks other children to play with.

Demonstrates Positive Sense of Self

❑ Makes activity choices without teacher's help.

❑ Shows satisfaction and pleasure in own accomplishments.

❑ Plays roles confidently in dramatic play.

❑ Displays enthusiasm about doing things for self.

Integrates Emotional Thinking

❑ Expresses a full range of emotions.

❑ Can express anger in words rather than actions.

❑ Allows aggressive behaviour to be redirected.

❑ Beginning to recognize effect of behaviour on others.

❑ Shows beginning skills in problem solving.

❑ Shows increasing number of appropriate choices of behaviour in interactions with others.

❑ Expresses emotional ideas in dramatic play.

❑ Accepts adult assistance to resolve emotional issues.

❑ Resolves emotional issues in a satisfying manner through play.

Source: Based on J.J. Beaty. (1994). *Observing the Development of the Young Child* (3rd ed.). New York: Macmillan, pp. 45–46.

BOX 5.8 GUIDELINES FOR OBSERVING PLAY

- ◆ What play activities are preferred?
- ◆ What play activities are avoided?
- ◆ What themes are common or recurring in the child's play (aggression, fears, dependency, control, nurturing, monsters, etc.)?
- ◆ What needs or emotions are expressed through play themes?
- ◆ How does the child attempt to resolve or deal with these needs and emotions in her or his play?
- ◆ How does the child respond to new or difficult challenges in play?

- ◆ How does the child deal with frustration or failure?
- ◆ What interpersonal skills (co-operating, negotiating, caring for others, empathy) are seen in social play?
- ◆ Does the child use play to calm down or to release tension? If so, what activities does the child choose for this purpose?
- ◆ What activities tend to overstimulate the child? How does the child handle this overstimulation?

BOX 5.9 SOCIAL PLAY PREFERENCES

TOY PREFERENCE, ACTIVITY PREFERENCE, PEERS

When playing with toys or objects, does child

- ◆ play by self?
- ◆ play parallel with others?
- ◆ play co-operatively with a group?

When constructing or creating something, does child

- ◆ play by self?
- ◆ play parallel with others?
- ◆ play co-operatively with a group?

When engaging in make-believe play, does child

- ◆ play by self?
- ◆ play parallel with others?
- ◆ play co-operatively with a group?

the result that many young children feel unaccepted and on the outside of meaningful play. Social acceptance and play skills are interconnected, and each depends to some degree on the other.

Observing children in their freely chosen play activities provides an intimate and rewarding glimpse into each unique personality. To observe the meaning and level of play of young children, begin by observing their solitary play. As we discussed in the previous chapter, play often reveals much about the child's emotional state and/or any areas of upset. Box 5.8 suggests some questions to help you understand the content of children's play.

You can also observe the amount and type of social play. Some children prefer to play alone or parallel to others, but independently. Most children engage in a mix of solitary and social play (see Chapter 4). Box 5.9 provides a guide to observing the social play of each child to determine whether a child is experiencing a wide variety of play opportunities.

If your observations to this point suggest that a child does not regularly enter into meaningful social interactions in play, you may want to observe further to assess specific skills in this area. Guralnick, in his checklist "Assessment of Peer Relations" (in Littman n.d.), identifies a number of skills that children need for maintaining successful peer interactions. These include

❖ skills to enter play successfully, such as requesting permission to join or proposing joint activities;

❖ skills in conflict resolution, such as regulating one's own level of emotion, negotiating strategies, and being able to compromise;

❖ skills in maintaining play, such as demonstrating a shared understanding and complying with the rules of the play, and adapting to the pressures and changing patterns of play.

Careful and detailed observation of a child's play and social interactions might indicate areas in skill development that require coaching or teaching of specific strategies to improve the quality of peer relationships and satisfaction from social play.

Communication and Language

Children's ability to communicate effectively underlies success in social and cognitive areas. Are they able to communicate basic needs and wishes, for example, hunger or what they want to play? Record samples of children's conversation, looking for their ability to follow the conversation and take turns with another person (pragmatics). Vocabulary level and ability to sequence words and sentences are examples of children's expressive language ability. How they respond to directions, questions and general conversation tells you about their receptive language abilities.

Can children make themselves understood? Do they primarily use single words and simple two- or three-word sentences? Can they convey more complex meaning through complex sentences with conventional grammatical structures such as negatives, questions, and clauses? Do the children speak clearly enough to be understood by others? Can they produce most speech sounds, or do they have articulation problems?

The most effective way to observe language is to take a language sample — writing down everything that a child says, as well as what others say. The context is important for assessing a child's understanding. Do not forget to include descriptions of nonverbal communication, such as shaking the head or shrugging the shoulders. Also, using a tape recorder is a good idea.

Cognitive Development and Learning

Cognitive development — all thinking abilities — is complex and includes numerous skills and abilities. Observe children's knowledge of concepts involving objects, shapes, size, spatial location, time, and number. Look for indications that children are using preoperational thinking (as described in Chapter 4) to understand such relationships as same and different, and to group and sequence objects in a logical manner. Record examples of the children's general knowledge and awareness of their immediate world.

Other areas to observe are auditory and visual memory, attention span for both self- and teacher-directed activities, and the ability to carry a task through to completion. You should look for clues to a child's ability to understand cause and effect and to solve problems. It is valuable to note differences in the way children learn, such as a preference for visual or hands-on learning, a reflective versus impulsive style, or an ability to think creatively when problem solving.

Physical Well-Being and Motor Development

Early childhood educators often observe physical well-being as part of the arrival routine. Some centres use a standard health check each day to ensure that children appear healthy and ready to take on the day's adventures. Consider their overall appearance, colouring, and activity level, as well as indications of possible illness, such as nasal congestion or ear infection.

Be aware of any long-term physical conditions — allergies or other health problems — and their implications for a child's ability to handle the daily routine. Observe children's eating, sleeping, and toilet habits as well to make sure that their basic needs are being met. Observe their vision and hearing abilities. Earlier in the chapter, we included a checklist of indicators for problems in these areas (Box 5.6).

Such large-motor skills as jumping, running, catching, throwing, and climbing are easily observed on the playground or during active play, especially if one adult leads the children in a group activity while another checks their skills. Small-motor skills — the ability to manipulate small materials such as blocks, pegboards, and Lego, to control crayons to make deliberate markings, and to fasten buttons or zippers — can be observed during free play and during routines of eating and dressing.

Be sure to evaluate the quality of movement as well as the specific large- and small-motor skills. Is a child awkward or does he have poor co-ordination? There are wide differences in both ability and co-ordination, which will suggest the need for specific planning in the motor areas of the program.

Behaviour

Often the most puzzling aspect of a child's development is behaviour. This is one area in which observation can be useful and informative. Children behave in many ways in response to situations and factors that adults may or may not be able to identify. Using observational techniques can help you understand a child better and make the behaviour seem less unpredictable.

One area to observe is the response of children to each of the aspects of the program. How do they handle such routines as snacks, lunch, or rest time? How do they behave in those transition times that require extended waiting? Is their behaviour different in teacher-directed activities than in other play time? Do they handle the demands of group times without difficulty?

Another area to observe is the ability to initiate and carry out responsibilities such as picking up and putting away toys and equipment or assisting in tasks assigned by an adult. How well can a child keep track of clothing and other personal belongings?

A third area to observe is response to the directions of an adult. Most children are able to follow directions without too much difficulty, although occasional resistance is normal. Sometimes a child challenges the authority of the adult or refuses to follow direction. When this happens, it can usually be worked through with a consistent, firm, and gentle insistence on the part of the adult. When a child continuously has trouble complying with your expectations and the "rules of the room," further observation is warranted.

Finally, observe for an overall behavioural style. Look at the activity level of the children, as well as their ability to remain focussed while they complete a task. Pay attention to indicators of independence and dependence, assertiveness and aggressiveness. Observe for methods of handling stress, such as regression, self-comfort (using objects, thumb, or body movements), lashing out, or withdrawing. Also, look for consistency in the behavioural patterns of each child, as well as factors that might explain inconsistencies in a given child's behaviour from day to day.

Often the most valuable result of observing a child's behaviour is identifying the behaviour and approach of the adult that elicits the best and most consistent response. All children respond differently to behaviours of those around them. Incorporate what you learn into your planning and program development.

INTERPRETING DEVELOPMENT FROM OBSERVATIONAL INFORMATION

Observing is a first step in evaluating children's development. The real value of your observations comes with insightful interpretations that enable you to determine a child's progress. Interpretation means taking what you have observed and adding it to other information to help complete the picture of the child's development. Look for patterns in observations that take place over a span of time or in a variety of situations. Once you have formed initial impressions, you should go back and do further observations to confirm your interpretations.

In forming impressions and interpretations, do not read more into a particular situation or behaviour than what is really there. Many inexperienced observers make the mistake of seeing an isolated behaviour and interpreting it as the child's normal behaviour. Take the example of Gauze, who cries frequently and is clingy with staff. You might see this as an indication of an overall pattern of anxious or withdrawn behaviour. However, in this case you would be mistaken, because Gauze's behaviour is the result of an ear infection and is quite atypical for her.

Whenever you make interpretations about a child's development, remember that all areas of development are interconnected. If a child experiences difficulty in one area, this often has an influence on other areas. For example, Willie's language is delayed because of earlier temporary hearing problems. He is slow in grasping concepts and general knowledge, because for more than two years he did not hear what was being said to him. His expressive language is delayed, affecting his ability to interact successfully with peers who are articulate. These factors have affected his self-esteem and willingness to take risks, so that he often appears hesitant and on the fringe of the goings-on in the program. Supportive and sensitive responses from the educators are helping Willie to gain confidence, and developmentally appropriate communication strategies will eventually minimize the impact of his earlier problems.

Recognizing Developmental Achievements

One of the main reasons why we observe children is to evaluate their development in comparison to what is expected of their age and ability. We use developmental milestones and

developmental norms as a guide. Developmental milestones are important skills in each developmental area that most children usually demonstrate at *approximately* the same age. Developmental norms tell us when we can expect certain behaviours and achievements. They represent the average age at which specific developmental skills are achieved by most children in a given culture (Allen & Marotz 1994). You can find charts outlining development in the boxes throughout this book. A valuable resource is a book by Allen and Marotz (1994) entitled *Developmental Profiles: Pre-Birth through Age Eight,* which provides extensive lists of behaviours in each area of development for each year of age. These descriptive lists can provide a solid starting point for an observation when your purpose is to identify developmental achievements. *However, remember that each child progresses through the sequence of development in a different manner and at a different pace.*

You can recognize developmental achievements by comparing your observations with the developmental milestones and norms. When a child appears to be achieving the developmental milestones expected for his or her age, record examples of these achievements in each of the areas of development discussed earlier. Highlight a child's interests and areas of enjoyment. These will be valuable for staff meetings and parent feedback. Continue to monitor children's progress at regular intervals.

Identifying Strengths and Needs

Because developmental patterns and achievements are different for each child, one useful way of interpreting your observations is to create a profile of development for each child. In a profile, you evaluate each aspect of development in terms of strengths and areas needing improvement. Strengths include areas of advanced achievement, high interest, or special ability or talent. Keep in mind these strengths in your planning to ensure that you are providing challenging activities as well as opportunities for leadership.

All children have areas in which they could benefit from more experience and practice. These can be identified for further observation and for program planning. Children might need to be encouraged to try things that present more challenge or difficulty. Some children might have areas of development that represent real delays and challenges, in which case deliberate planning and strategies will need to be implemented in consultation with parents and specialists.

Identifying Concerns

At times you might discover through observation that a child is not achieving developmental milestones as expected within a reasonable range of time. If so, that child might need special attention (Allen & Marotz 1994). Children with communication, sensory, motor, or other learning needs might show an uneven pattern of development in that they are achieving within the norms in some areas but not in others. Use running and anecdotal records to determine the extent to which these possible delays are affecting a child's participation in the group and overall learning.

If you discover that a child is not achieving milestones in more than one area of development, you might have uncovered a more serious problem. Carry out several observations to assess how well the child is handling each aspect of your program and to further evaluate the child's skills in each area of development. Look for patterns that can help you to better understand the nature of the child's difficulties. Spend some time in a play interview to see if the child performs differently in the one-to-one situation. Look for evidence of short attention span or distractibility. Analyze the similarities and differences in behaviour to help form your impressions and interpretations.

Be cautious when you attempt to interpret the development of preschool children through the use of developmental norms. As we have mentioned several times, children do develop at their own pace — sometimes they seem to have reached a plateau, and then they suddenly leap ahead. Developmental norms represent only the average age at which children demonstrate a particular skill, which means that many do so earlier and just as many do so somewhat later. All of these children would still be devel-

oping "normally." You must keep in mind the wide diversity in developmental timetables and focus your attention on areas in which children demonstrate *significant* differences.

Keep in mind that your role as an early childhood educator does not qualify you to diagnose or determine exactly what the child's developmental difficulties might be. That is best left up to the specialists who have the expertise to make diagnoses. Your role is to provide the observational information and to determine and identify when the child's development does not seem to fit the usual patterns. When you have these concerns, they need to be discussed with parents and colleagues.

Using Observational Data

The real goal of observation is not just to learn what children are like, but to find the best ways to help them develop and grow (Beaty 1994). Through the process of observation, you have become very familiar with the children and their ways of interacting with the environment. You are aware of their developmental levels and have determined their strengths and preferences. You have seen how they use play to express interests and needs. You have formed impressions about their sense of well-being and the quality of relationships with others, and have identified areas that the children need to develop further. You have a sense of each child's behaviour in many different situations. It is now possible for you to create the best possible environment for each child. You will be able to choose a style of interaction to which each child is most likely to respond positively.

You know whether a certain child needs time and space in order to comply with direction, or whether gentle physical guidance is best to avoid a struggle. You know how to offer comfort and support in a way that a child can accept it. You know how to motivate each child to participate fully, and you are able to adapt your style to suit the individuality of each child.

Similarly, you are now able to plan learning experiences that will best facilitate each child's further development. Knowing the level of development of each member of your group allows you to provide developmentally appropriate learning experiences. Knowing individual strengths helps you to include all children in experiences that help them develop to their full potential. Anticipating children's reactions to different situations and events and modifying routines and schedules as needed will make each day a little smoother. In making each of these aspects of your program more responsive to the needs of the children in the program, you are well on your way to providing a child-centred program.

COMMUNICATING YOUR FINDINGS

Recording Observations

The value of information obtained from observations is increased when it is recorded well. You might have several pages of anecdotal and running records, as well as checklists and samples of a child's work. When you want to speak to parents or colleagues about a child, you will need to make concise notes or reports. By going through all of your material, you can highlight what you think is most important. Briefly summarize the main observations and any specific conclusions you have made. Be sure your observations distinguish between factual material and your own

impressions. Include such details as the date, the child's full name and age, the setting, and the observer's full name. Treat these records as individual and formal items within the child's file. Remember that parents have the right to see the information you have compiled on their child. Maintain the file as a well-documented, unbiased profile of their child's developmental progress.

Confidentiality of Records

Any records that you maintain must be confidential. This means that they must be kept in a place where they can be accessed only by staff of the centre. They must not be shared with anyone outside the centre without the family's written consent.

Confidentiality also applies to discussions and verbal sharing of information about the child. You should not discuss a child's behaviour or development with anyone outside the centre unless you have the parents' consent. An exception is a situation in which you suspect a child is being abused. In this case, you must report your concern to an appropriate agency, such as the Children's Aid Society. You must ensure that discussion with other staff members occurs in a place that is private and cannot be overheard by members of other families or visitors in the centre.

Discussing Assessments with Colleagues

There are several reasons why you might wish to discuss your observations with colleagues. The first reason is to obtain input on your observations and conclusions. If you have observed something that is puzzling, ask your colleagues to make observations as well. Once they have had a chance to form their own impressions, you can benefit from discussing the child at a staff meeting. Present your observations and questions in an organized manner, being clear about what you would like from the others (opinions or advice about what to do). Be careful to present any concerns objectively and with the goal of doing what is best for the child. It is all right to share your feelings about the child provided that you do so in a professional manner and take responsibility for the way you feel ("I am upset that nothing I have tried seems to be effective," not "I've given up on that kid. He is not interested in behaving the way he should"). This is not the time to vent your feelings of frustration or anger.

A second reason for discussing a child with colleagues arises when you have ideas for a certain approach or strategy as a result of your observations. If you want to try a new approach with a child, share your idea with your co-workers as a way of confirming your decision and gaining their support. Be clear about whether you wish them to try out your ideas as well, or whether you would just like them to watch for signs that your approach makes a difference. Open discussion and co-operation among staff help to ensure that a child does not become confused by contradictory approaches while you attempt to modify your style of interaction or programming.

A third reason for discussing your assessment occurs when you wish to consult with, or refer to, an outside specialist such as a psychologist, pediatrician, or speech therapist. When contacting these specialists, be clear about what you want from them. Are you asking for further assessment, programming guidance, or help for the child or parents? Before you make a referral, you need the parents' written consent. Then you will be able to share your summarized observations as well as any steps you have already taken to assist the child. Be prepared to act as an advocate for the child and family, ensuring that their needs are addressed by the specialist.

As an early childhood educator, you are an important member of the multidisciplinary team serving the child and family. You see the child on a consistent basis in a familiar setting. Your well-documented and objective observations and impressions are a valuable part of further assessment and intervention when it is needed.

Discussing Assessments with Family Members

There are two main reasons for discussing your observations with family members. The first is that they have the right to know about any observations, assessments, interventions, and concerns about their child. The second reason is that whatever information and observations you have gained will be just as helpful to the family in their relationships with the child as they are to you.

Discussion of observations with family members is most beneficial in the context of an ongoing and comfortable relationship. You should share descriptions of the child's activities and achievements regularly and informally as a way of developing and maintaining a relationship between yourself and the family and communicating to the family your interest in their child. When the family members are comfortable with and trust you, the family conference will be much easier for you and for them.

Once your observations are completed, recorded, and summarized, you are ready to schedule a conference to discuss your findings with the parents and other family members as appropriate. Be sure to allow plenty of time for your meeting, and choose a private place. Do not attempt to share detailed information or concerns as children are being dropped off or picked up.

Prepare for the conference so that you know what you want to communicate. Be sure that you provide many opportunities for family members to share their own observations and knowledge of their child and to ask any questions. Many parents appreciate receiving a copy of your report or summary so that they can refer to it later, without having to try to remember everything that you have told them. Box 5.10 provides some suggestions for a successful parent conference.

Discussing Assessments with Children

Children who are being observed or who are participating in tasks for the completion of a checklist often have questions about what you are doing. Putting them off or giving vague responses is not appropriate because it can increase their anxiety. Answer their questions honestly and accurately in words they can easily understand. Telling Raoul that you are interested in seeing what each child is learning in your program and how different each child is from the others is an answer that should satisfy without raising concerns about his own performance. Give concrete examples such as, "I wrote down how much you enjoyed doing that painting and that you said it was a green airplane," and "I am interested in seeing which children jump on one foot and which children jump on two." Make sure the child is aware that there is no right way or one behaviour that you wish to see, but that you are interested in what makes each child special. Enlist the children's co-operation and interest by inviting them to draw pictures or call you to see what they have done. When you have completed your observations, it may be helpful for children to hear what you have found.

BOX 5.10 GUIDELINES FOR A SUCCESSFUL PARENT CONFERENCE

◆ Begin with an overview of what you see as the child's unique and positive qualities.

◆ Identify any areas that you would like to discuss in more detail.

◆ Share your observations, interpretations, and any concerns clearly.

◆ Question parents as to their observations, perceptions, and reactions to your opinions.

◆ Discuss the whole child, including strengths and areas of concern.

◆ Ensure that results of checklists are presented in the context of the child's overall nature.

◆ Use anecdotes and examples to illustrate any checklist items.

◆ Never compare children.

◆ Talk about any specific approaches or activities the child is successful at and responds well to.

◆ Offer parents the opportunity to express their feelings, concerns, and goals.

◆ Remind parents how quickly children develop and change.

They will beam with pride and pleasure if you point out to them accomplishments that you have noted.

An honest and concerned discussion about areas in which you see the child needs support can be effective in encouraging extra effort: "I see that riding the trike is hard for you. If you wish, I will help you a little every day until you can do it for yourself." When discussing any area of difficulty with the children, be sure to let them feel your optimism in their ability to achieve difficult tasks with extra effort.

It is especially important to encourage children to express any of their own feelings about what you tell them. You might find it helpful to offer some possible words, such as "Sometimes it is frustrating … " or "I know I'd feel upset … " to help them put their feelings into words. The children may have questions — honest and simple answers are best. If you do not have the answer, be sure to admit it, and then try to find out.

Never underestimate the benefits of this type of discussion or the ability of children to participate in it — you might be surprised at the relief that some children feel at having a chance to discuss their feelings and achievements seriously and privately. You will be impressed and pleased with the outcome of these discussions. You will hear children use your words to praise the efforts and achievements of others, and to explain their own abilities and needs.

SUMMARY

Ongoing observation provides two main benefits: it enhances your understanding of the common and unique aspects of child development, and it provides you with the means to recognize and evaluate all areas of development of children in your care. With your understanding of child development, you can provide a curriculum that is responsive to the strengths and needs of all children and you can intervene when necessary to support their developmental needs.

The main techniques of systematic observation include such descriptive methods as anecdotal and running records and such predetermined methods as time and event sampling, rating scales, and checklists. Play interviews are also useful as an interactive observational technique.

Effective observation needs a focus, and this chapter provided suggestions for observing emotional, social, communicative, cognitive, physical, and behavioural development. Interpretations of observations should consider milestones of development as well as particular areas in which children demonstrate developmental and experiential diversity. Valid observations must be carefully and objectively interpreted in light of theories and norms of child development.

Conclusions drawn from your observations will benefit the child's family and your co-workers, as well as the child. The child's family has a right to know how their child is progressing and to be informed of any intervention you believe would be helpful. When sharing information, respect confidentiality and maintain the family's and the child's right to privacy.

REVIEW QUESTIONS

❶ What are the benefits of observation for the early childhood educator?

❷ Describe each of the techniques for observation and explain when each is best utilized.

❸ Give examples of what can be observed in each of the following areas of development: emotional, social, communicative, cognitive, physical, and behavioural.

❹ Why do you need to be familiar with sequences and norms of child development when interpreting your observations?

❺ What is the best approach for communicating your findings to family members?

DISCUSSION QUESTIONS

❶ Your director thinks that observations are useful only when a child appears to be delayed in an area of development. What would you say to convince him or her that observations are important for all children?

❷ Discuss the role of ongoing observation in the development of a child-centred curriculum.

❸ What steps must you take to ensure that the information you gather on a particular child is valid and provides an accurate interpretation of her or his development?

❹ The staff of a child-care centre complete checklists evaluating skills in late fall and spring in order to give feedback to parents. Is this approach adequate? Valuable? What are the weaknesses in this approach?

❺ You have concerns about a child but are not sure that anything is really "wrong." When is the best time to approach parents, and how would you go about it?

ACTIVITIES

❶ Show a videotape of a child participating in various activities in an early childhood education program. Have each of your fellow students write a running record, and then compare your recorded observations. Discuss differences and replay the tape for confirmation and clarification.

❷ Show a videotape of one or two incidents of children's behaviour. After a short period of time, have fellow students write anecdotal records. Compare your results, and then discuss the potential dangers of relying on memory over an extended period of time.

❸ Using several of the techniques described in this chapter, observe a child in an early childhood education setting. Form tentative impressions based on what you have observed. Discuss your observations with someone who is familiar with the child for confirmation.

❹ Observe several incidents of children's aggressive behaviour. Record what you see using the ABC method, and analyze the behaviour for patterns and explanations.

❺ Conduct one or more play interviews with individual children as described in this chapter. Comment on what you were able to observe. Tape a language sample as well, and analyze it according to developmental norms.

FURTHER READING

Allen, K.E., and L. Marotz. (1994). *Developmental Profiles: Pre-Birth through Eight.* **Albany, NY: Delmar.**
This book is a good source of developmental sequences and norms. The authors emphasize developmental principles as a foundation for observing children. Each chapter outlines what to expect at a given age in the areas of physical, motor, perceptual-cognitive, language, and personal-social development.

Beaty, J.J. (1994). *Observing the Development of the Young Child* **(3rd ed.). New York: Macmillan.**
This book is an excellent resource for the observation of children. The author provides a checklist of developmental milestones in emotional, social, motor, cognitive, language, and creative development. Beaty summarizes relevant theory in each area and offers suggestions for programming.

Crain, W. (1992). *Theories of Development: Concepts and Applications.* **Englewood Cliffs, NJ: Prentice-Hall.**
Crain summarizes the work of a wide range of theorists, such as Erikson, Piaget, Kohlberg, and Montessori, who have attempted to explain development in many areas.

Greenspan, S., and N.T. Greenspan. (1986). *First Feelings: Milestones in the Emotional Development of Your Baby and Child.* **New York: Penguin Books.**
This book is a guide for parents to observe the emotional development of their children. Chapters on infant development describe early tasks, while later chapters provide detail on the emotional milestones facing 3- and 4-year-olds.

ADDITIONAL RESOURCES

Littman, Elaine, ed. (n.d.). *Making Friends: Early Childhood Social Integration.* **Vancouver: Making Friends.**
An educational package that includes a video series, an assessment tool, and a guide to these materials. The emphasis is on observing and assessing play and social skills needed to maintain successful peer relationships. The package includes many suggestions for developing these skills. Available from Making Friends, 4508 West 12th Avenue, Vancouver, BC V6R 2R5.

REFERENCES

Allen, K.E., and L. Marotz. (1994). *Developmental Profiles: Pre-Birth through Eight.* Albany, NY: Delmar.

Anderson, Z. (1976). *Getting a Headstart on Social Emotional Growth.* Omaha, NE: University of Nebraska Medical Center.

Beaty, J.J. (1994). *Observing the Development of the Young Child* (3rd ed.). New York: Macmillan.

Black, J.K., M.B. Puckett, and M.J. Bell. (1992). *The Young Child: Development from Prebirth through Age Eight.* Toronto: Maxwell Macmillan.

Chess, S., and A. Thomas. (1987). *Know Your Child: An Authoritative Guide for Today's Parents.* New York: Basic Books.

Crain, W. (1992). *Theories of Development: Concepts and Applications.* Englewood Cliffs, NJ: Prentice-Hall.

Essa, E. (1992). *Introduction to Early Childhood Education.* Albany, NY: Delmar.

Greenspan, S.I., and N.T. Greenspan. (1986). *First Feelings: Milestones in the Emotional Development of Your Baby and Child.* New York: Penguin Books.

Guralnick, M.J. (n.d.). Assessment of peer relations. (Checklist). In E. Littman, ed., *Making Friends: Early Childhood Social Integration.* (Kit). Vancouver: Making Friends.

Hayden, A.H., R.K. Smith, C.S. von Hippel, and S.A. Bear. (1978). *Mainstreaming Preschoolers: Children with Learning Disabilities.* Washington, DC: U.S. Government Printing Office.

Neisworth, J.T., and S.J. Bagnoto. (1987). *The Young Exceptional Child: Early Development and Education.* New York: Macmillan.

Rimer, P. (1990). *Child Abuse: A Handbook for Early Childhood Educators.* Toronto: Association for Early Childhood Education, Ontario.

Santrock, J.W. (1992). *Life-Span Development* (4th ed.). Dubuque, IA: Wm. C. Brown.

Wortham, S.C. (1990). *Tests and Measurement in Early Childhood Education.* Columbus, OH: Merrill.

CHAPTER 6
Facilitating Emotional Development

✐ **Overview**

✐ **Emotional Well-Being**

✐ **Milestones of Emotional Development**

  ◆ A Sense of Security

  ◆ Forming Relationships

  ◆ Communicating Effectively

  ◆ Developing a Sense of Self

  ◆ Creating Emotional Ideas

  ◆ Emotional Thinking: Fantasy, Reality, and Self-Esteem

✐ **Supporting Emotional Well-Being**

✐ **Floor Time: The Importance of Interactive Play**

✐ **Linking Social and Emotional Development**

  ◆ Development of Social Skills

  ◆ Educators as Models

  ◆ Coaching Social Skills

✐ **Nurturing Socioemotional Development**
- ◆ The Self
- ◆ Family
- ◆ Friends
- ◆ The Community
- ◆ Canadian Society
- ◆ Global Concerns

✐ **Summary**

✐ **Review Questions**

✐ **Discussion Questions**

✐ **Activities**

✐ **Further Reading**

✐ **Additional Resources**

✐ **References**

OVERVIEW

Children's emotional well-being has to do with their sense of safety and security and their relationships with others whom they trust — relationships that are loving, satisfying, and supportive. This sense of well-being includes feeling confident enough in their own skills and abilities to explore the world, take risks, and express their ideas and feelings without fear.

Early childhood educators have a number of tasks and challenges in providing for children's emotional well-being. The most critical factor is the quality of the relationship the adults establish with the young children. The emotional development of the older preschoolers is also influenced by the quality of relationships with peers.

In this chapter, we discuss in detail the emotional needs of young children and the importance of their having meaningful relationships with the adults and peers in the early childhood setting. We also discuss guidelines for sensitive and responsive interactions with children, support for developing social skills, and curriculum applications.

By the end of this chapter, you will be able to

❖ describe the characteristics of an emotionally healthy child;

❖ explain the processes and milestones underlying the achievement of emotional well-being;

❖ describe the qualities of adult–child relationships that promote emotional well-being;

❖ explain the role of peer relationships in enhancing emotional development;

❖ describe the components of the early childhood setting that promote emotional and social development.

EMOTIONAL WELL-BEING

Imagine an infant who is fed and kept warm and comfortable, with all the physical needs supplied, but who is kept in isolation and is never held, is never touched, and never hears an adult's voice. This baby would never feel love or any kind of emotion — a horrifying thought. Perhaps in imagining the absence of emotional connection for an infant, you can understand the necessity and importance of this connection.

If you read the work of developmental theorists, you will find that for many years they have emphasized the significance of meeting emotional needs for lifelong well-being. In Abraham Maslow's theory on the hierarchy of needs, the emotional needs are secondary only to the essential physical needs (in Crain 1992). The emotional needs include security, acceptance, and love, among others. On a still higher level are the self-fulfilment needs for beauty, order, symmetry, and self-actualization.

Recently, professionals have recognized more clearly the extremely important role that early childhood educators and care-givers play in meeting the emotional needs of young children during the time away from their parents (Greenspan 1990; Lieberman 1994). Discussions that had focussed on the importance of learning in the early years have been replaced by concerns about the ideal environment for ensuring emotional and mental health. Children need meaningful relationships with care-givers. In fact, Lieberman argues that emotional nurturing is the most important role of the early childhood educator, because emotional well-being is the essential foundation for all other areas of development.

Young children rely on adults to provide security, comfort, affection, admiration, encouragement, understanding, and protection from strong emotions — those of others as well as their own strong and confusing emotions. In quality attachment relationships with parents and care-givers, the consistent meeting of these emotional needs leads to a sense of trust in others and a positive self-concept, which allow children to begin each day with a sense of competence and confidence. A positive self-concept is enhanced by successful peer relationships, through which children develop social skills.

As more younger children enter early childhood education settings, we need to consider how care-givers and educators can best meet the emotional needs of young children.

MILESTONES OF EMOTIONAL DEVELOPMENT

Emotional development refers to two key processes: the development of a sense of oneself and the development of meaningful relationships with others. Emotional development is influenced by many factors: the individual characteristics of a child and the adults close to her or him, a child's experiences in dealing with the world, and the quality of attachment relationships that develop between the child and care-givers and peers.

In describing the complexities of emotional development, we draw on the work of several theorists and practitioners. Dr. Stanley Greenspan (1986, 1989, 1990), a professor of psychiatry and a practising child psychiatrist and psychoanalyst, wrote about six milestones of emotional development. In this chapter, we

BOX 6.1 SIX MILESTONES OF EMOTIONAL WELL-BEING

1. Child experiences a sense of security and calm that allows for meaningful interpersonal experiences.

2. Child experiences a strong attachment based on trust and the knowledge that she/he is valued and can share in a mutually pleasurable relationship.

3. Child is able to communicate needs effectively, so that she/he comes to expect prompt and sensitive response to these needs.

4. Child develops a sense of self, experiencing success in asserting needs and in self-direction, developing confidence,

and a sense of pride in her/his abilities and accomplishments, leading to a sense of self-esteem.

5. Child feels safe to express the full range of emotions, knowing the adult will support her/him and provide protection if there is loss of control. Child begins to replace behavioural communication of emotions with verbal means.

6. Child clarifies the relationship among ideas, emotions, behaviour, and consequences. Child shows increasing ability to make good choices in interactions with others.

Source: Based on Stanley Greenspan and Nancy Thorndike Greenspan. (1986). *First Feelings: Milestones in the Emotional Development of Your Baby and Child.* New York: Penguin Books.

integrate other relevant theories into Green-span's framework of emotional development.

A Sense of Security

Before anyone, child or adult, can participate in any situation effectively, the person must feel secure and calm. New or unfamiliar situations tend to create anxiety for all of us, so it is easy to understand this basic concept.

There will be children in your program who are not able to achieve or maintain enough of a sense of security and safety to feel calm. Without feelings of security and calm, they will not be able to achieve a level of interest and involvement that allows them to participate fully in and benefit from your program. What reasons might children have for feeling tense, anxious, overwhelmed, or insecure in a child-care setting?

SEPARATION ANXIETY

The anxiety experienced by young children who are separated from their parents is one of the most common factors affecting their sense of security and calm. At first, an early childhood setting is unfamiliar to young children and somewhat overwhelming. They need familiar adults who can reassure them, interpret situations that seem frightening, and provide the support needed to move into new situations. They need the security that only their familiar parent or other family members can give. However, often these family members are not available, so the children become distressed. They might feel they have been abandoned in an unfriendly and overwhelmingly distressing situation.

Children express separation anxiety through many different behaviours. Some cry intensely, resisting all attempts by adults to offer comfort. For these children, who have no clear concept of time, the period of separation is painfully long. They often stop crying only when they are exhausted. Other children might attempt quite quickly to transfer their needs for emotional closeness and dependency onto a caregiver. These children might accept comfort from this adult to reduce the obvious distress of feeling alone, but they still cry for the absent parent and ask several times a day for assurances that the parent will return. Some children express their stress through anger and aggressiveness, and actively resist an unfamiliar adult's attempts to comfort them. Others are so overwhelmed by the anxiety created by separation that they withdraw to a place where they can feel somewhat safer, and avoid all forms of involvement with people or activities.

In whatever way children express the distress of separation, care-givers must realize that this is a normal reaction that deserves respect from adults. You need to identify and accept the distress children feel and not expect or pressure them to "get over it." Offer empathic support to the children so that they will come to see you as an alternate source of emotional security as quickly as possible. Do not just leave a distressed child who resists your efforts, but continue to gently encourage from a distance — if a child is more comfortable with you at a distance — with smiles, interest, and sensitivity. Children will reach out to you when they have assured themselves that you continue to be accessible and that they can trust you. Some will take longer than others.

Separation is difficult for many young children because they face two tough emotional demands at the same time: the experience of losing contact with the parent, and adjusting to new people in an unfamiliar situation. The distress of separation can be lessened somewhat (but still not totally) by separating these two demands. For example, have the parent spend

BOX 6.2 STRATEGIES TO REDUCE SEPARATION ANXIETY

◆ Have the child and parents visit your centre when there are only a few children there. They should explore the centre together.

◆ Suggest that the child visit the parents' places of work or school so that the child can visualize where the parents are during their absence.

◆ Keep a small selection of family photographs available so that the child can look at them and be reminded of this special relationship.

◆ Parents can leave a note or a personal object, such as an old piece of jewellery or watch, with the child to remind him or her that they care.

◆ Encourage the child to bring a transitional security object from home, such as a stuffed toy, book, blanket, or other favourite item. Allow the child to have access to this item at any time.

◆ Encourage parents to visit with the child as often as possible before the first time that the child will be left alone. Use these visits to begin to build a relationship with the child while he or she is still being supported by the parents.

◆ When the child is being left, encourage the parents to stay for a brief time to give the child time to adjust to being there. The par-

ents can involve the child in an activity, and then you should join the two of them there. Try to keep this time calm and unrushed.

◆ When the parents are ready to leave, make the goodbyes affectionate, reassuring, and relatively quick. Offer your support to the child so that the parents will be reassured that the child is not being left alone and upset.

◆ Allow the child to watch the parents leave, and reassure him or her that "Mommy (or Daddy) will be back after work."

◆ Acknowledge and accept the child's feelings and right to be unhappy. Assure him or her of your support until the parents return.

◆ Encourage the child to use the transitional objects or pictures to comfort him- or herself and to get involved with something he or she can share with the parent later, such as a painting or drawing.

◆ Remain available to the child during the time it takes to work through this normal separation distress. Remember, you are substituting for the parents in the role of security base.

◆ Call the parents to let them know that the child is OK. This is a hard time for parents, too. Reassured parents will help to support the child through this stressful time.

enough time in the centre with the child until the place is no longer as unfamiliar and frightening. Also, make the initial separations short and gradually lengthen the period of separa-

tion from the parent as the child becomes confident that the parent will return. Be sure to convey to anxious children that you are available for security and support.

THE INFLUENCE OF TEMPERAMENT

Children's individual characteristics and temperament affect how they react to new situations. As we mentioned in Chapter 4, children have three general types of temperament.

The majority of children are outgoing and flexible and move easily into new situations, coping effectively with expectations and with change without experiencing extreme distress (Chess & Thomas 1987; Leiberman 1994). These children more easily achieve a sense of calm and generally participate in most activities with little anxiety or distress. Children who are slow to warm up (Chess & Thomas 1987) or are more fearful (Leiberman 1994) need more support as well as time to move into new or uncomfortable situations. Allow them to observe from a distance and decide on their level of involvement.

Some children have significant difficulty in coping with and adapting to the demands of a new situation, and might react with resistance or extreme upset (Chess & Thomas 1987). These children experience emotions and frustrations more intensely than others, which can create tension for child and adult alike. There is no one style of adult interaction that works best for a child with this temperamental style. You will have to observe, consult with parents, and experiment to see what supports the child most effectively. Intense children need your understanding and encouragement. You can help them learn strategies and acceptable behaviours for times of distress, such as withdrawing to a quiet, calm place or engaging in a relaxing activity.

To help each child experience a sense of comfort in your program, you need to be familiar with the various temperaments outlined in Chapter 4. You can observe new children carefully to determine how their temperament affects their response to your program.

THE INFLUENCE OF EXPERIENCE

Children come to early childhood settings from a wide range of backgrounds. Some children are confident in group settings, with peers and unfamiliar adults, and are eager to enter into any activities. For others, your program might be their first experience in a group, and the number of other people and choices of activities might feel overwhelming. Some children come from other parts of the world, and everything in their new environment seems strange. The more the early childhood setting is different from home, the more likely that children will need time and gentle support before they begin to participate comfortably.

Imagine Elizabeth, who comes from an isolated rural area with a great deal of poverty, coming into a busy, well-equipped child-care centre with many rooms and nearly 60 children. Is it any wonder that for weeks she stood back and observed, uncertain, without playing, and that several months passed before she talked to other children or adults? At the same time, at home she talked excitedly about her experiences at the centre. In the meantime, the sensitive teachers respected her choice to observe and to communicate nonverbally with gestures and pointing, knowing that this would help her to overcome her high level of anxiety.

For some children, experiences of abuse, family breakup, death of a family member, and other traumatic events contribute to their anxiety, anger, fear, and mistrust. These children have strong needs as a result of their pain and distress (Gartrell 1994). To children with strong or unfulfilled emotional needs, the world might seem to be a hostile place, and they have little expectation of support from the early childhood setting. These children need extensive and patient support in dealing with their strong needs and they require time to allow them to see the care-givers as a source of security and safety.

Children who have recently immigrated to this country need a particular kind of support. Early childhood educators should realize the uniqueness of these children and try to understand the incredible changes that they experience. Remember, some of these children may never have experienced an urban setting, a cold climate, or even a separation from their parents. The terrifying changes these children experience, coupled with cultural misunderstanding, have an impact on their emotional development. Their self-concept can be threatened, resulting in acting out or withdrawing. This is a time when gradually establishing a relationship with recent immigrant children and their families is of critical importance.

Juan and Maria came to Canada to escape from a country where their father had fought against an oppressive government. In their short lives, they have already experienced death, destruction, and fear as a part of daily life. They and other family members do not speak or understand English, making communication very difficult. It will take time and commitment to help them and their family to experience the early childhood setting as a safe place where they can finally stop being afraid.

Preschoolers who are learning English as a second language might have difficulty communicating their needs and emotions. When they are not understood by adults and other children, they likely feel uncertain, anxious, and frustrated. Of course, these feelings affect their ability to interact with others. Unable to make themselves understood, children in this situation sometimes feel rejected and become aggressive or withdrawn. Using nonverbal communication (gestures, smiles) can help to let children know that they are welcome and that you are interested in what they are feeling. Your response also provides a model for other children, giving them some ideas of how to interact despite communication barriers (Chud & Fahlman 1985).

As an educator, part of your job is to assist children to maintain their sense of being in control and feeling calm. Children respond differently to strategies for calming: some accept support and comfort from adults, some prefer time alone, some use a security item such as a toy or favourite blanket, and some respond to talking or to music. You can help children recognize when they feel overwhelmed or upset, and can encourage them to use whatever helps them to feel calm again. Whatever children use for comfort should be seen in a positive light and should never be used to isolate or embarrass them.

A few children have great difficulty in calming themselves and will require your patient support. Try to learn what will help the hyperactive or overanxious child. Some children need to be taught such strategies as relaxation or withdrawing from situations into a quiet activity. A back rub, a special cuddly toy, or deep breathing may be helpful. Do not underestimate the value of such relaxation techniques — as children discover a sense of calm, they may be able to use the new technique frequently and spontaneously.

Remember, all young children are dependent on adults to meet their emotional needs. It is up to you to attempt to determine what factors may be preventing a child from actively and happily participating in your program. It is also up to you to consistently offer your encouragement and support at whatever level children will accept until they begin to feel safe and secure with you.

Forming Relationships

Closely related to the first milestone of feeling secure is the need to develop a close and satisfying relationship with at least one care-giver. As children begin to feel more secure, possibly as the result of your efforts, they will work to strengthen the ties between the two of you. Each child needs to establish a relationship in which she or he feels accepted, valued, and genuinely liked. In forming a relationship with another adult, children discover that they can give and receive pleasure in a mutually satisfying relationship.

In the parent–child relationship, this attachment is crucial and forms the basis for the child experiencing trust in others (Erikson 1963). A secure attachment, which provides a sense of psychological security for young children, increases the confidence with which the children go about exploring the world (Ainsworth 1979) and has also been related to later social competence (Santrock 1993).

Although the relationship with a secondary care-giver is not as intimate or permanent as the parent–child relationship, in the parents' absence, it must serve some of the same needs. Each child needs to feel special and close to you, and secure in the knowledge that you are there for him. This quality relationship plays an essential role in the development of positive self-concept and high self-esteem. Children view themselves through the eyes of others — if others like them and see them as special, children incorporate this sense of acceptance and worth into their own view of themselves. If adults are frustrated or disappointed with a child, or if adults maintain a distance in their relationship with her, she will begin to see herself as unworthy. This negative self-view becomes part of her self-concept and influences future relationships.

With many children, a relationship with a care-giver develops naturally and easily, as many children bring the skills they have learned from the relationship with parents to this new relationship. For some children, this relationship may not come easily. One factor that influences relationships is called a "goodness of fit" (Chess & Thomas 1987). Each of us has preferences for certain characteristics and qualities in other people. Some of us are more comfortable with outgoing, physical, and active styles, while others prefer a soft-spoken, reflective, and observant approach. We all have a tendency to treat boys and girls differently based on our perceptions of gender differences and societal roles and expectations. Each of us has expectations based on our own style and on the types of experiences we have had with others. We need to recognize these as personal preferences and take care not to value one style of temperament or behaviour over another. Although we might enjoy and find our relationships with some children more easily maintained, we must work to develop an accepting, meaningful, and respectful relationship with each child as a basis for healthy emotional development.

Sometimes when children come from other ethnic, racial, or economic groups, or even geographical regions, you might feel uncomfortable with them because they seem unfamiliar. It is important, as an early childhood educator, to become aware of your specific biases and then work at not negatively influencing the children because of your biases. Diligent observation of your interactions with young children will help you to identify behaviours that you may need to change in working toward a "better fit."

Do not feel uncomfortable about admitting to yourself any feelings of hesitancy you have toward a child. In recognizing how you feel, you can then concentrate on changing your reactions in positive ways. Remember, your reaction forms part of a child's perception of whether he or she is likable or acceptable. Having admitted your hesitancy, you can then begin to build a relationship by sharing common experiences — possibly creating with play dough, playing with water, or running around the yard. Focus on what can be shared rather than on what cannot be shared, and you will find that the diversity of children adds to your own personal growth and development. There are many more similarities among people than differences, even if we do not share a common language or lifestyle. You, as well as the other children, will find it interesting and rewarding to learn phrases in another language, to appreciate differences in the way we all live, and to discover that we are more alike than different.

It may seem that some children make relationships difficult. It is not surprising that a child with a lot of hostility or mistrust has a more difficult time engaging in a meaningful relationship. However, you must not give up your efforts. "The more difficult [a relationship] is, the more the child needs it. … Understanding and empathizing with the child will not always be easy, but the situation that arises because you don't won't be easy either" (Greenspan & Greenspan 1989, p. 26). Look for positive qualities to which you can respond, and work to build a relationship that tells the child you care. The time spent in satisfying interactions with a caring person slowly builds self-esteem and improved relationships.

Communicating Effectively

The third emotional milestone is developing effective communication skills. Again, most children develop communication skills naturally.

BOX 6.3 DETECTING BIAS IN INTERACTIONS WITH CHILDREN

◆ Do you pick up on verbal and non-verbal expressions of interest in a similar way with all children?

◆ Do you offer the same amount of physical freedom to all children?

◆ Do you allow all children the opportunity to express their feelings?

◆ Do you help some children more than others?

◆ Do you respond differently to similar behaviours of all children?

◆ Do you provide opportunities for children to play together or alone?

◆ Do you assist children in getting started at an activity or allow them to call you for help if they prefer?

Source: Based on L. Derman-Sparks and A.B.C. Task Force. (1991). *Anti-Bias Curriculum.* Washington, DC: National Association for the Education of Young Children.

Most preschool children will come to you with good communication skills and the confidence that you will understand and respond to their requests and sharing of ideas.

You may be wondering why communication is an emotional milestone. This is another example of the interrelationship between developmental areas. Remember that we have defined emotional development as the development of a self-identity as well as the ability to participate in satisfying relationships. Think of how important communication skills are in relationships: each of us needs to have ways to express our ideas, needs, and feelings effectively, and to have confidence that other people understand and can help us.

Children who are effective communicators experience many advantages. They can express their needs in a way that is acceptable to adults and will most likely have their needs met. Children with effective communication skills can identify problems and ask for help. They can assert themselves with peers and adults in speaking, which is more likely to accomplish what they want. Compare this with what happens to a child who is not an effective communicator.

There are several reasons why children may have difficulty with communication. The most obvious reason is that they may be delayed in the use of language, which means they cannot express themselves adequately. Another obvious reason is that you might not speak a child's language. When these children attempt to communicate through gestures, poorly articulated words, or another language, you likely will not understand them and will have difficulty responding to them. The children then feel frustrated, anxious, and unsure about whether they can trust you. This predicament is not anyone's fault, but neither is it acceptable.

Children might also be ineffective communicators for emotional reasons. Earlier in the chapter we referred to Elizabeth, who was so overwhelmed that she did not speak. Her cautious use of gestures and body language were so subtle that unless the adults observed her carefully, they did not see or respond to her attempts at communication. Another child, Jason, might be described as having an intense temperament. He is also impulsive. Whenever he is frustrated, he experiences his emotions so strongly that he cannot put his feelings and needs into words. Instead, he kicks and screams to communicate his unhappiness. The staff mistakenly refuse to respond to his needs unless he puts them into words, which only increases his feelings of frustration, lack of support, and mistrust.

In all cases of ineffective communication, you must concentrate on reassuring children that you will attempt to understand and respond to each effort to communicate. Whenever possible, you should attempt to communicate through the child's chosen means, incorporating your words as backup. Use of and response to nonverbal communication helps to let children know that they are welcome and that you are interested in what they are feeling. This means that for Elizabeth, you accept her nonverbal style and respond with body language, gestures, and facial expressions, sometimes also using words, but with no demands that she speak in return. For example, if she tugs on your arm and points to the sink, it is best to nod, smile, ask if she wants a drink, and take her hand while walking to the sink. Communication received!

With Raúl, who speaks only Spanish, your use of frequently needed phrases such as "¿Te gustaría jugar?" ("Would you like to play?") or "¿Quieres ir al cuarto de baño?" ("Would you like to go to the bathroom?") helps him feel valued and accepted. He is much more eager to learn to speak English with you when you speak Spanish with him. For Jason, you need to show that you understand how he feels and what he wants by labelling the situation for him rather than expecting him to do so unsupported: "It looks like you are angry because you didn't get a turn at the computer before snack. I can understand your anger, but I can't let you push Robbie to show how you feel." Jason needs to experience understanding for how difficult it is for him to communicate appropriately rather than to experience rejection or lack of support. Understanding helps to build the sense of security and acceptance that enables him to move to a more effective stage of communication.

If we put pressure on children with ineffective communication skills to become better at communicating in the manner we prefer, we are subtly placing a value judgement on them and making them feel less valued than others. The resulting anxiety, stress, and loss of confidence further inhibits communication attempts, discouraging communication altogether and placing a barrier into the development of a trustworthy relationship.

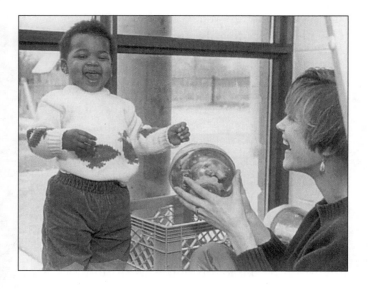

Developing effective communication skills and experiencing success in communicating is a significant factor underlying the next milestone, which is seeing oneself as competent and capable of making things happen.

Developing a Sense of Self

The next milestone to be achieved is the development of a positive and accurate sense of self. Preschool children constantly take in information that clarifies their views about who they are and how valuable they are to others. The development of identity includes knowledge about personal characteristics (boy, girl, big, pretty, a pain, strong, too little, brave, smart, clumsy) and the relative value of one's own sex, race, and abilities. These issues are discussed in more detail in Chapter 7.

To begin to build an image of themselves as having skills and competence, children need many successful experiences in many areas of their lives. Communication is one of those areas, motor skills is another. Think of the child who does his first somersault or makes the trike pedals go around, or skips, or draws a circle for the first time. He experiences an enormous sense of achievement and pride. When you admire a child's efforts and share his pleasure in his accomplishments, you are helping to build a positive sense of self. Successful experiences build a sense of competence and confidence, the basis for independence and autonomy.

In the process of coming to understand who they are and what they are capable of, children need freedom to try things for themselves, to make decisions, and to experience a degree of control over their own lives. As they make choices and determine their own behaviour, they will face the consequences of their choices.

Children learn from the results of their mistakes. Their discomfort with the results of their behaviour can become motivation to resolve a problem — cleaning up a mess or changing their behaviour, for example. However, consequences must be at a developmental level that children can handle without creating excessive anxiety, guilt, or distress. When either natural or imposed consequences of children's mistakes are too severe, self-doubt and an unwillingness to take further risks may result (Erikson 1969).

In this process, the following behaviours indicate that a child may be experiencing self-doubt:

❖ lack of confidence;

❖ excessive concerns about pleasing others, doing it right;

❖ excessive needs for approval, direction, and assistance;

❖ limited skills in seeing options and in solving problems;

❖ frustration and difficulty with perceived failures;

❖ resistance to limits and direction;

❖ negative reactions to others.

The early childhood educator should be observant and sensitive to indications that a child might not be feeling positive about her own skills and competence. In general, the way to enhance the sense of self is to respect the child's attempts at mastering new or challenging situations and to ensure, through careful planning, that each child experiences more success than failure. Admire with the child both the effort and the achievements, no matter how small they seem. A sincere and heartfelt compliment goes a long way toward helping a child to see herself positively.

Creating Emotional Ideas

The preschool years are a time of intense, confusing, and often conflicting emotions. The relative calm of the first year is followed by the emotional roller-coaster ride that begins in the toddler period. Many of the emotions experienced by young children result from the frustration of not having their needs and wishes responded to promptly. Although it is obvious to adults that young children cannot have everything that they think they need, this fact is not obvious to the children and often creates distress.

The perceived unwillingness of a trusted adult to give children what they want creates a level of doubt and anxiety that underlies their distress. Young children do not know how to interpret a refusal and may see it as a rejection or withdrawal of caring. As a child's wishes become more extensive, learning to deal with frustration becomes an important aspect of emotional development, along with understanding that relationships are becoming increasingly complex. Children discover that the same person can be both giving and withholding, permissive and restrictive, loved and hated. These contradictions are upsetting and confusing for young children and must be experienced and dealt with many times over before they can integrate these apparent contradictions into their concept of other people who are important to them.

Communication is a component of emotional ideas, and again, you can see the interconnection of developmental areas. Children with well-developed skills in understanding language become aware of the motives and reasons behind others' behaviour and reactions. When they can understand the reasons, they are less likely to resist. Language skills also enable children to communicate their feelings and to test their own understanding. You can see this development in understanding in a conversation between a 2-year-old and her mother.

Child: I pee on the floor, I make you angry (frowning).
Mother: It's better to pee in the toilet, because it's not as messy.
Child: I pee in the toilet, I make you happy (smiling).
Mother: Yes, I like it when you pee in the toilet.
Child: I pee on the floor, I make you angry (frowning).
Mother: You're right, I don't like it when you pee on the floor. We need to pee in the toilet.
Child: I pee on the floor, I make you angry (frowning). I clean it up with a cloth, I make you happy (smiling).
Mother: Yes, when you pee on the floor, it needs to be cleaned up. Good for you to clean it up.

It is interesting that the child has already made the connection between the correct label, the appropriate facial expression, and the behaviour that creates the emotional reaction. She is beginning to understand that her mother can be both angry and happy, and, more importantly, that she can influence how her mother reacts to her by her behaviour. If she is distressed about making her mother angry, she has options for behaving in ways that avoid the anger or resolve the issue to restore the positive feelings. This child is not likely to feel victimized or overwhelmed by her mother's disapproval, because she feels competent and confident in her ability to influence the situation and the relationship.

You can see the value of effective communication in helping a child deal with the puzzling and confusing world of emotions and relationships. Imagine a chid without these communication tools trying to figure out this dilemma. There could be many more puddles on the floor, or conversely, much more anxiety about the occasional accident because of not being able to predict the mother's response.

For this milestone to be achieved, the adult has to be understanding and accepting of the child's expressions of emotions, even when these expressions are intensely negative. There is nothing wrong about feeling the way you do, and children need to hear that: "I realize that you are angry. I would feel angry too if someone took my toy. Tell Sadie how you feel." What is important is to learn how to let others know how you feel in acceptable ways. Again, this is often less of a problem for a child with positive self-concept, trust in others, and good verbal skills.

Children with intense feelings, because of their temperament or because of strong needs, have more difficulty in working through this milestone. Let the children know that they do not have to handle difficult situations alone, but that you will always help out. Let them experience that, with your help, the situation works out more positively. This means that you have to use positive, rather than negative, guidance techniques (see Chapter 8). If children are punished for making poor choices each time you get involved, they are not likely to ask you for help.

Sometimes preschool children become totally overwhelmed by their emotions and lose control. The children's safety is a first priority, and at the same time, the individual child's sense of psychological security is also a priority. Loss of control is often very frightening to a child, and she might lash out in panic. Comfort the child, staying with her to reassure her that you are not angry or frightened by the outburst. As the child relaxes, be sure to rebuild her feelings of safety and security, and let her know that she does not have to deal with such a loss of control alone. Help her to get involved in an activity with you, and demonstrate that your relationship is still intact. Your understanding and continuing support mean a great deal to a child with strong needs or inner pain.

Emotional Thinking: Fantasy, Reality, and Self-Esteem

The final milestone may well be one that is ongoing throughout your relationships. Older preschoolers become more aware of the possible conflicts between their own ideas, feelings, and behaviours and the consequences and reactions of others. Children begin to understand the notion of accidental versus deliberate behaviour, along with the idea that co-operating and sharing decision making help to maintain positive relationships. Children understand more clearly the impact of their behaviour on others and make decisions with a clearer expectation of the consequence.

In this stage, children are also working to differentiate fantasy and reality. They may be fearful of their own fantasies or those of others, or confused as to the reality of television and movies. As their experience broadens, they clarify this boundary and begin to take control of the world of their imagination.

Preschool and young school-aged children continue to work through this last milestone for some time, dealing with many different relationships with siblings, peers, and adults. Through fantasy, play, and social interactions, children continue to increase their awareness of emotions, reality, and causality — they

develop and practise skills to handle the challenges of daily life. Although some children may have difficulty with this task, it is an amazing feat of development that many 4- and 5-year-olds have many of the skills they need to function with sensitivity, competence, and autonomy in a range of social situations and relationships.

SUPPORTING EMOTIONAL WELL-BEING

Achieving the six milestones of emotional development is a task that challenges young children every day. Children who successfully meet the challenges feel calm and eager to venture out into the world each day, confident and open to new opportunities. Emotionally healthy children bring this sense of positive self-worth and competence into relationships with others. These children become co-operative and responsible group members, showing concern and understanding for the feelings of others.

How can you assist and support these processes? There are a number of guidelines you can incorporate into your relationships with each child in your program.

Support children in achieving a sense of security and calm. Provide whatever assistance they need. If you observe that George becomes overly active and agitated in the gym, offer him some quiet time with you in a sheltered corner, perhaps playing with blocks or listening to soothing music.

Help children develop the skills they need to regulate their physiological and emotional state. Help them to recognize their body's signals of upset or overstimulation, and to withdraw from situations when they feel those signals. Learn and teach deep breathing and relaxation techniques to children. Use quiet, soothing music as a calming technique.

Observe each child's temperament, needs, preferences, and means of communication, and base your interactions on knowledge of the individuality of the child. Give time and space to a slow-to-warm-up child, but do not withdraw. Model slow and calm speech and actions to an excitable or intense child.

Enter into one-to-one interactions. One-to-one interactions show acceptance, affection, and interest, and help to develop meaningful and satisfying relationships. Spend a few minutes each day with each child in an activity of the child's choice. Individual attention may seem demanding, but the children will benefit and you will enjoy getting to know them better.

Respond with predictability and empathy to each child's needs. Trust that children know what they need. Accept their perceptions, and be flexible in your support and the choices you offer in an attempt to meet these needs.

Support and encourage each child's sense of autonomy and impact in expressing needs and having them met. Keep daily routines flexible, and give children independence in using the washroom, getting a drink, or having time away from the group to observe and/or rest. Encourage children to independently assess and meet their own needs, and respond to individual differences.

Express admiration for children's efforts and accomplishments, and give encouragement in the face of failure. This means more than a token comment of "Good job." Admiration means taking time to give careful attention to what a child is doing, and to give meaningful and descriptive compliments: "Shelley, I have been watching the way you worked so hard on that building — all those different rooms and strong walls. Tell me more about it." When the building topples, acknowledge the frustration or upset as legitimate: "I know you are upset. You have worked so long to get it how you wanted it. Would you like to fix it? Would you like some help? How can we do it differently this time?"

Recognize, accept, and support children's expression of powerful emotions. Label emotions and help children see reasons for the way they feel. All children experience strong emotions sometimes — anger, despair, and frustration are part of life. Be sure to acknowledge children's right to feel those feelings. Do not pressure them to suppress their feelings by expecting them to stop crying before you respond. Respond by labelling the feeling and acknowledging the appropriateness of the feeling: "I know it makes you angry when we have to come inside before you are ready. I can let you stay here for a minute to give you time to calm down."

Support children when they feel overwhelmed by emotions. Reassure the children of your continued availability and caring, even in times of upset or loss of control. Loss of control is frightening for young children, and they need to know that you will not abandon or withdraw from them because of their strong feelings: "Wendy, I know you are upset, but I am here to help you. I won't let you or anyone else be hurt. Let's work this out together." Gently hold the child if necessary to prevent someone from being hurt.

Help children verbalize and express feelings in acceptable ways. "When you are frustrated with your friends, you can tell them or tell me. Say 'I don't like that.' You know I can't let anyone throw toys, because someone might get hurt."

Discuss the connections between feelings and relationships with others. Help a child see connections between feelings, behaviour, and the reactions of others: "When you get upset and call Tony 'stupid,' he gets upset and unhappy, too. Let's find another way to work this out together."

Help children to express feelings and to resolve issues safely through the use of play and fantasy. Play is a familiar activity for children, and as such role-playing is an excellent way to resolve issues and to come up with solutions. Use puppets, doll-house figures, and dolls to engage children in this type of play: "Allan, this bear is sad because he has no one to play with. How can we help?" Because the issue is distanced from the child, he is more likely to see a solution than when he is talking about himself. The next section describes the use of interactive play in more detail.

FLOOR TIME: THE IMPORTANCE OF INTERACTIVE PLAY

Children use play to gain a better understanding of complex relationships and emotions. They express emotions and practise strategies for problem solving in nonthreatening and controlled situations, such as in the dramatic play centre or with family figures in a doll house. With a little guidance and lots of support from you, children make excellent use of this play experience.

Greenspan and Greenspan (1989) advocate using "floor time," a means of supporting children through interactive play. They describe floor time as both a philosophy and a way of being with children that is respectful, supportive, and caring. During floor time, you get down on the floor with a child and try to follow his or her lead, doing whatever interests the child. This is a spontaneous, unstructured interaction in which you are the "assistant director" in the child's play, observing and following the play to facilitate expression of emotional ideas.

Greenspan and Greenspan (1989) suggest several steps to follow in floor time:

❖ Be patient in helping the child to take the initiative. As you follow her lead, support her emotions by recognizing and accepting them.

❖ Help the child elaborate on the theme of his play. Be subtle; do not pressure, intrude, or change direction.

❖ Help the child switch back and forth between feelings and details of the situation as a way of clarifying cause and effect.

❖ Help the child see all aspects of the play situation.

❖ Help the child explore reasons for the doll/figure's feelings.

❖ Help the child to summarize and expand on the theme by summarizing it in your own words, and then encouraging her to do the same.

In a busy early childhood setting, there is little time for individual play with one child at a time. However, the principles of interactive play apply to any interactions with one child or a small group of children during free play or outdoors. The important components are the attitudes and processes through which you convey acceptance, affection, and support, regardless of the activity. Only when a child seems particularly troubled or distressed is it necessary to try to arrange an extended time for uninterrupted individual floor time.

Greenspan and Greenspan (1989) describe several benefits of spending time in interactive play with young children, many of which are evident in the example described in Box 6.4.

❖ Children experience a sense of closeness and interest.

❖ Children experience acceptance and security through gestures, words, and nonverbal communication.

❖ Children experience independence, assertiveness, and initiative by directing the play and determining the degree of closeness.

❖ Children experience a sense of competence and positive self-esteem as they practise cognitive, motor, creative, and communication skills.

❖ Children experience a sense of connectedness to important others, allowing them to take risks in sharing intense and, sometimes, conflicting emotions, while still being assured of love, security, and support.

❖ Children experience warmth, closeness, and respect, facilitating the integration of their emotional, cognitive, and physical experiences.

LINKING SOCIAL AND EMOTIONAL DEVELOPMENT

Two areas, social and emotional development, are so closely intertwined that many people link them in the term "socioemotional development." Linking these terms gives strength to the obvious fact that our sense of self is clearly influenced by how others see us. As well, how we respond to others is related to how we see ourselves. Children with a positive self-concept and high self-esteem are likely to approach others with confidence and expect to be accepted as worthwhile. This positive approach encourages others to accept and value their company — a further validation of their sense of self. Thus, a discussion of emotional development would not be complete without considering socioemotional development.

We have described emotional needs for acceptance, belonging, affection, recognition, and approval. Along with adults, children's peers also help to satisfy some of these needs. Friends are usually one of the first social groups children experience outside their family, and this influence is significant. Children in early childhood settings spend several hours a day with peers, and the degree to which they feel accepted and liked by their peers affects their self-concept and self-esteem.

Although young children's friendships are often unpredictable and changeable, they are

BOX 6.4 AN EXAMPLE OF FLOOR TIME

Craig, 4 years old, was experiencing an intolerable level of distress as a result of a combination of factors. He had an articulation problem, and most people could not understand what he was saying. Work with a speech and language therapist had made him very sensitive about his difficulty, but had not improved his articulation. As a result, Craig had become silent in most situations. His self-esteem and sense of competence were, understandably, reduced. Craig's awareness of tension in his parents' marriage, partly due to disagreement about how to handle his withdrawal and unhappiness, added to his distress and feelings of helplessness.

Jean, a caring and sensitive early childhood educator, used the principles of floor time to assist Craig in expressing some of his turmoil. In a playroom with Craig, Jean remained in the background while Craig explored and eventually chose an activity — mini-basketball. He tossed the ball toward the hoop several times without much enthusiasm and without getting it through. He let Jean have a turn when she held out her hand. Jean also missed. The game became an interaction, with Craig and Jean taking turns. Jean missed frequently, while Craig moved closer to the basket and began

sinking more of his tosses. Jean admired his competence with smiles, cheers, and applause.

Soon Craig forgot to give Jean her turn, and his scorekeeping showed him winning soundly. Wisely, Jean followed Craig's lead. She enjoyed seeing him become more animated and actually laughing and talking to her without being self-conscious. She commented that he was a good basketball player and that he was getting many of his shots in. She did not comment on how close he was standing to the hoop. Craig replied, "Yeah, I am good, aren't I?" — an important observation for a child who had felt such obvious self-doubt.

The play continued, with Craig clearly in control and enjoying his experience of success. Craig eventually offered Jean more turns, and even suggested that she stand closer so that she could sink more shots. He became sensitive to the possibility that she might be getting discouraged. He became much looser, and Jean laughed to see him try to sink the ball without facing the hoop. As he began clowning around, the tension seemed to melt and Craig's spirits lifted. His need to perform diminished as he worked through his feelings within the safety of floor time spent with a caring and sensitive person.

still important to socioemotional development. Within friendships, social awareness and empathy develop, including understanding of the feelings of others and awareness of the impact of one's own behaviour. Maintaining friendships requires the development of complex social skills of co-operation, negotiation, and conflict resolution.

Development of Social Skills

Effective communication is one of the most basic social skills. Interactions with others require some form of communication, usually verbal exchanges. People share ideas, wishes, requests, and information in social interactions. Likewise, listening to the ideas, feelings, and wishes of others is necessary for successful co-operation with peers. Children who are not effective communicators because they speak a different language or because their own language skills are undeveloped are at a distinct disadvantage in social situations. Encouraging peers to be responsive to a child's unique style of communicating is essential if meaningful socializing is to occur.

Learning how to enter into play that others have begun is another necessary skill (Guralnick in Littman n.d.). If Karen barges in and takes over the hospital centre, the other children will not want to play with her. She needs to learn to observe first, and then ask if she may join in. Sometimes children can be successful by starting to play parallel to other children, starting a conversation, and gradually beginning to play together.

Children need a "shared understanding" of the way things work within a group (Guralnick in Littman n.d.), including knowing how props are used and how play is governed. They need to learn that toys are for sharing and that they must either ask or wait for a turn. In co-operative play, children must understand various roles and be prepared to share control in the give-and-take of a group.

Young children experience conflict within themselves when their needs differ from those of others and their feelings become the source of conflict with others. They need to learn conflict-resolution skills, but this is a sophisticated and complex demand on young children. Expressing one's own needs or rights in an acceptable manner without losing control of one's feelings requires maturity and also confidence in the willingness of others to listen and respond. No wonder many conflicts need your assistance.

As you can see, effective social relationships require some high-level skills. When children experience difficulty in play, your observation and support in developing new skills enhances socializing.

Educators as Models

Observing any group of children reveals that socioemotional development is part of everything they do. Tears, laughter, frustration, and anger are all quick to surface. In child-care settings, children are expected to interact with others almost continuously. This is hard work! One of your tasks as an early childhood educator is to assist children with this process, something that is integrated into everything that you generally do routinely. It is part of the respect you show for them in your responses, the way you model social interactions, and the way you encourage them to express their feelings.

Children often learn skills for getting along in the group by observing those around them. They frequently imitate adults, and for this reason you must be sure that you speak respectfully and model the techniques for interaction that you would like them to learn. Children also observe and imitate other children. As a way of letting children know what you expect, you can acknowledge them for positive strategies: "Emma, I am pleased to hear you asking for a turn. Terry, that was great that you told her you will give her the drum when you are finished."

Coaching Social Skills

Many early childhood educators assume that children make friends and interact successfully with peers without help. Unfortunately, this is not the case for all children.

Children develop in all areas on their own timetable, and the area of socioemotional development is no exception. Their developmental diversity affects their socioemotional development. For example, children who are physically challenged may have difficulty playing certain games with others, while children who are delayed in language development may have difficulty expressing their needs and feelings to their playmates. Children with developmental delays might not have the "shared understanding" needed to participate in more complex play scenarios. An increasing number of children entering our child-care centres seem to have difficulty in socioemotional development. For some children, playing with their peers evokes many emotions — anxiety, fear, hostility, or anger — and they have difficulty making friends and expressing their emotions in a socially acceptable way. These challenges can limit their opportunity to develop meaningful social interactions.

Michael J. Guralnick has developed the "Assessment of Peer Relations and the Inventory of Resources" (in Littman n.d.) to guide early childhood educators in programming to assist all children to make friends. He suggests that by observing and assessing children's social needs based on their interests and abilities, educators can become mediators by planning activities that involve skills such as taking turns, entering into a group activity, and resolving conflicts. This work represents a shift from seeing children who have difficulty being with peers as a behavioural concern, to seeing them as having social needs. Guralnick's work encourages early childhood educators to analyze each child's ability to regulate emotions during play and understand social rules and roles. The results of this analysis should be combined with information regarding what works best to help this child play, and should be used to plan intervention so the child can make the best of contact with other children. The example in Guralnick's video *Programming for Friendship* (in Littman n.d.) describes a child who liked trains and responded well to new things at circle time when they were accompanied by songs and chants. The teacher used this information to introduce a train game and then transferred this activity to free-play time. This technique helped the child become more successful with peers during free-play time. The teacher built on the child's interest to provide him with a script (or content of play) to act out in a play situation. Guralnick's work offers a valuable strategy for teachers to use to facilitate children's friendships.

NURTURING SOCIOEMOTIONAL DEVELOPMENT

The child-care environment should say to each child "You are special" by providing individual cubbies, display places for children's projects, and a spot for their personal belongings. Making children feel special fosters their self-esteem and enhances a sense of belonging. The environment should also convey a sense that the culture of every child in the program is valued (Chud & Fahlman 1985) by including objects that are familiar to them. A respect for the culture of each child helps each one feel valued. When children feel good about themselves, they do not feel threatened by differences and are able to respect others' heritage.

When you arrange the room, remember to provide space and activities children can use when they want to be alone. A learning centre for a single child, a pile of pillows, or a large cardboard box offers children a break from the stress of groups. Provide duplicates of some materials so sharing is not required in every situation. On the other hand, also arrange space and equipment in a way that encourages children to play with others. If working with a set of large blocks requires two children, they are more likely to co-operate.

Likewise, the arrangement of a housekeeping or family centre invites more than one person.

Interacting with peers is a large part of emotional and social development, and adult involvement changes the interactions. Two children working on a block structure is different from a child and an adult building together. To foster development of peer interactions, be sure that most materials in the room are available for children to use independently of adults, and that all the toys and equipment are developmentally appropriate. Display toys at a level and in a way that makes them inviting and accessible to the children.

The environment can also be designed to provide acceptable avenues for physical movement. Children require physical release for their feelings, and for this they need plenty of space. By providing sufficient room and equipment for large-muscle activities, you offer children the opportunity to express feelings through body movement. Opportunities for sensory experiences — sand and water play, for example — also offer relief from tension.

Plan activities that encourage the children to share and co-operate: mural painting, wagons in the playground that call for a puller and a rider, large puzzles, making fruit salad (each child prepares one fruit for the salad), or a giant box sculpture. The activities selected should come from all areas of the program and encourage children to participate and share with others. In this way, the social goal of sharing is integrated across the other subject areas.

So far, we have described indirect ways of promoting socioemotional development. If encouraging social and emotional development is part of everything the educator does, do you also need to develop programs to encourage these skills? Absolutely! Even adults, who have much more experience than

young children in this area, can have difficulty in interactions with others. Since this is a challenging area in development, appropriate curriculum experiences can help. Programming can help children gain these skills in a positive, rather than negative, way. This means that you can help children learn how to interact and express their feelings in ways that are acceptable at times when they are not upset, and these experiences can help them when times are tough.

The socioemotional curriculum should promote children's sense of themselves and assist each child in turning outward and connecting with family and friends, the community, Canadian society, and global concerns.

The Self

The goal of curriculum planning about the self is that each child learns that "I am me and I am special." Each child in your care is unique, likable, and lovable. A carefully planned curriculum should, and will, result in children feeling that they are like others in some ways and different from others in other ways.

Mirrors, tape recorders, magnifying glasses, scales, and tape measures encourage children to explore their individual characteristics. Remember, this should be a nonjudgemental activity. Encourage children to compare themselves — "My eyes are brown and yours are blue and we can both see" — to identify similarities and differences without placing value on physical characteristics. Children can also compare themselves against their own previous records in height or length of their bangs. Having an inexpensive camera around is an asset. Taking pictures of the children in action and displaying the photos throughout the classroom helps children to learn about themselves and feel good about what they do. Including pictures from home is also a good strategy. The creative curriculum can also be used to promote self-awareness. Making hand- and footprints provides a basis for discussion about similarities and differences among us.

Preschool children are becoming aware of the differences between males and females. Avoiding stereotyping by gender means avoiding attributing some characteristics only to boys and others only to girls. For example, using such terms as "firefighter" instead of "fireman" removes sexual stereotyping. Encourage children to participate in all areas of the classroom. However, be respectful of the cultural differences that may interfere with the comfort of some children in participating in some activities. You can find more information on cultural diversity in Chapter 4.

Young children are naturally observant and curious about differences among people. They notice, comment on, and question what they see, often without intending to evaluate or offend. Situations in which children make these comments offer excellent opportunities for addressing diversity in all its forms (appearance, race, ability) in an accepting and positive way. For example, "You're right. Rose's skin is a different colour, just like Tien's. We all look different in our own way, but we are all the same, too. Can you tell me something the same and something different about yourself?"

Children with physical or sensory disabilities often need specialized equipment, and their peers are curious about this as well. Explain the purpose of the equipment in a way that clarifies how it helps the child to do things we all do: "Erin's scooterboard is like a skateboard. She needs the scooterboard to get her to the toy shelf or to the bathroom." If possible, let children try the equipment themselves so it seems less strange.

Children imitate the adult's attitude of acceptance and casualness regarding differences, and they become more aware of how many ways they are the same.

Family

Along with encouraging children to feel special, another goal is to encourage feelings of "I am part of a family and my family is special." Traditional family structures have changed, and each child's family structure must be accepted without judgement. Each family has unique beliefs, special ways of living, and celebrations that are important to them. Good curriculum planning respects these differences.

Including the families of the children in your centre as part of the curriculum is an excellent way of ensuring respect for them. You can plan for visits from family members to share parts of family life. For example, a parent with an infant could share information about the care of a newborn. A grandparent could lead a cooking activity or demonstrate a fix-it project from around the house.

The dramatic play centre is an excellent environment for helping children to gain an understanding of family. Playing the roles of adult family members can be encouraged by including clothes that adults wear, equipment that they use around the house or at work, dolls to represent babies and siblings, and supplies to care for the "babies." Make sure your selection of materials for this centre reflects a variety of cultural traditions rather than just the mainstream. Babies sleep in baskets as well as in cradles and are carried in carriers as well as pushed in buggies, and many different types of kitchen utensils are used in addition to North American pots and pans. Clothing should also reflect and celebrate ethnic and cultural diversity. Pictures, photographs, and decorations (such as a Native dream catcher above the bed) should convey an acceptance of people of different ages, gender, race, and ability in performing household and occupational tasks. Use your dramatic play centre to challenge stereotypes of all kinds and to stimulate acceptance and respect for different lifestyles and traditions.

Children can also benefit from the many excellent books that are available about family life. When you select books, remember the range of family structures that the children in your class represent. Divorce, remarriage, adoption, foster placement, and same-sex families might be among the experiences of the children in your care. When you deal with family topics, display acceptance of each child's experience of family in the books available. Box 6.5 offers some examples.

Friends

Preschool children are in the midst of the difficult process of moving from being egocentric toddlers to playing in groups. They are moving from seeing the world only from their point of view to being able to understand and consider the thoughts and feelings of others. This is a challenge, and learning about friendships is part of this challenge. Through experience and curriculum activities, children come to realize that friends are special and should be accepted for who they are, and that we each have our own set of friends.

The activities suggested in the previous section, "The Self," can help children celebrate the uniqueness of their friends. Co-operative

---

BOX 6.5 BOOKS ABOUT FAMILY LIFE

When selecting children's books, include books that represent the wide range of family structures that are familiar to children. Consider some of the following:

Galloway, Priscilla. (1985). *Jennifer Has Two Daddies.* Toronto: Women's Press.

Hogan, Paula Z. (1993). *Will Dad Ever Move Back Home?* Chatham, NJ: Raintree Steck-Vaughn.

Paris, Susan. (1986). *Mommy and Daddy Are Fighting.* Toronto: Seal Books.

Schein, J. (1988). *Forget Me Not.* Toronto: Annick Press. (on grandparents and the elderly)

Stinson, Kathy. (1984). *Mom and Dad Don't Live Together Anymore.* Toronto: Annick Press.

Stinson, Kathy. (1992). *Steven's Baseball Mitt.* Toronto: Annick Press. (on adoption)

games and activities can also help children appreciate the unique strengths of others. Resources for co-operative game ideas are listed at the end of the chapter.

As children learn about friendships, they sometimes need help finding words to express their feelings. Curriculum planning should include activities that focus on feelings. Creative movement and large-muscle activities complement the use of feeling words. For example, you can play music and allow the children to move to the feelings the music evokes. Box 6.6 lists books for children that would be useful for this area of the curriculum.

The Community

Preschool children are curious about the world around them — even their neighbourhood is often a source of fascination. They recognize themselves as part of a family that interacts with the surrounding community. Through your curriculum, children can be made aware of the interconnected nature of that community. They can also learn to recognize the diversity within a community by exploring how people within it help each other.

A walk around the local neighbourhood can introduce the many helpers in the community surrounding your centre. Children will be fascinated by a new building under construction on the corner, the light stand being repaired, or the back room of the local grocery store. A phone call to neighbouring services can often get you access to your own community, and through this you are able to expand children's understanding of their neighbourhood.

Make the connections between the child, the family, and the community. Point out and visit places where parents and other family members work and go to school. Walk through the neighbourhood to look at or visit the children's homes. When you introduce the concept of community, you do not want it to be seen as something external to the children but as something connected and meaningful.

For children to gain a better understanding of community, reinforce these activities with hands-on experiences by adding props to the dramatic play and block centres to promote role-play about the community. Tools and toy construction vehicles can be added to encourage construction play. Groceries, cash registers, play money, and shopping carts can be added to create a grocery store. The activities

---

BOX 6.6 BOOKS ABOUT FEELINGS

Boynton, Sandra. (1983). *A Is for Angry.* New York: Workman.

Brisson Murphy, Joanne. (1985). *Feelings.* Windsor, ON: Black Moss Press.

Crary, Elizabeth. (1992). *I'm Frustrated.* Seattle, WA: Parenting Press.

Munsch, Robert. (1979). *The Dark.* Toronto: Annick Press.

Simon, Norma. (1991). *I Am Not a Crybaby.* New York: Puffin Books.

Vecere, Joel. (1992). *A Story about Courage.* Chatham, NJ: Raintree Steck-Vaughn.

Wilhelm, Hans. (1985). *I'll Always Love You.* New York: Crown.

Zolotow, Charlotte. (1969). *The Hating Book.* New York: Harper & Row.

at a library can be explored by adding books, tables, stamp pads, and a date stamp. The list of possibilities is endless. Let the curiosity and interests of the children in your care be your guide.

Children can also become aware of the community through real-life experiences. Take advantage of the need to shop for groceries for the centre, clean up the local park, or hire a tradesperson to fix the leak in the bathroom sink drain to involve the children.

Canadian Society

Picture a group of 4- and 5-year-olds changing from being intent and active in play to becoming quiet and respectful as the Canadian national anthem is played on the intercom. Although the concept of something as abstract as Canadian society is difficult for preschool children, the expression on the children's faces shows that the concept is not beyond their comprehension.

As preschool children are beginning to understand things that are beyond their immediate experience, curriculum can be designed to promote an understanding of Canadian society. Activities can focus on the concept of what it is to say "I am Canadian." At the same time, keep in mind that some children may have been born in other countries and may have relatives there. The richness of having children from different countries can be cited as a characteristic of Canadian society.

Children need to learn these concepts in a concrete manner. Comparing flags, weather, geographic features, and agriculture helps to make the concept of Canada more concrete. Graphs and pictures can also be used. Involve family members to demonstrate that we are all part of the same Canada, even when we are

different in race or traditions. Help children to connect on a personal level by exploring their own family history within Canada.

Pride in being Canadian can be taught by incorporating Canadian events into the curriculum. Olympic games, national holidays, and special traditions can all provide a basis for curriculum activities that help children to better understand what it means to be Canadian.

Global Concerns

Children, even at preschool age, are aware of global concerns. They see dead fish floating on the shoreline at their local beach and garbage in their park, and television carries news of disasters. These things worry children. A curriculum designed for healthy socioemotional development cannot ignore these issues. It can, however, focus on the positive things about our world as well as taking control of the things we can do to preserve it.

Children develop an appreciation of the beauty of our natural environment during leisurely walks through the park or forest, or along the edge of a stream or lake. Spend time with the children quietly enjoying the sky, the clouds, the rain, and mud. Help them experience the sense of peace and well-being that comes from feeling connected to nature.

Observe and learn about the needs and habits of animals, and make connections to people's needs. Through these experiences, children begin to recognize both the importance and the challenges of looking after our world, and they are much more likely to feel they can make a difference.

For example, children can become part of a reduce, reuse, and recycle program at the centre. Purchasing decisions can be discussed with the children with the three Rs in mind. The dramatic play and block centres can become a recycling zone. Children can also take part in clean-up efforts at the centre or on the playground.

When you talk about environmental issues, be careful not to instil a sense of personal guilt for our society's collective abuse of the world. Young children can easily become overwhelmed by the problems that adults create. Keep the focus on individual responsibility for children to clean up after themselves and being responsible for their own behaviour. Again, remember Elkind's advice not to hurry children and risk creating stress (1981, 1988).

SUMMARY

Emotional well-being develops within the relationships that children have with their family, care-givers, and peers. A sense of emotional well-being reflects feelings of security, the knowledge that they are loved and cared for by others, and the ability to communicate and accomplish what they set out to do. Young children are emotionally dependent on adults for this sense of well-being, and early childhood educators have an important responsibility in this crucial area of development.

Emotional development occurs through the resolution of a series of tasks or milestones, each of which presents a particular challenge for the child and calls for a particular response from the early childhood educator. Sensitivity to the child's needs and knowledge of the milestones underlie the quality of your relationship and the type of interactions that support emotional well-being.

Emotional and social development are closely intertwined. Therefore, early childhood educators must support social relationships through modelling and by coaching attitudes and skills that enhance interpersonal interactions in the early childhood setting.

Through curriculum planning, you can support children's socioemotional development. The curriculum for socioemotional development does not stand alone, but is integrated throughout the children's natural interactions and experiences. A carefully designed environment, including the selection and display of chosen materials and activities, can promote healthy social and emotional development.

Curriculum should be planned to promote each child's sense of self and should encourage children to become aware of the interdependent nature of families, communities, Canadian society, and global concerns.

REVIEW QUESTIONS

❶ Describe each of the six milestones of emotional development and the processes by which children can achieve them.

❷ Describe the influence of others on emotional well-being. Give examples of reactions or behaviours of others that can hinder the achievement of a sense of well-being.

❸ Describe the type of relationship an early childhood educator should endeavour to build with each child.

❹ How can the environment that an early childhood educator provides play a role in the development of skills in the socioemotional area?

❺ Why is careful curriculum planning in the socioemotional area important for children in our care?

DISCUSSION QUESTIONS

❶ A child who is new to your centre is experiencing separation distress. The parent wants to sneak away while the child is distracted. Is this a good idea? Why or why not?

❷ Two children have enrolled in your centre after moving from China. The children speak to each other in Chinese, but do not attempt to communicate with anyone else. How can you communicate with them? Should you expect them to speak English with you?

❸ A child who happens to be the youngest in your group and is also somewhat immature is experiencing frequent rejection from her peers when she tries to play with them. How can you help her?

ACTIVITIES

❶ Observe two different adults interacting with children. Identify examples of relationship-building behaviours and the children's reactions. Identify examples of behaviour that violate or harm the relationship, and the reactions of the children to these behaviours.

❷ Early childhood educators model social skills for children every day. Think about how you model social skills. Give an example for each of the following social skills: sharing, taking turns, co-operating, helping, showing caring, appreciating another's uniqueness.

❸ Observe a child for ten minutes, then record your observations using a running record. Analyze your observations and identify the emotions that the child may be feeling. Describe how he or she expressed these emotions. Compare your answers with a classmate's and discuss the differences.

❹ Create ideas for a dramatic play centre that reflect a respect for diversity in areas of gender, ability, race, and culture.

FURTHER READING

Adock, D., and M. Segal. (1983). *Play Together Grow Together.* **New York: The Mailman Family Press.**
This book gives curriculum suggestions for enhancing social skills such as co-operating and making friends. It advocates using both free play and group times to enhance interactions and social skills.

Beaty, J.J. (1994). *Observing the Development of the Young Child* **(3rd ed.). New York: Macmillan.**
This book is an excellent resource for the observation of children. The author provides a checklist of

developmental milestones in emotional, social, motor, cognitive, language, and creative development. Beaty summarizes relevant theory in each area and offers suggestions for programming.

Cech, M. (1991). *Globalchild: Multicultural Resources for Young Children.* Menlo Park, CA: Addison-Wesley.
A Canadian resource with suggestions for creating an environment that celebrates our cultural diversity.

Greenspan, S., and N.T. Greenspan. (1986). *First Feelings: Milestones in the Emotional Development of Your Baby and Child.* New York: Penguin Books.
This book is a guide for parents to observe the emotional development of their children. Chapters on infant development describe early tasks, while later chapters provide detail on the emotional milestones facing 3- and 4-year-olds.

Greenspan, S., and N.T. Greenspan. (1989). *The Essential Partnership. How Parents and Children Can Meet the Emotional Challenges of Infancy and Childhood.* New York: Penguin Books.
Discusses the relationship between adults and children working and playing together in partnership, and includes practical explorations of real-life situations for parents and educators.

ADDITIONAL RESOURCES

Committee for Children. (1991). *Second Step: A Violence Prevention Curriculum.* Seattle, WA: Committee for Children.
This kit is highly recommended as a social skills curriculum for 4- to 6-year-olds. It contains a video, puppets, visual aids, and a teacher's guide. Units include empathy training, impulse control, and

anger management. Available from the Committee for Children, 172 20th Avenue, Seattle, WA 98122 (Ph: 1-800-634-4449).

***Floor Time: Tuning in to Each Child.* (1990). New York: Scholastic.**
This video features Dr. Stanley Greenspan discussing and demonstrating techniques of interactive play, effective communication, and support for use by parents and early childhood educators to enhance emotional development of young children.

***Life's First Feelings.* (1984). Boston: WGBH. Coronet Films and Video.**
A PBS NOVA documentary on emotional development in infancy. This video highlights the theories and research of several researchers, including Dr. Greenspan.

Littman, Elaine, ed. (n.d.). *Making Friends: Early Childhood Social Integration.* Vancouver: Making Friends.
An educational package that includes a video series, an assessment tool, and a guide to these materials. The emphasis is on observing and assessing play and social skills needed to maintain successful peer relationships. The package includes many suggestions for developing these skills. Available from Making Friends, 4508 West 12th Avenue, Vancouver, BC V6R 2R5.

REFERENCES

Ainsworth, M.D.S. (1979). Infant—mother attachment. *American Psychologist* 34: 932—37.
Chess, S., and A. Thomas. (1987). *Know Your Child: An Authoritative Guide for Today's Parents.* New York: Basic Books.

Chud, G., and R. Fahlman. (1985). *Early Childhood Education for a Multicultural Society.* Vancouver: Pacific Educational Press.

Crain, W. (1992). *Theories of Development: Concepts and Applications.* Englewood Cliffs, NJ: Prentice-Hall.

Derman-Sparks, L., and A.B.C. Task Force. (1991). *Anti-Bias Curriculum.* Washington, DC: National Association for the Education of Young Children.

Dworetsky, J. (1993). *Introduction to Child Development.* St.Paul, MN: West.

Elkind, D. (1981). *The Hurried Child.* Reading, MA: Addison-Wesley.

Elkind, D. (1988). *Miseducation: Preschoolers at Risk.* New York: Alfred A. Knopf.

Erikson, E.H. (1963). *Childhood and Society.* New York: W.W. Norton.

Gartrell, D. (1994). *A Guidance Approach to Discipline.* Albany, NY: Delmar.

Greenspan, S. (1990). Emotional development in infants and toddlers. In J.R. Lally, *Infant/Toddler Caregiving: A Guide to Social-Emotional Growth and Socialization,* pp. 15–33. Sacramento, CA: California Department of Education.

Greenspan, S., and N.T. Greenspan. (1986). *First Feelings: Milestones in the Emotional Development of Your Baby and Child.* New York: Penguin Books.

Greenspan, S., and N.T. Greenspan. (1989). *The Essential Partnership.* New York: Viking Penguin.

Guralnick, M.J. (n.d.). Assessment of peer relations. (Checklist). In E. Littman, ed., *Making Friends: Early Childhood Social Integration.* (Kit). Vancouver: Making Friends.

Guralnick, M.J. (1992). *Programming for Friendship.* (Video). In E. Littman, ed., *Making Friends: Early Childhood Social Integration* (Kit). Vancouver: Making Friends.

Hyson, M.C. (1994). *The Emotional Development of Young Children: Building an Emotion-Centered Curriculum.* New York: Teachers College Press.

Lieberman, A.F. (1994). *The Emotional Life of the Toddler.* New York: The Free Press.

McKay, D.K., W.E. Mitchell, B.M. Flemming, D.S. Hamilton, and J.D. Hicks. (1993). *Creative Teaching in Early Childhood Education* (2nd ed.). Toronto: Harcourt Brace Jovanovich.

Santrock, J. (1993). *Children.* Dubuque, IA: Wm. C. Brown.

CHAPTER 7
Supporting Children's Self-Concept

- 🖋 **Overview**
- 🖋 **What Is Self-Concept?**
- 🖋 **Theoretical Perspectives on Self-Concept**
  - ◆ Carl Rogers
  - ◆ Erik Erikson
- 🖋 **Supporting Self-Concept in the Early Years**
  - ◆ The Importance of Trust
  - ◆ The Importance of Autonomy
  - ◆ Initiative and Risk Taking
- 🖋 **A Sense of Identity**
  - ◆ Gender Identity
  - ◆ Race, Culture, and Identity
  - ◆ Identification with Others
- 🖋 **Mastery, Competence, and Self-Concept**
- 🖋 **Self-Esteem**
  - ◆ Acceptance and Affirmation
  - ◆ Admiration and Encouragement
- 🖋 **Social Competence and Peer Acceptance**

✏ **Observing Children's Development of Self-Concept**

◆ Play and Self-Concept

◆ Signs of Positive Self-Concept

◆ Signs of Negative Self-Concept

◆ Changes in Behaviour

✏ **Summary**

✏ **Review Questions**

✏ **Discussion Questions**

✏ **Activities**

✏ **Further Reading**

✏ **References**

OVERVIEW

I am glad I'm who I am;
I like myself.
Even when I do the wrong thing
I know I am the right person.
— *Jessie Orton Jones*

If someone were to ask you, "What do you think of yourself?" what would you say? How would you explain what you are like and how much you value yourself? Your self-concept would be the determining factor in your answer, whether you felt good about yourself at that moment or whether you felt yourself to be a success in life, or a failure, or perhaps somewhere in-between.

No one is born with a self-concept. Children develop a self-concept gradually as they grow and as they relate to the people around them. The respect you have for children and your response to them becomes internalized and reflected in the way they feel about themselves. Their frequent experiences of mastery and competence in meeting daily challenges also contribute to a positive self-concept.

This chapter is an exploration of how a child develops a self-concept. We draw on theoretical perspectives to describe how identity, experiences, and interpersonal factors influence a child's self-concept, and we describe some signs you can use to understand how children see themselves. We also offer suggestions on how you can encourage a positive self-concept in children.

By the end of this chapter, you will be able to

❖ define the terms "self-concept," "self-esteem," and "self-image";

❖ explain theoretical viewpoints regarding the development of self-concept;

❖ describe the importance of interpersonal relationships in enhancing self-concept and self-esteem;

❖ identify factors that influence the development of self-concept;

❖ use appropriate observation techniques to identify the development of a positive self-concept;

❖ explain how encouragement and positive feedback foster a healthy self-concept;

❖ demonstrate what early childhood educators can do to foster the development of a positive self-concept.

WHAT IS SELF-CONCEPT?

Imagine this scene that takes place during the first half hour on a Monday morning at a day-care centre. Jared, Mari, and Elizabeth, who are 3-year-olds, each arrive with their parents for their first day at the centre. Jared says hello to the teacher, but he hangs onto his father's hand and refuses to let go when he has taken off his coat. However, when he discovers another boy getting out some play dough, he pulls his father to the table and begins playing. After ten minutes, he is willing to say goodbye to his father.

Mari grabs her mother from behind, buries her face in her mother's coat, and does not want to look at the teacher. Mari's mother finally lifts her up, but Mari clings and begins crying. "No, don't go," she wails, "I can't stay here."

Elizabeth takes off her coat, hangs it up herself, and tells the teacher her name and her little brother's name. She gives her mother a kiss and then joins the children working with play dough and begins chatting with them. The teacher immediately notices how self-confident the little girl is.

Meanwhile, another staff member suggests to Mari's mother that she sit in the reading corner with Mari where the two of them can read a book. Mari seems frightened and insists on sitting on her mother's lap the whole time she is reading. Her mother spends the morning at the centre with Mari sitting on her lap.

Mari needed a week of having her mother stay with her at the centre before she began playing with other children. Even in the following months, Mari still cried some mornings when her mother left, but she gradually participated in more and more activities.

Why did these three children react so differently to this new situation? There could be many reasons, but one of them could be simply in the way they felt about themselves. When children feel good about themselves, they are free to learn and to explore. When Mari wailed, "I can't stay here," she communicated that she was not up to exploring this new place. Did she feel too small? Did she feel she did not know enough? Did the adults close to her give her responses that made her feel incapable in new situations? Or was she naturally so cautious that she needed several weeks to get used to going to day care? Mari's teachers may never have found answers to these questions, but it was clear that she would need a great deal of encouragement.

Judging by the different responses of these three children to a new situation, each one has a different self-concept. Self-concept means simply the whole image a person — whether child or adult — has of herself or himself. Self-concept is related to self-esteem, self-identity, self-worth, self-image, self-respect, self-acceptance, and self-love. The terms "self-concept" and "self-esteem" are often used interchangeably, but they do have different meanings.

Self-concept is the picture one has of oneself, incorporating knowledge of physical and personal characteristics, gender and ethnic awareness, and a sense of one's capabilities and limitations. **Self-esteem** is a value judgement one makes about one's personal worth based on how one sees and accepts one's characteristics. Children who see themselves as valued by others and as competent come to have a positive self-concept and high self-esteem. Children who have a negative self-concept also have low self-esteem because they do not value themselves or feel that others value or appreciate them. They incorporate this disheartening view of their lack of worth into their self-image.

Educators sometimes get the impression that a positive self-concept is something they can "give" to the children. This is a mistaken notion. However, you certainly can influence how children feel about themselves, not necessarily just by what you do, but by the person you are and the respect you show for them.

THEORETICAL PERSPECTIVES ON SELF-CONCEPT

No one's self-concept is fixed or always the same. As is the case for adults, children's self-concept fluctuates, often depending on the response they receive from other people close to them — their parents, peers, and teachers.

When people study child development, sometimes they tend to fasten onto a single aspect. As you study different theories, keep in mind that the theorists may each have focussed on a specific aspect of child development, but the parts of the puzzle they each found have to do with a whole child. Children's self-concept is not an isolated part of themselves, but it is a part of their total development. "How children feel and think about themselves is integrally tied to their physical, social, moral, emotional, cognitive and personality development" (Curry & Johnson 1990, p. 5). As children enhance their cognitive growth by exploring and learning new skills, so too can children enhance their sense of self.

Carl Rogers

During the 1960s and 1970s, the American psychologist Carl Rogers (1974) explored the idea that people need to experience unconditional positive regard. In other words, no matter what the children do, they need to feel that their parents will still love and respect them. Those who feel loved for who they are, not for what they do, develop a positive self-concept. Children who feel loved or valued only for what they do experience low self-esteem, negative self-concept, and self-doubt. "High achievers" may receive praise for learning to read early or because they are good at sports or because they "sit nice and quietly" during story time. However, with this approval also comes terrible pressure to always be the best no matter what they try to do, and a dawning realization that they are worthy only when they do well, and that they are unworthy when they fail. Under this kind of pressure, children can hardly risk making mistakes, which are a part of any learning experience.

From Rogers came the concept that one can "disapprove of the behaviour, not the child." All children are worthy of respect, even when you do not like their behaviour.

Erik Erikson

Erik Erikson was a psychoanalyst whose impact on education continues. He became a Montessori teacher in Vienna in the late 1920s, and he also trained under Sigmund and Anna Freud. After he went to the United States in 1933, through his clinical work he

TABLE 7.1 ERIKSON'S EIGHT STAGES OF DEVELOPMENT

STAGE	DESCRIPTION
Stage 1: Infancy	Trust vs. mistrust
Stage 2: Toddlers	Autonomy vs. shame and doubt
Stage 3: Early Childhood	Initiative vs. guilt
Stage 4: School Age	Competence vs. inferiority
Stage 5: Adolescence	Search for identity vs. role confusion
Stage 6: Young Adulthood	Intimacy vs. isolation
Stage 7: Adulthood	Generativity vs. stagnation
Stage 8: Old Age	Integrity vs. despair

Source: Based on E.H. Erikson. (1963). *Childhood and Society* (2nd ed.). New York: W.W. Norton.

expanded his psychoanalytic theory to take into account social, cultural, and environmental factors in people's lives.

Erikson's psychoanalytic work, along with his experience and interest in education, led him to develop a theory that is still used widely in education to understand human development. He said that beginning at birth, children go through stages, and each stage is dependent on the previous one. Erikson's theory (1963) is that eight stages cover the life span of a person. The first three stages have to do with the development of self-concept in the early years.

STAGE 1: TRUST VERSUS MISTRUST (BIRTH TO 1 YEAR)

Infants develop trust when they receive prompt and consistent attention to basic needs for food, comfort, affection, and emotional security. With consistent care, children feel worthy and develop a sense of trust that they will be taken care of. Infants develop a sense of mistrust if their needs are not met promptly and if adults caring for them are unfeeling. Not being able to trust adults contributes to a negative self-concept, because the child comes to see the self as unworthy.

STAGE 2: AUTONOMY VERSUS SHAME AND DOUBT (1 TO 3 YEARS)

During the second stage, children develop a growing curiosity and a great urge to explore the environment. They also have a greater desire for independence. The heartfelt "no" of toddlers is an important achievement of this stage, indicating the children's confidence to assert themselves.

Because of children's physical development and their expanding abilities, adults need to provide a safe environment and an atmosphere of encouragement so the children can expend their energy in active play. In this stage, toddlers learn to decide for themselves how to handle issues such as toilet control. If adults enjoy and encourage children's curiosity and independence, they develop and gain mastery in new areas without shame and doubt, which translates into a positive self-concept.

STAGE 3: INITIATIVE VERSUS GUILT (3 TO 6 YEARS)

As children develop more independence, they also develop a capacity to take initiative. They need the latitude to plan and carry out

---

BOX 7.1 AN EXAMPLE OF TRUST VERSUS MISTRUST

TRUST

Four-month-old Kendra wakes up in an agitated state. Her mother responds immediately to her cries by taking her out of the crib and gently stroking her back while singing softly. After several minutes, Kendra's cries subside and she relaxes against the warmth of her mother's body.

MISTRUST

Eight-month-old Neil is in his highchair, demanding food. His mother is frustrated with his two older siblings and ignores him. Neil's cries escalate, and he begins to bang his hands on the highchair tray. His mother angrily shouts, "Can't you see I'm busy now!" Neil looks at her in confusion. His cries and movements subside, and he slumps into his chair with downcast eyes. When his mother finally gives him his plate, he makes no eye contact with her.

their ideas without fear of the consequences of a possible mistake or unexpected outcome. At the same time, they need guidance from adults so they can learn socially acceptable

---

BOX 7.2 AN EXAMPLE OF AUTONOMY VERSUS SHAME AND DOUBT

AUTONOMY

Two-and-a-half-year-old Peter is eager to go out in the first snowfall of the year. He drags his boots, snowsuit, hat, and mitts from the closet. He puts on his boots first, then struggles with the snow pants. His father, seeing this, says, "Let's try the snow pants before the boots and see if that works better." Peter willingly agrees, and to his pleasant surprise it works. He finishes dressing with the encouragement of his father.

SHAME AND DOUBT

Three-year-old Mahi has had her third toileting accident of the morning. Her exasperated teacher says to her, "Now what will we do? You've run out of all your extra outfits. You'll have to wear these horrible green pants." English is a new language to Mahi, and even though she cannot understand the words, she senses the disapproval. Mahi starts to cry and is of little help in the changing of her clothes. For the rest of the day, she shuns any interaction with other adults or children.

BOX 7.3 AN EXAMPLE OF INITIATIVE VERSUS GUILT

INITIATIVE

Adam and Alec, both 4, storm into the room yelling, "Everybody to the spaceship! The warlords are coming!" They dash to the cardboard spaceship in the dramatic play centre. The early childhood educator had envisioned the spaceship as part of her unit on transportation to coincide with a Canadian astronaut's current space mission. She realizes that for the children, this concept of space travel is too difficult. Their immediate reality is the Saturday morning cartoon television superhero. Instead of letting the boys race around the room, she encourages them to have a superhero meeting to plan their strategies to safely evacuate members of the community. In doing so, she draws upon such

skills as organization, thoughtfulness, consideration for others, and sharing resources.

GUILT

In the afternoon, another early childhood educator sees Adam and Alec continuing their superhero play. At this point in the play, they are defending the community while the invisible civilians enter the spaceship. To her, these boys are waving pretend weapons around the room. She rushes over and says, "Out of that spaceship! You'll ruin it! We don't play like that here." Adam and Alec look at her in confusion. Their play was all right in the morning, so why not now? They wonder what they have done wrong.

BOX 7.4 A LEARNING ENVIRONMENT TO FOSTER POSITIVE SELF-CONCEPT

You can foster a positive self-concept in children in the way you plan the child-care environment.

1. Try to put yourself in the child's position. Get on your hands and knees to discover where your line of sight takes you. Lie on the floor on your stomach or back, or sit on the floor to see what your view will be. Is it bare ceilings and floors? Consider the sights and also the sounds, temperature, and smells. Are there draughts that blast in your face when you are on the floor?

2. Next, watch children using the environment. How does the setting work for them? Are there loose rugs or other things on the floor that they trip over or that impede the mobility of a child with a wheelchair or walker? Are doorknobs too hard to manage or doors too heavy? Can the children manage taps, light switches, and other features? Of course, sometimes you do not want them to be able to open doors or operate light switches. These features vary from setting to setting, taking safety into account.

3. Look at the furnishings in the room. A setting that is designed solely for the comfort of adults — big chairs, pictures high on the walls, and breakable, untouchable items — tells children that their needs and interests do not matter. However, a room with child-sized chairs and comfortable cushions and rugs communicates that their needs are important. Here are some other suggestions for room arrangement that communicate to children that they are worthy:

◆ displaying artwork at child's-eye level, thoughtfully placed and perhaps matted;

◆ installing child-sized sinks and toilets, or at least providing easy-to-use step-stools;

◆ bringing into the room beautiful objects, which communicates that you think the children can appreciate beauty;

◆ bringing into the room a few fragile objects, which communicates that you trust them with treasures. However, there does need to be a balance between having some delicate (but not dangerous) items and expecting children to curtail their movements and actions so much that they get the impression that the beautiful glass vase is more important than they are!

forms of behaviour and social responsibility. An educator's role is to be sensitive in balancing adult guidance with children's freedom to deal with one another, learning to be fair and developing a social conscience. Failure to do so robs them of their personal sense of initiative.

In the following sections, you will see how the issues described by Erikson continue to influence the development of self-concept.

than those who are left to "work it out alone." Young children depend on the support of adults, and when their needs and feelings are ignored their sense of powerlessness and lack of worth is reinforced.

Offer security and comfort. By being sensitive to children's verbal and nonverbal messages of their needs for support, attention, and affection, you can respond appropriately. This is how children learn that adults care about them and can be trusted with important and sensitive issues.

The Importance of Autonomy

Erikson (1963) and Curry and Johnson (1990) have identified autonomy as an important aspect of self-concept. As children form clearer pictures of themselves, they express their individuality through a strong desire to do things for themselves. During the early years, many power struggles erupt as children realize they are separate individuals, not extensions of their parents. Power struggles often develop over eating, sleeping, and toileting because young children realize that these are activities that only they can perform. With peers, young children attempt to assert their will and desire to choose for themselves, resulting in power struggles among children as well.

Consider the reasons for these power struggles. Young children have a developmental drive to become more self-determining. However, in most areas of their lives, adults hold much of the power and make most of the decisions for children. Thus, it is difficult for children to find opportunities to master this developmental task. A developing realization of some areas where they have some control — eating, sleeping, and interacting with

SUPPORTING SELF-CONCEPT IN THE EARLY YEARS

The Importance of Trust

Children's self-concept begins in infancy and develops as they grow and mature. To feel good about themselves, children need to be sure that others are trustworthy. Sometimes children who have not experienced a secure and predictable atmosphere in the early years continue to feel unsure later on about whether they can trust others.

What are some of the ways you can provide an atmosphere that fosters children's sense of trust in the early childhood setting?

Make children's world predictable. With sensitive and appropriate responses to their needs, children learn that their actions cause predictable responses in adults. For example, when children feel frightened or upset, they should be able to count on someone being willing to soothe them. Children who are given a prompt response recover more quickly less-powerful peers — gives them a sense of power. It is natural and healthy for children to use these opportunities to make some choices and decisions for themselves.

Often, however, children lose even these power struggles to parents and other adults, who are bigger and more powerful. Consistently losing leaves the children feeling helpless and deflated, and they may either give up or determinedly fight to hang on to some degree of control at all costs. Educators must make sure that they offer children many reasonable choices to foster autonomy and self-determination.

BOX 7.5 BUILDING BLOCKS FOR POSITIVE SELF-CONCEPT

◆ **Approval.** Educators can express approval of children verbally ("You did a great job," "You've really improved"), by physically being available (listening to and playing with children), and by taking time to share interests (coming to see the Lego building or discussing home topics).

◆ **Acceptance.** It is easy to accept children when they fit easily into your program and get along well with other children. However, it is more difficult when they are not doing well or are lagging behind their peers. Children will not accept themselves if others do not. Acceptance conveys a sense of valuing children for who they are today, without pressure to be better or different.

◆ **Affection.** This can be expressed verbally and physically. What is important is that all children feel that you truly like them and enjoy their company.

Achieving autonomy is especially important for children with physical or developmental limitations that affect what they can do independently. Some children will not find it easy or possible to be mobile or to develop self-help skills. The educator must develop strategies and alternate ways of achieving independence so that all children can experience the satisfaction of autonomy.

Initiative and Risk Taking

Independent and self-determining children develop a strong sense of self-confidence, which allows them to take initiative. They feel free to try new challenges, to tackle difficult tasks, and to take risks to meet their own goals.

Taking initiative underlies independent functioning and leadership, qualities that adult members of our society need. Most preschool children spontaneously show initiative in many areas, such as helping themselves to supplies and toys, reminding peers and adults of the schedules or rules, choosing for themselves what and how to play, and stretching to develop new skills such as hanging upside down from the climber. Because of inexperience and immaturity, the preschooler does not always consider the situation carefully and may make errors in judgement while showing initiative (spills, messes, accidents, hurt feelings). However, the intent of the child is usually to feel more grown up or to demonstrate new capabilities, not to cause a problem.

As with the issue of autonomy, there are hurdles to initiative for children with physical or developmental challenges. You must guard against any tendency to see the child with special needs as less competent or as needing additional protection in ordinary circumstances. Encourage all children to show initiative and take risks. An anonymous quotation displayed on a playroom wall of one centre sums it up well: "A bruised knee will mend. Bruised courage lasts a lifetime."

Another threat to initiative is guilt (Erikson 1963). All children need encouragement to take initiative without becoming burdened with guilt, which destroys self-confidence. When children's initiative-taking leads them into difficulty, you should empathize with their feelings, recognize their original intentions as valid, and encourage ways of remedying the situation. You should not express disapproval or frustration with the consequences resulting from well-intentioned initiative. Respond to the child's intentions: "I know you meant to help, and I really appreciate that. It just didn't work out very well this time. Next time we'll try carrying one at a time. For now, let's get a broom and clean it up." An approach like this will not produce excessive guilt or discourage further attempts at initiative.

To help children maintain a sense of initiative, use the following guidelines:

❖ *Be receptive to children's ideas* and give them a positive response in situations in which they have taken the initiative, even if their idea is inappropriate. For example, in a painting activity, some children want to paint themselves all over. An appropriate response is, "That would be fun! Let's put your idea on our list for outdoor summer activities when we have wading pools set out. For now, how about painting faces we can use for masks?"

❖ *Define a boundary for an activity.* Provide access to different materials that can be used, and then allow the children to create their own play within these parameters. For

instance, when the children begin tussling, you can designate part of a room and some movable equipment as a site for physically active play.

❖ *Balance activities that challenge the children with helping them develop an awareness of consequences.* If they set up a target in a place that happens to be in front of a window, praise the idea of the game and point out the hazards of the location, and then help them find another spot.

A SENSE OF IDENTITY

It might be an interesting experiment to ask, say, ten people, "Who are you?" What answers do you think they would give? They might tell you their names, or they might give another type of answer: "I'm a construction worker," or "I'm a mother," or "I'm an ordinary person," or maybe they would tell you that it's none of your business.

Perhaps you think the question "Who are you?" is the same one that we posed at the beginning of the chapter, "What do you think of yourself?" The questions are, in fact, different. "Who are you?" has to do with identity, which you formed through feedback from other people all your life. The expectations and messages sent by adults and peers give children important information about who they are and what they are like. A second source of feedback about the self is the experiences with successful mastery and failures. Children need to develop a sense of competence and capability to ensure a healthy self-concept. The next sections address these two processes in more detail.

Young children are beginning to form their identity. Identity formation has two parts: the ways in which a child is unique, and the qualities the child has that are similar to those of other people. As part of the process of discovering one's identity, children categorize the world around them and then construct an image of self in relation to this knowledge (Curry & Johnson 1990). This construction of the self is made up of such categories as sex, age, and physical characteristics. Early in the toddler stage, the categories are not yet stable, or consistent, in nature. For example, a 2-year-old boy might say, "I am a boy, and when I grow up I will be a mommy." By the age of 3, most children can apply gender labels correctly and consistently. They are also aware of some behaviours associated with each sex — common roles expressed in the notion that mothers nurture and fathers roughhouse. These are learned behaviours that children observe in the adults around them and from adults' conversations. You will notice that young children often appear quite rigid in their ideas about differences between categories: "You can't do that, you're a girl." As an early childhood educator, you play a very important role in this process, both confirming and clarifying their perceptions of these categories and what they mean. You must challenge such rigidity in children's ideas, and help them to understand and accept diversity and the freedom to choose.

Gender Identity

How would you define gender roles? Apart from the obvious physical characteristics, what does it mean to be male or female? ("Gender" means the characteristics society attributes to men and women, while "sex" is the term generally used to communicate physical characteristics.) When did you first realize that you were a boy or a girl? Was this a sudden or a gradual realization? Think of the multitude of impressions and "facts" that adults give to children daily that tell them what it means to be male or female.

When you compliment little girls about how pretty their clothes look and boys about how strong they are, you are delivering a message about your expectations that girls are important for how they look and what they have, and boys for how their bodies work. Further, if you emphasize the possessions children bring with them and the clothes they wear, you are inadvertently sending the message that what they possess is more important than who they are.

Socially defined roles for each sex are passed down from generation to generation, with a few modifications to fit the shifting societal winds. Young children do not have a constant understanding of these roles. Although Rachel knows that her dad is a male, at the age of 3 she asks, "Daddy, did you ride a bike when you were a little girl?" Children of this age do not yet understand that usually your sex at birth remains throughout life. Acquiring an understanding of gender parallels expanding cognitive growth. For example, children as young as 2½ can look at a toy catalogue and explain which toys are for boys and which ones are for girls. They acquire this knowledge through an increasing use of language, an awareness of gender roles, and the reinforcement of these roles by the adults they know.

The main task of young children in the area of gender development is discovering what it means to be male or female. Young children identify closely with the parent of their sex, and imitate her or his characteristics and behaviours. Children spend a lot of time role-playing mommies and daddies — the girls usually playing mommy and the boys daddy. Although you may not want to discourage this play, you do need to broaden the concept of adult roles. Not everyone can be a mother or father, nor does everyone who has the physical capacity to be a parent want to. You can encourage boys to play the mommy and girls to play the daddy in their games, so that children can break down the stereotypical attributes of these roles. Both women and men can be nurturing and strong.

You can broaden children's concepts of occupations that are open to them. Through the use of literature and other media, for example, you can depict women in nontraditional jobs and jobs that, until recently, were not easily accessible to them. Both boys and girls need to realize that they have a choice in what they want to be in their adult lives. Adding hard hats and other articles that are not gender-specific to the dramatic play centre allows children to take on different roles without the props dictating whether the role is male or female.

Make sure your toys include dolls of both sexes and some that are anatomically correct, so that boys feel comfortable playing with and nurturing them. This type of play can help them to realize that it is all right to cuddle infant boys as much as infant girls. One book for children that clearly addresses this issue is *William's Doll* by Charlotte Zolotow (HarperCollins, 1985).

Race, Culture, and Identity

Children's identity as part of racial, religious, and ethnic groups gradually develops through early childhood and is consistent by the age of 4. Self-esteem and self-concept are directly tied to children's positive or negative feelings about being part of a specific cultural group, and depend on how others around them react to this part of their identity.

In a British study (Milner 1983), children of West Indian, Asian, and English descent were given dolls that resembled their racial group and one other racial group. All of the English children correctly identified the doll that looked most like them. However, 76 percent of the Asian and 52 percent of the West Indian children chose the correct doll. Only 24 percent of the Asian and 48 percent of the West Indian children indicated that the white doll looked most like them. When asked what doll they would prefer to be like, 100 percent of the English children preferred the white doll. As well, 82 percent of the West Indian and 65 percent of the Asian children selected the white doll. This study obviously shows the need to present all cultures positively so that children can identify with their own group and be proud of who they are.

By the age of 2½, children can understand the differences in sex. By age 3, children are aware of differences in skin colour and other physical characteristics. Children from different racial or cultural backgrounds often do not see themselves reflected in the mainstream society.

Kids look to all of the images around them. I keep thinking of our son, Douglas. He was about five when he announced that he didn't want to be Black because he wanted to be a fireman/paramedic like on the TV show "Emergency." He was a child who hadn't really been exposed to prejudice but was taken by the program and wanted to be a paramedic. But he didn't see anyone who looked like him so he concluded that he'd have to change his skin colour to be able to be a paramedic. *(Derman-Sparks 1991, p. 38)*

This example illustrates two things: the need for attitudes that convey an acceptance, respect, and valuing of the worth of diversity in race or culture, and the value of having a variety of visual materials (pictures, books, manipulatives) that reflect people of different races and cultural backgrounds. In storytelling, educators can include families of different cultures — felt pieces or pictures can easily be used in most stories where the plot line is not culture-specific. In the housekeeping–dramatic play area, artifacts from different cultures, such as a rice cooker, tortilla press, clothing, and hammocks can be introduced in group time and then placed in the play area. Most games for children have a universal nature. You can tell children that such games as chase and tag are played all over the world.

Introducing dolls resembling a variety of races is often seen as a quick way to incorporate multiculturalism into a centre. However, take care to ensure that these dolls are a true representation of the culture and not a stereotype. Black dolls with smooth, silky black hair do not represent the reality of coarse, kinky black hair. Nor is a doll with Caucasian features and black skin a true representation. Children may not make any comments about the colour or features of the doll, but messages are being given to them nonetheless.

Identification with Others

Children need to feel they are special and that the adults close to them have a special feeling for them that is different from their feelings for other children. At the same time, children also like to feel that they are similar to other people they like — people who are beautiful, smart, or strong, or who have other characteristics the children admire. However, young children do not identify with everyone they know, only the ones who are important to them.

Children try to imitate the mannerisms and expressions of the people they admire because they believe that by doing so, they will become like the model (Kagan 1971, pp. 12–14). As a child, Ping admired her mother in everything she did — Ping also wanted to be well-educated, a world traveller, and a business executive, even though within her community this was most unusual. She emulated her mother in her style of dress even though the colour and style combinations did not suit her. She felt that dressing as her mother did would enable her to reach the same goals. This feeling prevailed into adulthood.

Young children often see their parents and teachers as smarter, stronger, and more competent, and as having more power and more freedom, and they want to have these qualities too. Children are attracted to others on the basis of the qualities they wish to possess. The more positive qualities they see in a person, the more likely they are to view that model as attractive and to attempt to imitate his or her behaviours. Children also admire and imitate fictitious characters, most notably cartoon or media personalities, many of whom also possess any number of desirable qualities and power.

Payam never missed an opportunity to watch all of the superhero cartoon shows on television, as well as collecting as many related toys and accessories as his parents would allow. He believed that these heroes were more competent and smarter than himself, and that they had unusual physical abilities and skills. At the same time, they always looked out for the underdog and triumphed over the evil forces. Payam liked them for these reasons and tried to emulate them. He seemed to think that these perceived qualities would give him an edge over other people.

MASTERY, COMPETENCE, AND SELF-CONCEPT

It is true that educators should base their respect for children on who they are and not on what they can do. At the same time, attaining mastery of (achieving control over) their bodies and surroundings does contribute to the development of a positive self-concept in children. This is why mastery is an important part of curriculum.

Take a moment to think of something you do well: dancing, singing, gardening, playing squash, or fostering friendships. When you are engaged in this activity, how do you feel about yourself? How do other people respond to you? Part of feeling good about yourself comes from the things that you can do, and this is indeed an important part of who you are. Children begin to think of themselves in terms of their achievements, and they will be able to state, "I am good at drawing," or "I can jump really high, see?" Their feelings of accomplishment increase when adults foster the skills children need to become more independent: opening doors, getting dressed, going to the bathroom, and feeding themselves. Helping with daily household chores — such as setting the table for meals — also can increase a sense of mastering the environment.

Positive self-concept depends on children having many successes as they practise and master the tasks they take on. They need to experience the pride and satisfaction of working hard to achieve something and being successful. They need to be able to say to themselves and others, "Look what I did!" and

know that their accomplishment was worth something. If children experience too many more failures than successes, their self-concept will be diminished. They will begin to say "I can't" or "It's too hard," and soon they will come to see themselves as incompetent and therefore less valuable. These responses underscore the need to provide activities that children can master with a little effort, but that are not excessively difficult.

The issue of positive self-concept is especially important for children with special needs as they grow and realize their limitations in contrast with the abilities of their peers. You need to be creative about finding and emphasizing the talents and gifts that children with special needs have, especially those that can be shared with others. Examples include teaching friends sign language, learning how to navigate the classroom without sight, and demonstrating adeptness with a walker or a wheelchair. Special aids and braces can, where appropriate, be shared with others if the children who own them are willing.

Kira has severe cerebral palsy and is in a wheelchair. She is not able to speak clearly enough to be understood. A computer-operated communication board is attached to the tray on her wheelchair. Pictures of everyday activities are shown on the board, and when Kira or her friends push the appropriate picture, a voice says the word. In this way, Kira not only communicates her wants and needs to others, but they can also share in this technological "toy" that is especially designed for her.

Discussions about "same" and "different" can help children. For instance, you can emphasize that we all like to listen to stories, but some of us hear the words and others watch signs to understand. The notion that some children need extra help with eating, toileting, or behaviour can also be explained in positive ways by discussing the similarities and differences — we all loved the ice-cream cones, but Marcos needed someone to hold his for him.

Jean has worked with many children who are faced with developmental challenges. When children comment or protest to her about things they cannot do, she encourages them to accept their limitations as a part of themselves but not to feel less competent or less valuable because of their differences. Her answer to each child is, "You're right, you can't do it the way your friend can, but you can do it this way." Her intervention ensures a success for the child, often resulting in an appreciative smile, a further effort to master the challenge, and, of course, a positive self-concept.

SELF-ESTEEM

Self-esteem is the value a person attaches to her or his self-concept. According to Curry and Johnson (1990), preschool children begin to test and evaluate their self-concepts. If their self-concepts have been built upon a good foundation, they should feel secure in the knowledge that they are loved and accepted by the people who are important to them. With this view of themselves in place, children begin to test it against the way that other people see them.

Acceptance and Affirmation

There are several sources of others' affirmation that help children to feel they have value. The first is their name. Children recognize their own name within the first year of life and show pleasure in hearing it from others in conversation and in song. Using the children's given names, or nicknames that are in common use at home, and pronouncing them correctly is important to them. Children love to see and hear their names, and need to hear their names used frequently in a positive and caring context. Names on cubbies, artwork, and photographs of the children helps to instil positive self-images.

You can offend children by making fun of their names, even unintentionally. Perhaps you think it is cute to call Suzie "Suzie-Q," but to Suzie that is not her name. She may even begin to wonder what is wrong with her name and carry it further to what is wrong with her. Even adults are annoyed if their names are mispronounced or misspelled. The correct pronunciation of children's names is important and requires extra effort from educators if they are unfamiliar with certain names, especially those in different languages. It is equally crucial not to emphasize the child's name when frustrated or angry, such as, "JEREMY JACKSON, HOW MANY TIMES DO I HAVE TO TELL YOU!"

Some children, when they enter a group setting, think of their name as a hindrance, especially if it is unusual or if they think it is "babyish" or has unpleasant connotations. Some children even insist on calling themselves by a different name to rid themselves of the supposed bad image that they feel their given name suggests. Adopting a new name they choose themselves, or that is given by peers they respect, gives them confidence. You need to be aware of the names that children call themselves and use those names. For example, when Randall started school, he thought his name was too stiff and formal and the name Randy was too babyish. He seemed to experience a self-identity crisis based purely on his inability to come to terms with his given name. After he took on the name of Jake, he assumed the personality of the person whom he felt the name signified: a strong, silent, confident person. His identity crisis was resolved.

Personal possessions are also important to self-identity. Each child should have a personal space (cubby or basket) and access to personal possessions, such as security objects or special "home toys." The young child can build on a sense of her own uniqueness and value if her personal possessions and belongings are also valued and respected. A cornerstone of the early years is the "mine" syndrome. Young children are often insistent on what is "mine," and in some cases this can extend to toys at the centre if the child has been using them or wishes to. The "mine" assertion is a healthy,

necessary part of a child's development of self-hood and is a prerequisite to what adults like to call "co-operation." Children can co-operate and share only after they are comfortable with their own concept of self. Children need to possess before they can share, a reality that has implications for educators as they plan the environment. For example, you should make sure that you have more than one of the most popular toys so that more than one child at a time can "possess" the toy.

Admiration and Encouragement

All children need recognition for their efforts and encouragement for difficult tasks. If Ingrid tackles sweeping the lunchroom floor and then becomes overwhelmed by the task, your encouragement can be just what she needs whether or not she is able to complete it: "You put a lot of work into sweeping the floor." If she does complete the task, your comment, "Ingrid, you worked hard at sweeping the floor and you finished the big job," also lets her know that you noticed how hard she worked. However, if you say, "You are a good girl Ingrid, because you swept the floor," you are using a generality that places a value on the child because of something she did and gives a confusing message.

Similarly, the comment, "That's the most wonderful painting I have ever seen in my whole life!" is not likely to have an authentic ring to it. Encouragement and commenting on children's *efforts* — not always on the end product — does more to build children's self-concept than just telling them they are "good." You also need to be sure you do not jump to conclusions about the meaning of children's paintings and make comments that are inappropriate.

Four-year-old Molly worked diligently on a painting. It included two people standing in a window holding hands. The teacher praised her for her lovely painting, but Molly was not finished. She used green paint to cover up the people and the window. Then she repeated the process with orange and brown and red. By the time she was finished, the people and window were no longer visible, and grey-brown blotches remained. The teacher asked Molly why she had "messed up" her beautiful picture. Molly went home, most upset that her picture had not been appreciated. She explained to her mother, "It was a picture of Daddy and me looking out the hotel window watching the fireworks, and when I put the fireworks in the picture, Sarah didn't like it anymore." If Sarah had asked Molly to tell her about her painting instead of passing judgement, she would have avoided deflating the child.

When children's behaviour annoys adults, it is much easier to find fault than to provide encouragement. A child who is constantly knocking books off shelves can be annoying. It is hard to think of something positive to say in this situation. First, redirect the child or stop the behaviour, but in such a way that the child does not lose self-esteem. One option is to say, "It is very hard for the other children to choose books if they are scattered on the floor. Come help me put them back on the shelf and then you can choose one for yourself." This approach makes clear why the action is not appropriate and suggests an alternative, but at the same time the child does not have reason to feel deflated. This is a much better approach than saying, "You always make a mess of those books!"

Preschoolers often tend to view themselves as all good or all bad. Adults must provide a reality check, since children may need help to develop a realistic picture of themselves. No one can be "all good" or "all bad" at everything. Children's excellence in one area and lack of skills in another does not mean that they are lesser individuals.

Older preschoolers often experience a decline in self-esteem (Newman & Newman 1978). They become increasingly aware of the discrepancies between their own skills and the skills of others. You might hear these children say: "I'm stupid!" "I can't do anything right!" "I can't do it, I'll never learn to do this," and "I don't care!" Some may seem to wallow in self-pity, questioning their identity; they might feel worthless, restless, bored, or depressed. To adults, this is a frustrating stage because no matter what they say, the children do not respond. During this crisis, children need to experience more successes and a reduction of pressure to achieve. Understanding children's need for respect, and then responding to them with respect, which means avoiding attitudes and comments that leave them feeling worthless, are the best ways adults have of helping children build a positive self-concept. Their self-esteem will recover, especially if they have a secure foundation of acceptance from the adults who are important to them.

SOCIAL COMPETENCE AND PEER ACCEPTANCE

Being accepted is crucial to the growth of children's positive self-concept. In their play, children often communicate their acceptance of one another, as this example shows. Jude and Leslie, both 4-year-olds, were playing in the puppet centre. Jude, with a dinosaur puppet, and Leslie, with a cat puppet, had this conversation:

Leslie: Where are you going?
Jude: To the field to eat popsicles.
Leslie: I like popsicles. Can I come too?

BOX 7.6 SUPERHEROES — WHY DO BOYS LIKE THEM SO MUCH?

Many adults have trouble with young boys' displays of "he-man" behaviour when they emulate their favourite cartoon characters. Although some girls also have superheroes, this phenomenon does seem to be much more common in boys. Even if the toy weapons and other props that are sold relating to these characters are restricted in some child-care centres, the behaviour usually persists. Perhaps there is something to learn in analyzing the place of superheroes in children's lives. One common characteristic of ancient mythological heroes, fairy-tale characters such as Jack and the Beanstalk, Batman, Superman, Teenage Mutant Ninja Turtles, and others is that they are supremely powerful. What a contrast with the typical young child, who constantly hears "No" and "You're too little"! Some experts feel that young children actually need to fantasize about situations in which they have complete control. Children must be allowed to use their idols in play as vehicles for working through issues. Carlsson-Paige and Levin (1992) suggest that children benefit from "open-ended" toys and games that offer a range of play possibilities and decrease the imitation of television's aggressive and violent themes.

Jude: Sure, but it might be scary. There are lots of monsters there, bigger than even me and I'm a big dinosaur.

Leslie: Well I'm good at hiding, especially because I can see in the dark. You're too big to hide.

Jude: Yes, but I'm stronger than monsters because I'm so big.

Leslie: OK, so we will be safe. We can each do something against the monsters. We are good at things.

Jude: Yes, let's go.

Not being accepted by peers says to children, "You are not worthy of our attention" and "You are a bad person and we don't like you." Children value the opinions of their peers and therefore attempt to modify their behaviour so they can participate in mutually rewarding social interactions. If children are not able to conform to acceptable patterns of interaction, their peers often shut them out of social situations. If children face rejection too many times from peers, they incorporate this view into their own view of themselves. When you see children consistently being rejected, help them develop the skills needed for social success, and also encourage their peers to be more empathic and accepting.

There are a number of ways you can help children develop the confidence and competence they need for acceptance by their peers.

Recognize and accept your own feelings. For example, you may be a person who has no problem with walking into a room full of strangers, and you see this as a positive trait. When children are continually shy and withdrawn, you may be tempted to push them into situations for which they are not ready because of your own way of handling social situations. Remember that not all children have your personality traits. On the other hand, if you are a person who is naturally quiet and shy, it may be easier for you to accept children with similar traits. However, you should still encourage children to enter into social situations as much as they are able. Your methods may be different from your more extroverted co-worker, but the end results should be the same.

Model your acceptance of each child, and spend time playing with children who need help in learning play or social skills. When you play with children, you can help them develop such skills as taking turns and co-operating. Moreover, as you play with a child, the other children come to see that child as a valuable playmate and will often ask to join in. You will have created a situation in which you can assist the children to have successful peer interactions.

Set up situations in which children trying new skills will have success. Leo, a shy 4-year-old, is new at his day-care centre. He has attended for two weeks, but he still has difficulty settling into activities. He spends a great deal of time alone and wandering about the room. One day, the teacher read a story about a turtle who overcame his shyness through the help and understanding of the other creatures who lived by the pond. Later, the teacher let the children act out the story. The next day, the teacher suggested a different group of children act out the same story, and this time Leo participated. Leo played the role of the turtle, and the expression on his face showed his pleasure and enjoyment in being able to take this important part. This experience seemed to be a turning point for Leo, and he began being able to focus on activities to a greater extent.

Several other strategies for facilitating social skills are described in Chapter 6. As we mentioned, coaching specific skills can be beneficial for improving the quality of children's social experiences.

OBSERVING CHILDREN'S DEVELOPMENT OF SELF-CONCEPT

Play and Self-Concept

The growing and changing self-concepts of children during the preschool years are demonstrated in their play. We can learn how children perceive themselves through careful observation of dramatic play. In their play, young children often act out nurturing themes, usually in the form of dyads: parent–child, doctor– or nurse–patient. Some children like to be in the powerful role or in control of the situation, while others enjoy the attention given to the "baby" or "patient."

Other children, especially boys, are preoccupied with aggression, power, and vulnerability. Many want to play the part of superhero, whom they perceive as being accepted by others, powerful, moral, and competent. If you are concerned that superhero play often leads to increased aggressiveness, refocus the play on the characteristics so admired. Maybe the superhero can save people from an earthquake or flood or hold up a crumpling building. A hero, with supervision, could find lost children or valuables for others. Superhero play does not need to have violent overtones; creative scenarios that you suggest can lead the players to become the caring, competent, and powerful characters they so admire.

Children's dramatic play also reflects individual concerns with a wide variety of roles and situations. As children have wider experiences with an increasing number of people, they play out their observations and concerns to gain understanding. A child with a healthy self-concept often switches among roles and shows resourcefulness in solving play problems. A child who is constantly stuck in one role, particularly a victim's role, may be showing indications of insecurity, negative self-concept, and hopelessness. Additional support through play and successes can change the play themes to those of competence and confidence.

One benefit of dramatic play is that children can take on through their play any qualities they wish. They can be nurturing, brave, dependent, and cared for by others, star dancers, champion ballplayers, or anything else — there is no reality to remind them of their limitations or vulnerability. They can imagine and achieve great things, and feel competence and

power not experienced in other areas of their lives. Of even greater importance is their discovery that they have a private, inner world into which they can retreat, where no one knows what they are thinking.

Signs of Positive Self-Concept

An evaluation of a child's self-concept cannot be made simply based on certain specific behaviours. Feelings of self-worth ebb and flow depending on age and circumstance — even children who generally have a positive self-concept will not *always* feel good about themselves. However, children who have a positive self-concept generally have these characteristics (Hodgins 1992):

❖ display poise and confidence;

❖ display positive social interactions;

❖ are equally comfortable being the leader or the follower;

❖ are able to make friends;

❖ use their curiosity to make discoveries;

❖ are assertive but not overly aggressive;

❖ enjoy sharing information: "Come see my wonderful spaceship!";

❖ are risk takers who may occasionally get into trouble because of their adventures;

❖ are self-directed and can do things on their own initiative.

Parents of children who have a healthy dose of self-confidence can tell you that sometimes their resulting determination — or is it stubbornness? — becomes frustrating, and educators also have the same experience. Nevertheless, self-confident children are much more free to be who they are than children who have a negative self-concept.

Signs of Negative Self-Concept

Children might have different degrees of self-confidence in different places and circumstances. For example, a child who appears to be self-confident at day care may be the opposite with siblings and/or parents, and vice versa. To help you find out which children have a negative self-concept, look at patterns of behaviour that are consistent over a period of time. Children with a pattern of negative self-concept tend to be consistent in the following behaviours in a variety of circumstances:

❖ avoid situations that provoke anxiety, and rarely take risks;

❖ are defensive in situations in which blame may be assigned. They rush to defend themselves or to make excuses for their actions: "I didn't do it";

❖ are more likely to believe that they are the cause of disasters. The egocentric thought processes of young children mean that they assume that they can cause, for example, divorce or other family troubles. As they get older, children with a negative self-concept still believe this to be true in all situations, whereas children with a positive self-concept do not take the blame for everything that occurs around them. Therefore, be sure that you do not make blanket statements that children can misconstrue: "Someone has eaten all the cookies!" Children with a negative self-concept will blame themselves regardless of their innocence. They may even tell other adults that "X" was mad at them and does not like them;

❖ are often aggressive rather than assertive. Aggressive children feel power when they hurt others. This power can give them a false sense of confidence. For example, where assertive children may inadvertently hurt another child in a rush to get a toy, aggressive children intentionally do so;

❖ are ineffective in expressing needs;

❖ behave inappropriately to get the attention they feel they need because they do not have the inner resources to give themselves their own support and approval for their actions;

❖ have a constant need to criticize others. In doing so, they are affirming to themselves that others are as inadequate as they feel they are: "Look! Look! Russell didn't put his boots in the right place!";

❖ resist change;

❖ have great difficulty making choices in everyday situations.

Changes in Behaviour

INSECURITY AND WITHDRAWAL

Using your observational skills and keeping written records regularly helps you to identify changes in behaviour. Of course, knowing the children and having a good rapport with their families also helps. A sudden change in behaviour for one day does not necessarily signify a long-term problem. Like adults, children experience changes in moods depending on their health, the time of year, or some unusual situations at home, such as the birth of a sibling, or for inexplicable reasons. If you notice a change in a child, use your observation techniques (see Chapter 5), talk with the parents, and consult with your colleagues to decide what steps, if any, need to be taken.

Mark's behaviour is one example of how children react to change. Mark, a bright, vivacious 3-year-old, attends a nursery school 3 mornings a week. When he began, he adapted well to the routine after an initial week of separation anxiety. He participates in all the activities and has good social relationships with the teachers and children. In the past month, he established a unique friendship with 2 other little boys. His mother was anxious that he fit in at nursery school. She is a single parent and Mark does not have any siblings, and he does not see his father regularly. After one visit with his father, Mark had a hard time settling back into the routine, both at home and at nursery school.

In January, Mark returned to school after Christmas bubbling with excitement and news about his Christmas vacation. He constantly mentioned a new friend, Dwayne. At the end of the second week of school, one of the adults at the day-care centre asked Mark how his friend Dwayne was doing. Mark looked at the floor and muttered "fine." Later in the morning, the educator again referred to Mark's friend. Mark looked at her, panic in his face, burst into tears, and ran from the room. One of the other adults hurried after Mark, seeking to comfort him. When his mother came to pick him up, the director of the centre mentioned the incident and the mother was evasive in her response. For the next few weeks, Mark did not mention Dwayne. The staff noticed that sometimes he came to school looking as though he had slept in his clothes. He seemed pale and withdrawn and did not participate in activities, preferring to sit quietly in the book corner, staring at books. When his friends approached him, he rebuffed them. At circle time, he did not participate. When his mother dropped him off or picked him up, she hurried in and out without speaking to anyone.

What is your initial reaction to this situation? If you were asked to advise the staff, what would you say to them? Perhaps you would summarize their description of what has happened in this way:

❖ changes in physical appearance: skin colour, cleanliness, care of clothing;

❖ changes in social relationships: withdrawal from others;

❖ changes in interactions with the parent;

❖ parent becomes withdrawn, secretive, and unreliable.

Having noted these changes, you can begin to look for a pattern in the behaviour to try to understand what has happened to Mark and his family. From the above description, do you think you have enough information to try to help Mark?

If you answered no, you are right. Mark has talked about his friend Dwayne, but considering the reaction of Mark's mother, you will need to know more about this person since Mark is not forthcoming with the information. At this point, it would be advisable to suggest a meeting with Mark's mother to talk about the change in him and his apparent unhappiness. This request should be made in a sensitive, diplomatic manner that is nonthreatening to the mother. She may be grateful for the opportunity to discuss a family situation. On the other hand, she may be resentful of the intrusion into her private life. If so, you should back away, but at the same time let her know that you are available whenever she would like to talk with you. In any case, your concern is with Mark. Stories about friends can be an opening for you to initiate a one-to-one conversation with him concerning Dwayne. At all times, you should support Mark and let him know that he is a worthwhile person and that he is loved even though he is unable to respond at the moment.

After two months of the doldrums, Mark gradually became more and more like his old self. One day when his mother came to pick him up, a man accompanied her. Mark shyly introduced him as his friend Dwayne. His mother quietly told the teachers that she and Dwayne had been married on the weekend. She explained that Mark was having a hard time accepting Dwayne as a permanent part of their lives. She had not felt comfortable talking to the staff because she was still sorting out her own feelings about remarriage.

INSECURITY AND AGGRESSIVE BEHAVIOUR

Children's self-concept is reflected in their behaviour. However, not all children react the same way to the same circumstances. You have likely met people who cover their feelings of insecurity with bravado. Some children disguise their negative self-concept in behaviour that frustrates and confuses you. It is too easy to assign such labels as "clown" or "bully" instead of trying to understand the child's insecurity. The following example illustrates how a child might cover his insecurity by behaving exactly opposite from the way he really feels.

In the gym, the children are trying out a new climbing apparatus for the first time. Some of the children hang back and seem reluctant to try it. Stefan, on the other hand, pushes everyone aside, wants to be the first one up the ladder, and shouts, "I can do this, it's easy!" But when he gets to the top of the ladder, he panics and freezes. The other children yell at him to keep going. The teacher

has to intervene and rescue Stefan. After that, he does not go up the ladder, and he pushes the other children who are waiting in line.

Stefan's behaviour shows how some children cope with their feelings of insecurity. Other children might feel vulnerable and use aggressive behaviour to protect themselves against perceived threats. These children might lash out in situations because they anticipate aggressive behaviour toward them from others. Reassuring these children that you will not allow anyone to hurt them is the first step in reducing aggressiveness caused by the insecurity.

SUMMARY

In this chapter, we have discussed how self-concept develops and ways of fostering a positive self-concept in children. We looked at the theoretical underpinnings of self-concept, the work of Carl Rogers and Erik Erikson. We examined how identity, gender, culture, and social interactions affect self-concept. Through observation, you can recognize negative and positive self-concept in children, and you can offer them your help and encouragement out of respect for them as people.

REVIEW QUESTIONS

❶ Explain the difference between self-concept and self-esteem.

❷ Discuss why self-concept is important to the healthy emotional development of children.

❸ Comment on the contributions of Carl Rogers and Erik Erikson to the study of self-concept.

❹ Why is mastery important to children's self-concept?

❺ List five signs of positive self-concept and five signs of negative self-concept.

❻ Discuss the part that identity, gender, special needs, culture, and social settings play in the development of self-concept.

❼ How can early childhood educators influence the development of self-concept?

DISCUSSION QUESTIONS

❶ Children with a negative self-concept tend to avoid situations that provoke anxiety. What do you do when confronted with anxiety-provoking situations, such as an exam or a new social situation?

❷ Create a heraldry shield to express your personal sense of identity. Include your interests, how you describe yourself, where you are now, and where you are going. Share this shield with your classmates. How does their sense of self differ from yours?

ACTIVITIES

❶ Write down fifteen things that you like about yourself. Is this a difficult task for you? Why or why not?

❷ Think of a child who is taking you to "the end of your rope." In three minutes, write down on a sheet of paper fifteen positive things about that child. For the next week, focus only on the positive in this child. Did you notice a change in the child's behaviour? Did you observe any changes in your own behaviour toward the child? Did you feel differently about the child at the end of the week?

❸ Plan two activities suitable for preschool children that will enhance their self-concept.

❹ Select a child-care environment with which you are familiar. Make a list of environmental features that encourage mastery, initiative, and independence. Make another list of features that discourage mastery, initiative, and independence. Suggest ways to change these components.

FURTHER READING

Beal, Carole R. (1994). *Boys and Girls: The Development of Gender Roles.* New York: McGraw-Hill.

This book looks at the development of gender roles through socialization patterns, cultural distinctions, and biological diversity of boys and girls.

Briggs, D. (1975). *Your Child's Self-Esteem.* **New York: Doubleday.**
This book deals with how self-esteem affects the entire life of the child.

Hart, L. (1990). *The Winning Family: Increasing Self-Esteem in Your Children and Yourself.* **Oakland, CA: Life Skills Press.**
This book suggests ways in which families can work together to bolster self-esteem in all family members.

Mendler, A. (1990). *Smiling at Yourself: Educating Young Children about Stress and Self-Esteem.* **Santa Cruz, CA: Network Publications.**
This book gives practical hints that early childhood educators can use to help children deal with stress.

REFERENCES

Anselmo, S. (1987). *Early Childhood Development: Prenatal through Age Eight.* Columbus, OH: Merrill.

Berk, L.E. (1991). *Child Development* (2nd ed.). Boston, MA: Allyn & Bacon.

Bolby, J. (1969, 1973). *Attachment and Loss* (2 Vols.). New York: Basic Books.

Bushey, J. (1992). I like me! The importance of self-esteem. *Today's Parent* 9 (2): 26–30.

Carlsson-Paige, N., and D.E. Levin. (1992). *Who's Calling the Shots? How to Respond Effectively to Children's Fascination with War Play and War Toys.* Gabriola Island, BC: New Catalyst/New Society Books.

Curry, N.E., and C.N. Johnson. (1990). *Beyond Self-Esteem: Developing a Genuine Sense of Human Value.* Washington, DC: National Association for the Education of Young Children.

Deagle-Fong, T. (1992). Superheroes: What's the appeal? *Today's Parent* (September): 42–43.

Derman-Sparks, L. (1991) Self-esteem: Helping children feel good about themselves ... and others, too. *Scholastic Pre-K Today* (November/December): 36–43.

Erikson, E.H. (1963). *Childhood and Society* (2nd ed.). New York: W.W. Norton.

Hodgins, D. (1992). Helping children like themselves. Seminar presentation, National Association for the Education of Young Children.

Kagan, J. (1971). *Understanding Children: Behaviour, Motives, and Thought.* New York: Harcourt Brace Jovanovich.

Maccoby, E.E. (1980). *Social Development: Psychological Growth and the Parent–Child Relationship.* New York: Harcourt Brace Jovanovich.

Marshall, H.H. (1989). The development of self-concept. *Young Children* 44 (5): 44–51.

Milner, D. (1983). *Children and Race.* Beverly Hills, CA: Sage.

Newman, B.M., and P.R. Newman. (1978). *Infancy and Childhood Development and Its Context.* New York: John Wiley & Sons.

Rogers, C.R. (1974). In retrospect: Forty-six years. *American Psychologist* 29: 115–23.

CHAPTER 8
Guiding Children's Behaviour

✎ **Overview**

✎ **The Guidance Relationship**

   ◆ Understanding Children's Behaviour

   ◆ Personal Attitudes and Values

   ◆ Building the Guidance Relationship

   ◆ Goals for the Guidance Relationship

✎ **The Guidance Process**

   ◆ Clarifying the Terms

   ◆ Setting Limits

✎ **The Language of Guidance**

   ◆ Verbal Techniques

   ◆ Nonverbal Techniques

✎ **Guidance Techniques**

   ◆ Indirect Guidance Techniques

   ◆ Direct Guidance Techniques

✎ **Summary**

✎ **Review Questions**

✎ **Discussion Questions**

✎ **Activities**

✎ **Further Reading**

✎ **References**

OVERVIEW

Balancing the needs of individual children with the needs of the whole group is one of the main challenges in guiding children's behaviour. Creativity, flexibility, and sensitivity to the needs of each child are essential for this task, because you, as an early childhood educator, are responsible for establishing and maintaining an environment that offers appropriate boundaries for children's development.

This chapter explains techniques that can help you to understand and support the kind of behaviour in children that leads them away from depending on others to set limits into learning to control their own behaviour and to discover the impact their behaviour has on others. As you use these techniques, you will be nurturing the children's self-concept, self-esteem, and respect for one another. You will also be developing a warm and trusting relationship with the children. This kind of positive adult–child relationship is essential for guiding children.

By the end of this chapter, you will be able to

❖ explain the difference between guidance and punishment;

❖ explain the goals of guidance;

❖ describe the guidance relationship;

❖ understand the techniques you can use to guide children's behaviour, both directly and indirectly.

THE GUIDANCE RELATIONSHIP

Zachary is applying to an early childhood education program at his local college. One of the requirements of the application process is to visit and observe two different early childhood centres.

At Centre A, in a large playroom, Zachary sees sixteen children playing in eight different learning centres. The noise in the room ebbs and flows, and the children are all concentrating on individual work or are playing in small groups. Both of the two adults are interacting with the children. One is quietly moving from one activity centre to another, chatting and laughing with the children. The other lends moral support to four children who are building a magnificent block castle.

When two children start yelling at each other, one of the adults quickly moves beside them, kneels down with an arm around each one, and says, "Tell me what is happening." Each of the children has a different idea of what they want to do next on the castle, and with the educator's input they work out a plan they both like so they can complete their project. In the end, both children are proud of their castle.

At Centre B, Zachary sees the same number of children. However, in this playroom there are only three activity centres in corners of the room. The high noise level makes Zachary feel agitated, and in the midst of all the commotion he sees a girl quietly sitting at a table sucking her thumb. At the same time, he notices children racing back and forth across the room, yelling at one another, and from time to time the adults yell at the children because otherwise no one can hear them. Toys and equipment are strewn everywhere. One of the adults is trying unsuccessfully to separate two children who are fighting and crying. The other adult stands at a counter writing in a notebook, her back to the children. Her only interactions with the children occur when she turns around and shouts, "Quiet, please!" After this the noise subsides only briefly, and then the children continue their chaotic behaviour.

Zachary walks out the door of this playroom with his stomach in knots. He thinks this centre is not a very happy place, and he has some niggling thoughts that perhaps early childhood education is not the place for him after all. As he thinks about his experience, he realizes that he is confused about why two centres with the same number of children and adults in playrooms of similar size can give him such dramatically different impressions. He also realizes that he has some opinions as well as some questions about what he saw. Did the adults have anything in mind that they wanted to accomplish with the children? Was each centre as he saw it that way all the time, or was Centre A sometimes like Centre B? Why were the behaviours of the children so different in the two centres? Did the children in Centre B feel they could count on the adults? Why was the atmosphere in the two places so different? How much effect did the set-up of the two rooms have on the children? The more Zachary thought about his experience, the more he became determined to find answers to his questions.

Zachary's questions are likely similar to those you would have asked if you had visited these two centres. In studying this chapter, you will find the answers for yourself. In fact, you may feel you already know some of the answers based on what you read in previous chapters, since we discussed in detail the importance of the adult–child relationship for the emotional well-being of the children. We also described the ideal relationship as being one that enhances children's sense of security, trust, acceptance, worthiness, autonomy, and independence. The relationship can be threatened if the adult is not sensitive to these aspects of development while attempting to ensure children's appropriate behaviour.

In any relationship, there are two partners, and the guidance relationship is no different. To learn how to guide children's behaviour, you must understand the outlook and needs of each of the partners. Each is a part of this relationship, and their needs influence the nature of the relationship. As you develop your own approach to guidance, you must be sensitive to the other partner, the young child. At the same time, you must evaluate your own values, attitudes, and expectations to be sure that you value the child as an equal and respected participant in the relationship.

Understanding Children's Behaviour

Young children learn and communicate through what they do and how they act. The behaviours that we see in young children are most often the normal and appropriate ways for them to explore their environment and develop social skills. So many things are new for them, and they experience situations and people in ways unique to themselves, ways that we as adults have forgotten from our own childhood. Children try new activities and work to gain new skills, master new challenges, and interact with their peers. In the process, from the adult point of view, they often make mistakes or poor choices. They spill paint, break toys, take things from other children out of turn, and sometimes even hurt one another, not because they are misbehaving, but because they are playing and focussing on what they want. Making mistakes is a part of their learning. Most children willingly try to correct their mistakes and inappropriate behaviour with supportive guidance from adults they trust.

Young children often need guidance to help them get along with one another. They have a struggle because they feel a strong need to get what they want, and at the same time they are also becoming aware of the outside expectations for co-operation and respecting the needs of others. Your role as an educator is to facilitate communication and help them learn how to work things out. Children need to find ways to assert their own needs and rights without violating the rights of others.

All children sometimes have mistaken behaviour. They are more likely to behave inappropriately when they are tired, upset, or distressed than when they are feeling good. You need to recognize frequent anxiety, resistance, aggression, or upset as a form of communication, telling you that all is not right in the child's world. Children who feel unloved, uncared for, unprotected, or unaccepted suffer distress because their legitimate emotional needs are not being met. It is not surprising that children with unfulfilled needs express these needs and attempt to resolve them through their behaviour. You will see extremes of behaviour because of children's intense needs. Sometimes you will feel that they constantly need your guidance.

Recognizing that children's behaviour results from developmental levels, temperaments, prior experiences, and present life circumstances is the first step to building the guidance relationship. Young children often have special needs for support. Once relationships are firmly founded, based on trust, empathy, acceptance, and support, the children will begin to accept the educator's assistance in developing more appropriate strategies for expressing and meeting their needs.

Personal Attitudes and Values

As professionals in early childhood education, we need to be aware of our attitudes and values and of the effect that our personal history has on our guiding techniques.

Attitudes are derived from personal experience. Most adults who take care of children reflect in their ideas and behaviours how their own parents treated them and how they were disciplined. Some people react against the way they were raised, while others tend to follow the model that their parents set.

How were you disciplined as a child? Did you feel your parents listened to how you felt about things? Did you feel the rules in your family made sense? What are your feelings now about your childhood experiences? As you begin to guide the behaviour of children in your class, try to discover how your own attitudes may influence your behaviour. You can use the questions in Box 8.1 as an exercise to increase your awareness.

BOX 8.1 QUESTIONS TO INCREASE AWARENESS OF ATTITUDES AND VALUES

Do you really believe

◆ in the worth and dignity of young children?
◆ that each individual child is unique?
◆ that each child has an instinctive drive to grow and develop?
◆ that a strong positive self-concept is essential to learning?
◆ that appropriate child-guiding techniques encourage children to develop to their potential?
◆ that appropriate child-guiding techniques encourage children to develop from dependence to independence?
◆ that appropriate child-guiding techniques encourage children to move from reliance on external control (i.e., early childhood educator's limits) to internal control?
◆ that when children are allowed to be active manipulators of their environment, their experiences become meaningful?
◆ anything that causes children to feel less liked, wanted, accepted, capable, worthy, or respected interferes with their ability to learn and their healthy self-concept?
◆ that the purpose of positive child guidance is to assist children to accept and integrate failure as a part of life experience?
◆ that the purpose of positive child guidance is to set the stage for children's success?

How do your answers compare with the approach to guiding children's behaviour as discussed on pages 171–72?

Building the Guidance Relationship

There are three aspects of the relationship between the children and the educator that affect the guidance relationship.

1. *Children need to be able to trust in the educator's ability to empathize and to respond to their needs.* They are able to trust the educator if they have a history of trusting relationships with adults, and if the educator behaves in a way that is dependable and responsive to the children's needs.

2. *Children need to feel valued and respected by others.* They need to experience the adult's acceptance and support in all interactions, including the adult's efforts to guide behaviour. Children respond when they are guided with understanding and concern for their perspective.

3. *Children need to experience freedom to make choices and decisions within the guidance relationship.* The educator offers alternatives and communicates faith in the children's ability to make wise decisions with caring support.

In the following example from an early childhood education playroom, you can see how the educator honoured her relationship with Brianne and Jared as she offered needed guidance.

Brianne is concentrating on her painting when she reaches across the table for the red paint. She knocks over a paint pot, and blue paint spills onto Jared's paper. He shouts at her and starts crying. Brianne becomes distressed and tense as Ann, the teacher, approaches the table. "What happened?" Ann asks in a completely nonjudgemental way. Jared shouts that

Brianne ruined his picture, and Brianne dissolves into tears. Ann comforts Jared and also asks Brianne what happened.

Having determined that the paint spill was an accident, Ann also offers support to Brianne: "I can see that you are upset by what happened. What can you do to solve this problem?" Brianne appears relieved and offers to get Jared more paper. She looks anxiously at Jared and says, "I didn't mean to do that," and seems relieved when he accepts the paper and begins again. Both children start painting again and Brianne cheerfully says, "I'm painting a red cow and a blue horse. What are you making?" "The circus," replies Jared.

In this incident, Ann placed a high value on Brianne's self-esteem and, at the same time, she defended Jared's rights. She placed no blame, but accepted the feelings of both children. The problem was resolved in a way that allowed both children to maintain their self-esteem and self-confidence. Both children learned that when they make mistakes they do not have to suffer recriminations, and that they can count on Ann's support when they get into difficulty. Imagine the difference in outcome for all three people, and the impact on the other children, if Ann had responded with frustration or anger and had required Brianne to leave the paint area because she accidentally knocked over a paint pot.

This example illustrates why teachers must consider carefully the way they influence children to follow guidelines for behaviour. The many positive strategies for guiding behaviour ensure respect for the children's emotional needs, whereas more negative techniques hinder emotional development and also harm the relationship with the adult.

Just as Ann made a choice about her responses to Brianne and Jared, so we as educators make choices in every situation. Our responses have an impact on our relationship with the children and affect the atmosphere in the playroom. Our responses also set the tone for what happens. The nurturing tone of Ann's interaction with these two children resulted in effective guidance in behaviour. This is the kind of nurturing tone that is essential for supporting children so that they can reach their full potential.

Goals for the Guidance Relationship

In the early childhood education profession, we value certain qualities in children: self-confidence, self-esteem, independence, autonomy, and self-control. However, these qualities are not necessarily valued in all of society. Sometimes we experience pressure to conform and to obey, and not to question authority. Your attitudes and values influence how you react to children who have the qualities we mentioned. Your attitudes either encourage (by being sensitive, nurturing, accepting) or jeopardize (by being controlling, judgemental, inflexible, distant) children's optimal development. You need to examine your expectations for children's behaviour in relation to the goals for their development.

Your goals for the guidance relationship should be consistent with the overall goals for child development and well-being. The behaviour of young children reflects their emotional needs, their level of development, and their inexperience. Young children sometimes struggle with self-control, particularly when they are under stress and their emotional and cognitive resources are lowered. For example, Sonia becomes angry when she is asked to come in from the playground. She has just started her turn with a tricycle and is enjoying riding it. She ignored the first two requests to come in, and when an adult approaches, she expresses how she feels by hitting and struggling. Her frustration is natural and understandable when you consider that she just finally got a turn on the tricycle after waiting for a while. In light of your goals, in this instance you acknowledge her feelings, offer empathy, and restate your expectations in a positive way, and then gently support her compliance.

Goals for positive guidance include

❖ a positive self-esteem so that children feel important and worthy even when they are upset or make mistakes;

❖ a positive self-concept so that children recognize and accept that mistakes of judgement or behaviour can be resolved satisfactorily;

❖ a sense of autonomy and self-discipline;

❖ security in the knowledge that the adults will continue to provide support and acceptance even when children's behaviour is not acceptable;

❖ increasing self-control and freedom to make choices regarding acceptable behaviours and means for solving problems;

❖ increasing awareness of the needs and rights of others, combined with empathy for the feelings of others;

❖ acceptance of feelings and support in expressing them in acceptable ways;

❖ assurance that the adults will treat all the children fairly, avoiding inequity in the use of power;

❖ a genuine, trusting relationship.

Although there will be times when you might be tempted to use a guidance technique that quickly solves a problem or conflict —

dividing up a set of pegs over which two children are arguing — remember that you have choices about the way you intervene. You must work to avoid choosing the fastest or easiest solution, and instead choose techniques consistent with your long-term goals for the children and for the relationship you want to foster.

Through your guidance strategies, you can support children in a multitude of circumstances, accept their mistakes as learning opportunities, and preserve their integrity and dignity.

THE GUIDANCE PROCESS

Punishment has no place in Early Childhood Education, because it builds resentments, fears, antagonisms and timidity instead of the healthy, happy child you will hope to rear.
— *Hildebrand 1985, p. 48*

Clarifying the Terms

In any group of early childhood educators, whether they have minimal experience or are veterans, the topic of conversation inevitably turns to coping with children's behaviour: Sam, who won't settle down at nap time; Monika, who balks at eating her lunch; or Whitney, who "won't listen" to the rules. One of the first steps you can take in finding effective ways to cope is to clarify the words you use in talking about children's behaviour to understand their underlying meanings. We hear many words to describe our responses to children and their behaviour. Some of these are "guiding behaviour," "discipline," "managing behaviour," and "punishment." Do these terms all mean the same thing to you or are there differences? Looking at each of these terms will help you understand how they are used in this chapter.

Traditionally, "discipline" and "managing behaviour" have been used to describe the positive approaches of early childhood educators in helping children to acceptable behaviour. For example: "I know you are in a hurry, Jenny, but it is important to walk in the hall. When you run, you are more likely to trip and get hurt. Let's walk together to the playground." Here the teacher reflects the child's feelings (in a hurry to get outdoors), states the limit (walk in the hall), explains the limit (walking minimizes danger of falls), and supports the child in adhering to the limit (accompanying the child in a friendly manner).

The term "punishment" refers to techniques used to eliminate inappropriate behaviour. This approach does not provide an opportunity for children to learn, but aims to stop immediately the behaviour that the adult dislikes. For example: "You are a bad girl, Jenny. I've told you a dozen times not to run in the hall. You sit here on the floor until I tell you that you may get up and go to the playground." Here the teacher tells the child what *not* to do (run in the hall), removes privileges or administers uncomfortable consequences (sitting on floor), and criticizes or demeans the child (labelling her a bad girl). As in this example, a cold relationship between the adult and a child is more likely to include punishment, because a child has little motivation to co-operate with an adult outside an atmosphere of trust.

Over time, the meanings of the terms "discipline" and "punishment" have become closely linked, although their original intent and impact were different. People often assume the term "discipline" has the same meaning as "punishment." Recognizing the confusion that can result from these terms, we have chosen to use the phrase "guiding children's behaviour" to mean the gentle process of supporting children in their developing awareness of and ability to act in socially acceptable ways. This kind of gentle guidance process is possible only when the adult has built a strong, positive relationship with the children.

Setting Limits

In guiding behaviour, be sure to clarify for yourself and for the children what you expect. You can think of limits as fences that provide boundaries so everyone knows what is acceptable behaviour and what is not. As any parent can tell you, children seem to naturally try to break through fences — this seems to be a part of growing up. Nevertheless, the fences, or limits, need to remain in place for children's safety and well-being.

When you stop children's unacceptable behaviour, you are setting limits. Learning the limits is the way children find out what behaviours are acceptable and what behaviours are unacceptable — in other words, how to get along with other people. You can use two basic principles to help you in deciding what are reasonable and consistent limits: children must not be allowed to hurt themselves or others, either physically or verbally, and children must not be allowed to destroy property and materials. To determine fair and reasonable limits, consider the following guidelines:

1. Setting limits should be a process that involves the children whenever possible. If children participate in setting limits, they also experience opportunities to practise problem solving. You might say to a group of children arguing over bikes, "We have only four bikes and you all want to ride as soon as we come out on the playground. What can we do about this?"

TABLE 8.1 **GUIDANCE VERSUS PUNISHMENT**

GUIDANCE	PUNISHMENT
Attempts to shape desirable behaviour	Attempts to eliminate undesirable behaviour
Associates a negative behaviour with an alternate positive behaviour	Associates a negative behaviour with a negative response
Encourages internal control	Controls behaviour by external forces
The child is given responsibility to modify her/his behaviour	The punisher assumes responsibility for modifying the child's behaviour
Emphasizes appropriate behaviour	Emphasizes inappropriate behaviour
Ignores minor inappropriate behaviour in favour of dealing with major issues	Responds strongly to even minor inappropriate behaviour
Considers causes of behaviour	Does not consider underlying causal factors
Is nonthreatening	Produces fear
Attempts to help children see possible consequences of actions	No attempt is made to help children learn from inappropriate behaviour
Helps children learn to balance their needs	Does not help children to consider the needs and feelings of others
Helps children feel good about making appropriate choices	Children "behave" only to avoid penalty
Encourages exploration and initiative	Teaches children to be wary of new situations
Creates feelings of respect and encourages responsiveness	Creates feelings of hostility, resentment, and guilt
Helps children become increasingly independent	Encourages dependence on external rules
Takes every opportunity to help children learn and grow	Reduces opportunities for learning
Used by loving, warm, yet firm adults in touch with their own feelings	Used by unsure, insecure, and unaware adults

(continued)

TABLE 8.1 (continued)

GUIDANCE	PUNISHMENT
Adult guides behaviour	Adult controls behaviour
Is used by knowledgeable, sensitive adults	Is used by uninformed adults
Bolsters self-esteem	Defeats good self-esteem
Is an ongoing process	Is a one-time occurrence
Sets an example to follow	Insists on obedience
Accepts children's need to assert	Makes children behave
Fosters children's ability to think	Makes children behave
Gradually decreases the controls the adult places on children in order to provide increasing opportunities for children to self-govern their behaviour	Assumes control for telling children what to do, which inhibits their learning to handle freedom

Source: Based on A. Gordon and K.W. Browne. (1993). *Beginnings and Beyond: Foundations in Early Childhood Education* (2nd ed.). Albany, NY: Delmar, p. 215.

2. Limits must be developmentally appropriate. The limits that you set are most effective when they are thoughtfully matched to the individual child's developmental level. You might be frustrated by what feels like children's inappropriate behaviour. Perhaps a closer look at the situation will reveal that your expectations for a particular child are unrealistic and that she is acting in a most suitable way for her age and stage. It then becomes your responsibility to change your expectations of her rather than to require her to change a very natural (although perhaps inconvenient) behaviour to fit with your needs.

3. Establish limits that are consistent, yet flexible enough to meet the individual needs of the child. For example, you might allow Huong to play with the play dough without sharing it after a particularly distressing separation from his mother, even though you have a general understanding that play dough must be shared.

4. Limits must be meaningful and must contribute to the positive experience of children and educators. Limits should not restrict play, movement, or choices unless the restriction is necessary to protect a child's safety or individual rights.

Often many rules in the child-care environment are in place simply because they "always have been." But history or habit is not a sound basis for rules. Rules need to be reviewed periodically and discussed among the members of the staff. When you feel clear about which rules you think are essential to the happy flow of the daily routine, discuss them with the children so they also can be clear about expectations. This helps to build an atmosphere of trust and caring.

THE LANGUAGE OF GUIDANCE

The process of positive guidance is made up of many parts: what we say, the way we say it, the things we do, and the environment we create. Examining the language you use is a good place to start in looking at the process of guidance.

Verbal Techniques

Our primary mode of communicating with children is through our words. Therefore, it is important to consider how we can make what we say have the most positive impact on them. Using the following techniques will enhance your success in verbal guidance.

State directions positively. Your directions should tell the children what to do rather than what not to do. Keep directions positive, simple, and to the point — avoid using too many words or the children may lose the point of the message or tune you out. Explaining the reasons for your instructions helps children to understand your request. For instance, you might say, "Ride your tricycle on the path. I'm afraid the children playing on the grass will run into you there," or "Put your snow boots in your cubby so no one trips over them."

Use a normal tone of voice when you speak to children. Increasing or decreasing the volume of your voice can be effective in reinforcing your message. A quiet tone of voice can be extremely effective in gaining the children's attention because they may have to strain to hear what you are saying and, as a result, may be more focussed on the message you are trying to convey. Yelling at children is never necessary, although in an emergency situation calling loudly across a room may be unavoidable. For example, if a child is about to hit another and you are physically unable to get there to intervene, you can call out loudly, "Stop, Phyllis! Put that block down."

Use normal speech patterns (words and pitch). Beware of overusing guidance phrases or falling into a rut of excessive "teacher talk," for example: "Use your walking feet," "You need to … ," "Use your words." When these phrases are used in combination with other directions they can be quite effective, but using them continuously creates an artificial way of speaking. The above examples can easily be

BOX 8.2 GIVING DIRECTIONS

Giving directions is such a large part of verbal guidance that it may be helpful to outline specific techniques.

1. Be sure you have the children's attention before you give directions. Get down to their level to ensure you are face-to-face and to establish eye contact. Respect children's dignity and do not require that they look directly at you as long as they are paying attention. A child who is forced to make eye contact may not be able to focus on listening at the same time.

2. Establish physical proximity to the children. A gentle touch can help a child to pay attention.

3. Give directions one step at a time to prevent young children from becoming confused.

4. Give a clear reason for your directions whenever possible.

5. Assess the children's understanding so that you can be sure to choose words or phrases with which they are familiar. Ask them, "What did I ask you to do?"

6. Address children by name to help them focus on the direction.

7. Focus on what the children are to do, avoiding negative lead-ins such as "How many times do I have to remind you?"

8. Use "you" and not "we" when you give directions to only one child.

9. Provide choices to allow children a sense of control whenever possible.

10. Avoid giving instructions through questions that imply a choice when no real choice exists. Questions about choices can get you into trouble if a child answers "no" when you do not really mean to offer a choice (e.g., "Shall we put our coats on and go outside?" "Would you like to come for lunch?").

11. In certain circumstances, you can give directions to a child by asking a question: "Where do the blocks go when you are finished using them?"

12. Keep your sense of humour, and use it!

changed so that you have a wider repertoire of verbal directions. For instance, you might say, "Please walk inside," "It is important that you ... ," or "Tell him that ... ." When you use a variety of appropriate directions, children are less likely to "turn a deaf ear" and instead pay attention to what you are saying.

Describe the children's behaviour and its consequences. This will help them to understand how their actions affect themselves and others. However, when you use this technique, avoid labelling or centring out children ("Oh, Robert, how could you ... ?") because the result is an erosion of their self-esteem. When you describe children's behaviour and its consequences, they learn new information about their actions — what constitutes socially acceptable behaviour — and they can apply it to future experiences. This process helps children to move from needing external adult control to relying on inner self-control. Imagine the difference in how children feel if a teacher uses these inappropriate and appropriate verbal directions: "That was bad. I don't like it when you hit!" or "Be gentle. It hurts when you hit. Tell him that truck is yours." With younger children, you may have to give them the actual words and tell a child to say, "That truck is mine."

Be specific about what children have done. You need to be specific to reinforce positive behaviour. When you give children genuine praise on a consistent basis, they are less likely to seek attention in negative ways. For example, you might say, "You did a great job putting on your snowsuit," or "Wow, you put all that Construx back in the bin. There were lots of pieces to put away!" This is much more effective than just saying, "Good boy. That was nicely done."

Support children to express emotions. A major part of our role is to help children find and use words to express their feelings. The range of emotions in children in the preschool years expands, and they need support to express these emotions in socially acceptable ways. For instance, Joel has just hit Sabina because she took his doll. The teacher says, "Joel, tell Sabina you are angry and want your doll back." With your support, children can learn to accept all of their feelings (both negative and positive) and can learn to express feelings verbally rather than in physical ways like biting or hitting.

Nonverbal Techniques

Nonverbal guidance techniques include those things you do to reinforce the words you say. In other words, your body language must suit your directions, because children become confused if you communicate mixed messages. If you smile while you tell the children not to shove each other as they wait to go outdoors, they will think you do not mean what you are saying and they will be confused.

BODY LANGUAGE

The following nonverbal guidance techniques are effective for conveying clear messages to children.

Get down to the children's level. Squat, stoop, kneel, or sit on a low chair. These attempts to equalize your height and size show respect for the children. When you are face to face with a child, your verbal and nonverbal communication is more effective.

Be aware of the effect of your body posture. Standing with your arms crossed or your hands on your hips conveys a message that you are not approachable. Also avoid keeping your hands in your pockets and yawning. These gestures may convey the message that you are bored or uninterested.

Your body language should accurately convey the mood of your message. For example, you can show reassurance or affection by a smile, a wink, your arm around the child's shoulder, or a hug. You can convey concern or frustration by the shake of your head, a serious facial expression, or holding out your hand to caution a child.

You can use touch to communicate messages. A gentle touch on the arm or back may reassure or act as a cue to change the behaviour. If a child is about to hit another child, what can you do? Perhaps you can gently hold the child's fist while acknowledging his feelings: "I know you are angry at Shawna because she pushed you. But hitting hurts and is not OK." You can then support the child in finding an acceptable alternative to dealing with this incident: "Let's go and tell her that it was your turn to hammer at the workbench."

As we have indicated earlier, specific cultural backgrounds can influence how we interpret various aspects of body language, and the importance of this reality merits further discussion. In some cultures (for example, Native Canadian), it is disrespectful for children to make eye contact with adults. Touching a child if you are not a family member is also unacceptable in some cultures. Other cultures warmly welcome friendly touching, but never of the head. Physical proximity may also be an issue — in some cultures more personal space is the custom, while in others people are most comfortable speaking to one another standing close together. As an early childhood educator, keep in mind the culturally diverse customs and expectations as you interact with children.

LISTENING

Listening is an active process that helps you understand "where the child is at." When you are in touch with the children, guidance techniques can be adapted to meet individual styles and needs. Being a good listener means that you

❖ maintain appropriate contact at the children's physical level;

❖ show respect for the children by being genuinely interested in what they have to say;

❖ allow time to let children finish their thoughts, and ensure that neither you nor other children interrupt while someone is trying to say something. Silence is essential to facilitate effective listening;

❖ use "reflective listening" — paraphrasing what the children have said to be sure you understand. For example, Flavia tells you, "Yua's a bad boy. He took it … it's broken now. I hate him!" You respond, using reflective listening: "You are upset with Yua, aren't you, Flavia? He took something and now it's broken. Can you tell me more about what happened?";

❖ support children in expressing themselves without putting words into their mouths;

❖ avoid jumping to conclusions. Give children the time they need to explain the situation from their point of view;

❖ pay full attention to the children while they are speaking.

GUIDANCE TECHNIQUES

"Guidance can either be indirect or direct. Indirect guidance includes all the teachers' behind-the-scenes work" (Hildebrand 1991, p. 103). Direct guidance includes your on-the-spot reactions to and interactions with the children. These techniques are used together as a part of the total guidance process. To clearly identify the differences between indirect and direct guidance techniques, however, we list them separately.

Indirect Guidance Techniques

One of the most successful guidance strategies is the careful design of the physical space and program. Children with ample room to play, attractive and accessible toys and materials to use independently, and a well-planned balance of activities are much less likely to become frustrated, bored, or over-controlled. Chapters 9 and 10 provide detailed discussions of planning the environment, schedule, and curriculum in ways that reduce the need for more direct intervention.

You can use a number of indirect guidance strategies to keep your program running smoothly as you supervise a preschool room. Maintain an awareness of the atmosphere in the room, and assess the children's interest in their activities. Are they concentrating on what they are doing? Are the groups of children focussed on their play? Does the program you have scheduled channel the children's energy in a positive way? For example, if several children begin chasing one another, you need to assess whether they are bored, excited, over-stimulated, or tired. If you know the children well, you can determine whether they have enough developmentally appropriate activities available or whether they need more options to help expend their energy in creative ways. You might also ask yourself whether your expectation for their behaviour is clear. After you have analyzed the situation, you can choose from among the following alternatives:

1. Introduce a new activity: "Bill and Andrew, I have a great new game. I would like you to help me teach the rest of the children." In this situation, you have deliberately decided not to address the boys' running, but instead, to redirect their energies.

2. Rearrange the schedule so the children can be outside earlier if you detect that they need more opportunity for gross-motor activities.

3. Introduce an active indoor exercise activity as a way of allowing the children to expend their energy in more appropriate, safer ways.

Anticipate the need for a change of pace before the activity at hand deteriorates. Even with exciting, absorbing activities, children have limited attention spans. Be aware of the cues that signal waning interest. For example, during a small-group activity, watch for a case of the "wiggles" or "sillies," inattention and looking about for something else that interests them, lack of eye contact, and chatting with or poking their neighbours. If any of these occurs, you have a number of indirect guidance techniques from which to choose:

1. Address a child directly with a question having to do with the activity at hand, thereby positively refocussing her or his attention.

2. Ask the child to help you with the task at hand.

3. Change gears and choose to do an active song or activity.

YOUR POSITION IN THE ROOM

Your physical presence alone can have a positive impact on children's behaviour and a calming influence on the atmosphere of the room. Indirect guidance can be given simply by careful strategic positioning — choosing where to stand or sit in the playroom.

Remember, the children pick up on the adults' cues and model their behaviours. In our anecdote at the beginning of the chapter about Zachary's visit to Centre A and Centre B, it is not surprising that the children yelled at one another in Centre B, since yelling was the way the teachers tried to get the children's attention.

Although you will find yourself constantly interacting with specific children, playing games, sampling play-dough cookies, or helping to solve an engineering problem in the block area, it is essential to remain alert to all activity around you. Frequently scanning the room, even while you are focussing on one or two children (also known as having eyes in the back of your head) is a skill necessary to ensure a happy and flowing program.

Use your skills in active listening to help you predict that a situation between children could potentially erupt. Often you can redirect behaviour before the situation gets to the breaking point.

RESPONDING TO CHILDREN'S INDIVIDUAL NEEDS

Your familiarity with the individual characteristics and needs of all of the children in the program is essential in selecting the most suitable indirect guidance techniques. Here are some of the techniques you might find effective.

Take time to stand back and carefully observe the children's behaviour. In this way, you will come to know each individual. Perhaps you notice that when Richard plays in the housekeeping centre, the children inevitably end up fighting unless you sit close by. With closer observation, you also notice that Richard always bosses others around and that this is the source of the problems that arise. When you remove him from the housekeeping centre, the conflict dissolves.

Confer often with the parents to increase your understanding of the children. Perhaps in talking with Richard's parents — not by telling them about Richard's behaviour in the housekeeping centre, but by learning more about what his boundaries are at home — you can understand his need to dominate the other children and how to direct his behaviour and the dynamic he sets up in a group of children.

REDUCING CHILDREN'S STRESS

Children's inappropriate behaviour often results from their need to reduce stress (running, yelling, not listening, not participating). Stress

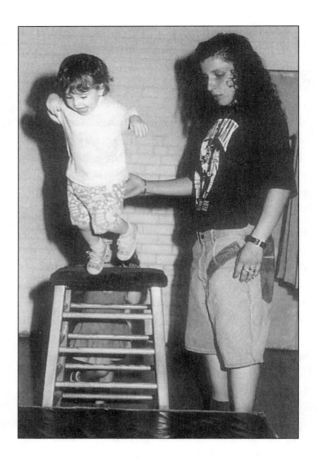

lowers one's emotional resources and results in less mature levels of behaviour or self-control. Table 8.2 provides strategies for reducing stress and stress-related behaviour.

Direct Guidance Techniques

Sometimes all the planning and preventive techniques are not enough to eliminate the need for more direct guidance. When children are struggling to achieve or maintain self-control, or when conflicts escalate, you can use the following strategies to intervene.

Use active problem solving with the children. To help children move from external control to internal control, we must help them learn how to solve problems. For example, you might verbally lead the children

TABLE 8.2 STRESS RELIEVERS FOR CHILDREN

Stress Reliever	Examples
1. Plan a special day.	Pyjama day, teddy bear day, backwards day, red day, beach party
2. Plan a special event.	Show a video, invite a surprise visitor, organize a treasure hunt, invite the entire family to a muffin morning or an afternoon tea
3. Play a variety of co-operative games.	Co-operative musical chairs, hot potato
4. Arrange "soft spots" in the playroom.	Large, soft cushions or beanbag chairs piled in a cozy corner with soft lighting, soothing music, and blankets to snuggle under
5. Change the daily routine.	Move traditional inside activities outside, do activities usually done in the afternoon in the morning, arrange to have a picnic snack or lunch
6. Do guided children's aerobics.	Disney's *Mousersize*
7. Offer a wide range of musical experiences.	Classical, pop, rock, music from other countries; provide a variety of musical instruments
8. Plan cooking activities.	Make fortune cookies, play dough, a "friendship salad," latkes, milkshakes
9. Use the great outdoors.	Fly a kite; gather a bouquet of wildflowers, grasses, and leaves to make centrepieces for the lunch tables; go on a "let's care for our environment walk" and clean up garbage, then follow up with a lesson on recycling; plant a garden
10. Introduce pets into the program.	Guinea pigs, gerbils, rabbits, cats, and hamsters make great child-care centre pets; encourage the children to be active in caring for these pets
11. Surprises!	Greeting stickers in children's cubbies to greet them as they arrive, secret messages hidden under milk glasses
12. Water, water everywhere!	Introduce new items to the water table, e.g., foil confetti, small bars of soap, baby dolls, measuring items, and containers for pouring

through the steps of resolving problem situations: "Sam and Kadish, it seems you both want the red shovel. What do you think you can do to solve this problem?" You must allow plenty of time and opportunity for the children to formulate and verbalize their plans. You can help support the process by asking open-ended questions and, if necessary, offering suggestions. For example, "Do we have any other shovels?" Do not be afraid of a few moments of silence. Giving children the opportunity to think about alternatives sometimes requires silence. Try to leave the onus of the responsibility for resolving the problem with them.

Redirect the children from an inappropriate behaviour to another, more appropriate, one. If a child is tossing blocks, you might say: "I'm afraid someone will be hurt with one of those hard blocks. Come over here and throw beanbags at this target. Let's count how many you can get through the bull's-eye." The key to making this technique successful is to offer alternative activities that are as fulfilling to the children as their original activity. You must accurately assess the situation before you can determine what the best alternatives may be. Whenever possible, offer more than one choice to allow children to have some control over the situation. If they make the choice themselves, the chances are that they will feel more commitment to the new activity.

Distract the children's attention to something more positive. For example, "Manuel, it's hard to say goodbye to Daddy, isn't it? It must make you feel sad. Remember, Dad will be back to pick you up when you are playing in the playground this afternoon. After we wave goodbye, let's play with the Teddy Bear Bingo you had so much fun with yesterday." Notice in this example that you are not

denying the child's feelings. You are recognizing and supporting his sadness, and then reassuring him and supporting him in the ritual of saying goodbye. Only when all of these steps have been taken do you try to distract Manuel with the Teddy Bear Bingo. Using this technique does not always have to be preceded with as many steps as in this example. Distraction can be as quick and easy as offering another red shovel or blue car when two children reach for it at the same time. It is important to be aware of the situation almost before it erupts and step in quickly, for distraction rarely works when two children are thoroughly embroiled in a power struggle.

Lead the children through the steps needed to change behaviour. You can talk the child through the necessary steps — a verbal process — or take the child by the hand and use the "hand-over-hand" method — a physical process. Often direct guidance is a combination of both verbal and physical support. This technique can work well with children who run away once directions have been given. Calm, supportive words and physical support can help to eliminate chasing games. In many cases, this technique can avert a lot of frustration for both you and the child.

Use physical guidance that is calm and gentle, yet firm. As a child is about to hit another, you can hold the child's hand: "I'm not going to let you hit. Hitting hurts." The key to effective physical guidance is that the children feel that you are supporting them. Therefore, you must be calm and in control of yourself both in body language and in the tone of your voice. Any such physical movements as reaching out to hold a child's hand must be done calmly and deliberately. There should be no fast, jerky movements that might appear threatening. Always tell the children what you are doing and why. Sometimes children must be held to protect them or others. Occasionally, some children have severe, adverse reactions to being touched or held. Respect each child's needs whenever possible. You may have to move other children away from the area or carry a distressed child to a safe spot to "let loose" without hurting anyone.

Ignore minor inappropriate behaviour. Sometimes this technique works well, especially when children have been inundated with directions and commands: "Do this," "Do that," "Stop that," "Don't do that." Too many commands make the environment feel like a negative place. Early childhood educators have the responsibility to avoid creating this tone by thinking carefully before they "spit out a command." Ask yourself: Will the children's behaviour hurt themselves or others? the environment? What would be the impact of not responding to the behaviour? If the children's actions will have a negative impact, then do not hesitate to intervene quickly and redirect the behaviour. However, the ability to pick and choose issues is most important — children have an uncanny ability to tune out nagging adults.

These are some examples of behaviours you may choose to ignore: Betsy sticking her tongue out at something she does not like; Matt working very hard to put his shoes on all by himself but putting them on the wrong feet (ignore the shoes being on backwards, but praise the effort required to put them on). However, it is not a good idea to ignore such behaviours as hitting or pushing others, taking another's toy, or ruining another's artwork.

Avoid allowing situations to become power struggles. A child's staying power is amazing in the face of the ultimatum, "You may not get up from the table until you drink your milk." Apart from being punitive, boring, and an absolute waste of time, this kind of ultimatum is a totally inappropriate response because you are initiating a power struggle that renders you completely powerless. Children who react in numerous infuriating ways are attempting not to lose face and are trying in any way possible to regain and control the situation to win the power struggle. This sets up an unhealthy relationship between child and adult. The directions that you give should be suitable for both the child and the situation and not just be rigid ultimatums.

Avoid making children say they are sorry. This is *not* an effective direct guidance technique. Little learning results from the use of this technique because you are providing all of the external control and the children develop no strategies for self-control. They quickly learn that saying "Sorry" lets them off the hook with little effort. Holding children accountable for their actions through natural consequences is much more effective. If Stephanie hits Jason, you can ask her to hold a compress to Jason's head. If Joshua deliberately kicks over Steven's block structure, you can have Joshua build it up again. If Dana tears a page from a book, you can ask her to get the tape and help make the necessary repairs.

Use withdrawal techniques for situations in which neither indirect nor direct guidance techniques are effective. Usually children respond appropriately to the positive guidance techniques we have described, but occasionally a child experiences such frustration, anger, or distress that neither indirect nor direct guidance techniques are effective. In this case, the child needs the opportunity to regain composure away from other children, with the support of the adult (Clewett 1988; Marion 1991). You can assist the child by reflecting her intense emotional state and observing that she needs some time to calm down. Direct the child to a quiet and private area of the classroom where she can remain until she can regain control of her emotions. You need to remain accessible the whole time, offering comfort, support, and encouragement in whatever form is acceptable (some children accept and respond to being held, while others resist physical contact). When the child regains composure, the two of you can work out a solution to the problem that originally upset her.

Children who experience occasional or frequent intense emotional outbursts need the caring support of an adult to learn to control the expression of strong needs and feelings. They need to develop strategies that enable them to withdraw from situations with which they cannot cope before the situation totally breaks down. Those children who experience sensitive support in expressing and controlling their intense emotions are more likely to withdraw on their own initiative when they need some time alone to calm themselves.

The use of withdrawal is clearly not intended as a negative consequence for uncontrolled behaviour, and should not be perceived as an unpleasant or punitive time of isolation. As intended, the child should see withdrawal as a positive alternative to loss of control, an option that the child will learn to ask for from time to time, especially in stressful situations. For withdrawal strategies to be effective, children must not feel isolated, rejected, or abandoned. Rather, they should discover that moving away from a troublesome situation is helpful in reducing distress.

This strategy of withdrawal to increase self-control should not be confused with the once-common "time-out" strategy, in which a child

was directed to a specific location for a set time period to think about his or her unacceptable behaviour alone. In time-out, the child often felt humiliated and rejected and suffered diminished self-esteem. Young children are often so distressed by anxiety, isolation, and loss of control that they are incapable of thinking about their behaviour or coming up with alternative ways of meeting needs. Time-out is therefore often unsuccessful in changing behaviour, and may even intensify unacceptable behaviour because the children can feel increasingly resentful toward the adult and negative toward themselves. Quite rightly, the time-out technique is losing favour as an acceptable form of guidance for young children.

The following example provides an illustration of a situation in which supportive withdrawal helped a child regain a sense of calm and well-being.

It has been raining all morning. Jordan is dropped off at the centre rather brusquely by his normally relaxed dad, who today is agitated because he is already late for a meeting with the company president. Danny, Jordan's favourite teacher, is away ill and his best friend, Chelsea, has decided that she wants to play alone. Jordan wanders aimlessly around the room dabbling in various activities until he spies the computer. There is already a line-up but he is so excited he is willing to wait. Finally it is his turn! But no sooner is he settled in than the teacher, Sharma, comes to tell him it's "tidy up" and he needs to turn the computer off. This is the final straw — Jordan responds with an adamant "No!" His frustrated teacher leans over and switches the machine off. Jordan gives her a forceful punch on the arm. She responds with a surprised and loud "OUCH! That really hurt me, Jordan." Jordan can no longer cope — he crumples to the floor, wailing and rolling around. Sharma, realizing the stress he has been through this morning, says sympathetically, "You've had a rough morning." At this, he starts to scream loudly and kick out, and the other children, attracted by the noise, begin to wander over and stare. Sharma makes the decision to give Jordan some withdrawal time.

She calmly, yet firmly, picks him up (holding him in a "football hold" on her hip so his flailing arms and legs are less likely to strike her. Also, holding Jordan this way allows her to protect other children, if need be, with her free hand). Calmly and in a matter-of-fact way she says, "Let's go to the quiet area. I'll help you while you calm down."

Taking her cue from Jordan's level of agitation, Sharma sets him gently down on the floor and moves aside. She chooses to say and do nothing until Jordan begins to calm down, and only then moves closer and gently puts her hand on his back. Jordan does not resist her touch and she gently rubs his back. As he stops crying and appears to be able to listen, Sharma

speaks: "It's been a really hard morning. Do you want to tell me about it?" Jordan shakes his head and Sharma does not insist. She says, "Let me know when you feel ready to join the other children in the gym." She sits quietly, waiting for a few minutes, and then he says, "Will you play basketball with me?" Sharma enthusiastically agrees and they go to the gym, where Chelsea runs up to say hi.

In this kind of situation, when mounting pressure on Jordan led to the outburst, Sharma's most important goal was to help him regain control while maintaining self-respect, rather than lecturing him about misbehaviour. Your sensitivity and intuition will guide you to know that children are usually aware of their inappropriate actions. Instead of focussing on these, it is more important to relieve some of their stress to help them regain their sense of self-control and to be able to cope more positively with the rest of the day.

If Jordan frequently behaved this way (i.e., was always hitting out when frustrated), Sharma would have ensured that before he returned to play with the children they would have discussed the consequences of his hitting and would have talked about more appropriate ways for him to express his anger. However, since his behaviour was directly related to the particulars of the day, Sharma did not feel that discussing his behaviour was necessary.

The staff's commitment to the techniques that Sharma used meant that they had to creatively adapt the daily schedule (delay coffee breaks or gym time) to allow Sharma to spend time supporting Jordan through his distress.

As in this example, all guidance strategies should reflect your sensitivity to the child's needs and your desire to help the child come through the situation with self-esteem intact while you preserve the relationship.

SUMMARY

In this chapter, we have explored a variety of aspects that have an impact on the guiding environment in an early childhood education program. We described two centres that illustrate differences in atmosphere and tone, the difference in the teachers' approach, and the impact on the children's behaviour.

We considered the importance of a positive approach to guidance and presented the goals of guidance. To achieve these goals, we looked at the fundamentals of the guiding environment: what we say and how we say it, and what we do: our body language, our position in the room, our responsiveness to children's needs and styles, and setting limits while being flexible and responsive.

We explored the importance of creating a warm and responsive environment that encourages children's positive self-esteem. The essential role of effective guidance is supporting children in their ongoing development toward becoming independent, self-directed, empathetic, and responsible individuals. As early childhood educators, our own growing-up process and the values and attitudes we formed have an impact on how we relate to children. In becoming self-aware, we are empowered to make choices that have a positive impact on the guiding environment.

REVIEW QUESTIONS

❶ Outline the differences between the terms "guiding behaviour," "discipline," and "punishment."

❷ List the main goals of guidance.

❸ What are limits, and what are the main determining factors in setting limits?

❹ Describe the verbal and nonverbal guidance techniques that are effective with young children.

❺ Compare indirect and direct guidance techniques.

DISCUSSION QUESTIONS

❶ Discuss the difference between supportive withdrawal and time-out from the child's perspective.

❷ Try to remember an incident when you have been humiliated by someone. Discuss the impact this had on you.

❸ Discuss the style of parenting you grew up with. Is how you interact with children similar to this or different? What are some reasons for your answers?

❹ Discuss why a warm, nurturing tone in children's environment is so important.

❺ Sally and John are pulling back and forth on the same doll. Each is shouting, "I had it first!" Discuss what your role is in this situation. What techniques of guiding would be most beneficial to foster a positive outcome?

❻ Ashley has been playing in the sandbox for quite a while. During this time, you have had to remind her twice not to throw sand at others.

She has just thrown sand at someone again. Discuss what you should do and say.

ACTIVITIES

❶ Observe an early childhood educator at work with a group of children. Write examples of the directions the educator gives to the children. Beside each example, explain why the direction is or is not appropriate.

❷ Write a list of as many rules as you can think of that exist in child-care settings. Decide whether these are absolutely necessary. Based on the philosophy of this chapter, which of these rules could be revised or eliminated completely?

❸ Make a list of some of the overused phrases in "teacher-talk." Provide alternative ways that the same message could be given to the children.

❹ Observe four incidents of an adult guiding a child. Evaluate the effect of each technique on the child's self-esteem and the relationship between child and adult.

❺ Write a sample philosophy of discipline that could be given to parents to explain the goals and strategies used by centre staff to guide the behaviour of young children.

FURTHER READING

Beaty, J. (1992). *Skills for Preschool Teachers.* **New York: Macmillan.**
This book explores the basic roles of the early childhood educator in the preschool program. Basic classroom skills are discussed as they relate to the learning environment and to the individual developmental domains. The book is designed to allow students to use the self-taught module approach. Each chapter is a self-contained learning module.

Dreikers, R., and V. Soltz. (1964). *Children: The Challenge.* **Markham, ON: Fitzhenry & Whiteside.**
This classic resource addresses many issues that parents face in rearing young children. Such areas as the fallacy of punishment and reward, setting appropriate limits, helping to build independence, and general communication skills are all age-old issues for which the authors have given advice that is still beneficial and relevant today.

Ferris Miller, D. (1990). *Positive Child Guidance.* **Albany, NY: Delmar.**
The underlying theme of this book is the importance of helping children develop self-control. The approach is based on the belief that no single guidance strategy is appropriate for children of all ages. The book is a celebration of children's individuality.

Gartrell, Daniel. (1994). *A Guidance Approach to Discipline.* **Albany, NY: Delmar.**
This excellent book analyzes the role of the educator as "a professional, not a technician," and emphasizes the importance of a positive approach that responds to mistaken behaviour of children resulting from a variety of factors such as inexperience, social influences, and strong emotional needs.

Marion, M. (1991). *Guidance of Young Children.* **New York: Macmillan.**
Marion attempts to get the reader to see guidance as a process. Although there are no magical answers for each interactional problem that educators face, the author has a strong conviction that positive child guidance is possible when educators believe they have choices about how to interact with children, have realistic expectations, learn developmentally appropriate guidance techniques, and

understand the long- and short-term goals of child guidance.

REFERENCES

Beaty, J. (1992). *Skills for Preschool Teachers*. New York: Macmillan.

Broman, B. (1982). *The Early Years in Childhood Education*. Prospect Heights, IL: Houghton Mifflin.

Clewett, A. (1988). Guidance and discipline: Teaching young children appropriate behaviour. *Young Children* 43 (4): 26–31.

Cohen, S., and G. Rae. (1987). *Growing Up with Children*. New York: CBS College Publishing.

Dreikers, R., and V. Soltz. (1964). *Children: The Challenge*. Markham, ON: Fitzhenry & Whiteside.

Essa, E. (1983). *A Practical Guide to Solving Preschool Behaviour Problems*. Albany, NY: Delmar.

Ferris Miller, D. (1990). *Positive Child Guidance*. Albany, NY: Delmar.

Gartrell, D. (1994). *A Guidance Approach to Discipline*. Albany, NY: Delmar.

Gordon, A., and K.W. Browne. (1993). *Beginnings and Beyond: Foundations in Early Childhood Education* (2nd ed.). Albany, NY: Delmar.

Hendrick, J. (1992). *The Whole Child*. New York: Macmillan.

Hildebrand, V. (1985). *Guiding Young Children*. New York: Macmillan.

Lay-Dopyera, M., and J. Dopyera. (1987). *Becoming a Teacher of Young Children*. New York: Random House.

Linberg, L., and R. Swedlow. (1985). *Young Children Exploring and Learning*. Newton, MA: Allyn & Bacon.

Machado, J. (1984). *Early Childhood Practicum Guide*. Albany, NY: Delmar.

Marion, M. (1994). *Guidance of Young Children*. New York: Macmillan.

Peck, J. (1978). *Young Children's Behaviour*. Atlanta, GA: Humanics.

Seefeldt, C., and N. Barbour. (1986). *Early Childhood Education: An Introduction*. Columbus, OH: Merrill.

PART 3
Setting the Stage for Learning

Children learn and develop fully when they feel welcomed and find meaningful experiences in the early childhood setting. Early childhood centres reflect the diversity of children and families in the variety of materials, the physical environment, and the wide range of experiences offered.

Children learn naturally as they explore and interact with things in their environment. A physical environment that encourages exploration and a wide variety of play opportunities is vital for optimal learning. Room and playground designs, learning experiences, routines, and schedules that are child-centred are best able to respond to the varied individual needs of young children.

CHAPTER 9
Designing an Environment for Children

✎ **Overview**

✎ **The Early Childhood Environment**
- ◆ Guiding Principles
- ◆ Developmental Considerations
- ◆ Creating a Positive Atmosphere
- ◆ An Environment for Play

✎ **Indoor Play Space**
- ◆ Open and Private Space
- ◆ Learning Centres
- ◆ Play Units
- ◆ Factors Affecting Arrangement of Space

✎ **Outdoor Play Space**
- ◆ Arranging Outdoor Space

- ◆ Outdoor Zones
- ◆ Outdoor Equipment and Facilities

✎ **Observing and Evaluating the Early Childhood Environment**
- ◆ Ensuring Safety

✎ **Scheduling**

✎ **Nutrition**

✎ **Summary**

✎ **Review Questions**

✎ **Discussion Questions**

✎ **Activities**

✎ **Further Reading**

✎ **References**

OVERVIEW

Can you take yourself back to your preschool years and remember the places you liked most? If you went to nursery school or day-care centres, do you remember the playrooms? How were the equipment and materials organized? If you have difficulty remembering this part of your childhood, try to imagine ideal indoor and outdoor spaces for preschoolers. As you try to visualize each space, remember that for many children this is their second home — they spend a lot of time in this place.

Planning and arranging indoor and outdoor spaces are among the most important tasks you will have as an early childhood educator. What you place in each room or area determines much of how the children feel there. Where and how toys, materials, and equipment are placed in each area contribute to children's sense of calm or chaos, and whether they feel safe. Careful planning determines the richness of play, children's social interactions, their ability to make choices, the noise level, the traffic flow, and safe supervision. Well-designed physical environments contribute to children and adults working and playing together.

In this chapter, we discuss planning the environment, which is often difficult, especially if the space was designed for other purposes and now must meet all the requirements of a quality program. Not only do early childhood educators have a responsibility to plan and prepare space for children, but also for the needs of staff and parents. Planning an environment for children also involves thinking about the schedule and daily routines for mealtimes and rest or sleep, along with understanding the guidelines for good nutrition. Considering the needs of the child in all areas guides this planning.

This chapter provides guidance and strategies for planning, arranging, and monitoring environments for children, staff, and parents. By the end of this chapter, you will have an understanding of

❖ the philosophy behind arrangement of space;

❖ layout of indoor and outdoor spaces;

❖ traffic patterns and flow;

❖ arrangement of furnishings and equipment;

❖ schedules and routines;

❖ nutrition guidelines.

THE EARLY CHILDHOOD ENVIRONMENT

In Chapter 8, you were introduced to Zachary, who visited two different day-care centres, where he found what seemed to be two totally different environments. However, the philosophy in the two centres was the same in that the adults all encouraged children to make choices and transfer learning through manipulative, hands-on experiences.

As Zachary later realized, in addition to the lack of presence of the adults, the way the room was arranged in Centre B was largely responsible for the chaos. The room had a large open space with the three activity centres in the corners, with no clear boundaries or zones and no pathways leading from one activity to another. The children simply raced around or wandered aimlessly. However, in Centre A, the learning centres were easy to identify, the pathways were obvious, and the amount of open space was limited. But the room did have an area with a soft rug that was adaptable for use for gross-motor activities when the children needed active play. Later, when Zachary made a report in one of his classes on his visits to these centres, he described the room arrangements as the dominant factor that affected the children's behaviour.

Guiding Principles

When you plan a place where children spend a significant part of their time away from home, it must reflect what you want for them in all aspects of their growth and needs. Planning starts by considering what the young child needs in order to thrive and to maintain a sense of physical and emotional well-being. The ideal early childhood environment meets the learning and developmental needs of the whole child.

Children need an environment that provides for their physical needs. They need opportunities and places to be active and to rest. Times for active movement and rest need to be planned as part of the daily schedule, but ideally children should have opportunities and areas for both throughout the day as individual needs arise. Routines and facilities for eating, toileting, and personal hygiene will be required several times each day, and should be planned to balance independence and healthy practice.

Young children away from home need a homelike environment to meet their emotional needs. The atmosphere should be comfortable, warm, friendly, and child-centred. The rooms should reflect the children who come to the centre in terms of personalized spaces and choice of pictures and decor so that they all feel a sense of belonging. The arrangement must convey a sense of order and calm to ensure that children feel secure and safe. Furnishings and arrangements should promote independence and self-help to promote the

autonomy and initiative we described in Chapters 7 and 8.

Young children who are growing and changing each day need adaptable, flexible environments. The arrangement of equipment and space and the choice of materials must encourage and enhance social interaction and learning through play, exploration, and active involvement. The environment must also provide for the adults involved — visiting family members as well as the staff.

In planning an environment for children, the early childhood educator must keep these principles in mind, while also considering such practical issues as places for personal possessions, storage of equipment not being used (beds, gross-motor equipment), and ease of maintenance and clean-up. When space is arranged efficiently and effectively, educators can focus their attention on pleasant and meaningful interactions with children.

Developmental Considerations

Preschoolers have specific developmental needs that must be considered. They need

❖ an atmosphere that conveys acceptance and respect for individual and family diversity;

❖ an atmosphere that encourages self-esteem and self-confidence;

❖ experiences and activities that encourage making choices;

❖ space and time to carry out personal choices;

❖ a variety of ways to explore, manipulate, and experiment safely;

❖ opportunities to become independent problem-solvers;

❖ opportunities to transfer learning from one situation to another;

❖ a holistic program that considers children's strengths, interests, individual learning styles, approaches, and backgrounds; and

❖ resources that reinforce social interactions and feelings of belonging.

Because preschoolers are at different levels in their play and learning, the environment must be planned with varying levels of challenge, so that success is possible for all.

Creating a Positive Atmosphere

When you step into an early childhood setting, you are immediately aware of a feeling or atmosphere, as Zachary was. Initially, you might not be aware of its source, although you will come to realize that it arises from a variety of sources, including the physical environment.

It goes without saying that the early childhood setting is primarily a setting for children. The atmosphere reflects the presence of children in the furniture (child-sized), the decor (bright, colourful, interpersonal, and personal), and the evidence of children's activities (art on the walls, projects ongoing in various areas of the room). Although an accumulated mess is not desirable, children who are busy and creative create clutter and they need the freedom to make a mess.

The physical atmosphere also reflects values of early childhood education in the choice of materials and pictures. A celebration of multiculturalism is apparent so that all children can see themselves and their families having a place in this, their second home. Children benefit from the richness that comes from an awareness of the traditions of diverse cultures and backgrounds. You can see evidence of children learning and developing in many ways —

specialized equipment or modifications to increase mobility, or labels in sign language. You also see indications that parents are a welcome part of the program in the coffee pot, books and magazines, and comfortable couches or chairs.

An Environment for Play

The quality and type of play is influenced by such environmental factors as toys and space. Different toys "pull for" different types of play. Blocks and other building materials pull for constructive and imaginative play, art materials draw out creative play, and puzzles and similar toys have a higher cognitive component. The early childhood setting must have a wide variety of each type of toy and material accessible for as much of the day as possible. If creative material or water play is limited to certain times of the day or is brought out infrequently, the children's play experiences are unnecessarily limited.

The placement of equipment and furnishings also affects social play. A water table placed in the centre of the room, with space for four children to face one another, promotes more socializing than the same water table facing the wall, where children cannot maintain eye contact as they play.

How learning centres are set up can reflect gender stereotyping. However, both boys and girls play in centres if you avoid sex-typed toys. In the housekeeping areas, for example, you can include dress-up clothes and tools and implements for making repairs, cooking, and cleaning. If you are aware of your own biases — and we all have them — and work to avoid setting up learning centres in a way that the children see them as the domain of only boys or only girls, you can go a long way in breaking down sex stereotypes.

INDOOR PLAY SPACE

As Zachary discovered, open, undefined space conveys an image of freedom of body movement, running, and boisterous activities with few boundaries. On the other hand, defined, organized space that provides clear direction or pathways communicates a completely different message. The optimal room arrangement consists of open space, defined learning centres, accessible places for toys and materials, clear boundaries, and pathways to guide children's movements. The way the room is arranged takes into account a development curriculum that provides for emotional, gross- and fine-motor skills, self-help skills, and the language and cognitive needs of young children.

Open and Private Space

The amount of open space available for play is one indicator of quality in a program (Wach & Gruen 1982). After completing a three-year study, Kritchevsky, Prescott, and Walling (1977) concluded that approximately one-third to one-half of the total floor space should be unobstructed. The ideal amount of open space also depends on the number of children. The remainder of the space should balance the open space with smaller self-contained play and learning areas, each with a different focus or goal.

As important as open space is an area of quiet, private space where a child can be alone to observe, relax, or experience a feeling of calm away from the others. You can achieve this effect with soft, inviting furniture, a pile of pillows, or a partially enclosed space.

Learning Centres

The early childhood environment and curriculum are based on the knowledge of what children are like, both individually and as a group (Kostelnik, et al. 1993). Preschoolers are ready for many challenges, but they need adults to help them make sense of the equipment, materials, questions, and situations they encounter.

How can you find out what learning centres are appropriate for your particular group of children? A starting point for your planning could be making a list of the children and writing down each child's interests and areas of development. Your notes can guide you in organizing the space to support children's explorations, and to provide activities that allow for self-selection and self-direction.

Many of the early childhood learning centres are planned for explorations related to daily living. The creativity and imagination of the staff, coupled with the needs and interests of the children, dictate the arrangement of learning centres.

Space arrangements should address all aspects of the curriculum and provide distinct play areas for different developmental areas. This list of learning centres provides for a variety of experiences. Box 9.1 offers more ideas, including appropriate materials for centres.

❖ sensory (water, sand, play dough)

❖ creative (paint, drawing, and collage materials for experimentation)

❖ dramatic play (housekeeping, community, dress-up)

❖ large and small block play (with such props as cars, people, animals)

❖ manipulatives (Lego, small blocks, stacking toys)

❖ miniatures (doll house, hospital, farm, cars, trains)

❖ language, reading, storytelling

❖ science, nature, discovery activities (weigh scale, magnifying glass, plants, objects from nature)

❖ music (tapes, instruments)

❖ cognitive activities and problem solving (puzzles, sorting activities, matching activities, mathematics or number activities)

❖ contemplative, space to be alone

❖ woodworking, building, sculpting

These centres should be planned to provide for a balance of individual and small- and large-group activities. Within each learning centre, a range of materials for varied levels of involvement and accomplishment allows children to make choices, move independently, and revisit old and encounter new experiences. Children need to have many opportunities to

test similar materials in different ways, and to transfer knowledge and integrate learning when centres with similar goals are located close together — for example, dramatic play areas close together can allow for play to spill over from one area to another. For example, Hira, who has just gone "shopping" at the shoe store, visits Kim and Francisco in the housekeeping centre to show off her new shoes. They invite her to stay for tea.

Sometimes several curriculum areas can be located close together or integrated into one area to make the best use of the available space. For example, locating the housekeeping centre close to the block area can bring about some interesting possibilities as children mature and become more creative and experimental. They might use the blocks to build missing furniture in their "house."

Carefully arranged learning centres allow materials to be available for use on a consistent and continuous basis. When structures or projects in process can be left to be continued later, children increase the complexity and scope of their play. Every effort should be made to design areas that allow this extension in play to take place. Everyone learns best by doing, trying new activities, making "mistakes," trying again, and entering wholeheartedly into new experiences. Children need repeated opportunities to experiment in an environment that is stimulating, challenging, aesthetically pleasing, safe, and organized.

Keep in mind that children need to be exposed to the same toys, equipment, activities, and experiences over a period of time. Familiarity with the things in their environment helps them gain confidence in their attempts so that they become competent in their skills and feel satisfied with their accomplishments. Only then are they able to move on to new challenges and to begin to feel

BOX 9.1 LEARNING CENTRES

DRAMATIC PLAY CENTRE

Child-sized kitchen equipment with
    pots and pans
Dishes and silverware
Tables and chairs
Telephones
Child-sized ironing board and iron
Child-sized cleaning equipment, including
    mops, brooms, dustpans
Assorted tubs, buckets, dishpans
Assorted dolls, including different races
Doll clothes
Doll bed, carriage, snugglies
Doll house, furniture
Assorted dress-up adult clothing and
    costumes
Hand mirrors
Full-length mirror

BLOCKS

Blocks (unit and hollow)
Block accessories (people, cars, safety signs)
Small blocks (sets of cubes, small coloured
    blocks)
Sturdy wooden vehicles: cars, trucks, boats,
    planes, tractors, fire engines, buses,
    helicopters

CREATIVE

Adjustable easels
Brushes
Liquid tempera paint in many colours
Painting smocks
Crayons
Coloured chalk
Clay
Scissors

Glue, paste
Paper: newsprint, white drawing paper, con-
    struction paper in a variety of colours,
    tissue paper, glazed paper for finger
    paints
Drying rack for paintings
Miscellaneous recycled materials (cardboard
    tubes, egg cartons, styrofoam, fabric
    scraps, rickrack, yarn, ribbon, glitter,
    buttons, feathers and other natural
    materials)

LISTENING, LANGUAGE, STORYTELLING

Computer and printer
Typewriter
Paper
Pencils and markers
Envelopes
Rulers
Tape recorder
Record player
Flannel board with stand

MANIPULATIVES/GAMES

Hand puppets
Puzzles
Games (lotto, checkers, chess, dominoes,
    Candyland, Chutes and Ladders, Hi-Ho
    Cherry-O)
Beads and strings
Sewing cards
Sorting collections (buttons, rocks)
Sorting trays
Tinkertoy (regular size and large size)
Lego blocks, bristle blocks

(continued)

BOX 9.1 (continued)

SCIENCE/DISCOVERY

Aquarium
Terrarium
Magnets
Magnifying glasses
Prisms
Metric measuring devices
Pattern blocks
Pegs and pegboards
Geoboards
Geoblocks
Base ten blocks
Unifix cubes
Scales
Rhythm instruments
Workbench with equipment

SENSORY

Scent bottles
Water table with top
Funnels
Straws
Bubble liquid
Food colouring (nontoxic)
Sand table
Plastic containers
Clay
Play dough

MUSIC

Tape recorder
Record player
Audiotapes
Instruments: a variety of wind, string, and
    rhythm instruments such as drums,
    shakers, triangles, flutes, xylophones,
    guitars, autoharps, ukuleles
Materials for making instruments: dried
    beans, plastic and metal containers with
    lids, shakers, spoons, combs, pot lids,
    wood dowels, coconut shells

WOODWORKING

Low, sturdy table or workbench
Small functional tools: hammers, saws,
    screwdrivers, pliers
Wide-headed nails
Softwood scraps

PHYSICAL EDUCATION

Balance beam
Tumbling mat
Rocking boat
Steps
Walking boards
Jungle gym
Fabric tunnel
Sawhorses (sturdy metal)
Climbing ladder, climbing rope
Assorted balls
Hula hoops
Bowling set
Outdoor equipment: wheeled toys,
    gardening tools, sandbox

Source: Adapted from J. Brewer. (1992). *Introduction to Early Childhood Education: Preschool through Primary Grades.* Needham Heights, MA: Allyn & Bacon. Adapted by permission of the publisher.

secure in taking new risks. Limited exposure to a specific medium makes children fearful in their attempts, reduces skillbuilding, and limits experimentation and exploration. For example, some educators say that children do not enjoy clay, so they make it available only occasionally. However, modelling with clay requires time for children to develop their interest — time for experimenting, and for finding the many possibilities clay provides. If clay is available only once in a while, children cannot develop an interest in it.

Learning centres are designed to foster children's creativity, imagination, and spontaneity. You set the stage by arranging the space and the materials placed within that space. The rest is up to the children's imagination, maturity, and experiences. Blocks may become boats, or dress-up clothes might suggest celebrating a holiday. The possibilities are endless, and children will expand their play more and more as the physical environment allows them to do so. Chapter 10 discusses the closely related area of curriculum planning in more detail.

Play Units

Within the learning centres, the educator provides a variety of play materials, toys, and equipment. One study (Kritchevsky, Prescott, & Walling 1977) suggests that playrooms should include three levels of play unit: simple, complex, and super units. **Simple** units are those that contain materials limited to use by one child, generally with a defined purpose — for example, a bike or swing. **Complex** units have more than one part or have two materials used together, for example, water with containers for pouring, which can be used by more than one child. **Super** units have three or more play materials — a dramatic play

area set up as a shoe store with a cash register, a telephone, receipts, materials to sell, and bags for wrapping, for example.

The definition and description of the units described by Kritchevsky, Prescott, and Walling offer a useful guide to ensure that you provide a range and variety of materials within each category. There are developmental benefits in a balanced number of play units. Complex and super units allow more children to participate in social interaction, while the simple play unit provides an opportunity for quiet solitude or for play with individual goals, such as mastery. Such a range allows the children to make choices based on their individual differences, temperaments, interests, developmental levels, maturity, and personal needs.

PATHWAYS

Clearly defined pathways to and from learning centres allow children to move about and choose activities independently. Carefully placed furnishings and shelves can block traffic that interferes with play and allow children to move easily between, say, the paint easel and the sink. Pathways that break up open areas also reduce aimless wandering and running. Children easily follow clear and visible pathways at their own eye level, with cues or indicators (signs and pictures) that help them identify areas and centres for specific play purposes. Rugs or coloured markings on the floor also help to define space.

Factors Affecting Arrangement of Space

Many provinces have legislation that deals with the physical environment of child-care centres. There are minimum space requirements per child (for example, each province requires approximately 3 m^2 per child of indoor space), and requirements for playground design and safety, use of space, and types of toys and equipment needed (Yeates, et al. 1990). These standards must be addressed within the design of the physical space.

Reading the regulations is certainly necessary, but having a clear understanding of the implications is another matter. Beyond the requirements listed under regulations, many legislating bodies include guidelines and procedures that centres must follow. These guidelines usually refer to preferred practices or suggestions that expand on the regulations. For example, the regulations might require that dramatic play equipment be provided in a quantity and size to meet the developmental level of the children in each age group. The guidelines might elaborate on the regulations by giving examples of the kind of dramatic play equipment to be used, where it should be placed, how staff can enhance or enrich the play by providing additional props, and so on. As an educator, you are responsible for knowing the regulations for your province or territory and municipality, and for ensuring that the centre complies with these regulations.

The need for supervision is another factor influencing room set-up. Small, enclosed learning centres might be ideal for the children's play needs, but these are difficult to observe and supervise. Thus, many centres divide play areas with low shelves so that the adults can easily see over them. Learning centres often open onto a common open space, again to allow educators to supervise all areas of the room from a central location.

Many centres share space with other groups: groups of children of different ages, such as older children after school, or organizations that use the same space in the evening. This situation affects educators' options in arranging a playroom, since equipment and furniture might have to be moved frequently or stored away.

Structural factors that require consideration when arranging space include the location of entrances, exits, fire doors, windows, access to washrooms, proximity of the playground, children's cubbies, availability of storage, natural lighting, and the location of the kitchen. Sometimes centres have several smaller rooms. Compatible learning centres can be set up in these smaller spaces, but these can create problems in adequate supervision. Whatever the circumstances, educators must provide an environment that adequately provides for the developmental needs of the children.

The needs of the children are the prime consideration in design of an early childhood setting, but the needs of the staff and the children's families also must be considered. Educators and other staff need a personal space to store their clothing, personal possessions, and books. They also need an uncluttered, comfortable workspace away from the children where they can do planning and recordkeeping. A place for small- and large-group meetings is valuable, even if it is in a multipurpose room.

Family members bringing and picking up children need a spacious and uncluttered transition area where the child's outdoor clothing and personal possessions can be kept, ideally in individual cubbies. During the transition to the centre, parents need a quiet place to say goodbye to their children, away from the bustle of a busy hallway and the activity of the playroom.

You can welcome and encourage the involvement of family members by providing a comfortable reception area, where an information board displays items of interest and upcoming events as well as photographs and news items about past activities. Magazines and books on relevant topics should be available, and perhaps even a pot of coffee. Like children, family members respond positively to a friendly atmosphere that conveys a message of belonging.

OUTDOOR PLAY SPACE

In the profession of early childhood education, the organization, grouping, and arrangement of indoor and outdoor space are both important to the learning and development of the whole child. The challenges of Canadian weather can seem daunting, and sometimes educators, like many other people, are inclined to close the door and stay inside until summer. Changing seasons can seem troublesome because they require storage space for bulky outerwear, mopping of wet floors, and time to allow children to develop dressing and undressing skills. Nevertheless, outdoor play provides benefits in all kinds of weather that children cannot experience indoors.

Outdoor play allows preschoolers to feel more freedom and spontaneity and to be more boisterous than they can be indoors. Although many centres have indoor space for gross-motor activities, the constraints on movement are less limited outside. Indoor and outdoor spaces should be complementary. Bringing indoors natural materials that children find expands their creative experiences, and singing, chanting, and fantasy play can take place on the outdoor swings, climbers, slides, and other play equipment.

Arranging Outdoor Space

When you observe children, you will notice a difference between indoor and outdoor play — they become much more spontaneous outdoors. Children and adults seem to feel less inhibited and constrained when they are outside. This special characteristic of outside time should be considered in the arrangement of the space. An important principle of outdoor playground design is that, when outdoors, children should be allowed to express themselves more freely, to become part of the natural surroundings, and to learn to respect and appreciate nature and the wonderful feelings it brings.

The concept of transfer of learning, with many ways and means of providing similar experiences, needs to be as much a part of the planning outdoors as it is indoors. Proximity of the playrooms to the playgrounds allows children to move about independently and use materials, toys, and equipment in two different settings. Ideally, outdoor areas should be usable in almost every weather condition. Pleasant weather conditions should allow staff to extend play materials both indoors and outdoors. Overhangs on buildings can extend outdoor activities. Large playhouse arrangements with extended roofs achieve the same purpose.

Safety must be the first and foremost consideration given to the arrangement and inclusion of various types of equipment. Studies by Esbensen (1984) concluded that the quality of the play equipment, where it was located, and the type of ground surface used determined the safe use of playgrounds. For example, cushioned surfaces under swings, slides, and climbers such as thick layers of sand, grass, and other materials that have good impact-absorbing qualities prevent serious injuries.

Outdoor Zones

The same principles for use and arrangements of indoor space apply outside as well. Distinct play areas, or zones, with obvious boundaries; open space; clear and uncluttered pathways; simple and complex equipment; proximity to washrooms, storage, and cubbies; ease of supervision for staff; and sufficient storage areas are primary considerations.

Consideration should be given to the natural terrain — hills and valleys — that will be incorporated into the permanent design. Fences, shrubs, trees, permanent play equipment, storage areas, hard surfaces for riding toys, and shaded areas are the first to be located within the space. The attractiveness, flow, and appeal of the playground should be a primary goal. Gardens where children can plant flowers and vegetables and bench swings that allow children and adults to sit together provide a homelike atmosphere.

Patio stones, interlocking bricks, concrete slabs, or asphalt provide hard surfaces for entrances and riding toys. Hard surfaces can be attractively constructed to avoid the cold and hard effect these materials sometimes portray. Weaving them through the playground can add to the attractiveness of the area as well as helping to define space for children. A wide range of textures adds to the tactile experiences as children sit, roll, play, and interact with their environment.

Zoning the playground, with pathways leading safely to and from each area, provides messages to children about what should happen in each area. Zoning supports sound curriculum design, but it is also a good safety measure for children using the playground. Boundaries must be clear and distinct so children can easily see them.

Just as for indoor planning, outdoor play areas should provide opportunities to meet all aspects of children's needs. Esbensen (1990) recommends the following outdoor zones:

❖ manipulative/creative (carpentry, construction, clay);

❖ fantasy (sand and water areas equipped with small figures, objects, and materials to create fantasy scenes;

❖ social (somewhere to sit comfortably to observe, chat, and enjoy the company of others);

❖ social/dramatic (playhouse or other area, complete with props to enhance pretend play);

❖ physical (wheeled toys and the paths on which to drive them, swings, climbing, and other stationary equipment);

❖ natural (natural and cultivated gardens with a wide variety of plants, grasses, vegetables, and flowers to be studied and cared for).

One aspect of children's play that is often overlooked is fantasy play involving superheroes. Children need opportunities to express power and control in their adult-regulated lives, and they need space for this type of play. Outdoor space is a more suitable environment

for children acting out roles of fearless characters of superhuman strength and endurance because this kind of play is exhilarating, exciting, and noisy. Given the nature of this form of dramatic play, it can sometimes be more acceptable to adults when it is planned for outdoors.

Outdoor Equipment and Facilities

Permanent climbing structures provide a variety of opportunities for children to use and develop their physical skills, and they need to be integrated into the overall plan of the space. These complex play structures enable children to play together in a variety of experiences. Well-designed equipment uses all gross-motor possibilities and can incorporate dramatic and fantasy play. For example, playhouses or structures that have some division for role-playing might form the basis for the climbing, balancing, and swinging apparatus.

Platforms built into large trees, when closely supervised by staff, provide a natural way for children to feel a sense of power and control. A sturdy staircase or ladder leads children to explore heights safely and give them a lookout place to view the world.

Areas for digging require deep sand, lots of space, and clear boundaries. Small sandboxes are not adequate. The area should allow many children to participate in the range of experiences that playing with sand allows. A built-in, child-size table in the middle of the area reminds children to keep the sand within the boundaries. They will gravitate toward the table or platform to set their pails, sift the sand, or add water. Another interesting addition to a playground is a digging area for larger shovels and digging objects. This area can have a mixture of sand, gravel, and dirt in a place where water might be added to give a variety of textures. Depending on the season, gardens might also be planted in this area.

Thought needs to be given to all four seasons when you are planning the playground, and you can plan it in ways that make winter outdoor time enticing despite the cold.

❖ Incorporate hills into play structures that might also double as winter sliding areas.

❖ Ensure that sliding areas are free of obstacles a long way from the bottom of the hill.

❖ Determine whether hard surfaces are safe and whether they can be cleared of snow.

❖ Evaluate water run-off to be sure that icy areas do not form and that the playground has good drainage.

❖ Assess the open area available for snow structures, winter games, digging in the snow, and making snowmen.

❖ Ensure that drying facilities are available for mitts, boots, and wet snowsuits.

❖ Use overhang areas to best advantage, or plan some covered or sheltered areas.

The overall plan should also include facilities for adults: benches, bench swings, or other places where adults can sit comfortably and observe and converse with the children. Of course, adults and children both need areas where they will be sheltered from winter wind. Adults need storage for their bulky outdoor clothing — they often leave snowsuits, boots, and warm clothing at school instead of taking them home each day. Adults also need a place indoors where outdoor clothing will dry overnight.

Family members need easy access into the outdoor area that does not require going through the entire building. A shelf or counter for checking in and out is useful at the entrance. A large window in the playroom overlooking the outdoor play space allows family members to watch the children's outdoor play from time to time.

OBSERVING AND EVALUATING THE EARLY CHILDHOOD ENVIRONMENT

As you have read in other chapters of this text, observational techniques play an important role in designing the environment. Educators casually observe how children respond to the physical environment as they interact on a daily basis. This observation can clue you in to areas of the room that seem to create more than their share of conflicts or problems. Careful observation and modifications might lead you to enlarge an area that is too small, or move certain toys from one place to another. You might see the need to create a new learning centre to expand interest, or to block an unwanted pathway that is encouraging running.

As important as these informal observations are, they are not sufficient. From time to time, you will find it helpful to do a more systematic observation of the environment of your centre.

Keep your eyes open for the following indicators of quality:

❖ a comfortable, inviting, homelike environment with individual personal spaces (cubbies or baskets);

❖ a culturally rich environment, where materials, toys, and decor reflect an unbiased acceptance of diversity;

❖ an arrangement that includes open space for group play, quiet space for solitude, and several clearly defined learning centres designed for a variety of developmental areas;

❖ specific centres planned for release of energy and emotions (sand and water play, active play, creative and sensory areas);

❖ all centres accessible throughout the day;

❖ clear boundaries between centres to control traffic flow and noise levels;

❖ the amount of space in centres proportionate to the activity being offered (larger spaces for gross-motor and group activities, smaller spaces for quiet, individual activities);

❖ a wide variety of toys, materials, and activities to stimulate curiosity and learning;

❖ toys, equipment, and set-up that encourage social interaction;

❖ children's creations displayed at their eye level;

❖ accessible, orderly arrangement of materials to encourage independence and self-direction;

❖ ease of supervision.

Ensuring Safety

It goes without saying that an environment for young children must ensure their physical safety. Each province and territory has regulations to ensure the safety of children in early childhood settings. Regulations for a safe environment include those of the licensing body as well as the local health and fire authorities. Every staff person should be familiar with relevant legislation. Preventive measures must be in place, with systems to monitor each aspect of the centre regularly and consistently. All adults should be alert to any health or safety issue and take action to correct problems, but it makes sense to assign one adult the task of completing a safety checklist on a regular basis.

A checklist is an effective way of ensuring that each area of the centre has been examined for health and safety hazards. Any areas identified as possible hazards should be noted, and a plan made to take care of the problem immediately. The plan should indicate when and how the repair will take place, and the date of the next inspection. Box 9.2 provides an example of a checklist that is suitable for an early childhood education centre.

SCHEDULING

In addition to the physical space, an ideal environment for young children incorporates a plan or schedule for the day to ensure that all their needs are consistently met. The opportunity for children to freely and fully participate within the well-planned playroom and playground also depends on the careful planning of the schedule.

Needing at least some predictable parts to life is characteristic of everyone, adults and children alike. At minimum, we all count on daylight in the morning and darkness at night.

In-between, we establish certain patterns to our days. Children need daily routines that provide predictable patterns, because they depend on the consistency of familiar routines to feel secure and confident. Early childhood educators provide these routines by establishing a schedule, which is simply a framework for organizing the experiences of the day.

A well-thought-out schedule balances children's needs for active and quiet times, group and individual play, eating and rest. Through planning a schedule, you can be sure that you include activities that encompass the range of children's needs:

❖ physical needs: rest, nourishment, gross- and fine-motor activity;

❖ social needs: building relationships, enjoying friendships;

❖ cognitive needs: discovering and learning;

❖ emotional needs: building positive self-concept and -esteem;

❖ creative needs: using the imagination and building creativity.

This variety of experiences is reflected in the following aspects of the schedule:

❖ child-directed learning experiences: large blocks of time for play, both indoors and outdoors, when children can circulate through the play space and choose a variety of activities;

❖ small-group times: for cooking, music, games, and stories;

❖ routines: resting, eating, toileting;

❖ transitions: ending one activity and beginning the next, which includes tidying up after play and preparing for outdoor time, rest, or lunch.

BOX 9.2 HEALTH AND SAFETY CHECKLIST

Inspection completed by _____ Date _____

Summary of concerns from last inspection _____

_____

_____ Date of last inspection _____

INSPECTION AREA	YES	NO	COMMENTS
Indoors			
◆ Surfaces that are easy to disinfect.	____	____	_____
◆ Floors that provide warmth and comfort	____	____	_____
◆ Rugs that are secure to prevent tripping	____	____	_____
◆ Nonslip floor surfaces	____	____	_____
◆ Rounded or padded corners	____	____	_____
◆ Climate control and draft-free environment	____	____	_____
◆ Good ventilation with all systems working	____	____	_____
◆ All areas well-lighted	____	____	_____
◆ Acoustic and noise levels appropriate	____	____	_____
◆ Safe, locked storage for hazardous materials	____	____	_____
◆ Controlled systems for food storage and refrigeration	____	____	_____
◆ Sanitary diapering procedures posted	____	____	_____
◆ Sanitary food-handling procedures posted	____	____	_____
◆ Hand-washing procedures posted	____	____	_____
◆ Electrical outlets at children's level have dummy plugs when not in use	____	____	_____
◆ No electrical or phone wires at children's level	____	____	_____
◆ Furniture is stable, washable, not peeling or chipped, and uses nontoxic paint	____	____	_____
◆ Safety glass in doors and windows, securely fastened	____	____	_____
◆ Child-size furniture and equipment to avoid accidents	____	____	_____
◆ Equipment and toys have no protruding edges and are in safe working order	____	____	_____
◆ Science and nature materials are nonpoisonous and safe	____	____	_____

(continued)

BOX 9.2 (continued)

Inspection Area	Yes	No	Comments
◆ Toys and equipment are stored safely when not in use	___	___	_____
◆ Toy shelves and cupboards are stable	___	___	_____
◆ Water in water play centre is changed after use	___	___	_____
◆ Sand is disinfected regularly	___	___	_____
◆ Woodworking equipment is organized and safely stored	___	___	_____
◆ Pathways in rooms are uncluttered, at child's-eye level, and easy to follow	___	___	_____
◆ Toilets and sinks are at child's level	___	___	_____
◆ Stepstools are wide, strong, and stable	___	___	_____
◆ Faucets used by children are temperature-controlled	___	___	_____
◆ Paper towels are readily available for children to use	___	___	_____
◆ Children can access paper cups and a drink of water easily	___	___	_____
◆ Kitchen is out of reach of children	___	___	_____
◆ Dangerous equipment in kitchen is well out of reach of children	___	___	_____
◆ Storage areas are uncluttered and have safe passages	___	___	_____
◆ All areas of the centre are cleaned daily (floors, washrooms, kitchen, counters)	___	___	_____
◆ Intensive cleaning is completed on a regular schedule (rugs shampooed; walls, doors, windows washed)	___	___	_____
◆ Staff areas are organized and uncluttered	___	___	_____

Outdoors

	Yes	No	Comments
◆ Playground can be accessed safely from building	___	___	_____
◆ Entire playground is visible	___	___	_____
◆ Playground has clear and safe pathways	___	___	_____
◆ Grounds are clean, garbage-free, and well-maintained	___	___	_____

(continued)

BOX 9.2 (continued)

INSPECTION AREA	YES	NO	COMMENTS
◆ Fencing in all areas is at least 1 m high			
◆ Fences are in good shape, latches working and secure			
◆ Bushes and tree limbs are strong and sturdy			
◆ Surfaces are free from holes and protrusions			
◆ Sandboxes are covered or inspected for debris			
◆ Equipment is confined to designated area			
◆ Drainage is working well			
◆ Washrooms and drinks are easily accessible			
◆ Gross-motor equipment is well-anchored			
◆ Equipment is free of holes, gaps, and rough edges			
◆ Equipment has no protrusions that clothes can catch on			
◆ Equipment has space between each area			
◆ Equipment is easy for the staff to supervise			
◆ Equipment is developmentally appropriate			
◆ Children are protected from sun, wind, and cold			
◆ Surfaces under equipment have good cushioning			
◆ Water in water play area is changed at least daily			
◆ Plants, shrubs, etc. are nonpoisonous			
◆ Swings are checked to ensure safety			
◆ Slides have no pinch points or protrusions			
◆ Riding paths are in good shape			
◆ Wood on equipment is smooth and splinter-free			
◆ Bolts and screws are recessed			
◆ Riding toys are checked for safety			

All CONCERNS OR PROBLEMS WERE REPORTED TO THE SUPERVISOR ON _____
BY _____

Schedules let children know the order of things to come. Being able to predict activities gives them a sense of security so they have the freedom to enjoy their play and their learning.

However, becoming a slave to your schedule is a mistake — everyone likes an occasional break from routines. In fact, there are times in a creative preschool program when the children's absorption in creative play might suggest a change in the schedule, and with experience you learn to recognize this kind of circumstance. The point of the schedule and routines is to provide consistency and predictability. In an atmosphere of security and trust that children feel within a structured environment, they can more easily enjoy unusual experiences: field trips, or having guests or a substitute teacher.

There are a number of steps you can take to make sure that your schedule meets the needs of the children.

❖ Provide plenty of uninterrupted play periods so the children can enter into and complete the activities they choose.

❖ Plan a schedule that minimizes routines in which all the children have to do the same things at the same time. Having children waiting in snowsuits until everyone is ready to go outside and lining up should be avoided. Arrange staffing so that the children can move through routines at their own pace and in small groups.

❖ Carry out routines with a minimum of waiting. Children need plenty of action and stimulation — forced inactivity breeds behaviour that requires intervention. Again, avoid situations in which children must line up.

❖ Plan a logical flow of experiences so the preceding activity appropriately channels children's actions for what follows. For example, tell a quiet story before rest time rather than planning energetic gross-motor activities, which can make falling asleep difficult.

❖ Encourage children to make choices by planning to have a snack available during a block of play time and leaving the decision of when to take a break up to the children. Also, washroom routines work best when determined by the children's needs and choices, not a schedule.

❖ Provide adequate warning of forthcoming transitions. Children need to know what to expect, when to expect it, and why. Reminders and explanations should be given to individuals and small groups of children to maintain the calm atmosphere of the playroom. Avoid shouting announcements, flashing lights, and ringing bells to alert children. Such techniques startle and frustrate children when they are suddenly interrupted, and may discourage co-operation. When loud and intrusive announcements are made to "tidy up," the overall tone and activity level of the room often escalate to unsafe levels.

❖ Keep transitions and routines flexible enough to meet the needs of individual children. If a child (or the child's family) is uncomfortable with using the toilet in the presence of others, provide a private time for that child. If children are unaccustomed to the food being offered, explore ways to accommodate them — perhaps they can bring familiar food from home.

❖ Offer a range of rest activities from sleep to quiet relaxation (such as reading or listening to music). Not all young children need to sleep every day, but all will benefit from a quiet, relaxing routine.

❖ Balance types of activities and expectations to suit the children's daily physiological rhythm. Morning is when energy peaks, so plan energetic activities for the morning, but reduce the amount of activity as lunch time approaches, when the children are tired and hungry.

❖ Schedules should reflect the needs of the children. It is easy to slip into the rut of imposing your priorities, for example, rushing slow eaters so that staff breaks start at exact times. Schedules should allow for flexibility at routine times.

❖ Allow the children to participate in planning the schedule as much as possible. They will be much more enthusiastic about following a schedule that they feel they "own." Negotiating with the children to shorten a circle time and go outdoors earlier than usual shows that you are responsible to them and respect their ideas.

NUTRITION

Young children who are fortunate enough to be well-nourished and cared for glow with good health. They are alert and responsive, and able to learn and grow. In contrast, undernourished children are often pale, listless, and unable to enter into play with enthusiasm.

As children grow, their diet should include foods from the four food groups, with a minimum of extra fats, salt, and sugar. These groups include breads and pasta, fruits and vegetables, dairy products, and meat (including fish, poultry, and legumes). A variety of foods from these four groups will keep children healthy. Many young children have individual patterns and preferences for certain foods as well as intense dislikes. Adults need to respect these food preferences and to honour them as much as possible when serving snacks and meals. Provide choices and some variety (breads, fruits, vegetables, cheese) so that children will not go hungry if they do not like the main dish. As long as the menu is made up of healthy choices, a child will not need to eat everything being served in order to get a balanced diet. Remember, a happy eater is a healthy eater, even if the child's diet seems somewhat unorthodox.

Healthy foods give children energy for play and learning. Early childhood settings should limit the servings of non-nutritious junk food and avoid offering sweet or salty snacks on a regular basis. Although children enjoy cakes and cookies — and these can be offered as an occasional special treat — for good nutrition ensure that snacks, as well as meals, reflect primarily the four food groups. The best snacks are raw vegetables and fruit, and fresh, clean, cool water and milk. Care should be taken in slicing vegetables and fruits for children so that they do not choke on the pieces. Your choice of foods teaches children good eating habits that will benefit them over a lifetime.

Children need plenty of good, nourishing food, but they should not have to confront too much at one time. Small servings, with as many "seconds" as the children want, are easier for them to handle than large, adult-size helpings, which discourage some children from eating.

Children go through growth spurts that affect their appetites. For a few weeks they might "eat like a horse," and then they enter a different phase when they only pick at whatever you serve them. By understanding these patterns, adults can adjust the size and number of servings without a fuss. Mealtime should be a pleasant experience, and not an occasion for argument and trying to get children to comply with the adults' ideas about how much food children should eat.

Early childhood educators can widen the children's experiences of a variety of foods. At the same time, children from cultures accustomed to different foods and children from families who have specific diets, such as vegetarian, need to be accommodated. A variety of foods — mangoes, pita, figs — can be an interesting alternative to apples and celery.

When you accept a child into an early childhood program, finding out about any food allergies is a priority. You need to know whether certain foods or food additives make a child ill. In general, plan snacks and meals that avoid foods that most commonly cause allergic reactions: peanuts, chocolate, and

spices. It is also best to avoid foods containing additives, for example, monosodium glutamate, which can cause headaches and hyperactive behaviour.

Learning as much as possible about good nutrition should be as much a part of your training as an early childhood educator as curriculum planning. Without a healthy diet, children cannot benefit from even the most excellent curriculum.

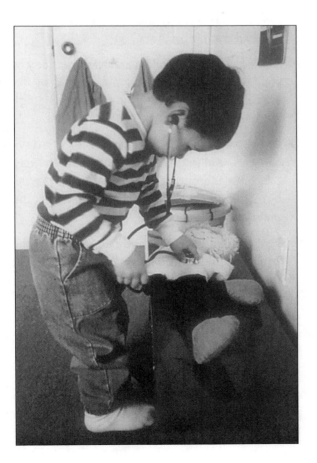

SUMMARY

Well-planned indoor and outdoor spaces stimulate motivation, willingness to face challenges, and excitement for discovery. Children play more fruitfully, gain independence, and feel confident and competent when the environment promotes developmentally appropriate activities and behaviours. Children need opportunities to make choices from a wide range of options, develop problem-solving skills, and become able to take risks in a safe environment. In a well-designed setting where supervision is easy, the stage is set for children to gain these skills while the adults are free to provide warmth, encouragement, and support, and to facilitate learning.

A well-designed program provides a sense of security and meets children's needs through child-centred routines and careful attention to individual differences in preferences and habits. Good nutrition practices round out the day in quality early childhood settings. Planning for the well-being of staff and family members ensures that all experience the early childhood setting as an inviting and supportive place.

REVIEW QUESTIONS

❶ Describe and compare the effect on children of well-planned indoor play space and poorly planned indoor play space.

❷ If indoor space is well-organized, why do children also need outdoor play space?

❸ Describe appropriate toys and materials for ten different learning centres that should be included in an early childhood education program.

❹ Why do we recommend that materials be available consistently and for long periods of time?

❺ What are the three types of play units that should be included in a playroom?

❻ What are the four components of a schedule?

❼ Describe the main principles to keep in mind when you plan a schedule.

DISCUSSION QUESTIONS

❶ The children do not seem to enjoy going outdoors in early winter. Discuss what you could do to make this time more fun for them. Include in your discussion the equipment, toys, and materials you would use, as well as the role of the adult.

❷ You have been asked by parents to describe the value of having learning centres set up in your room. What information would you include in your response?

❸ How can you prepare the physical layout and decor of the centre to give a message to parents that you want them to participate in the centre?

❹ One of your colleagues believes that children should try everything on their plate before being served fruit, which is normally the last part of the meal. Do you agree? Discuss this question from the point of view of a child-centred approach.

ACTIVITIES

❶ Observe the playroom in two different day-care centres. Make a list of the areas in the physical environment that support the developmental needs of the children. Compare the two playrooms and summarize the strengths and weaknesses of each. Then make a list of improvements you would suggest.

❷ Sketch the layout of the two rooms you visited. Then draw up your "ideal" design for a playroom and an outdoor space for an early childhood education program.

❸ Find out who is the child-care licensing body in your province or territory. Make a list of the areas that must be addressed to meet their regulations.

❹ Conduct an interview with the director of a day-care centre to find out the rationale for the way the centre is organized. How does the organization of the room and the scheduling reflect the philosophy of the centre?

❺ Visit another day-care centre and interview the adult who is responsible for the safety check. Ask to accompany this person as she or he does a routine check, then summarize what was done.

FURTHER READING

Dodge, D., and L. Colger. (1992). *The Creative Curriculum for Early Childhood.* **Washington, DC: Teaching Strategies.**
This helpful book covers a variety of topics including room arrangements, designing the learning environment, and setting up learning centres.

Esbensen, S.B. (1990). Designing the early childhood setting. In I.M. Doxey, ed., *Child Care and Education: Canadian Dimensions*, pp. 178—91. Scarborough, ON: Nelson Canada.

This chapter describes a process for designing and organizing indoor and outdoor play spaces into zones that encourage a variety of learning experiences, interactions, and play.

Frost, J.L. (1992). *Play and Playscapes*. New York: Delmar.

A detailed discussion of the planning of play spaces and the selection and design of equipment to enhance play experiences.

Marotz, L.R., J.M. Rush, and M.Z. Cross. (1989). *Health, Safety and Nutrition for the Young Child*. Albany, NY: Delmar.

Covers a range of topics that have an impact on the well-being and safety of children in group-care settings.

REFERENCES

Brewer, J. (1992). *Introduction to Early Childhood Education: Preschool through Primary Grades*. Needham Heights, MA: Allyn & Bacon.

Canada Mortgage and Housing Corporation. (1978). *Play Spaces for Preschoolers*. Advisory document prepared by P. Hill, S. Esbensen, and W. Rock. Ottawa: CMHC.

Canadian Standards Association. (1990). *A Guideline on Children's Play Spaces and Equipment*. CAN/CSA-Z614-M90.

Doherty-Derkowski, G. (1995). *Quality Matters: Excellence in Early Childhood Programs*. Don Mills, ON: Addison-Wesley.

Esbensen, S.B. (1984). *Hidden Hazards on Playgrounds for Children*. Hull, PQ: Université du Québec à Hull.

Esbensen, S.B. (1987). *The Early Childhood Education Playground: An Outdoor Classroom*. Ypsilanti, MI: High Scope Press.

Esbensen, S.B. (1990). Designing the early childhood setting. In I.M. Doxey, ed., *Child Care and Education: Canadian Dimensions*, pp. 178—91. Scarborough, ON: Nelson Canada.

Feeny, S., D. Christensen, and E. Moravcik. (1987). *Who Am I in the Lives of Children?* Columbus, OH: Merrill.

Frost, J.L. (1992). *Play and Playscapes*. New York: Delmar.

Kostelnik, M.J., A.K. Soderman, and A.P. Whiren. (1993). *Developmentally Appropriate Programs in Early Childhood Education*. New York: Merrill.

Kritchevsky, S., E. Prescott, and L. Walling. (1977). *Planning Environments for Young Children: Physical Space*. Washington, DC: National Association for the Education of Young Children.

Lovell, P., and T. Harms. (1985). How can playgrounds be improved? A rating scale. *Young Children* 40 (3): 3—8.

Ministry of Culture and Recreation, Ontario. (1982). *A Guide to Creative Playground Equipment*. Toronto: Government of Ontario.

National Association for the Education of Young Children. (1986, September). Position statement on developmentally appropriate practice in early childhood education programs serving children from birth to age 8. *Young Children* 41 (6): 3.

Sciarra, D., and A. Dorsey. (1979). *Developing and Administering a Child Care Centre*. Boston: Houghton Mifflin.

Wach, T.D., and G. Gruen. (1982). *Early Experiences and Human Development*. New York: Plenum.

Walsh, P. (1988). *Early Childhood Playground: Planning an Outside Learning Environment*. Melbourne, Australia: Martin Educational in association with Robert Andersen and Associates.

Yeates, M., D. McKenna, C. Warberg, and K. Chandler. (1990). *Administering Early Childhood Settings: The Canadian Perspective*. Columbus, OH: Merrill.

CHAPTER 10
Designing a Curriculum

✏ **Overview**

✏ **A Portrait of Early Childhood Curriculum**

✏ **A Curriculum for All Children**
 ◆ Reflecting Cultural Diversity
 ◆ Reflecting Diversity of Individuals
 ◆ Reflecting Diversity in Development

✏ **A Curriculum for the Whole Child**
 ◆ A Comprehensive Curriculum
 ◆ Safeguarding the Qualities of Childhood

✏ **A Developmentally Appropriate Curriculum**
 ◆ Planning for Individual Children
 ◆ The Influence of Piaget
 ◆ The Risk of Miseducation

✏ **A Curriculum Based on Play**
 ◆ Constructivist Theory
 ◆ What Do We Mean by Play?
 ◆ Developing through Play
 ◆ Learning through Play
 ◆ Characteristics of a Play-Based Curriculum

✐ **Making Decisions about the Curriculum**

◆ Responding to the Community

◆ Consulting with Children and Parents

◆ Legislative Requirements

✐ **The Emergent Curriculum**

✐ **Observing and Evaluating the Curriculum**

◆ Ongoing Observation

◆ Curriculum Evaluation

◆ Personal Reflection

✐ **Summary**

✐ **Review Questions**

✐ **Discussion Questions**

✐ **Activities**

✐ **Further Reading**

✐ **References**

OVERVIEW

The early childhood curriculum consists of all aspects of children's experience throughout the day. It encompasses caring and respectful interpersonal relationships, a welcoming physical space, flexible and satisfying routines, and stimulating experiences that enhance learning.

The early childhood curriculum is based on certain values and beliefs. Our profession celebrates individual children and their diversity of background, culture, ability, and personality. We recognize the benefits of diversity and design curriculum to build on it and to encourage individually charted developmental paths.

Through our curriculum, we celebrate and protect the experience of childhood — joyous, playful, exciting, active, and full of wonder — and with thoughtful planning and evaluation, we seek to ensure that children's eager, enthusiastic experience of life is safeguarded within their daily experiences and interactions. Of course, childhood also includes pain and insecurities, and for many children, poverty and family stress denies them much of the kind of childhood we described. The early childhood curriculum incorporates support and caring for children under stress.

The early childhood curriculum supports the whole child, providing care, emotional support, and learning opportunities. As part of protecting childhood, the early childhood curriculum is designed for the present, and does not pressure or rush children to achieve or perform. In the early years, children develop lifelong learning attitudes and abilities. Therefore, early childhood educators carefully nurture a positive self-concept, the developing sense of competence, and the increasing expression of initiative as vital to both present and future learning and development.

The early childhood curriculum is based on a strong body of knowledge and theory that guides educators in providing a program based on play, and in selecting developmentally appropriate materials and experiences that enhance learning for all children.

This chapter discusses the underlying values, principles, and practices of a curriculum for young children from a Canadian perspective. Planning a curriculum for young children is described as a process based on the needs and interests of children. The framework for designing a curriculum lays the foundation for the remaining chapters, which focus more specifically on areas of the early childhood curriculum.

By the end of this chapter, you will be able to

❖ understand the foundations of the early childhood curriculum;

❖ outline the principles of preferred and current practice in early childhood education;

❖ explain the methods for providing a multicultural, anti-bias, and inclusive curriculum for young children;

❖ understand the value of a play-based and constructivist approach to early childhood curriculum;

❖ explain the concept of developmentally appropriate practice in early childhood education;

❖ describe curriculum design and the process of designing an effective early childhood curriculum;

❖ outline strategies for observation and evaluation of curriculum.

BOX 10.1 PRINCIPLES OF EARLY CHILDHOOD EDUCATION

Early childhood educators

◆ welcome and value every child, *respecting and accepting diversity;*

◆ recognize their responsibility to meet the needs of the *whole child,* including physical care, caring relationships, and learning opportunities;

◆ use a curriculum based on knowledge of development and encourage learning through *developmentally appropriate practice;*

◆ recognize that children *construct knowledge* through their exploration and mastery of the environment, and use a *play-based curriculum* that supports the natural processes of development and learning.

A PORTRAIT OF EARLY CHILDHOOD CURRICULUM

It is Tuesday morning. Imagine you are visiting an early childhood playroom. You see immediately that the children are active and having a good time. Sara and Ishmael are giggling as they pour purple, bubbly water through funnels and tubes at the water table. You wonder if that is the source of the scent of peppermint. In the dramatic play centre, Robbie, dressed in high heels and a neck tie, is covering up his "baby" and serving tea and cookies (cut from construction paper) to Lesley, the teacher. Mavi and Simone, the firefighters, are halfway up the climber spraying the fire with their hoses, while René, another teacher, watches to ensure safety.

Across the room, Charise and Michel are serving themselves a snack, choosing from kiwi fruit, pita bread, and cheese. When Charise spills her juice, she immediately gets the sponge from the counter and wipes it up. "There, that's done," she states.

The sound of classical music provides the background for Sasha and Juanita's flannel board presentation. They are performing their version of Mrs. McDonald's farm for an audience of one visiting parent. Rhana is finishing a block tower, adding the last block as she stretches up on tiptoes. When the tower comes crashing down, Lesley moves quickly from the dramatic play centre to make sure Rhana is not hurt: "It's too bad that your tower fell down; you must be disappointed. You worked hard to build it so tall. Would you like to build it up again?" Her ready support comforts Rhana, who eagerly begins again.

At the fish tank, Douglas has just sprinkled food into the water and is carefully marking a check in the box beside "Tuesday" on the chart. Emmy runs over to feed the fish as well. Douglas says "No, Emmy," and carefully explains that the fish are fed only once a day because if they eat too much they get sick. He shows her the check mark he has just made. Lesley watches from a distance and smiles as she sees that Douglas has successfully resolved a potential clash with Emmy.

Bashir has just returned from his cubby, carrying his favourite doll and a small train. He clutches them close as he backs into Lesley's lap where she is sitting on the floor. She gives him a warm hug and a big smile. Both are content to sit and enjoy the contact and the company as they watch the others. Beside them, Marissa starts singing "Wheels on the Bus," and Lesley joins in.

As you look around, you notice that the walls at the creative area display Inuit stone printing and Japanese fans. You see a globe and a colourful poster of flags from around the world in the reading area. The dramatic play centre includes chopsticks and a wok alongside plastic sandwich fixings. In the dress-up area are saris, kimonos, a sombrero, a grass skirt, and many bright accessories. In the window hangs brightly coloured beadwork of Native Canadian origin. Signs and posters display words in several languages.

You cannot help but think that this is a great place for children. There are surprisingly few conflicts or disagreements — all the children seem to be involved and content. The adults are interacting with the children and are enjoying them.

To a visitor, this program may seem unstructured and unplanned. While children are busily playing, the adults' supervision appears to be minimal. However, what you are really seeing is an excellent example of what is currently considered to be the best possible curriculum for young children. It is the result of a blend of a philosophy that is child-centred, based on the early childhood educators' knowledge of children's development and learning characteristics — a program that is play-based with careful, behind-the-scenes planning and selection of materials and activities.

This could be a child-care centre, a nursery or preschool program, or a junior or senior kindergarten. In Canada, there are many similarities among programs and curricula for young children, regardless of the setting. A review of current literature on theory and practice (see the list of references) reveals that there is a common ground on which early childhood education is based. This common ground has been validated by the work of the Canadian Child Care Federation in its discussions with early childhood educators across Canada in its preparation of "National Standards for Training in Early Childhood Care and Education" (draft, 1994).

A CURRICULUM FOR ALL CHILDREN

Reflecting Cultural Diversity

An early childhood curriculum reflects the society in which it exists. Canada is a country formed on the foundations of three major cultures — the First Nations, the French, and the English — and embraces many other cultures. A Canadian early childhood education curriculum therefore incorporates the heritage and vision of these cultures.

Our Canadian Charter of Rights and Freedoms guarantees equal rights for all Canadians regardless of differences in culture, gender, age, religion, or ability. As Canadians, this belief underlies our sense of respect for diversity, our valuing of the individual's right to choose, and our attitude of tolerance toward different ways of doing things. A Canadian early childhood curriculum reflects these values of tolerance, understanding, and respect for the distinctiveness of other cultures and respect for fundamental human rights for all people.

We all share a multicultural heritage to some degree in that we have been, and continue to be, influenced by many different people, experiences, and cultures. Who we are is determined in part by the heritage and history of our families. Each of us reflects some common and some distinct aspects in our personal heritage, including family traditions, rituals, and celebrations, as well as differing degrees of knowledge of our larger societal values and traditions.

When we come from a common background of experience, we assume a common understanding of how and why things are the way they are. However, even with similar backgrounds we see the same experiences differently and must search to find a common understanding. It is erroneous to categorize people according to race, religion, gender, politics, economics, values, or lifestyle. For example, French Canadians are not all the same, English Canadians are not all the same, nor are all Asian Canadians nor all Canadian farmers or plumbers or artists. People all have individual differences, even though certain groups share a common belief system and cultural traditions and values.

The early childhood curriculum welcomes all children as valued individuals and incorporates positive approaches to cultural diversity. Creating a multicultural curriculum is not about singling out and perpetuating stereotyped images of diverse racial or ethnic groups; rather, it emphasizes and encourages children to understand, appreciate, and value diversity in all forms, including heritage, traditions, and customs. "Multi-cultural education does not attempt to eliminate differences. It builds on cultural and racial diversity as a strength in our classrooms and in our Canadian society" (Mock 1990, p. 110).

A multicultural approach to early childhood education recognizes the tremendous impact that education has on the attitudes and beliefs of children, and takes the initiative to provide a curriculum that values and fosters respect and appreciation for the diversity of people's lives. Multicultural education helps each child to

develop a positive self-concept that incorporates and values his or her unique personal and cultural heritage, and to accept others regardless of their background, lifestyle, culture, or race.

The early childhood education curriculum reflects cultural sensitivity most strongly through the attitudes of the teachers, who value and respect diversity and do not expect or require any children to conform to a particular model, but allow them each to be who they are. The evidence of a multicultural curriculum is in the choice of materials, furniture and decor, and activities and experiences. In Canada, all early childhood education programs must incorporate a rich variety of experiences from our First Nations and French heritages to emphasize their significant contribution to the development of our country and to balance the dominance of the English–Western European influence. In addition, the multicultural curriculum must reflect the rich diversity of the many other cultural groups who have made Canada their home.

DESIGNING A MULTICULTURAL CURRICULUM

All children have a variety of experiences outside the early childhood education setting. You must make every effort to learn about the lives of the children, noting what is familiar and unfamiliar to them, so that you can incorporate familiar experiences, materials, and language to help the children feel comfortable in your program. You must allow children to participate in unfamiliar experiences at their own pace. You can provide exposure these while helping all the children to recognize similarities and individual differences or preferences as valid and worthy of respect.

Language is one of the most unique parts of any culture. Therefore, a multicultural curriculum includes many languages and styles of communication. It is a good idea to learn a few basic phrases in the children's languages — a child's name, a greeting, and some key phrases for meeting basic needs, such as "Are you hungry?" and "Would you like to play?" Hearing you use their familiar language will go a very long way in helping children feel more comfortable and accepted.

Another part of the multicultural curriculum involves determining how to incorporate cultural diversity into all of the experiences you provide. Children benefit from having both familiar and novel toys, pictures, and materials, and from hearing both familiar and novel language and music. Including artifacts and music from all the children's cultures enhances their sense of self and pride. As well, exposure to experiences and customs from a mix of cultures increases awareness, understanding, and tolerance in all children. The

development of a shared understanding and awareness of similarities will begin the process of recognizing and eliminating stereotypes and injustices.

We want to emphasize that providing a multicultural curriculum does not mean that you plan isolated activities or themes that focus solely on different cultural traditions or stereotyped information for a block of time. The multicultural aspects of curriculum are embedded in all aspects of the program: pictures, materials, music, and food from many countries and cultures are always available. Language diversity can also be provided through posters, books, and music. Discussions of any topics should incorporate diverse points of view so that children become accustomed to, and accepting of, diversity rather than seeing "a multicultural experience" as something special, isolated, or unique.

BOX 10.2 INCORPORATING MULTICULTURAL INFLUENCES IN THE PHYSICAL ENVIRONMENT

WALLS

◆ Posters and photographs of activities representing people and activities from various cultures
◆ Wall hangings reflecting materials, patterns, and designs exposing children to textures, forms, and colours from various cultures
◆ Words to familiar and simple songs in many languages (complete with phonetic clues to ensure proper pronunciation)

FLOORS

◆ Mats, rugs, and cushions from various parts of the world
◆ Low tables with cushions, rather than chairs

SHELVES

◆ Toys and dolls from various countries
◆ Tapes of music from all over the world, with a variety of words, rhythms, and instruments
◆ Musical instruments from all over the world, chosen for their simplicity, variety of sound and tone, cultural distinctiveness, and durability

Source: Based on Pam Schurch. (1990). A multicultural perspective on programming for toddlers. In Anne Stonehouse, ed., *Trusting Toddlers: Planning for One- to Three-Year-Olds in Child Care Centers.* St. Paul, MN: Toys 'n' Things Press.

Reflecting Diversity of Individuals

Developing a self-concept is one of the major developmental tasks in the preschool years. The inexperience of young children usually means that they are just beginning to develop attitudes about certain qualities or activities that define or limit who they are and what they can achieve. Knowledge about similarities and differences is important to children, and they work hard to define themselves as members of a certain group based on their own beliefs of what it means to be a member of that group.

As you read in Chapter 7, children are susceptible to the attitudes and biases of others around them when trying to understand who they are. For example, adults often comment to young girls about how pretty they look, while young boys are told they are strong or brave. Children are socialized in these and many more subtle ways to develop a gender-based identity that reflects society's stereotypes.

Early childhood educators must be continually aware of, and sensitive to, their own biases and guard against communicating these unwittingly to children. You can reinforce the right of all children to make their own choices in play and activities without prejudging what is more or less appropriate for their gender, age, ability, background, or culture.

DESIGNING AN ANTI-BIAS CURRICULUM

In an anti-bias curriculum, the early childhood educator models and conveys respect for differences and encourages children to recognize that many options are open to them regardless of gender, age, ability, race, or culture. All materials, activities, and interactions are carefully selected and implemented to ensure that children are presented with a wide range of role models, choices, and information designed to minimize stereotypes in attitudes.

An anti-bias curriculum supports and encourages the expression of individual characteristics and interests without judgement. Girls, as well as boys, are supported in their play with trucks, blocks, and sports equipment. Boys can feel free to care for dolls, choose dresses and purses in the housekeeping centre, and make jewellery. The wise early childhood educator does not pass judgement on children's choices, knowing that they need to experiment and try out a wide range of activities and roles. For example, the 4-year-old who wants to be the baby may be expressing his own mixed feelings about growing up, or may be trying to see what it feels like to be a baby so he can relate to the new baby at home.

Like the multicultural curriculum, the anti-bias curriculum comes more from the choice of materials, vocabulary, and experiences than from isolated lessons or topics. An anti-bias attitude is embedded in all aspects of curriculum and is experienced by children as an acceptance and encouragement of diversity in roles, options, and preferences. Experiences and materials are considered carefully to challenge stereotypes and to ensure that children

BOX 10.3 AN ANTI-BIAS ATMOSPHERE

Respect for diversity is reflected in books, pictures, materials, visitors, and other experiences, which should portray

- diversity in family lifestyles, including single parents, one- and two-working-parent families, mothers and fathers in the home, extended families, interracial families, families with differently abled members, and families from different income levels;
- men and women of different ages and racial/ethnic groups doing jobs in the home;

- men and women of different ages and racial/ethnic groups doing a variety of jobs outside the home;
- children and adults from a variety of racial and cultural groups, shown in their families, at work, and at play;
- elderly people doing a variety of activities;
- differently abled people of all ages and backgrounds working, being with their families, and playing;
- diversity within each racial or ethnic group.

Source: Based on E. Jones and L. Derman-Sparks. (1992). Meeting the challenge of diversity. *Young Children* 47 (2): 12–18.

see a wide range of opportunities being modelled and portrayed, no matter who they are.

Anti-bias education is a comprehensive philosophy and methodology that empowers children in all aspects of their development and challenges all forms of bias, prejudice, stereotyping and discrimination. … In a world beset with inequality and injustice, the field of child care contains within it the hope, optimism and belief that we can make a difference. *(Chud 1993, p. 18)*

Reflecting Diversity in Development

The early childhood curriculum is a curriculum for every child. In an inclusive curriculum, each child, regardless of background, ability, or needs, should experience acceptance, belonging, and successful participation with peers in the program. As our society moves increasingly toward the integration of all people, regardless of individual challenges and needs, you are increasingly likely to have children with a wide range of developmental

diversity in your groups. A philosophy that includes all children is implemented through acceptance and respect within interpersonal relationships as well as through careful planning of the physical and learning environments. This approach to education is known as **inclusive education**, and also as **integration** or mainstreaming.

Inclusive education means that you welcome all children into your program, valuing each as a unique individual who has much to offer. You will need to develop an in-depth understanding of all aspects of development, including both typical and atypical patterns and stages, along with identifying children's levels and needs. You will also need to plan creatively to ensure that your experiences and activities are open-ended and that children of diverse abilities can benefit from the curriculum. Most children naturally benefit from a program without separate planning for individual children. However, sometimes additional planning is required for children with developmental differences or special needs.

DESIGNING AN INCLUSIVE CURRICULUM

To design an inclusive curriculum, you need to know and understand each child as an individual, and to understand the background of all the children. Your planning must take into account the children's individual experiences and the ideas, feelings, and knowledge they bring to the program (Kostelnik, et al. 1993).

Louisa, for example, has had limited opportunities to socialize because of health problems that required much medical intervention. She has had extended opportunity for cognitive development because her parents could provide these opportunities while she was at home or in hospital. In planning for Louisa, free play, as well as small- and large-group activities and games, are a priority. Ben and Sammy, on the other hand, are from families who constantly battle poverty. In their homes, toys, books, and creative supplies, as well as space for play, are limited. They will need as much exposure to free play, hands-on activities, and learning opportunities as possible to enhance cognitive and creative development.

Many children with special needs or developmental differences benefit from the well-rounded, comprehensive, and developmentally appropriate program you provide with little need for major modifications or intervention. Some children have needs that require adaptations in equipment, materials, and presentation. Consider each child individually to determine whether there is an area of your curriculum that needs to be emphasized or modified to meet individual needs. A questionnaire for parents can help you identify children who would benefit from additional exposure to specific areas of the curriculum.

Alison, for example, has spina bifida and as a result has limited mobility. She walks slowly, relying on the support of a walker. In planning the curriculum, it has been a challenge to ensure that her needs for appropriate gross-motor activities are met. It is not enough to depend on the outdoor equipment to meet this need; it has been necessary to ensure that each area is accessible and that a variety of materials that can be manipulated with only one hand are available. In planning for physical activities for the group, ensuring Alison's successful involvement has meant that many of the activities are designed for a sitting position, emphasizing arm and upper-body movements, rather than emphasizing running and jumping.

With thought and care in your planning, you can ensure that all the children in your program can participate successfully. You likely noticed that the terms "multicultural," "anti-bias," and "inclusive" are variations of the same principle with a different focus. All of these terms remind us of our goal of including and providing every child with meaningful and satisfying experiences. Because the terms overlap, they might be used in similar ways in early childhood education literature.

A CURRICULUM FOR THE WHOLE CHILD

The early childhood curriculum is based on what we know about the needs of young children. Maslow's hierarchy of human needs (in Crain 1992) reminds us that children have all kinds of needs. The early childhood curriculum must respond to all of these needs — to the whole child — to be effective (Hendrick 1993).

A Comprehensive Curriculum

Early childhood educators who support the "whole child" philosophy believe that all developmental areas are important, and that no one area deserves more attention in the curriculum than another. Children who do not have access to the full range of experiences will be disadvantaged. For example, programs that do not provide a range of musical activities are depriving children of a rich multicultural experience, a highly enjoyable source of relaxation or stimulation, and a sense of belonging and identification with diverse groups and ages. Limiting sensory or creative activities because of the messiness or space requirements denies children an outlet for creativity, and you run the risk of more stress-related behaviour. Programs that do not provide adequate literature and storytelling experiences limit the development of literacy.

Although we must address all areas of development in our planning, providing isolated activities that focus on only one area ignores the way that children learn and develop. Developmental principles and experience with children tell us that development in each area is interconnected with the other areas. When Jeremy does a puzzle of body parts, he is developing skills in planning and problem solving, as well as using visual attention skills, practising fine-motor skills to manipulate the puzzle pieces, and developing body concept and self-awareness. Upon completion of the puzzle, he experiences a sense of mastery, satisfaction, and pleasure in his accomplishment. Isolating each of these processes into individual activities for Jeremy would seem silly by comparison.

Through an integrated curriculum, you help children make connections among various experiences and bits of information by carrying a topic of interest into a number of aspects of the curriculum. Box 10.4 offers an example of how all areas of development can be enhanced through a variety of related experiences.

BOX 10.4 AN EXAMPLE OF INTEGRATED CURRICULUM

One of the teachers is expecting a baby and has shared this information with the children, who have lots of enthusiastic questions for her. This interest is incorporated into the curriculum in a number of ways. In the book corner are several books about families and babies. Specific props are added to the housekeeping centre, where the children are very eager to diaper, bathe, and feed their "babies." A parent with a new baby visits the centre and allows children to observe the infant, answering questions and validating the important role of the big sister and big brother. The mother displays some special infant toys, which are enjoyed by many children. Following a discussion of how infants have not yet learned how to walk, the children spend a hilarious period attempting to carry out their play without walking. This generates further discussion about the advantages of growing up and learning new skills, as well as sensitivity to a child in the group who has a physical disability and is constantly challenged by the task of walking. The children then begin to talk about themselves as babies, and parents are encouraged to send in pictures of each child as an infant and as a toddler. The photos become an excellent stimulant for discussions on individual similarities and differences, and on how everyone grows and changes as they get older. The children draw pictures to add to the photographs to make an individual journal for each child that celebrates his or her uniqueness.

Safeguarding the Qualities of Childhood

What does childhood mean to you? What words would you use to describe it? Young children are curious, active, joyful, enthusiastic, excited, inexperienced, and eager to try anything and everything they see. Young children approach each day as a new adventure, seeking out new experiences, taking on challenges, working with intensity to master new tasks, and doing this happily, noisily, and at a pace they determine themselves.

Childhood can, and should, be a time full of playful, exuberant, and wonderful opportunities and experiences. Adults sometimes envy children for their spontaneity and sense of wonder. As adults, we need to value and cherish this period of time when children are children.

Everyone knows that this image of a carefree childhood is not true for all children, but it provides a worthwhile vision for the early childhood setting. Young children are vulnerable to family pressures and stress. The curriculum for the early years should be comfortable and supportive, allowing children the freedom to be who they are. It should be a refuge from stress — not a contributor to stress — as much as possible, so that children can truly experience and enjoy their childhood.

A DEVELOPMENTALLY APPROPRIATE CURRICULUM

One of the main goals and responsibilities of the early childhood educator is to provide experiences that will enhance the child's development and learning. The best way to do this is through the natural process of learning (Elkind 1988; Hendrick 1992; Gordon & Browne 1993). Think about the incredible amount of learning that takes place in the first two or three years of life. Children do most, if not all, of this learning on their own, completely naturally, as they follow their curiosity, interact with other people, and explore and manipulate the environment during play.

Observing young children learning naturally and spontaneously gives insight into several aspects of the natural learning process of this age group.

❖ Children learn by being active, doing, touching, feeling, seeing, and trying out new experiences. They integrate all of these sensory experiences to form ideas and knowledge about their world.

❖ Children engage in learning spontaneously as they explore and manipulate their environment. They do not need to be pressured or coaxed to learn.

❖ Children learn through interactions with others through the processes of observing, imitating, and questioning.

❖ Children learn by themselves, although others have a role in facilitating and supporting the learning process.

Theories about how preschool children learn and develop support these observations and advocate active learning through play (Goffin 1994; Crain 1992; Bredekamp 1987). In the early childhood curriculum, we endeavour to create an environment that encourages this natural process of learning.

Understanding the common patterns and sequences of development of the young child is essential when we design a curriculum to enhance development and learning. The developmental perspective has been so strongly ingrained in our thinking about early childhood education that the concept of developmentally appropriate practice and curriculum is the core of current literature in the field of early education (Bredekamp 1987).

Human development research indicates that there are universal, predictable sequences of growth and change that occur in children during the first nine years of life. These predictable changes occur in all domains of development — physical, emotional, social and cognitive. Knowledge of typical development of children within the age span served by the program provides a framework from which teachers prepare the learning environment and plan appropriate experiences. *(Bredekamp 1987, p. 2)*

Planning for Individual Children

Throughout this book, we emphasize the need to understand the stages of development. However, in planning an appropriate curriculum for young children we also have a word of caution. Because of individual differences in the pattern and pace of development, no two children in a group will be at the same stage in all areas. Achievement of developmental milestones can vary in the early years by several months or more. The age levels we put on certain skills or characteristics are very general, and never match a child's age exactly. Thus, in a group of children all celebrating their third birthday, the range of development could

---

BOX 10.5 PRINCIPLES OF DEVELOPMENTALLY APPROPRIATE PRACTICE

- ◆ Developmentally appropriate curriculum provides for all areas of a child's development: physical, emotional, social and cognitive, through an integrated approach.
- ◆ Appropriate curriculum planning is based on a teacher's observation and recordings of each child's special interests and developmental progress.
- ◆ Curriculum planning emphasizes learning as an interactive process. Teachers prepare the environment for children to learn through active exploration and interaction with adults, other children and materials.
- ◆ Learning activities and materials should be concrete, real and relevant to the lives of young children.
- ◆ Programs provide for a wider range of developmental interests and abilities than the chronological age range of the group would suggest. Adults are prepared to meet the needs of children who exhibit unusual interests and skills outside the normal developmental range.
- ◆ Teachers provide a variety of activities and materials; teachers increase the difficulty, complexity and challenge of an activity as children develop understanding and skills.
- ◆ Adults provide opportunities for children to choose from among a variety of activities, materials and equipment; and time to explore through active ... engagement with materials and activities and extend children's learning by asking questions or making suggestions that stimulate their thinking.
- ◆ Multicultural and nonsexist experiences, materials and equipment should be provided for children of all ages.
- ◆ Adults provide a balance of rest and active movement.
- ◆ Outdoor experiences should be provided for children of all ages.

Source: Sue Bredekamp, ed. (1987). *Developmentally Appropriate Practice in Early Childhood Programs Serving Children from Birth through Age 8* (expanded ed.). Washington, DC: National Association for the Education of Young Children, pp. 3–8. © by NAEYC. Reprinted with permission.

appear to be from just over the 2-year level to just under a 4-year level. Moreover, for an individual child, one or more areas of development could appear to be "advanced" while other areas are not as well-developed compared with age norms. This variability is normal and natural.

The reality of variation in development affects planning. Just because the children in your group are approximately the same age does not mean they are all ready to learn the same things or are interested in or able to meet similar learning challenges. The overall guidelines for planning for 3-year-olds do not meet the needs of every 3-year-old. Individual appropriateness, or taking into consideration the developmental patterns of each individual child, is essential when planning for the development of every child. "Experiences should match the child's developing abilities, while also challenging the child's interest and understanding" (Bredekamp 1987, p. 2).

Danielle, an early childhood education student on field practicum, wanted to bring in a creative activity for a group of 3- and 4-year-olds. She had in mind having the children make a puppet face by cutting and pasting various shapes of paper onto a paper plate. She checked with Marian, her supervisor, to find out if this would be a suitable activity for the group. Marian advised her to sit with the children at the creative table for the next two days and observe what each child was able to do. As Danielle observed and made notes, she was absolutely amazed at the differences among the children. Mickie, age 4½, created a three-dimensional flower by carefully cutting circles and gluing them one on top of the other. Violet, the same age, could barely manipulate the scissors and confined her cutting to snips around the edge of the paper. Richard glued circles in the shape of a larger circle and then created a clown face in the centre, in propor-

tion. Sally wanted to make a face too, and was pleased when a few shapes stuck to the paper on which she had spread glue everywhere. Jeffrey drew a person with only a head and two stick legs, while Paula's person had clothing, fingers, hair, and ears. Feeling quite uncertain now, Danielle again approached Marian with her observations: "I think that some would find this puppet too hard, but Mickie, Richard, and Paula might find it too simple and be bored. What should I do?"

Marian wisely suggested that Danielle make the activity open-ended, without a specific end product in mind. A collage activity with the paper plates, some precut shapes, and lots of interesting scraps of material, yarn, and paper would provide plenty of variety and different degrees of challenge to allow each child to participate successfully. At the end of the next day, Danielle was most pleased to be able to display an interesting collection of unique collages ranging from a pig's face and a snowman to an apple with a worm, and including several abstract and colourful designs.

As Danielle learned, even a developmentally appropriate activity must be planned and tailored to individual skill and developmental levels. The early childhood educator must be observant, sensitive, and knowledgeable in order to recognize the individual patterns of development within the overall stages.

The Influence of Piaget

One of the most influential theorists on the concept of developmentally appropriate educational practice was Jean Piaget. His study of child development gave rise to the theory that the quality of thinking is different at various stages of cognitive development (Ginsburg & Opper 1969; Crain 1992). Like the younger child, preschoolers learn most effectively when they can incorporate sensory and motor information gained by active involvement and manipulation into the learning process. They are still a few years away from the next stage, when learning can occur through symbolic and mental representations of relationships, ideas, and concepts.

The 2- to 7-year-olds understand and deal with the world with a unique kind of logic based on their own inexperience and egocentric perceptions. Their understanding is enhanced when they can deal with concrete objects and real (or role-played) situations. The preoperational child's thinking is less effective when trying to deal with abstract concepts or mental manipulation of ideas.

Piaget's work has been a major factor influencing the belief in the importance of developmentally appropriate curriculum. Children's

learning occurs when the approach is matched to the characteristics and qualities of their stage of cognitive development. Effective curriculum therefore needs to provide many opportunities for observation and active involvement. Teaching approaches that expect children to listen passively or manipulate ideas in their heads or on paper are less effective and can be harmful. Read on!

The Risk of Miseducation

David Elkind is an educator who is concerned about the quality and type of education offered to young children. He warns that early formal instruction in academic and other specific skills (ballet, sports, music) is not appropriate for young children, and may in fact be harmful (Elkind 1988). Facing tasks that are beyond the child's developmental level or ability produces frustration, failure, and lack of learning. Too many such experiences diminish the natural motivation and drive of children to attempt and master new challenges, and can create a sense of incompetence or helplessness. Inappropriate educational practice can result in an unacceptably high cost for children in their poor self-concept, low self-esteem, and high levels of stress. Pressuring children to master skills before they are ready can also cause them to think that all learning is stressful and unnatural.

In the early childhood education profession, we believe that our role is to provide for children's learning consistent with current developmental levels and abilities. Educators should avoid curriculum experiences that are overly focussed on what children will do or need tomorrow in favour of meeting the needs and characteristics of the children as they are today. Pressuring or rushing children will not make them smarter nor will it speed up the learning process.

The best ongoing learning opportunity that early childhood educators can provide is an accepting and stimulating environment in which each child can master new experiences at his or her own pace. The successful learner of tomorrow is the child who participates eagerly and actively in play and learning today, experiencing satisfaction and success, which leads to positive self-concept and high self-esteem. These experiences encourage a willingness to take risks and make mistakes — essentials to ongoing learning and accomplishment.

A CURRICULUM BASED ON PLAY

Constructivist Theory

Constructivist theory, the idea that children construct, or create, knowledge through physical and mental activity, developed from the work of Piaget. Children learn through interaction with materials and people. This concept of the child's active participation in learning is central to constructivist theory, which represents another important building block in the foundation of early childhood education.

Physical activity means the exploration, manipulation, and mastery of the environment and the materials provided; mental activity is the thinking and organizing process that is stimulated by the hands-on activity. As they manipulate and try things out, children reflect on their observations and actions. New ideas and experiences are connected to previous learning as children build their own understanding of the world. You will find a more detailed discussion on constructivist theory in Chapter 14.

What Do We Mean by Play?

The implication of developmental theory is that preschool curriculum should be based on play (Hendrick 1992; Gordon & Browne 1993; Bredekamp 1987; Van Hoorn, et al. 1993). This principle has many applications in curriculum design and implementation.

Like most of us, you probably think you have a pretty good idea of what play is — children laughing, busy, running around, making up games, building, pretending to be someone else. Attempts to clearly categorize play have proven more difficult than you might expect. Does play have to be pleasurable? Is it play only if it is spontaneously chosen? What do we mean by play?

First, play is motivated from within the child and is voluntary. Requests to "go play" will not likely result in a meaningful play experience. Most children like to play, find play satisfying, and are motivated by many factors, but the motivation is theirs, not yours. Most children take their play very seriously and become intense and focussed on what they do.

Play belongs to the child. The child is the actor who controls the play and decides how it will be carried out. The child determines the content and the ending of a play incident, according to her or his own perceptions and needs at the time. Thus, a child may choose to play a parent one time, but a dependent baby the next. The doll may be "bad" or "good," the superhero aggressive or protective. Children often resist intrusion and object to others changing the play. Others are welcome to join in only with the consent of the child whose play it is.

Play has its own rules and reality, which are determined by the child. Some play is constrained by reality limitations, but much play is imagined or fantasy-based. Children create or change reality through play and get to experience life in a role other than their own. You will see children playing out situations in ways that do not always accurately represent their experiences. Young children do not fly, fight monsters, or put adults in jail except in play. Many parents are upset to see their children angrily spanking dolls even though they do not spank their children. But play is the way children experiment with their observations about life, and they try out both familiar and unfamiliar roles, both real and imagined issues.

Play has its own purpose. We often think of play as pleasurable, but it might not be. Children often use play experiences to work through emotional content, and this can be stressful, anxiety-producing, and emotionally draining. Children can choose play activities for the purpose of mastering a new skill, such as somersaulting, and at first they might not seem to experience much pleasure. However, the child who perseveres and masters the somersault will, indeed, eventually experience pleasure and pride in that accomplishment.

When play is voluntary, is under the child's control, and meets the child's needs, it is an extremely meaningful activity that is sure to contribute positively to the child's development in many ways.

Developing through Play

Play enhances development in all areas: emotional, social, cognitive, language, and physical development. Because it is the way much development and learning occur in the early years, you need to understand the characteristics and processes of play. The benefits of play for emotional well-being and social and prosocial development are discussed in Chapters 6 and 7. A brief summary reminds us that play provides an important avenue for children to develop self-knowledge, including understanding similarities and differences among people and categories of people, and where they fit in relation to others. Through play, children acquire concepts about self and others as members of different cultural groups, and develop attitudes and values of tolerance and acceptance of diversity.

Play also allows children to try out the roles of others, real and fantasy, which increases their understanding of others and of their own potential and options. Much of children's play involves taking on the roles of adults, such as parents and other adults in the community (police officer, storekeeper, doctor). As children develop an awareness of self through play, so too they develop knowledge and understanding of the thoughts, feelings, and roles of others.

Play provides the opportunity for children to express and become comfortable with a range of emotions, including acceptable ways of expressing and resolving powerful emotions, such as anger and aggressiveness.

Social play supports the development of skills in interpersonal relationships, such as caring for others, sharing control, and making decisions. Children become more skilful at being members of a group, and gain competence in many desirable social skills such as listening to others, recognizing and accommodating the viewpoints of others, co-operating, negotiating, and problem solving. Children develop friendships with play partners and learn to accept the need for give-and-take to maintain these friendships.

Learning through Play

When children play, they use external objects and words to represent their ideas about the world. This use of symbols in play reflects an important process in the development of children's thinking that enables them to explore concepts and relationships outside their experience. What are the aspects of cognitive development that can be enhanced through play-based learning?

PROBLEM SOLVING

During play, children encounter many different problems to be tackled and solved. The block building may be top-heavy and fall down, the animals may not all fit into the field created in the sandbox, or there may not be enough cups for everyone to have tea at the same time. To continue with the play, these "problems" must be solved. Sometimes the problems confronted in play belong to characters or figures used in the play. A rescue crew might rush off to fight a fire or save a person in need. A father might have to find suitable beds for his children, or a group of children might need to protect themselves from monsters.

Whether the problems are real or pretend, the children can gain important problem-solving skills. Successful solutions to both real and imagined problems create a sense of competence as well as teach strategies for tackling difficulties.

CREATIVITY

Problem solving often requires a creative or divergent thinking process. Although sometimes a problem has only one solution, more often there are many possible solutions. Creativity refers to the ability to think in unconstrained ways to come up with flexible and imaginative options. Play offers many opportunities to try out different ways of doing things, and to compare and evaluate different approaches and solutions to find the best one for each situation.

Creativity is an important cognitive skill that should be encouraged as much as possible. It is best encouraged through attitudes that value and reinforce different ways of doing or thinking about things, rather than having children look for the one right way. As discussed in depth in Chapter 11, children's creativity is enhanced through a variety of play experiences that allow for self-expression and individually unique approaches. These include creative expression of ideas through dramatic play, art, music, movement, and storytelling.

DEVELOPING KNOWLEDGE

Manipulation of materials, toys, and equipment through play increases children's knowledge of the physical and sensory qualities of the environment. The greater variety of hands-on experiences that children have, the wider their base of understanding and general knowledge. Children gain knowledge about their own bodies and how they function, as well as how things work in their immediate environment and in their community.

The development of knowledge does not just include factual information, but also knowledge of cause-and-effect relationships, and general understanding of concepts such as how things grow and change, and how things are influenced by other people and events. This higher level of knowledge about the interconnections among people, events, and the world is an essential foundation for all later learning.

DEVELOPING SKILLS

Children develop various skills through play. They develop fine-motor skills such as manipulating small objects (Lego, puzzle pieces), drawing, or using scissors and other tools. Children also develop such large-motor skills as hopping, skipping, and using play equipment — balls, bicycles, and climbing apparatus. Perceptual skills such as discrimination of shape or detail (through puzzles and games), memory skills, language skills, skills with counting and number or size sequencing, and vocabulary building are other abilities that children acquire and practise.

COMMUNICATING AND EXPRESSING IDEAS

While playing, children use language to communicate and express their ideas and feelings, especially during social interactions when they share ideas to influence play. In the social setting, the need for communication is obvious. Children use their language skills to contribute their own ideas and opinions and to assert their own wishes: "I want to be the doctor. Your turn to be sick."

Children also use language in solitary play as a form of self-guidance. Picture Dorothy creating a design from a set of shapes: "Now I want a yellow one to go here. No, that's too big. I need a round one, not that one." This language is not intended for anyone else, but is an outward expression of the thought processes that are at work. This type of self-talk facilitates the child's development of planning and problem-solving skills, and can be taught as a technique to help children in mastering complex learning tasks.

Characteristics of a Play-Based Curriculum

Play-based curriculum ensures that children will be engaged in **active learning** in exploration and hands-on experiences. Think about how much more children learn about fruit when they have real fruit to cut open and taste rather than only pictures, books, and plastic models.

In a play-based curriculum, learning is **process-oriented**, rather than being focussed on a teacher-determined task or product. This process of learning is different for each child. For example, in a preschool group of mixed-age children, a large set of colourful plastic blocks was presented as a new activity. Several children expressed interest in the blocks and eagerly dumped them on the floor. Martha and Jory began immediately to build a tall tower. Franco laid the blocks carefully side by side and created a long row, which he used as a road for two small motorcycles. Kathleen gathered a number of the blocks and began sorting them into piles by colour. Several times she asked another child to trade for a specific colour, because she was trying to keep the number in each pile the same. Paddy, one of the youngest in the group, was most interested in putting the blocks back in the tub and dumping them out again. This created some distress for Franco when Paddy started taking blocks from Franco's road. Paddy stopped when he heard Franco's loud protest, and was redirected by the teacher to blocks that were not being used. When Martha and Jory's tower collapsed, Martha decided to leave the block area, while Jory patiently began to rebuild.

In this scenario, the selection of materials encouraged open-ended play, and having enough for a number of children enhanced development in a number of areas. Clearly, Kathleen was practising cognitive skills, building concepts of categorizing and quantity, along with communication and social skills in her negotiations. Franco used such cognitive skills as planning, precision, and symbolic play. For Martha and Jory, fine- and gross-motor skills were as essential as cognitive skills to keep the tower stable. They used their ability to co-operate and share, although their differences in attention and persistence led to a different outcome. Paddy's use of the blocks enhanced gross-motor skills, and showed the effectiveness of the blocks in providing for participation and success at a variety of developmental levels. The unobtrusive presence of the teacher provided support for the success of the play for all. Allowing children to determine the process and outcome of the play ensured that this was a beneficial learning experience.

Play is self-expression and should be **child-directed** to be satisfying and meet children's needs (Spodek, et al. 1991). Adults should not interfere unnecessarily with the direction in which the child is taking the play, unless there is danger to any child or risk of damage to the toys or environment. For example, Roger is busily getting lunch ready for his baby in the housekeeping centre. He has a dish and spoon in his hand and is looking around the room thoughtfully. He spies the bin of macaroni in the sensory materials centre and runs over to scoop some into his dish. He returns to the kitchen area and begins to feed the baby the macaroni, looking extremely pleased with himself. "Good macaroni, isn't it baby? Do you like macaroni? I like macaroni with cheese. Eat some more. Are you all done?" Adding the macaroni into his play, Roger created an extra dimension of satisfaction and stimulated language.

Some adults would be inclined to stop Roger from bringing the macaroni into the doll centre, either because "it was intended for a sensory experience and should not be taken out of the sensory bin" or because of a fear that it would be "too messy" for the doll centre. However, neither of these reasons is valid — the macaroni in the doll centre posed no danger to anyone. In this case, Roger was fortunate to be in a program that is not bound by rules and encourages children to show initiative and creativity in their play. Roger will definitely benefit in many ways from the recognition by his teachers that the process of play is important, and that reducing rules and preconceptions about how children should play contributes to increased levels of satisfaction and learning.

MAKING DECISIONS ABOUT THE CURRICULUM

By now it is clear that the noisy, active Tuesday-morning program described at the beginning of this chapter did not occur by accident. Rather, it was the result of careful planning and selection of materials and experiences based on the principles we just presented. The early childhood education curriculum is much more than a variety of toys and activities; it is a thoughtfully designed program that provides developmentally and individually appropriate experiences within a child-centred, comprehensive, play-based approach.

Designing a curriculum is the way to translate theory about learning into practice (Gordon & Browne 1993). In the early childhood education field, there is no predetermined curriculum or list of expected outcomes. Unlike most other educators, early childhood educators are quite free to set their own goals and curriculum. This freedom, with its privileges and responsibilities, gives early childhood educators the unique opportunity to design and plan a truly child-centred curriculum, which emerges as the educator gets to know the children in the group.

Responding to the Community

Getting to know the children includes becoming familiar with their community and how the families interact with their community. You need to be aware and sensitive to the values and wishes of the community and families to whom you provide service. As well, with your knowledge and expertise about young children and their needs, a part of your role is communicating your philosophy to parents, interpreting children's needs and development in the process.

Be sure your planning responds to community needs, whether your centre is located in a rural, small-town, urban, suburban, or core-city area. Curriculum should reflect the daily routines of the community, ensuring that chil-dren are familiar with local activities such as farming, manufacturing, or business. Field trips, visitors, and a selection of topics for special focus will all increase the children's awareness of and involvement in the community.

Many communities have special celebrations that can also be incorporated into the curriculum, such as a maple sugar or apple butter festival, rodeo, pow-wow, or winter carnival. Try to incorporate the overall significance of a special event rather than just taking the children on a one-shot field trip. In-depth preparation and follow-up will help the children to see the connections between community events and the lives of their families and neighbours.

Consulting with Children and Parents

The planning of a child-centred curriculum cannot be fully completed before the children arrive. If you are to take into consideration the needs and interests of children and families, you will need time to get to know everyone as individuals. The child-centred curriculum emerges from a process in which the children express their individual interests and skills, and you base your selection of curriculum topics and activities on these interests. You arrive at your choices through a combination of observation, discussion, and consultation with children and families.

Legislative Requirements

In Canada, each province has a mandate to regulate child-care settings through provincial legislation. Although the content of legislation varies, in each province certain areas are covered (Yeates, et al. 1990): physical environments, health and safety, staff ratios, and staff qualifications.

To varying degrees, provincial legislation also provides guidelines related to curriculum, although this legislation is general and leaves many decisions to the boards, directors, and operators of centres. The legislation generally makes reference to the following curriculum areas:

❖ guidelines for activities and routines to ensure that care is appropriate to the age of the children;

❖ guidelines to ensure that activities include balance and variety, to address all areas of development and meet the needs of the whole child;

❖ activities that respond to individual needs.

Legislative requirements should be used as a starting point only, not as the total program. Because of the need to enforce legislated standards, most legislation is somewhat open to interpretation and defines standards for the *minimum* level of acceptable practice. Legislated standards do not describe or guarantee a high-quality program.

THE EMERGENT CURRICULUM

A curriculum that develops and evolves over time in response to the needs and interests of the children and their families is called an **emergent curriculum**. As we have already stated, the planning that occurs follows observation of children and knowledge of the group and the community, and includes special interests and events. The interests of young children change and expand quickly depending on what is happening in their families and community. Therefore, different topics and activities are paced in response to the children's level of interest and not according to a calendar or schedule. You might follow more than one topic of interest at the same time depending on the range of children's interests.

The children and their families help to choose topics and activities, and they participate in planning experiences. Most, if not all, families are more than willing to share skills, knowledge, and expertise with their children's program. In one setting where parents contributed to the curriculum, the children were able to see a heart-lung machine demonstrated by a nurse who was a relative of one of the children. One father shared his interest and expertise in geology, resulting in the children learning about rock formations. All members of the group enjoyed studying the photographs of plants and animals, as well as the samples of coral, that another child's grandmother brought back from her vacation.

Although the emergent curriculum encourages and builds from the support of the families in providing resources and expertise, the educator is responsible for planning and selecting the experiences and activities within the chosen topics. As discussed previously, you, the educator, are responsible for ensuring that the full range of developmental areas are addressed in planning and that a sufficient variety of experiences are provided. These responsibilities do not change in an emergent curriculum, but are met by incorporating your own knowledge of children's needs into the current topic of interest (Gordon & Browne 1993).

When child and family involvement in curriculum development is valued and encouraged, everyone benefits. Very often, you discover that children and their families have a wealth of information and resources to share with the group, which expand and enhance the resources of the centre. In a responsive

BOX 10.6 AN EXAMPLE OF THE EMERGENCE OF A TOPIC

Late one summer, a popular children's movie featured a whale as co-star. Many children saw this movie, and their play and conversations reflected their interest. Jeremy and Michael were playing with the toy animals one day, using the tigers and bears as ferocious beasts. Jeremy commented, "A killer whale could eat you in one minute." "No, it wouldn't," said Michael. "Whales don't eat people." "Yes, they do, that's why they are KILLER whales." "No, my mom says they don't eat people."

As the disagreement intensified, the children asked Jean, the early childhood educator, "Do whales eat people?" Jean was not sure, and rather than put them off with a half-answer, she said, "I don't really know, but let's try to find out more about whales. How could we do that?" Jean was aware that she did not know much about whales, and she knew that developing this topic would require that she research the topic. She and the children made notes together, which each child took home, as a start to finding information on whales. Jeremy said he could bring in some books from home. Michael had some whale souvenirs from a marine show he had visited, and brought them to share with the group. It turned out that the other children were also interested, and one of them brought the soundtrack from the movie and a magazine article about making the movie. A trip to the library yielded some more books and a movie about whales. Kelly remembered that her parents had a tape with whale songs, and it was donated to the listening centre. This tape resulted in some fascinating discussion about communication among animals.

As it turned out, one of the children had an aunt who was a marine biologist, and Jean made arrangements for her to visit. She was able to provide a wide variety of exciting materials and information, which got many children thinking about how they would like to be marine biologists when they grew up.

A comment from one of the children about having a whale for a pet got Jean thinking about an idea she had had earlier for a small aquarium for the centre. The children really enjoyed the trip to the pet store to purchase the fish, plants, and supplies they needed. Another offshoot from this topic was introduced by the marine biologist, who pointed out some of the environmental issues that threaten whales and other sea animals. The children talked about what they could do, and made plans to draw pictures and write letters to express their concern. In addition, they became much more conscious of the environment in their own playground, and began several projects to make it more friendly for animals and birds. As you can guess, this led to more research and study about birds, squirrels, and insects, as well as discussions on respect and responsibility for the environment.

approach to curriculum, both children and educators experience "the vitality of learning and growth" (Goffin 1994, p. 213).

Although the curriculum requires a great deal of thought and planning, it should not be limited by your plans. You have seen the value of a responsive and dynamic curriculum that flows from the children's own interests and experiences. Each day there are experiences and spontaneous activities that are beneficial to children that have not been preplanned. For instance, perhaps one day the cook is too ill to prepare lunch. You can see her absence as a major catastrophe or an opportunity for spontaneous curriculum. You and the children can take on some of the cooking tasks: preparing and serving lunches for younger children, setting tables, clearing, and loading the dishwasher. What better way to include the topics of nutrition, food preparation, and self-help skills?

The opportunity to provide the spontaneous curriculum occurs in all settings every day, but you need to be observant and responsive to take advantage of these wonderful learning opportunities. What makes the early childhood education curriculum truly meaningful for children is the educator's ability to recognize and respond to these brief and unexpected opportunities for children to take responsibility and learn. The story of the magic hat in Box 10.7 illustrates unforeseen opportunities for learning. Because Kerry had been observing throughout the sequence of the play, and had been involved herself, she recognized the benefit of a careful response to Brett's comments.

The spontaneous curriculum that emerges from the educator's interested and knowledgeable response to the "teachable moments" that occur for all children must not be overlooked as an ideal avenue for supporting children in their attempts to make sense of their day and incorporate meaning into each experience.

OBSERVING AND EVALUATING THE CURRICULUM

Even when you have designed and planned a curriculum for young children with utmost thought and care, some aspects of a plan might turn out to be inappropriate or uninteresting to some children. Children are not always predictable — nor would you want them to be — and this is why you need to constantly observe their participation in both planned and spontaneous aspects of your program.

Ongoing Observation

Curriculum evaluation need not be a frightening or overwhelming task. Much evaluation of the planned curriculum is carried out informally and intuitively. In an effective curriculum for young children, you will see much chatter, noise, activity, giggling, pride, interaction, and active involvement and exploration. This high level of enthusiastic participation is an indication that you have provided interesting, meaningful, and developmentally appropriate activities. Even observing occasional spills and accidents can be seen as evidence that the young child is struggling to demonstrate independence, initiative, and mastery of new challenges and skills. Evidence of attempts to clean up or resolve these accidents shows self-confidence and a maturing sense of social responsibility.

Observation is an important aid in evaluation. Simple observational techniques can provide a wealth of information to the sensitive and perceptive observer. A good place to start is by assessing the well-being and level of involvement of the children. Take a list of all the children and observe each one for short periods over several days. The anecdotal record and the checklist formats are the most helpful for this purpose. See Chapter 5 for more information on techniques of observation.

A second approach to evaluation through observation is to make a list of all the learning centres and planned experiences, and to observe these one at a time to see how effectively they are being used. Use either a running record or an anecdotal report, depending on how able you are to sit back and record

BOX 10.7 THE MAGIC HAT

Brett and Evan were playing intently in the bake shop, making cakes and pizzas and delivering them to other children and adults in the room. Kerry, the educator, was sitting at the snack table to be available for children as they took a break from their play to come for fruit and muffins. Brett and Evan rushed over with cardboard boxes loaded with "cakes." Brett asked politely, "Would you like to buy a cake? We just made it." Kerry said, "Yes, please. How much money is it?" "Four dollars," said Brett, "and thank you for buying it."

The two boys went off and returned briefly. Brett flung a second cake box at Kerry and said fiercely and loudly, "Here's your cake. Give me all your money right now!" Kerry played along, pretending to give him money. She said, "Would you boys like some snack?" They both said yes, and sat down. Brett said, "Please pass some fruit." They chatted about the cake sale while the boys ate.

Brett took his hat off and put it on the table. He said loudly to Kerry, "You'd better buy more cakes and give us all your money right now or you's be in trouble." He then put his hat back on, and said sweetly, "Would you like to buy another cake? I just made it and it's very good." Kerry said, "Maybe, what kind do you have?" "Chocolate." "OK, I'll take one." Brett hurried off to the bake shop where he

"made" a cake and, leaving his hat behind, he threw the cake at Kerry and said, "Gimme money right now." He ran back for his hat and then returned to the snack table and sat down. After pouring himself a drink, he said to Kerry, "This is a magic hat, you know. When I wear it, I can be good. When I take it off, I'm bad."

"I'm glad you explained that to me," Kerry said, "I was getting confused because one time you were so friendly and next time you seemed angry and mean." "When I take off the hat, I am mean," said Brett, "When I put it on, I'm nice." Kerry responded, "That's a very interesting game you're playing. I like it better when you have the hat on, because you are kind and friendly." "Me, too," said Brett.

"You know, Brett," Kerry said, "you don't need to wear a magic hat to be kind and good. You can choose how you act with other people. We can all be friendly and nice if we choose, even though we all feel angry sometimes. You can choose to be kind to your friends even if you don't have the magic hat, because the magic is inside you and you have it all the time. Do you know what I mean?" Brett nodded and smiled. He put his hat back on. "How about some more cake?" Kerry said. "I'd like banana cake this time if you have some." Brett said, "Sure do." He threw his hat away and came back smiling with a box of cake and a hug for Kerry.

your observations. Again, Chapter 5 provides more help in this area.

Curriculum Evaluation

In addition to regular observation, the process of in-depth curriculum evaluation should be built into your program. The depth and formality of evaluation techniques can be adapted and modified to suit any setting and purpose. Tools are available for the process of curriculum evaluation, such as the Environment Rating Scale (Harms & Clifford 1980). However, using a formal tool is not absolutely necessary.

Any process of observation, discussion, and revision of the curriculum is valuable.

One simple approach is to create a checklist from the guiding principles described in this chapter (see Box 10.8) and use it as a focus for observation by educators, administrators, board members, and parents. Once everyone has had opportunities to observe and identify areas for discussion, a meeting should be set to discuss observations and make suggestions for change.

Personal Reflection

Perhaps the most important component of the curriculum is the educator, so you need to reflect on your own role. As Pierce puts it

> The curriculum is not the schedule, or the equipment, or facts or skills, it is you — the early childhood educator. ... The best possible curriculum in any type of program involves sensitive, caring adults — who,

---

BOX 10.8 QUESTIONS FOR OBSERVATION AND CURRICULUM EVALUATION

- Do adults approach and interact with all children, consistently demonstrating warmth, acceptance, and respect for each individual?
- Is there evidence of language, food, toys, equipment, materials, visual images, and experiences that reflect the diverse backgrounds of all children in your group?
- Do all activities encourage and incorporate a variety of cultural perspectives and information to enhance understanding, appreciation, and valuing of cultural diversity?
- Does the curriculum offer each child a variety of opportunities to express and pursue personal interests, and to experience satisfaction and mastery in self-selected activities?
- Does the curriculum provide a variety of experiences in all developmental areas for most of each day?
- Does the routine provide adequate opportunities to meet basic needs in an atmosphere that is flexible, comfortable, and unrushed, recognizing the value of daily routines as an important part of the child's day?
- Are planned and spontaneous experiences meaningful, enhancing learning through a variety of related experiences, rather than focussing on isolated skills or individual developmental areas?
- Have you provided a range of experiences at the developmental level of each child, ensuring active and successful participation?
- Are all children welcomed and valued as contributing members of a diverse group?
- Are special needs accommodated in a supportive and accepting manner, ensuring that no child is segregated or treated differently from others in the group?
- Are materials, toys, books, and pictures selected to represent a range of genders, ages, races, and cultures, minimizing stereotypes that may limit development and negatively influence self-concept?
- Is there an emphasis on child-directed experiences that encourage each child to be in charge of her or his own learning through active participation and interaction with people, toys, and materials?
- Is your curriculum provided primarily through play-based experiences, with limited amounts of teacher-directed structured activity or formal instruction?

through their relationships with children, enable all the children to develop a positive attitude about themselves and others. *(1990, pp. 58–59)*

The relationship and interactions between you and the children form a foundation for the curriculum, and influence all aspects of the child's experience far more deeply than any other factor. Curriculum evaluation must, therefore, include self-evaluation. Reflect on your goals for children and your values and attitudes, and how these are conveyed through your behaviours. Make sure that you are open to change when you undertake an evaluation process.

SUMMARY

In this chapter, we have discussed the principles that form the foundation of a Canadian early childhood education curriculum, a foundation that is strong and well-supported by developmental theory. When your planning is based on these principles, you can be confident that your program is beneficial for all the children in your care.

We have advocated the need for the early childhood curriculum to reflect and respond to the backgrounds, interests, characteristics, and needs of all children in a group. A child-centred, play-based curriculum that provides a variety of opportunities for children to actively construct their own learning is most beneficial for optimal development and learning. We have discussed concerns and cautions against a curriculum based on teacher-directed formal education as being inappropriate, and potentially harmful, for young children.

We have made arguments in favour of a curriculum that is designed collaboratively, incorporating input from children and parents, to complement the expertise of the early childhood educator. We have also emphasized the benefits of a dynamic, emergent, and responsive curriculum, recognizing the value of a flexible curriculum in being able to meet the immediate needs and interests of the children. Ongoing feedback, observation, and evaluation of the curriculum helps to ensure that you are indeed providing a beneficial educational experience.

REVIEW QUESTIONS

❶ Describe characteristics of a Canadian early childhood curriculum.

❷ What do we mean by a multicultural, anti-bias, and inclusive curriculum? How can we best provide this for young children?

❸ Why do we follow a play-based approach to education? How can you implement this kind of program?

❹ What does constructivist theory tell us about young children's learning? How can you incorporate this theory into your program?

❺ What do we mean by emergent or responsive curriculum?

DISCUSSION QUESTIONS

❶ What purpose should education serve in society? How does this purpose relate to early childhood education settings?

❷ Read Elkind's *Miseducation: Preschoolers at Risk* (Knopf, 1988) or "Formal Education and Early Childhood Education: An Essential Difference" (*Phi Delta Kappan*, May 1986). Discuss the dangers of "miseducation" for young children.

❸ Should an early childhood setting address moral issues and values? Why or why not?

❹ The centre where you work uses the same basic curriculum plan every year. What would you say in a staff meeting to discuss the upcoming year's curriculum?

❺ Is it appropriate for an early childhood setting to claim that its only mandate is intellectual development? Why or why not?

ACTIVITIES

❶ Bring to class a picture of a young child whom you know and who is special to you. Discuss with a small group of your classmates what you hope this child will experience in an early childhood setting.

❷ Visit an early childhood setting and look for materials, play equipment, and books that convey either stereotypical or anti-bias attitudes. Have a discussion with a small number of young children about their thoughts based on one of these books. Share your observations in class.

❸ Observe a centre where children with special needs are included as part of the program. Observe and interview one of the staff to evaluate how effective this has been.

❹ Use the questions from Box 10.8 to observe the environment and curriculum in an early childhood setting.

❺ Gather a selection of foreign newspapers or textbooks from another field and try to make sense of the content. Describe the process by which you tried to make sense of the material. Compare your experience to the experience of a young child faced with unfamiliar information.

FURTHER READING

Bredekamp, Sue, ed. (1987). *Developmentally Appropriate Practice in Early Childhood Programs Serving Children from Birth through Age 8* (expanded ed.). Washington, DC: National Association for the Education of Young Children.
A comprehensive description of current practice in providing care and education for young children, including many examples of appropriate and inappropriate practices.

Deiner, P.L. (1993). *Resources for Teaching Children with Diverse Abilities: Birth through Eight.* Fort Worth, TX: Harcourt Brace Jovanovich.
This book provides information and invaluable practical resources for the inclusion of children with a wide range of developmental diversity into an early childhood setting.

Doxey, I.M., ed. (1990). *Child Care and Education: Canadian Dimensions.* Scarborough, ON: Nelson Canada.
An advanced analysis of the theoretical and sociological foundations for a Canadian approach to early childhood education, with contributions from a number of prominent Canadians in the field.

Elkind, David. (1986). Formal education and early childhood education: An essential difference. *Phi Delta Kappan 67* (May): 631–36.
An article urging us to protect the well-being of young children by ensuring that education is at an appropriate level and does not create undue pressure.

Elkind, David. (1988). *Miseducation: Preschoolers at Risk.* New York: Alfred A. Knopf.
A compelling book for parents that advocates approaches that value and safeguard childhood and refrain from subjecting the child to unnecessary pressure and stress.

Goffin, S.G. (1994). *Curriculum Models and Early Childhood Education: Appraising the Relationship.* New York: Merrill.
A book for the advanced student that reviews and evaluates a number of curriculum models for early childhood education. This book raises the possibility of negative implications resulting from strict adherence to any particular model and favours a responsive style of teaching offered by highly educated professionals.

Hall, N.S., and V. Rhomberg. (1995). *The Affective Curriculum: Teaching the Anti-Bias Approach to Young Children.* Toronto: Nelson Canada.
This recently published book discusses in depth the principles of an anti-bias curriculum and the process for designing anti-bias activities. Exploring one's own attitudes and values and developing sensitivity to diversity are seen as essential to the process.

Kostelnik, M.J., A.K. Soderman, and A.P. Whiren. (1993). *Developmentally Appropriate Programs in Early Childhood Education.* New York: Merrill.
An advanced textbook that clearly articulates the latest research and theory relevant to the practice of early childhood education.

Van Hoorn, J., P. Nourot, B. Scales, and K. Alward. (1993) *Play at the Centre of the Curriculum.* New York: Merrill.
A valuable book that emphasizes the value of a play-based curriculum. Constructivist theory provides the support for this approach.

REFERENCES

Association for Early Childhood Education, Ontario. (1985). *Good Care Educates, Good Education Cares.* Toronto: AECEO.

Bredekamp, S., ed. (1987). *Developmentally Appropriate Practice in Early Childhood Programs Serving Children from Birth through Age 8* (expanded ed.). Washington, DC: National Association for the Education of Young Children.

Brewer, J.A. (1992). *Introduction to Early Childhood Education: Preschool through Primary Grades.* Needham Heights, MA: Allyn & Bacon.

Canadian Child Care Federation. (1994). National guidelines for training in early childhood care and education, draft document. *Interaction* (Summer): 6–9. Ottawa: Canadian Child Care Federation.

Canning, P.M., and M. Lyon. (1990). Young children with special needs. In I.M. Doxey, ed., *Child Care and Education: Canadian Dimensions,* pp. 254–68. Scarborough, ON: Nelson Canada.

Chud, G. (1993). Anti-bias education: An approach for today and tomorrow. *Interaction* (Summer): 18–20.

Crain, W. (1992). *Theories of Development: Concepts and Applications.* Englewood Cliffs, NJ: Prentice-Hall.

Deiner, P.L. (1993). *Resources for Teaching Children with Diverse Abilities: Birth through Eight.* Fort Worth, TX: Harcourt Brace Jovanovich.

Doherty-Derkowski, G. (1995). *Quality Matters: Excellence in Early Childhood Programs.* Don Mills, ON: Addison-Wesley.

Doxey, I.M. (1990). A basic Canadian curriculum. In I.M. Doxey, ed., *Child Care and Education: Canadian Dimensions,* pp. 143–55. Scarborough, ON: Nelson Canada.

Doxey, I.M., ed. (1990). *Child Care and Education: Canadian Dimensions.* Scarborough, ON: Nelson Canada.

Elkind, D. (1986). Formal education and early childhood education: An essential difference. *Phi Delta Kappan* (May): 631–36.

Elkind, D. (1988). *Miseducation: Preschoolers at Risk.* New York: Alfred A. Knopf.

Essa, E.L., and P.R. Rogers. (1992). *An Early Childhood Curriculum: From Developmental Model to Application.* New York: Delmar.

Frost, J.L. (1992). *Play and Playscapes.* New York: Delmar.

Ginsburg, H., and S. Opper. (1969). *Piaget's Theory of Intellectual Development: An Introduction.* Englewood Cliffs, NJ: Prentice-Hall.

Goffin, S.G. (1994). *Curriculum Models and Early Childhood Education: Appraising the Relationship.* New York: Merrill.

Gonzalez-Mena, J. (1993). *Multicultural Issues in Child Care.* Mountain View, CA: Mayfield Publishing Company.

Gordon, A., and K.W. Browne. (1993). *Beginnings and Beyond: Foundations in Early Childhood Education.* Albany, NY: Delmar.

Greenspan, S., and N.T. Greenspan. (1986). *First Feelings: Milestones in the Emotional Development of Your Baby and Child.* New York: Penguin Books.

Hall, N.S., and V. Rhomberg. (1995). *The Affective Curriculum: Teaching the Anti-Bias Approach to Young Children.* Scarborough, ON: Nelson Canada.

Harms, T., and R.M. Clifford. (1980). *Early Childhood Environment Rating Scale.* New York: Teachers College Press.

Hendrick, J. (1992). *The Whole Child: Developmental Education for the Early Years* (5th ed.). New York: Macmillan.

Hendrick, J. (1994). *Total Learning: Developmental Curriculum for the Young Child* (4th ed.). New York: Merrill.

Jones, E., and L. Derman-Sparks. (1992). Meeting the challenge of diversity. *Young Children* 47 (2): 12–18.

Kostelnik, M.J., A.K. Soderman, and A.P. Whiren. (1993). *Developmentally Appropriate Programs in Early Childhood Education.* New York: Merrill.

Maxim, G.W. (1993). *The Very Young: Guiding Children from Infancy through the Early Years.* New York: Merrill.

Mock, K.R. (1990). Multiculturalism in early childhood education. In I.M. Doxey, ed., *Child Care and Education: Canadian Dimensions,* pp. 109–25. Scarborough, ON: Nelson Canada.

Morrison, G.S. (1991). *Early Childhood Education Today.* New York: Merrill.

Pierce, K. (1990). The child in the curriculum. In I.M. Doxey, ed., *Child Care and Education: Canadian Dimensions,* pp. 53–61. Scarborough, ON: Nelson Canada.

Regan, E.M. (1990). Child-centred programming. In I.M. Doxey, ed., *Child Care and Education: Canadian Dimensions,* pp. 171–77. Scarborough, ON: Nelson Canada.

Riley, S.S. (1984). *How to Generate Values in Young Children.* Washington, DC: National Association for the Education of Young Children.

Schurch, P. (1990). A multicultural perspective on programming for toddlers. In A. Stonehouse, ed., *Trusting Toddlers: Planning for One- to Three-Year-Olds in Child Care Centres.* St. Paul, MN: Toys 'n' Things Press.

Smith, C.A. (1993). *The Peaceful Classroom.* Mt. Rainier, MD: Gryphon House.

Spodek, B., O.N. Saracho, and M.D. Davis. (1991). *Foundations of Early Childhood Education: Teaching Three-, Four-, and Five-Year-Old Children.* Englewood Cliffs, NJ: Prentice-Hall.

Stonehouse, A. (1990). One perspective on programming for toddlers. In A. Stonehouse, ed., *Trusting Toddlers: Planning for One- to Three-Year-Olds in Child Care Centers.* St. Paul, MN: Toys 'n' Things Press.

Taylor, M. (1990). Foundations of early childhood education. In I.M. Doxey, ed., *Child Care and Education: Canadian Dimensions*, pp. 65–86. Scarborough, ON: Nelson Canada.

Van Hoorn, J., P. Nourot, B. Scales, and K. Alward. (1993). *Play at the Centre of the Curriculum*. New York: Merrill.

Yeates, M., D. McKenna, C. Warberg, and K. Chandler. (1990). *Administering Early Childhood Settings: The Canadian Perspective*. Columbus, OH: Merrill.

PART 4
The Learning Environment

Children learn through play. Learning opportunities are embedded in play experiences throughout the curriculum, open to choice and child-initiated exploration. Knowledge and skills are achieved by the child through the mastery of new challenges and information, facilitated by the observant educator who responds to the children's interests, efforts, and wonder. The early childhood curriculum is comprehensive, providing experiences that enhance all aspects of children's development.

CHAPTER 11
Nurturing Children's Creativity

✏ **Overview**

✏ **What Is Creativity?**

✏ **How Creativity Develops**

◆ The Senses

◆ Emotional Development

◆ Cognitive Development

◆ Physical Development

✏ **Culture and Creativity**

✏ **Observing Creativity**

✏ **Approaches for Nurturing Creativity**

◆ Creativity and Play

◆ Creative Programming

◆ A Rich Environment

◆ The Process Approach

✏ **Creative Art**

◆ The Link between Language and Art

◆ The Link between Cognition and Art

◆ The Creative Centre

◆ Art Experiences

- Music
- Creative Movement
  - ◆ Body Awareness
  - ◆ Creative Visualization
  - ◆ Making Space
- Linking Art, Music, and Creative Movement
- Linking Language, Creativity, and Discovery

- Summary
- Review Questions
- Discussion Questions
- Activities
- Further Reading
- References

OVERVIEW

Creativity is so delicate a flower that praise tends to make it bloom while discouragement often nips it in the bud.
— *Alex F. Osborn*

The essence of the creative person is being in love with what one is doing.
— *E.P. Torrance*

Imagine a room designed for preschoolers — large windows, walls hung with colourful paintings, and shelves of books, toys, drums and cymbals, plants, sand, water, clay, play dough, and a rich variety of other materials. In this environment, one of the children, Gina, has just discovered a box full of yarn, which she is carefully examining. She begins to twist pieces of the yarn together, trying to hold them with one hand and twist them with the other. She becomes frustrated as the yarn unwinds. As the teacher approaches, Gina looks up.

"These don't stick," she says.

"No, they don't stick together."

"You stick them," Gina demands.

"I can stick them on paper," the educator offers.

"No," Gina says firmly, "like this."

Then Gina points to her hair and the braided ribbon holding it.

"That ribbon is braided," the educator observes.

"Braided?"

"Yes, watch this."

The teacher takes three pieces of yarn and braids them together.

Gina watches. Then her friend comes to watch, too. "Look. Braids."

They both look at the colours of yarns as they twist and combine. They watch for a while, then put their hands on the teacher's hands as she braids. "Let's use red," says Gina.

"All right. Find some red."

Gina and her friend pick out three colours: pink, red, and peach. The teacher ties the ends to the three nails on a weaving board and starts the braid. Gina continues braiding with her friend's help. Other children move into the area, watching with fascination. Some ask for weaving boards too, while others choose yarn to glue onto paper. The teacher quietly assists, adding materials as they are needed. She also observes the new uses that the children find for the yarn. Some of their creations will be displayed, or used in other learning centres in the room.

The atmosphere is intense. The children are experiencing yarn in a new way and using it creatively. Some children observe for a few minutes, then leave. Others spend a long time working with the yarn with total concentration.

Now imagine another room of preschoolers. Six children are seated around a table with the teacher, who is showing them a beautiful origami bird.

"Today, we are going to make this bird just by folding the paper I have given you. Now, watch the first fold."

She slowly folds the paper in half, then asks the children to repeat the fold. A few copy her, while others wait for her to do it for them. By the third fold, one child tries to leave the table.

"Jason, sit down."

"I don't want to make the bird," says Jason.

"Look how pretty it is," says the teacher, holding up the original bird to show him.

Jason hesitates, then sits down, dejected. By the next fold, his paper is a crumpled ball that he is flicking at José. The teacher finally lets the children go.

What went wrong? Was the second group of children just being contrary? Both early childhood educators had prepared their art materials, making sure they were developmentally appropriate. Both enjoyed art, and each had a well-developed aesthetic sense. Why was the first activity so successful? What did the first teacher do to encourage creative expression? What might the second educator have done to make her activity a creative one?

This chapter offers answers to these questions through an exploration of creativity and its expression, as well as aesthetics. You will find out how to nurture, inspire, and encourage creativity in yourself and the children. In this chapter we also discuss the curriculum areas of play, art, music, and movement. Creative thinking is discussed in Chapter 14.

By the end of this chapter, you will be able to

❖ explain how creativity develops;

❖ describe how this development is enhanced throughout the early childhood curriculum;

❖ understand how cultural diversity can enrich creative programming;

❖ understand more about your own creativity. By developing this aspect of yourself, you can become a more creative and competent early childhood educator.

WHAT IS CREATIVITY?

Creativity is the process of discovering, experimenting, deciding, and problem solving to create something new from what you know and experience. Creativity is more than being "artistic." It is the capacity to construct, or create, something original or unique. Creativity

depends on and reflects sensory, physical, cognitive, and emotional processes.

Children are naturally creative, as creativity is one aspect of the natural process of learning. However, it is possible to discourage creativity by imposing rigid ideas and approaches on children. The responsibility of the early childhood educator is to provide a nurturing environment so that the creativity in every child can flourish.

Children express their creativity in many ways, including art, music, and movement; in their imaginative play; and in their thinking processes. The early childhood curriculum must support creative expression in each of these areas.

HOW CREATIVITY DEVELOPS

Creativity begins at birth. New parents can tell you how their infants explored the environment from the time they were born. Infants follow movement with their eyes and gaze intently at people and objects. These are the first signs of an infant developing sensory awareness and interacting with people and materials.

Even at this early stage, in an environment rich with sensations, the newborn's creativity develops in a logical and orderly sequence (for example, the baby learns to move her head before she is able to use her hands). Sensory experiences provided for newborns include bright pictures on the nursery walls, talking and singing to the baby, bright mobiles hanging above the diapering table, and the trickle of warm bath water over the skin. Parents might see these simple, routine parts of the newborn's environment as nothing out of the ordinary in caring for their baby, but they are some of the essential elements for early development of creativity.

In the toddler stage, children's environment expands rapidly and they interact eagerly with toys and materials. They develop co-ordination as they grasp a chair to pull themselves to their feet. They can balance themselves on their feet as they reach for a toy — eye–hand co-ordination — and examine it with both hands. Outside, they may resort to "all fours" and pick up blades of grass and pebbles, which they explore with their mouth. By the time they are steady on their feet, toddlers are into everything to satisfy their intense need to explore. This drive to explore is the core of creativity.

Preschoolers play creatively with materials that interest them and share their ideas with their peers. For example, they often play with figures of people or animals, and in the process, these figures take on personalities and the children make them talk to each other. In this kind of creative play, fantasy almost automatically develops. Preschoolers' free use of fantasy and fascination with new materials makes their self-expression, including paintings and drawings, extraordinarily creative and uniquely personal.

Each stage of children's development represents the interdependence of the four domains: sensory, physical, cognitive, and emotional. Their creativity reflects and benefits their development in each of these areas.

The Senses

In their first few weeks, infants' tactile perception sharpens, as does visual and auditory acuity. The aesthetic sense emerges early in life as infants show preference for certain tactile, visual, and auditory experiences. Whatever is personally gratifying is aesthetically beautiful. Infants respond to objects that have curvature, contour, complexity, symmetry, and movement. Contrasting colours — such as black and white — attract their attention. They also like objects that roll, spin, and twirl.

Infants' discrimination skills begin to develop as they reject dull and immobile objects and reach for more aesthetically pleasing ones. During this solitary play time they begin to develop personal aesthetics, and the children's own perceptual clues alone decide what is aesthetically pleasing and what is not. The sensations provided through the senses, such as feeling or mouthing a block or ball, provide pleasure.

Toddlers begin to be aware of others during parallel play. They notice a playmate's rejection of certain smells, tastes, and sights. In this way, the aesthetics of others start to influence personal aesthetics. The process of comparison and adjustment begins.

This process continues as the whole environment shapes and moulds aesthetics. The comments of playmates, teachers, parents, and neighbours influence the children's growing aesthetics. An adult who celebrates the wonders of nature can inspire children's aesthetic sensitivity. As a result, what was not pleasing to the 18-month-old child might be pleasing to the 5-year-old. As the environment enlarges for the school-age child, the aesthetics of peers and the influence of media are increasingly important. The school-age child is constantly adjusting personal aesthetics in response to the messages of the environment.

Emotional Development

Children's self-concept and self-esteem develop through creative activities. The pleasure and pride associated with personal creation and self-expression cannot be overstated. Creative experiences provide unique opportunities for children to experience and articulate "Look what I did!" If creativity and individuality are valued, when children try new things they do not experience the results as "failure," and they do not experience self-doubt. All children like to feel good about themselves. Creativity nurtures this high self-esteem, and when children feel that their creativity is valued — the music heard, the drawing enjoyed, the dance praised — their self-esteem soars.

Creative activities also help children express and control emotions and explore the emotions of others; in fact, such theorists as Lowenfeld (1968) see creativity as an expression of emotional well-being. Children and adults alike express their feelings through art, music, movement, and play, and thus release their emotions.

An unstimulating or unsupportive environment, or a lack of expressive media, can stifle children's creativity. With their creativity stifled, children lack an emotional outlet. They cannot express feelings and ideas as easily or as satisfactorily, and might become withdrawn, repressed, frustrated, and angry. Without a natural outlet for creativity and self-expression, children look for other outlets, and their behaviour can become erratic or aggressive.

Creativity is the key to healthy emotional development because it provides children with an outlet for self-expression, a chance to share and understand the emotions of others, and models of emotional growth.

Cognitive Development

Creativity is closely related to one aspect of cognitive development — divergent thinking. Divergent thinking means the ability to think about things in many ways, to see different aspects of a situation, or to come up with a variety of solutions to a problem.

In your interactions, encourage and model divergent thinking by asking the children for a variety of ideas and by validating each as "one way to do it." You need to help children see that they all have good ideas, and that they need not be concerned whether their way is the only right way. Children who are encouraged to think for themselves and to see their own ideas as important will be the risk takers we described in Chapters 6 and 7, and will be the most successful learners.

Physical Development

Much human creativity is expressed through the physical body. Art, music, movement, and play all involve the body and certain motor skills in the process of self-expression.

For young children, acting and doing is essential to all areas of development, and this is especially true for creativity and self-expression. We must encourage all children to express their ideas, feelings, and fantasies through many avenues, including those that involve physical action.

CULTURE AND CREATIVITY

Canada's cultural diversity enriches early childhood education programs and can stimulate creativity. You can tap into the richness of music, dance, art, costume, and language, and nurture and celebrate cultural expressions. Children enjoy learning songs in different languages, not just the dominant language of your group. They also respond to music that reflects diversity: reggae, pop, classical, calypso, throat singing, and more. When you choose stories, you can include those that reflect many cultures and many languages. Cultural diversity adds to the richness of stimuli. It expands the meaning of creativity, and can inspire the children to explore the cultural diversity around them.

Families are the cultural link providing clues to cultural practices. Ask the children's families to share their creativity in the following ways:

❖ share a story from their own culture;

❖ bring a traditional dress or hat to show the children;

❖ talk about a special holiday and let the children taste foods that are served for special celebrations;

❖ show a picture or a design that has special meaning in their culture;

❖ play or sing a song in their language and teach it to the children.

Given sufficient opportunity to express their new knowledge of others through play, children develop attitudes of comfort and acceptance that enhance their own development.

Cultural practices can influence children's attitude toward creativity. Some children are taught to listen and observe rather than to ask questions. They watch dramatic plays rather than acting themselves because they may have been taught that wearing costumes is disrespectful, bold, and frivolous. Children from these groups might feel uncomfortable participating in a dramatic play.

Other children are taught to be clean at all times. For them, playing in sand and water, finger painting, and moulding clay might seem distressing unless they can be reassured about the mess and provided with practical solutions.

Some children are taught to take on traditional male and female roles. In this case, boys might feel awkward washing dishes, bathing dolls, or cooking; girls might feel uncomfortable hammering or wearing a hard hat. These traditional attitudes extend to clothing, too. Girls who are taught to be covered at all times might not want to participate in body painting or having their body outline traced on paper. Boys who are taught that jewellery is only for girls might not want to make necklaces or string bead bracelets.

You can help by being sensitive to different cultural practices and seeing them as a source

of strength for the whole group. Perhaps the child who cannot wear masks is adept at yoga and might be willing to share a rhythmic breathing exercise with the whole group. The child who hesitates to finger paint may know how to make origami figures and might be willing to teach other children. Incorporating an acceptance of diversity conveys a message that involvement and creativity are personal experiences, all equally valid.

OBSERVING CREATIVITY

Children's creativity flourishes in an environment where they feel safe and accepted. By being alert, you can frequently detect opening points in their activities that allow you to facilitate expanding creativity. In other words, if you are observant you will be able to catch and enhance the moment.

Jerome, a 5-year-old, gave a hint of that kind of moment, and the educator picked it up. Frequently, Jerome made clay figures, perhaps half a dozen, with one bigger than the others. Once when he built a smaller one with a big head, the teacher asked him about it.

"He's smart," Jerome explained.

"So that's why his head is bigger than the others?"

"Yes, and he can think really good."

"Why don't you make a portrait of him — just make his head, large, and show his face and his expression?"

Jerome squished up all the figures, added more clay to his pile, and began working with intense concentration. He created a large, expressive portrait that drew praise from the other children as well as the adults. The next time he worked with clay, he wanted to make another head. This experience gave Jerome a feeling of acceptance because he discovered there was something he could do really well.

Perhaps a child in your classroom becomes interested in the light streaming in the window and spontaneously begins dancing. You can use that moment by bringing out supporting materials — a tambourine or other instruments — and perhaps other children will join in the dance and make music. Someone might notice the shadows of tree branches creating movement on a table or on the floor, and some of the children may be inclined to express the pleasure of that moment by getting out the paints or crayons.

Sometimes even an accident can take children into a new direction — a pot of paint spills and creates an interesting pattern or blend of colour, or the shaker lid falls off and all the sequins spill out. If you are alert, you can use this kind of unexpected incident as an opportunity for children to explore.

At the same time, you can observe how individual children react to stimuli. Some children tire quickly and move from one play episode to another. Others work with intensity and are completely absorbed in what they are doing. Often, these are the children who discover new ways to use materials, from which you can learn.

In the opening example of this chapter, the teacher had an awareness of how and when to help Gina. Through observing and responding with appropriate materials (weaving boards, glue) one child's interest and creativity led to creative experiences for a number of children.

Another benefit of observing the children's play is that you can find out their language patterns — their sentence structures and the level of their vocabulary. You can also get a glimpse into children's views or approaches to life by observing social groupings and who plays the role of the mother or father, who plays the child, who plays the bus driver, and who goes along for the ride. This type of observation is important in expanding your understanding of individual children and the entire group, and for feeding your ideas of creative approaches to learning.

It is easy to remember some of your observations — humorous and disastrous — but you will forget most of them unless you write them down. Recording your observations may seem to be adding to your numerous responsibilities, but you will likely discover that your records become a resource for planning creative activities. With practice, you will be able to jot down concise notes during the day and then fill in details after the children have gone home. Your accuracy on what you see improves with experience as you learn, almost intuitively, to observe children's body language, facial expressions, and conversations.

Astute observation is essential to the creative experience. Keep your senses tuned to the children's need to explore and express their creativity, then follow their lead.

APPROACHES FOR NURTURING CREATIVITY

"What a creative painting!" "She's a very creative teacher." "That is such a creative approach." What do these statements mean? Is creativity just some wild, eccentric magic that only the gifted few who call themselves artists possess? Is it rare, or can everyone be creative every day?

Creativity is innate to everyone, and every person on earth has the potential to live creatively. If this is true, then it seems that doing creative work is possible, and even beneficial, for everyone every day.

There are many approaches to creative learning and teaching. Some educators feel that creative learning occurs through the creative arts: visual art, music, dramatic play, and movement. A growing number of educators

---

BOX 11.2 OBSERVING CREATIVITY

Heather was playing in the sandbox. With a shovel, she had made roads and fences and placed animals in fields. When she picked up the ducks, she frowned and began to dig a pond. She put the ducks beside the pond and began looking around the room. She smiled when she spotted the water table, and then filled a large pitcher and poured the water into the sandbox. She looked so dismayed when the water seeped into the sand and flattened the sides of her pond.

Joey, the early childhood educator, had been observing Heather from a distance. As Heather looked his way, he moved to the sandbox and crouched down beside her. "What's the matter, Heather?" She pointed. "I can't make a pond." "I see," said Joey. "I wonder what other way you could do it." "The water just went away," Heather said, "I can't make it stay." "Well, what could you do to keep the water from going away?"

After a few seconds of deliberation, Heather saw a pie plate in the cooking centre and said, "I can use this!" Having solved that problem, Heather checked out the cooking centre again and added several "trees" (coloured forks) around the pond.

now recognize that creative learning also occurs at the science table, the block centre, or the sand table. Experimenting, building unique structures, and designing a landscape require divergent thinking, which underlies all creative learning and teaching.

Creativity and Play

Children naturally express creativity through play. Although we often associate imaginative play with what we see in the dramatic play centre, children express creativity when they build a school or circus with blocks or a space station with Lego.

Play naturally invites creativity because the materials are open-ended and can be used in divergent ways. During play, children express their own ideas and view of reality in the direction they take their play. There need not be limitations on either their imagination or their creativity.

In Chapter 10 we described the role of the educator in enhancing play without imposing constraints. These same principles apply here. Allowing children to direct the course of play and supporting the decisions they make sets the stage for creativity in play.

Creative Programming

One early childhood educator begins the fall program each year with an empty table. On the first morning, the children go with him on a collection walk. The treasures they collect and bring back to the room form the basis of that first day's program. His sensitive appreciation for the "beautiful junk" they collect sets the tone for the creative program that year.

This does not mean that there is no structure. He has planned in advance and studied the children's profiles, identified available resources (people, places, things), and organized materials. His approach does mean that the program is child-led and child-motivated. Because control resides not with the teacher but with the children, they have freedom for creativity, spontaneity, and personal responses.

Remember that a program does not produce creativity — the child does. Creativity is self-motivated and self-directed. It is a natural part of the child's state of being and cannot be produced by the educator. It requires real and open choices, not labelling activities right or wrong. If a child wants to crumple up paper into balls rather than draw on it, this is also a creative response.

A Rich Environment

If you refer to the beginning of the chapter, you will notice the description of the room in which Gina found the yarn. Creating a rich environment where children's creativity can flourish seems such an obvious part of early childhood education, but at the same time it requires thought and careful attention.

Researchers have noticed that in the surroundings of well-known creative people, two environmental factors recur: density and control. Creative environments are dense — full of materials that stimulate the senses — and rich. They are also controlled, imagined, and manipulated by the creator.

What does this mean for you as an early childhood educator? First of all, it means that your overall input must be dense and rich — you support creative efforts as they occur and also plan for their occurrence. This positive input is key. A study by Margolin in 1968 first showed that children's creativity increased in proportion to their educator's.

The creative educator encourages children to enjoy their own bodies, experiment with sound, make messes, and learn from all these experiences. There is, after all, no right way to dress up, to build, to draw, or to cut out. All creative actions are valid, and you need to accept, encourage, and praise the individual differences in creativity.

Preschool children learn and develop through concrete experiences that involve their senses. As active learners, they inspect, touch, manipulate, and explore for all aspects of sensory input, including sound, taste, and smell. If you create a dense environment — materials that can be seen, heard, touched, smelled, and tasted — you increase the potential for learning and creativity dramatically.

Just as important as density is control. The creative educator shares control and learns with the children, recognizing that creativity is self-motivated and is not imposed from the outside. As we have seen in Chapter 10, the most effective educators are not afraid to let the children lead and to learn from them. When children are in control of their own experiences and learning, they are free to be creative.

For instance, a group of children might see an accident on the street. Although they are clearly affected by it, they find it difficult to express these feelings. They want to understand and express what they feel about it, but they cannot find a method of expression. You can use this incident as a springboard for creativity. You can prompt reflection by asking the children questions in a comforting and straightforward manner, supporting their feelings through verbal and body language and supporting their idea of acting out the incident. As the children move to the block area, you can add such props as a stretcher, ambu-lances, a medical kit, white gowns and masks, or a paramedic bag.

As the dramatic play unfolds, observe and support the activities — add a tape recorder for recording a news bulletin of the accident, or paper to write a newspaper story. Throughout this creative play, the children are the creators and they are in control. They have no control over the accident that occurred, but they have control over their expression of their reactions.

You have likely heard people say, "My program will never be creative — I can't draw or sing or dance." This familiar lament reflects a fundamental misunderstanding of what creativity is. Artistic ability, dance skill, vocal pitch — these are not fundamentals of the creative educator. More to the point is a fundamental commitment to providing a rich, challenging environment in which the true creator, the child, is in control.

The Process Approach

An environment that encourages creativity allows children to make discoveries, try new

experiences, and learn from them. They will be able to imagine, "If I climbed that tree and then fell, what would happen?" These kinds of possibilities can be experienced in the context of making up a story and then acting it out without injury actually occurring. In essence, the creative process includes all those "what ifs" of divergent thinking.

The process is the important part. We can return to the example of Gina and her friends' experience of the yarn, in contrast to the children who were told their object was to make a bird by folding paper. The children experienced the yarn in several different ways and became engaged in the process of braiding or sticking yarn on paper, whereas in the teacher-directed paper folding the end result was the object, and there was no room for the children's creative exploration of paper and then discovering they could make birds.

Laura Mills (1990) reminds us that "Focus on the product only makes children value play that makes things. Focus on the process of play helps children value their own actions and builds self-confidence."

CREATIVE ART

Art for children is about sensory exploration and imagination, and there is no right or wrong way to do it. Art activities for young children are process-oriented and emphasize the experience rather than the end product. Picture a group of children all trying to reproduce a paper-tube bunny like the one that has been displayed by the teacher. Little creativity is required. In suggesting this activity, the adult has given an obvious message along with more subtle messages. Overtly, the children have learned to

> **BOX 11.3 CREATIVITY AND EXPERIENCE**
>
> **A person who never made a mistake never tried anything new.**
> — Albert Einstein
>
> **To understand the world knowledge is not enough; you must see it, touch it, live in its presence and drink the vital heat of existence in the very heart of reality.**
> — Teilhard de Chardin

❖ copy a model (the educator's model, usually);

❖ follow verbal directions;

❖ work in an orderly sequence;

❖ complete a task; and

❖ manipulate scissors, glue, and materials.

Covertly, or subtly, the children have also learned to

❖ compare products and abilities;

❖ feel inadequate or frustrated if their product does not "turn out";

❖ feel guilty if there is no object to take home;

❖ "do art" only if there is an end product;

❖ adapt to adult direction.

The early childhood curriculum is designed to offer experiences in which the goal is the process rather than an end product, even when there may be one. The art is the doing: manipulating the materials, solving problems, enjoying discovery, following one's curiosity, experimenting, and taking pleasure in the experience.

In other words, if Jody makes a "mess" and stirs together blue and yellow paint and discovers that she has green, it does not matter that the house and car and tree in her painting are hardly identifiable. In fact, if she only experiences the pleasure of the squishiness of finger paints, that is fine, too. Children themselves can best determine how they experience what we call "art."

The Link between Language and Art

Art is a universal language, and a language that is natural for children. "Words are an imperfect language for children. Their sensations and experiences find more exact and complete expression in another language, the language of art" (Lewis 1973, p. 51).

As they observe their environment, children often want to talk about their experiences and they have many questions: How did "they" make the tapestry? Why did "they" use those colours? How do "they" make plasticine? Why is the charcoal soft? By working with art materials, children form concepts and express them as they experiment with new vocabulary. Creative children are often very fluent and can express ideas clearly.

Sometimes children like to talk while they work. This experience becomes therapeutic as they give visual form to their feelings and thoughts while they also talk about what might be happening at home. If children are feeling angry, they might find release in hammering nails into a board, smashing clay, or painting a picture that portrays their emotions. One reason why art is often used by professionals in working with children and adults who have been abused is because it draws on inner feelings and provides a vehicle for expressing them, resulting in the release of emotions.

Children's body language is another form of creative expression. They respond to materials with big arm movements — painting with a wide paint roller, pounding clay, rolling out handmade paper, lacing gimp. While the angry child is hammering nails, the quiet child is gently weaving ideas on a loom, painting with watercolours, or feeling soapy finger paint on shiny paper.

Art inspires receptive, expressive language and body movement. Looking at art, experiencing art, and creating art, children are moved to use language. Similarly, language inspires art. Hearing a sound may move children to draw it or create an instrument to reproduce it. Singing a song or telling a story may inspire children to draw the story in episodes or sculpt one of the figures from the story. The Navajo speak of weaving tales, and many books describe quilts as story beds. In addition to the art of the language, stories become another form of art when they are woven in fabric.

The Link between Cognition and Art

When young children first encounter what we call "art materials" — paper, crayons, paints, markers — they react as they would to any novel item. They explore by touching, handling, waving the material about and probably putting it into their mouths. They have absolutely no notion that these materials can be used to make a representation of something. In fact, they have no notion of making representations at all.

Soon, however, they discover that certain materials leave marks on other materials, and next, they begin to deliberately make marks. Even then they still have no concept of making a picture of anything. They are simply fascinated by the effects of moving a marker back and forth on a piece of paper or squishing one colour of paint into another. We call this phase "scribbling." While scribbling, children practise making all kinds of shapes, controlling where lines go, seeing how colours mix, and experimenting with patterns. They also improve the co-ordination and strength of their hand muscles in the process. By doing so, they not only prepare for more drawing and painting later on, but also for printing and writing. Scribbling is therefore a phase that deserves our respect and observant interest.

Eventually, at their own pace, children start to make a connection between what they see and the marks they have made on paper. Sometime between the ages of 3 and 4, they start to refer to what they have done as a representation of something. An adult may not think such scribbles resemble any object, but they have meaning for the child. Four-year-old David holds up what looks like a blizzard of lines and squiggles and explains solemnly, "This is the olden days when I was 3 and my brother was throwing snowballs at me." So begins the representational stage. Often the first recognizable figure is a human being. It usually looks like a tadpole, with arms and legs coming directly out of a big head. Later, children add more body parts to their figures, which look more and more realistic. They also begin drawing houses, trees, flowers, cars, animals, and birds, at first suspended in space, but later placed on a baseline across the bottom of the picture that represents the ground. They may show the sky as a blue band across the top, complete with a sun. Colours and sizes are often unrealistic — a flower might be as big as a tree and a dog purple and yellow. This is not because children do not know that flowers are smaller than trees or what colour dogs are, but

simply because photographic realism is not their objective. For children ages 3 to 5 or 6, a picture is not so much a snapshot of visual reality as it is an unfolding drama. Only at age 7 or 8 do children want their drawings to look realistic. In the following incident, Rita Jo was fortunate that the staff at the child-care centre had an understanding of the relationship between children's thinking and the creative process.

Mary Smoke, supervisor of the Band child-care centre in a northern community, was collecting a picture painted by each child to display for parents' night. She noticed 4-year-old Rita Jo making a charming painting of herself playing in the yard. She had painted the house, the sun, some giant wildflowers, a tree, and herself in the tire swing her father had put up for her. Just as Mary approached to ask Rita Jo for the painting, she was dismayed to see her take a brush and paint the entire picture inky black. Stifling her disappointment, Mary asked in a friendly tone, "What happened here, Rita Jo?" Rita Jo explained, "I played all day long and now it's night time, so I went to bed." Mary grinned and went on her way, reminded again that for children, painting is not an end in itself but an attempt to express the ongoing drama of their lives.

Although many features are common in preschoolers' representations, each child has his or her own unique style. It is important for self-esteem and creativity that each child be left free to develop a personal style and to choose what to do with art materials. When adults show children "how to draw," give them colouring books, or require them to do pre-digested art activities following an adult-made model, they interfere with creativity and can cause children to lose confidence in their own abilities and ways of expressing themselves.

BOX 11.4 THE CREATIVE CENTRE

MATERIALS TO COLLECT

Rubber, plastic, and paper tubes of all sizes

Cloth pieces and yarn ends

Feathers

Wood blocks, driftwood pieces, corks, tiles, shingles, plywood

Shells, pebbles, buttons, beads, sequins

Carpet pieces and wallpaper samples

Cardboard boxes and wooden crates

Paper of all colours, textures, sizes (tin foil, waxed paper, wrapping paper, rice paper, origami squares, cellophane)

Fresh and dried flowers

Children can become too dependent on others to tell them what to do and how to do it, a phenomenon called "learned helplessness."

The Creative Centre

The creative centre is a place for materials that allow open-ended ways of using them and that encourage exploring many possibilities: paint, markers, crayons, and paper; mud, clay, sand, rocks, plasticine, and play dough; fabrics and fibres; plexiglass and plastics; ice, snow, and water; found objects and recyclables. You can gather these materials by asking the children's families for contributions.

After you have collected materials, display them attractively in the creative centre. The materials themselves ask to be manipulated, and your way of arranging them can encourage creative experimentation. For example, selecting bottle caps to be used with vegetable dye and cloth strips for printing encourages

children to look for other "printers" among household items. Bringing in stones in summer and snow in winter as materials to be painted suggests a new understanding of the word "canvas." When you go on a field trip, take along glue, streamers, yarn ends, and cloth scraps and let the children experiment with these materials in combination with things they find.

The creative centre is the heart of a creative program. It must reflect the needs of the children and offer choices that meet those needs; however, the selection, combination, and presentation of the materials is your work.

Art Experiences

Art experiences in the early childhood education program vary from the sensory exploration of materials to the more complex exploration of technology. Sensory exploration is important for children of all ages. You can offer such continuous materials — which flow and can be spread, stretched, and changed by manipulation — as sand, clay, mud, snow, water, play dough, cornstarch-and-water goop, and finger paint, as well as such discontinuous

materials as pine cones, bark, leaves, flower petals, shells, beads, or rocks. You can extend sensory exploration of discontinuous materials by adding such joining materials as glue, tape, staples, nails, and metal fasteners so that the children can combine these materials.

Children enjoy expressing their sensory exploration through drawing, painting, weaving, and construction. They can use pine branches, feathers, string, crayons, paint, markers, and charcoal for drawing on such surfaces as looms, papers, boxes, wood, rocks, and fabric. Giving children the freedom to use their imagination to combine drawing tools and surfaces as they like, in both traditional and nontraditional ways, allows their creativity to thrive. If you have the equipment, children enjoy using technology to express what they see around them. Taking photographs, filming, and photocopying, along with using computer graphics, allows them different forms of expression. Regardless of the media the children choose, in an early childhood program the emphasis is on the process, not the product.

MUSIC

For most people, music evokes emotions, and at the same time it is an expression of deep feeling. Playing music and singing provide a creative expression that cannot be experienced in any other way. Music also allows for expressing a wide range of emotions: joy, sadness, fear, love, grief, anger.

Very young children respond to the rhythm of music, and most children especially enjoy drums, tambourines, cymbals, and a variety of instruments they can make themselves. In developing the curriculum for music, your role is to provide objects the children can explore to create their own musical instruments: dowelling and bamboo lengths, gourds, yogurt containers, wooden spoons, pots, pans, boxes, and coconut shells.

Place a variety of empty, halved coconut shells in the music centre and observe how the children use them. They might make clicking, scratching, or echoing sounds by clapping two shells together or by clapping a shell against the floor. The children might also use these halved coconut shells in dramatic play for horses' hooves clumping against the floor, for example.

Songs and chants are also an integral part of every early childhood education program. You can communicate the most simple messages through song, from "hello" in the morning to "time to go home now" at the end of the day. Singing is a natural medium for children, and many children sing spontaneously throughout the day.

Songs can be drawn from folk traditions as well as contemporary music. Children do not need to have their songs sanitized or made cute. Nor are songs just another medium for rote learning. By drawing from the richness of rock and roll, classical music, blues, rap, and songs from different cultures, you can enrich your music program with simple songs that children love.

Songs and chants can be combined with simple clapping or more complicated group games to become action songs. Action songs, which are popular with children, involve the whole body in the music and help develop movement co-ordination. Poetry evokes similar responses. Dennis Lee's poem "Alligator Pie," for instance, often leads children to clap out the beat to the poem with their hands or by slapping their legs. A variety of learning opportunities emerge from this spontaneous experience: creating rhythm, creating loud/soft sound, working together, body awareness, and body percussion. Once these activities have been introduced to children, they incorporate various styles of music into their play and into their own musical creations.

CREATIVE MOVEMENT

Body Awareness

Free movement is natural to children, who use their bodies and limbs as natural props. For example, during outdoor play children move their bodies with and against the wind — they enjoy whirling and twirling with the wind. In the fall, they make fluttering movements with their arms and fingers in response to falling leaves. Gallahue (1982) and other theorists maintain that **kinesthesis**, or the sense of body position in space, should be well-developed by age 5. Without it, the development of children's basic locomotor and non-locomotor skills is delayed. For this reason, your program needs to include many opportunities for movement.

Children need space and freedom to explore, so their environment should include climbing structures, balance beams, slides, and swings so that they can develop static and dynamic balance. Tunnels and obstacle courses, trips through and under materials, also give children experiences in using space, along with close interactions with people so that they feel personal space and its limits. Preschoolers can take on greater challenges on tricycles and riding toys that provide motion experiences. They also need to discover the feeling of swinging high on a swing, sliding fast down a snowy hill, or gliding across the ice.

Hand and Foot Collage

You can provide sensory experiences for preschoolers by having them dip their hands and feet into paint and using these as paint-brushes. They can also stand against a wall or lie on the floor while a friend traces their body outline. When they look at the drawing, they can identify their hands, feet, and face. The final part of the experience is to draw in their own features, hair, and clothing. This activity is an affirmation of self as well as an aesthetic experience.

Creative Visualization

Although nothing in the world may be new, the world is new to the creative educators who discover it anew. These educators use all five senses, are alive to textures, feel the softness of velvet and the richness of taffeta, splash in mud puddles and enjoy the squishy feeling. They lead field trips down a 10 m long alley to discover beautiful junk, interesting shadows, tantalizing smells, and a variety of shapes. They use language that is rich and varied and open to the language of others. Creative educators celebrate the joy children feel in their own bodies.

The kind of sensitivity we are describing can be developed through creative visualization, or guided imagery, exercises (see Box 11.5). These are similar to the daydreaming experience of the creative spirit. You can do creative visualization anywhere at any time. The only essential ingredient is a peaceful environment. You can use creative visualization exercises with children, encouraging them to make visualization part of their daily routine. As they are getting comfortable, expect a few giggles. This is their way of expressing nervous energy. The key here is not to rush the process but to be consistent and not give up on it. From our experience, it may take as long as three months for the children to feel comfortable with this kind of relaxation.

BOX 11.5 CREATIVE VISUALIZATION

Here are some suggestions for creative visualization for adults.

◆ Imagine a space, then try to mentally draw this space. Imagine a warm space from your own childhood. Draw it. Colour it. Now imagine a lonely space from your childhood. Draw it. Colour it. Reflect on the chosen colours.

◆ Close your eyes. Relax. Be comfortable. Get in tune with your breathing. Listen to the sounds of your own heartbeat. Now listen to the sounds around you. Get in tune with them.

◆ Meditate on a sound or colour, then weave that into a story. Tell the story to yourself.

◆ Walk in your garden, a local park, or a forest. Watch a sunset from your window. Think about yourself as part of all this beauty.

Making Space

Creative movement and dramatic play require that you organize indoor space in such a way that the children have free floor space. Dancing in a circle in a tiny space is frustrating and certainly not very creative when body movement is inhibited and children bump into one another. Children need space to be able to respect the personal space of others.

There are practical things you can do to clear space for movement. Hang costumes on wall hooks, arrange props on wall shelves, and put face paints or masks on trays beside a wall mirror. You can hang things from the ceiling too. If the children paint a piece of canvas, for example, it can be suspended from the ceiling along with mobiles.

To make a stage, hang microphones from the ceiling and put coloured bulbs in the ceiling lights. Photographs, children's drawings, found objects — these too can hang from the ceiling to create a stimulating environment for movement and dramatic play.

If possible, use outside areas for dramatic play as well. If you put props and costumes on a trolley, the children can wheel it outside. They can use blankets for sleeping bags, picnics, tents, space capsules, hammocks, or storage bags. In winter, playground equipment can be removed and the children can use the snowy yard for all kinds of movement: chipping ice with their boots, forming images with snow, sliding through rough patches, digging snow holes, making snow angels, and turning the play yard into an ice palace.

On grey days, play music outside for dancing and sliding, or bring out bunches of balloons or bright paints to paint a snow palace. Using space creatively provides incentive for creative activities.

LINKING ART, MUSIC, AND CREATIVE MOVEMENT

Imagine a child who connects paper tubes together to make a long jointed creature, then begins to chant and pull this creature in a writhing dance through the room. Is this art, music, or creative movement? This child's play requires gross-motor skills, co-ordination, and balance in pulling the creature through the room. However, look at the other skills that are being developed:

❖ fine-motor skills in cutting tape and then taping together the joints;

❖ classification skills in selecting only tubes of the same diameter;

❖ problem-solving skills in using tape rather than glue or staples to make flexible joints;

❖ imaginative skills in creating a scenario, then acting it out to create a dance;

❖ expressive language skills in developing words to accompany the dance.

Development in one creative activity, such as movement, is connected to development in another creative activity, such as art. The child who is inhibited when moving is very often equally lacking in manual dexterity, and finds roller painting and sculpting difficult.

By linking art, music, and creative movement, you can provide outlets for children's overall creative development. Some very simple, open-ended creative activities that strengthen these links are

❖ painting and sculpting in response to mood music;

❖ dancing against a backdrop of slides of paintings;

❖ playing instruments that are made by the player;

❖ dancing in masks and costumes that are made by the dancer;

❖ flying and running with kites made by the children themselves;

❖ videotaping group singing, and then editing the tape.

LINKING LANGUAGE, CREATIVITY, AND DISCOVERY

Without artificial time and space boundaries, the language, creative, and discovery curricula naturally blend. Children weigh and measure sand, exploring its texture while discovering mass, weight, and volume. They mix colours, blending pigments to find the right colour that satisfies them. In all these activities they use language to describe, ask questions, and reflect on the creative process.

Appreciating art is both a cognitive and an aesthetic task. Looking at a painting, children observe media and method, learn about both, then solve the puzzle of the painting. All parts fit together to make a unified whole. Appreciating art leads children to solve problems as well as appreciate the aesthetics of the artist and to think over the mysteries they find in art. The early childhood educator facilitates this process by supporting and encouraging the divergent thinking process that underlies the language, creative, and discovery curricula. She or he understands the need for time and space in the creative process.

Time means providing adequate time for the links to happen. Children need to discover relationships and build on them, and this requires unpressured time. That cheerful refrain, "Now it's time to tidy up," can be a threat to the creative child and a requiem for creativity. For example, if children begin to role-play experiences and create costumes and masks, you need to be flexible enough to postpone a scheduled snack until the play process is complete.

Space means positioning experiences to foster the links. The sand table is placed near the water table. Measuring cups, funnels, weigh scales, clear containers, and scoops are nearby. Similarly, the tape recorder is put in the dramatic play area to encourage children to record experiences or to use music as a part of movement. In other words, the creative program meets the needs of children first, and is flexible enough to encourage spontaneous creativity and finding the natural links among language, creativity, and discovery.

SUMMARY

Children are naturally creative. The development of creativity is influenced by sensory experiences, emotional and cognitive factors, and motor skills. Young children need a stimulating environment for their creative development.

In this chapter, we have discussed approaches for nurturing creativity through an open-ended and rich program that emphasizes the process through which children play and learn. Creativity can be encouraged in all components of the curriculum through experiences that link various means of expressing creativity. We have suggested that art, music, creative movement, and dramatic play are avenues for

children's creative expression. By providing activities and materials for children in these areas, you are nurturing their creativity and giving them opportunities to grow and develop.

REVIEW QUESTIONS

❶ How would you define creativity?

❷ How can you nurture children's creativity?

❸ Give three specific examples of how cultural diversity enriches an early childhood program.

❹ What are the characteristics of a rich environment in an early childhood program?

❺ Describe three activities that link art, music, and creative movement.

❻ Describe three methods of creative visualization. How can creative visualization be used in creative movement?

DISCUSSION QUESTIONS

❶ Use your five senses to describe a beautiful experience. What makes it beautiful for you? Would it appear beautiful to a child?

❷ What media would be developmentally appropriate for a drawing activity for preschoolers? Why?

❸ How might parents identify a creative program? Are there warning signs for the "uncreative" program?

❹ How would you plan for a half-day nursery school program for 3-year-olds using the creativity guidelines outlined in this chapter?

ACTIVITIES

❶ Locate free sources for at least 25 varieties of paper that you might use with the preschool child.

❷ Develop a plan of action if
   a) there were no wood in the room;
   b) you could be anywhere in the world for an hour;
   c) there were no motorized vehicles in your city.

❸ Collect recyclables from your play yard and sort them. Suggest as many uses for each recyclable as you can.

❹ Go on a sculpture walk in your local community with a group of children. Try to look at the sculptures through their eyes, observing their reactions and jotting down their comments. How would you revise the sculpture walk if you did it a second time?

❺ Borrow a set of art slides from your local library. Choose slides from the set that you feel would inspire creativity in the children you teach. Which slides did you reject? Why?

❻ Review at least three computer graphics programs. Select one that would be appropriate for the children you teach.

FURTHER READING

Cass-Beggs, Barbara. (1978). *Your Baby Needs Music*. Vancouver: Douglas & MacIntyre.
This was Barbara Cass-Beggs' first book and perhaps her finest. It presents a collection of simple lullabies and folk songs for children up to the age of 2, together with suggestions for movement exercises to stimulate their involvement. At the end there is an excellent section on musical instruments that can be made by children of all ages.

Goleman, Daniel, Paul Kaufman, and Michael Ray. (1992). *The Creative Spirit*. London, UK: Dutton.
Daniel Goleman introduces the term "flow state" to describe the flow of sensory experiences and ideas. In the flow state, time does not matter, and the child is lost in the flow between conscious and unconscious. Goleman's insight into creativity incorporates many earlier theories of Amabile and others.

Lowenfeld, Viktor, and W. Lambert Brittain. (1987). *Creative and Mental Growth*. New York: Macmillan.
By describing creative development right up to adolescence, this book provides a background for teachers of school-aged children. It also features aesthetic development charts for easy reference.

McKay, Donald K., et al. (1993). *Creative Teaching in Early Childhood Education: A Sourcebook for Canadian Educators and Librarians* (2nd ed.). Toronto: Harcourt Brace Jovanovich.
This reference book has seven theme chapters: self-concept, families, celebrations, seasons, animals, transportation, and my world. Each chapter offers extensive and detailed creative theme activities. The introductory section, "Basic Resources," provides a very complete collection of patterns, recipes, and play props.

REFERENCES

Amabile, T. (1989). *Growing Up Creative: Nurturing a Lifetime of Creativity*. New York: Crown.

Brooks, P. (1972). *The Empty Space*. Middlesex, UK: Penguin.

Cass-Beggs, B. (1978). *Your Baby Needs Music*. Vancouver: Douglas & McIntyre.

Fauth, B. (1990). Linking the visual arts with drama, movement, and dance for the young child. In W.J. Stinson, ed., *Moving and Learning for the Young Child.* Reston, VA: American Alliance for Health, Physical Education, Recreation, and Dance.

Fralick, P. (1989). *Make It Multicultural: Musical Activities for Early Childhood Education.* Hamilton, ON: Mohawk College.

Gallahue, D. (1982). *Understanding Motor Development in Children.* Toronto: John Wiley & Sons.

Goleman, D., P. Kaufman, and M. Ray. (1992). *The Creative Spirit.* London, UK: Dutton.

Jenkins, P.D. (1980). *Art for the Fun of It: A Guide for Teaching Young Children.* New York: Prentice-Hall.

Lehnert, G., and I. Lachmann. (1990). *Growing Up through Games and Play.* Toronto: Sport Books.

Lewis, H.P. (1973). *Child Art: The Beginnings of Self-Affirmation.* Berkeley, CA: Diablo.

Lowenfeld, V. (1968). On the importance of early art expression. In W.L. Brittain, ed., *Viktor Lowenfeld Speaks on Art, Creativity*, pp. 20–27. Washington, DC: National Art Education Association.

Lowenfeld, V., and W. Lambert Brittain. (1987). *Creative and Mental Growth.* New York: Macmillan.

Margolin, E. (1968). Conservation of self expression and aesthetic sensitivity in young children. *Young Children* 23: 155–60.

McKay, D.K., et al. (1993). *Creative Teaching in Early Childhood Education: A Sourcebook for Canadian Educators and Librarians* (2nd ed.). Toronto: Harcourt Brace Jovanovich.

Mills, L. (1990). Make child care work into play. *Interaction* (Spring): 24–25.

Schirrmacher, R. (1988). *Art and Creative Development for Young Children.* Albany, NY: Delmar.

Torrance, E.P. (1962). *Guiding Creative Talent.* Englewood Cliffs, NJ: Prentice-Hall.

Wasserman, S. (1990). *Serious Players in the Primary Classroom: Empowering Children through Active Learning Experiences.* New York: Teachers College Press, 1990.

CHAPTER 12
Facilitating Motor and Sensory Development

✐ **Overview**

✐ **Stages in Motor and Sensory Development**
   - ◆ Motor Development
   - ◆ Sensory Development
   - ◆ Special Conditions

✐ **Cultural Factors in Motor and Sensory Development**
   - ◆ Environment
   - ◆ Sex Differences

✐ **Observing Motor and Sensory Development**

✐ **A Learning Environment for Motor and Sensory Development**
   - ◆ Balancing Challenge and Mastery

   - ◆ Encouraging Exploration
   - ◆ Supporting Emotional Well-Being

✐ **Learning Centres**
   - ◆ Large-Muscle Activities
   - ◆ Enhancing Physical Well-Being
   - ◆ Small-Muscle Activities
   - ◆ Sensory Experiences

✐ **Summary**

✐ **Review Questions**

✐ **Discussion Questions**

✐ **Activities**

✐ **Further Reading**

✐ **Additional Resources**

✐ **References**

OVERVIEW

This chapter describes motor development during the preschool years and outlines two basic principles that influence the course of large- and small-muscle development: physical maturation and experience. We also discuss preschoolers' fundamental movement skills and their sensory competence: vision, hearing, taste, smell, and touch. Although the age at which children achieve motor skills varies, you can detect some general patterns through careful and informed observation. Research into cultural and sex differences in motor development suggests that there are some slight differences in the rates at which some groups of children develop motor skills, but there are far more similarities.

In this chapter, we discuss observing childrens' motor and sensory skills as a means of developing curriculum and as a method for identifying possible impairments and developmental problems at an early stage. Finally, we present issues related to creating developmentally appropriate and safe motor and sensory programs with an emphasis on understanding patterns of motor development to encourage optimal motor performance, individualized programming that provides opportunities for challenge and mastery, and the need to celebrate the process (the doing) of these activities rather than the end result (the product).

By the end of this chapter, you will be able to

❖ describe phases of motor development that occur during the preschool years;

❖ identify the sensory abilities of preschoolers and their perceptual tasks;

❖ discuss the contributions of nature and nurture to motor and sensory development;

❖ identify the components of a learning environment that promote motor and sensory development.

STAGES IN MOTOR AND SENSORY DEVELOPMENT

Soon after his father brings him to the early childhood centre, Joshua greets Charnjit and suggests they play in the drama area. Together they begin to dress up as the regal characters they have pretended to be for the past two weeks. Joshua quickly puts on a gold lamé party dress backwards (to avoid all those tricky fasteners) and a pair of matching high heels. He grabs his paper-towel-roll sceptre and begins parading around his kingdom, carefully balancing on his shoes.

Charnjit ties up a kimono and puts a feathery hat on her head. She then puts on a pair of elbow-length white gloves, arranging each finger in its appropriate spot. For the final touch, she dons a pair of flaming pink high-heeled shoes. Soon Paula joins them and begins ironing tea towels with gusto. She carefully sprays each one with a little water from the spray bottle using two hands (one to hold the bottle and one to squeeze the trigger) and then energetically slaps the iron on the towel and draws her arm back and forth, her whole body swaying. "When I get these ironed we can set the table for our tea party!" she suggests. The other two children agree and begin to gather dishes and food.

Dramatic play like this "royal tea party" is a regular occurrence at many early childhood education centres. As well as being entertaining and engaging for adults and children alike, these experiences are full of opportunities to develop and refine language skills, expand cognitive concepts, and help children master the give-and-take of social play. In addition, they are rich motor and sensory experiences. Joshua is co-ordinating a lot of perceptual and motor skills in staying balanced and upright in those high shoes. Similarly, Charnjit is experiencing a change in her tactile awareness by exploring a familiar environment with gloves on, and Paula is giving her large muscles a workout at the ironing board.

Motor Development

Theorists agree that motor development proceeds in an orderly and predictable sequence. Most of us learned to roll over before we were able to sit up, and we learned to walk before we could run. Motor development follows two fundamental principles: it proceeds from head to foot and from the centre of the body outward. Infants gain control of their head, neck, and upper extremities before they master their lower bodies, legs, and feet. They can control their trunk and shoulders before they master activities that use their hands and fingers. Children usually develop their fundamental gross-motor skills before their fine-motor skills. This makes sense when you consider that you need to be able to control and co-ordinate your arm movements (gross motor) before you can master the finger and hand dexterity (fine motor) required to use scissors or to turn the pages of a book.

Patterns of motor development are influenced by physical maturation and experience. Logically, motor development depends on muscle development and maturation of the brain and central nervous system. Such environmental factors as nutrition and opportunities for movement also affect developmental patterns. Undernourished children whose diets are lacking in calories and/or protein may experience slower brain growth and motor development (Lewin 1975). Similarly, children who have few opportunities to practise their motor skills experience slower and less complete motor-skill development (Dennis 1960). Preschoolers need lots of vigourous physical activity to develop their gross-motor skills and integrate information from all their senses.

Gallahue (1982) describes motor development as having four general phases: the reflexive movement phase, the rudimentary movement phase, the fundamental movement phase, and the sports-related movement phase. These phases of motor development begin before birth (pregnant women can tell you about an unborn infant's kicking) and end in adolescence. Gallahue divides each phase into smaller stages of development and outlines how phases of motor development generally overlap and build upon one another. According to Gallahue's model, children's motor development is a continuous process of building, refining, and combining skills and abilities.

The first two phases described in Gallahue's model begin before birth and include motor development during the first two years of life. During this time, infants gradually gain increasing control over reflexive movements. In other words, they begin kicking when they feel like it instead of kicking as a reflex.

The third phase of motor development, the fundamental movement phase, describes motor development between the ages of approximately 2 and 7 years. Fundamental movements are basic movement patterns that fall into 3 large categories:

1. Locomotor skills: walking, running, leaping, jumping, hopping, galloping, sliding, skipping, climbing, and riding a tricycle;

2. Stability and balance skills: bending, stretching, twisting, turning, swinging, body rolling, dodging, and beam walking;

3. Manipulative skills: grasping, throwing, kicking, trapping, bouncing balls, catching, stacking, and pinching.

With practice and encouragement, children develop increasing skill in these areas. Preschoolers become more adept at controlling and refining their movements as their bodies mature and as they engage in a wide variety of motor activities. Healthy preschoolers have ample motivation to practise their motor skills — they are always on the move. On average, the third year of life is the most physically active year.

Finally, in the fourth phase, sports-related movement begins after the child has mastered the fundamental movements, often at about age 7, and continues through to the late teen years. Children refine and combine their fundamental movement skills acquired during their preschool years to develop more complex skills and participate in more demanding activities.

Careful observation of preschoolers' motor performance helps you see their development. You can identify the changes in the quality of their walking, jumping, stair climbing, catching, and handling of objects as they mature. For example, compare how a 2-year-old plops a book onto the carpet with how a 6-year-old can place it carefully. Or watch a group of preschoolers kicking a ball — who chases the ball, and who figures out where the ball will probably end up and runs to block its path? When making your observations, you will notice how growing ability in cognitive and other areas of development (social, emotional, language) interact with motor and sensory skills to contribute to mature levels of performance.

DIVERSITY IN MOTOR DEVELOPMENT

You can expect to find tremendous variability in the ages at which children achieve motor skills but are still considered within the normal range. However, the majority of children acquire these skills in the same sequence. For example, some children learn to peddle a tricycle as early as 21 months, while other normally developing children are not able to do this until after their third birthday. Similarly, a few children have mastered the heel-to-toe walk as early as age 3, while other perfectly normal children do not have this skill until age 5.

In addition, preschool children's motor-skill performance can vary considerably from day to day. Children who are tired, sick, hungry, or worried are often unable to perform skills of which they are capable when they are feeling better. Children who are in the elementary stages of acquiring a skill may also be inconsistent in their performance as they continue to practise and consolidate their skills.

Sensory Development

You can tell that newborn infants have hearing ability because of their response to noise. Also,

their eyes follow the movement of objects between 18 and 38 cm away (Harris & Liebert 1987), so there is no question that they also have visual ability. They react to tastes and smells and can respond to touch (Lahey 1992). During the preschool years, children's basic sensory abilities are fully developed but their perceptual processes (the processes of extracting and interpreting information from sensory stimulation) continue to develop.

Think about the enormous amount of information that is available to you through your senses — which you are probably ignoring — as you read this chapter. Take a moment to listen to the sounds around you and to feel the temperature of the air. Become aware of your body's position and how your feet feel, and to notice the smell of the room or space you are in. Now, if you were to focus on all of this information at once and try to read the rest of this chapter at the same time, you probably could not concentrate on the words you see or retain the relevant information. You were not born with the capacity to ignore sensory information, but you had to learn to so that you can focus on specific things.

Even though young children must learn all this, they have a tremendous ability to concentrate, which becomes obvious when you watch them eat — then they become totally focussed. In fact, one 3-year-old boy consistently told his mother to stop bothering him when she talked to him while he was eating.

During the preschool years, children become increasingly skilled at paying attention to relevant information and ignoring irrelevant information. For example, they can pick out different shapes and designs better than younger children, but they are not as skilled as adolescents. They are also better than younger children at visual, auditory, and tactile dis-

crimination but still not as good as adults at these tasks. They may be able to distinguish between the letters T and O but they have trouble with O and D or b and d.

Finally, during the preschool years children continue to develop their abilities to integrate information from the various sensory modalities. Children learn to link the visual image of a cat with the auditory "meow" and the tactile softness of the animal's fur. Providing children with a rich variety of sensory experiences that engage all their senses helps them integrate sensory information, discriminate among stimuli, and establish which information is most important in a particular situation. In addition, the richer the sensory experience, the more powerful the potential memory that will be encoded.

VISION

Preschoolers learn about visual phenomenon such as size constancies (things look smaller when they are farther away but actually they stay the same size) and shape constancies (things appear to be shaped differently when they are viewed from different angles but in fact their shape stays the same). For example, a 4-year-old who had often seen airplanes take off and disappear in the distance went for a plane trip with his father. After the plane had taken off, the boy turned to his father and said, "Things don't really get smaller up here" (Matthews 1980).

HEARING

The neural pathways from the ears to the brain are not completely mature until children are 4 years old (Goc Karp & DePauw 1989). During the preschool years, auditory acuity (clarity) improves as they develop their auditory discrimination skills. They can perceive the difference between two sounds of similar pitches or pick out a single voice or instrument among a variety of other sounds. Again, lots of experiences in listening and combining auditory information with information from the other sense modalities helps preschoolers to develop their auditory skills.

TASTE AND SMELL

The sense of taste (gustation) and the sense of smell (olfaction) are responses to chemicals in the environment and give us messages about what we eat, drink, and breathe. These two senses appear to be fully developed at birth. Newborns like and dislike smells and tastes that adults commonly like and dislike (Harris & Liebert 1987).

Unfortunately, North American society has a preoccupation with eliminating certain smells and valuing only a selected few, probably as a result of advertising. Companies producing certain products have convinced us that certain smells are nasty, and therefore we all need a variety of personal and household products that disguise these naturally occurring smells. All of this seems to contribute to an "olfactory-deprived" environment. People are rarely encouraged to use their sense of smell, and yet information from this sensory modality can provide useful information about plants and animals (Lahey 1992) as well as enrich sensory experience. There has been speculation that our sense of smell is related to our emotions, because many people experience strong feelings when they are exposed to certain smells.

TOUCH

The sense of touch includes at least three other senses: proprioception, kinesthesis, and tactile sensitivity.

Proprioception is the sense that tells you where your various body parts are in relation to one another and the space around you at any given time, without using your vision. Information about orientation and balance comes from a sensory structure located in the inner ear. This structure is called the **vestibular apparatus**, which is made up of sacs and canals of fluid and receptor cells that are sensitive to changes in the levels of fluid as the head tilts and bends. Too much stimulation, which can occur when you are on a roller coaster or a bumpy airplane ride, can cause dizziness and nausea.

Kinesthesis is the sense that tells you the speed and direction you are going in when you are moving. Information about the location and movement of each body part comes from kinesthetic receptor cells in the skin, muscles, joints, and tendons. The senses of proprioception and kinesthesis work together and are essential for motor development.

Tactile sensitivity includes the skin's responsiveness to pressure, temperature, and pain. Humans' tactile sensitivity is very well developed during infancy. During the first year of life, infants can discriminate among objects solely on the basis of touch. They are very sensitive to and interested in the changing temperature of objects, and they appear to experience pain in the same way that adults do (Shaffer 1989). During the preschool years, children learn to identify, label, and interpret these sensations and integrate them with information coming from their other senses. For example, preschool children learn that red apples feel smooth, firm, and spherical; have a crisp texture; make a crunchy noise when chewed; taste and smell sweet; have seeds in the middle; and can be made into a variety of things that have different textures (pie, sauce, crumble). Providing children with a wide variety of experiences that give them opportunities to experience the world through all their senses helps them to integrate sensory information and understand their world and themselves better.

There is no question that children need gentle and caring touch from birth for overall development. Harry Harlow's (1962) experiments with baby monkeys demonstrated that warm, soft tactile stimulation is essential in promoting healthy development in monkeys. Rene Spitz's (1946) research (reported in Shaffer 1989) into the development of children raised in orphanages who were deprived of skin contact provides evidence that infants and young children require human contact to thrive. Providing touch sensations is an important part of what educators and care-givers do. Young children need to be hugged and rocked. They also need to understand their right to control the way their bodies are touched by others. Children should not have physical contact forced on them, and they need affirmation from adults that they have a right to distinguish between touches they like and those they do not like. Working with families to help children learn to keep their bodies safe is an important part of our role as early childhood professionals. The National Film Board of Canada has a series of videos called *Feeling Yes, Feeling No: A Family Program* that is designed to help families, educators, and young children learn how to talk about and protect children from abuse.

Special Conditions

Special conditions have an impact on the rate and sequence of children's sensory and motor development. For example, a severe visual impairment may slow down children's rate of motor development. Mobility and orientation of one's body in space are greatly affected by the ability to see.

Such orthopedic impairments as cerebral palsy and spina bifida can have an obvious impact on motor development and may prevent children from ever developing certain motor skills. In addition, children whose mobility is limited have a harder time accessing a full range of sensory experiences. Without sensitive and creative parents and educators, these children might not experience the pleasure of splashing their toes in a wading pool on a hot summer's day or rolling in a snow drift.

Similarly, special health conditions — diabetes, asthma, and congenital heart defects, for example — can have an impact on children's motor development and create unique demands on motor curriculum. Adapting sensory and motor activities to meet the developmental needs of children with diverse abilities can be especially challenging. You will often be required to "bring the world" to children to make sensory and motor exploration accessible.

CULTURAL FACTORS IN MOTOR AND SENSORY DEVELOPMENT

Motor and sensory development appear to take place at the same approximate ages throughout the world. Maturation (nature) limits the ages at which children are first capable of sitting, standing, and walking, and children's experiences (nurture) and opportunities to practise these skills affect the age at which they can act on their capabilities (Shaffer 1989).

Environment

Environmental practices arising from cultural customs affect the rate of motor-skill development in early childhood. Babies who are carried in vertical slings or held upright on their mother's lap walk earlier than those who spend most of their time lying down. Babies' vertical posture in a sling or vertical carrier helps them develop strength in the legs, neck, and trunk, which in turn aids the development of the motor skills of standing and walking (Dennis & Dennis 1940). Most studies that have compared the motor performances of children of different races have concluded that race is not the determining factor in these differences — custom is. Young children who are active and are allowed to explore their environment and try out their motor skills tend to have superior motor performance.

Sex Differences

In the current dominant culture of North America, assigned sex roles influence the kinds of early motor experiences children have. If you spend some time watching children in a school playground, you will often notice differences in the play of boys and girls. Studies show that by the first grade, boys do better in running, jumping, and tasks involving eye–hand co-ordination, while girls have higher skill in balancing and gymnastic activities (Plimpton & Regimal 1992). These findings are consistent with current child-rearing practices that indicate that boys spend more time in aggressive, large-motor, and sports-oriented play, while girls often play more quietly and participate in dance and gymnastics.

As far as we know, there is no reason why children of both sexes and all cultural groups cannot develop a full repertoire of mature motor skills if they have opportunities and encouragement. Research in motor learning indicates that children who have a wide variety of motor experiences when they are young are better able to learn new movement and sports-related skills when they are older (Schmidt 1988).

OBSERVING MOTOR AND SENSORY DEVELOPMENT

If you were the adult observing Joshua, Charnjit, and Paula, the children mentioned at the beginning of the chapter, what would you record about their play that morning? How would you know what opportunities to provide that would help them acquire new skills (challenge) and perfect the skills (mastery) they already have? In the first place, to give your observation meaning, you would have to know at least three things about the children:

1. Which motor and sensory skills have they previously mastered?

2. Which motor and sensory skills are the children currently practising and consolidating?

3. What is the next skill the children need to learn?

To answer the first two questions, you need to observe the individual children. Because the ages at which their fundamental motor skills mature vary, observe the motor skills of each child. You may be working with the junior preschool group, but within that group the children likely have a wide range of motor skills. Observe children in their natural environment, over a period of days, during both the morning and afternoon and in a variety of

settings (climber, gym, block centre, circle time) to get the most accurate picture of their motor skills. Record your observations, and if you have concerns about the motor development of a child, discuss your observations with the child's family and, with the family's permission, seek appropriate resources to have the child assessed. The local department of public health, the family's doctor, and hospitals are good places to go for help. In addition, a list of resources is included at the end of this chapter. Very few of us like to hear bad news, and we often avoid discussing concerns about a child's motor skills, hearing, or vision because we do not want to upset the child or the family. This is dangerous because of the negative consequences to a child's overall development. Sensory and motor impairments can often be treated and even eliminated, especially if they are discovered early. It is so important to work with families to make sure that their child is developing normally and to obtain the best possible treatment as early as possible.

To answer the third question, you need a more detailed knowledge of the sequences of motor-skill development. Box 12.1 outlines

the developmental sequences of a variety of fundamental motor skills and gives a rough idea of what to expect at various ages. Again, keep in mind that the ages at which children acquire these skills can vary considerably and still be considered normal. Children with sensory, intellectual, or motor impairments may proceed through the sequences at a slower rate and may not develop certain skills at all.

A LEARNING ENVIRONMENT FOR MOTOR AND SENSORY DEVELOPMENT

Young children seem never to stop moving. Parents often comment on how tired they would be if they moved as much as their preschoolers. Of course, children's constant physical activity and sensory exploration are integral to their development and growth.

As they try out new motor skills, children often call out, "Look at this!" or "Watch me!" as they demonstrate their newest motor achievement. They love to try almost anything new, and they are often alert to sights and sounds that adults take for granted. Many preschoolers have only a fleeting interest in fine-motor activities, but this is to be expected since gross-motor development precedes fine-motor development.

If children naturally do these things, why bother developing motor and sensory programs for them? Research into preschool motor development suggests that free play alone, regardless of how well-equipped the play area is, does not promote well-developed motor skills (Poest, et al. 1990). Children need some guidance from adults or older children to expand their repertoire of movements and help them to develop a variety of large-muscle skills. In addition, a developmentally appropriate

BOX 12.1 SEQUENCES OF FUNDAMENTAL MOTOR-SKILL DEVELOPMENT

BALANCE AND STABILITY

2 years	Stands on a low balance beam
	Performs a basic roll
3 years	Walks 3 cm wide straight line
	Walks a short distance on 10 cm wide beam
4 years	Walks 3 cm wide circular line
	Walks a short distance on 10 cm wide balance beam using alternate feet
	Walks 5 to 8 cm wide beam
5 years	Balances on one foot for 3 to 5 seconds
6 years	Can use axial movements (bend, stretch, twist, turn) to throw, catch, and kick

LOCOMOTOR ABILITIES

Walking

2 years	Walks up stairs alone with 2 feet on step
3 years	Walks down stairs alone with 2 feet on step
4 years	Walks up stairs alternating feet
4–5 years	Walks down stairs alternating feet
	Walks with arms swinging
5–6 years	Walks heel to toe, like an adult

Running

2 years	First true run — not a hurried walk
3 years	Runs stiffly and has difficulty turning corners
4 years	Runs more smoothly, with more control
5 years	Strong, efficient running; ability to start and stop easily

Jumping

2 years	Jumps down from object with both feet
3 years	Jumps up from floor with both feet
4 years	Jumps over objects, leading with one foot
5 years	Jumps up (about 30 cm), down, and forward (about 90 cm)

Hopping

3 years	Hops up to 3 times on preferred foot
4 years	Hops 4 to 6 times on same foot
5 years	Hops 8 to 10 times on same foot

(continued)

BOX 12.1 (continued)

5—6 years	Hops distance of about 15 m in about 11 seconds
6 years	Hops skilfully with rhythmic alteration

Galloping

4 years	Basic but inefficient gallop
6 years	Gallops skilfully

Skipping

4 years	One-footed skip
5—6 years	Skilful skipping

MANIPULATIVE ABILITIES

Large-Muscle, Gross-Motor Skills

Throwing

2 years	Body faces target, feet remain stationary, ball thrown with forearm extension only
3—5 years	Same as above but with body rotation added
5—6 years	Steps forward with leg on same side as throwing arm

Catching

2 years	Chases ball; does not respond to ball in air
3 years	Responds to ball in air with delayed arm movements
3—4 years	Basket catch using body
	Fear reaction — turns head away from ball
5 years	Catches ball using hands only (small ball)

Kicking

2—3 years	Kicks with straight leg and little body movement (kicks *at* the ball)
3—4 years	Flexes lower leg on backward lift
4—5 years	Greater backward and forward leg swing with definite arm opposition
5—6 years	Mature kicking pattern (kicks *through* the ball)

Striking

2—3 years	Faces object and swings in a vertical plane
4—5 years	Stands to side of object and swings in a horizontal plane
5—6 years	Rotates trunk and hips and shifts body weight forward in a mature pattern

(continued)

BOX 12.1 (continued)

Small-Muscle, Fine-Motor Skills

2 years
- Opens doors using doorknob
- Uses fist grasp to hold crayons and markers
- Scribbles vigorously with crayons and markers
- Stacks 4 to 6 large blocks

3 years
- Shows improved control of crayons or markers when drawing — uses vertical, horizontal, and circular motions
- Begins to hold crayon or marker between first 2 fingers and thumb (tripod grasp)
- Pounds, rolls, and squeezes clay
- Builds tower of 7 or more blocks
- Turns pages of book one at a time
- Manipulates large buttons and zippers on clothing
- Pours liquid from a pitcher into another container

4 years
- Holds crayon or marker using a tripod grasp
- Forms shapes out of clay (cookies, snakes, animals)
- Reproduces shapes and letters (O, H, T, and V)
- Paints and draws with deliberateness
- Builds a tower of 10 or more blocks using dominant hand
- Becomes more accurate at hitting nails and pegs with hammer
- Threads small beads on a string

5 years
- Shows a hand preference
- Cuts on a line with scissors (not perfectly)
- Reproduces many shapes and letters
- Builds three-dimensional structures with small blocks by copying from a picture

Source: K.E. Allen and L. Marotz. (1994). *Developmental Profiles: Pre-Birth to Eight.* Albany, NY: Delmar; and D.L. Gallahue. (1976). *Motor Development and Movement Experiences.* Toronto: John Wiley & Sons.

movement program can facilitate physical fitness and perceptual-motor abilities (those that co-ordinate what we experience through the senses with the motor response we make, i.e., the mind and body working together).

Children use motor patterns and sensory information to construct and organize knowledge. The job of early childhood educators is to provide an environment full of stimuli that will give children the best opportunity for motor and sensory development.

Balancing Challenge and Mastery

If you were asked to take responsibility for a child-care program without any help from anyone and before you had any training, you would likely be overwhelmed and feel completely inadequate, and you might even decide this work is not for you. Similarly, programs that do not take into account the level of the children's development can undermine their sense of themselves.

Children need a program that provides opportunities for exploration, skill acquisition, practise, and mastery. They need to be able to build on skills they have already acquired, but at the same time they also need challenge. You can incorporate a range of skills into your program since the pace of children's development varies. For example, if you put out beads to string to develop finger dexterity, you can also provide a variety of bead sizes and lace or thread sizes so that all the children can participate successfully. Similarly, if you offer a mystery box that contains a variety of items with different smells to enrich sensory experience, choose some strong-smelling ones (vinegar, curry powder) and some more mild-smelling ones (mango, leather) to challenge a range of olfactory sensitivity.

The best materials and equipment lend themselves to multiple uses. Toys and games that can be used safely only one way fail to challenge children's creativity, provide little opportunity for problem solving, and are generally appropriate for children at only one level of skill development. Research into playground safety suggests that traditional, single-use playground equipment creates hazards because children at different levels of development try to use it in ways for which it was not designed (Bowers 1988). The traditional metal slides found in many playgrounds is a good example, because they are too high for young children and not challenging enough for many older children. As a result, older children often try to crawl up the slide, climb on the side bars, or go down the slide backwards, head-first, or with another child. All of these creative activities that children generate to challenge themselves and have fun on a traditional slide increase the risk of injury. Lower, wider, and less steeply sloped slides that have multiple levels eliminate many of the safety hazards because they allow children at different levels of skill development to use the equipment safely in a variety of ways.

Encouraging Exploration

At the beginning of Chapter 11, we contrasted two groups of children in child-care settings. In the first example, Gina explored what she could do with yarn. If the educator had said, "Gina, that is not what this yarn is for. You're supposed to weave with it on a frame," imagine how different the outcome would have been. Gina's interest would likely have died right there, and the other children would not have benefited either.

Gina's teacher provided not only materials but an emotional environment that encouraged exploration. By way of contrast, the teacher who wanted the children to make birds was focussing on the outcome, or product, instead of paying attention to the process. When educators value exploration itself, children will enter into motor and sensory activities for the experience itself, although in the process they also improve their skills. Nevertheless, it is the experience itself that counts. To create an emotional environment that promotes motor and sensory exploration often requires that you abandon adult ideas about products, messes, getting finished, wasting time and materials, and directing children's activities. In other words, you must follow the children's lead because they are exploration experts.

Supporting Emotional Well-Being

Children also need opportunities to develop their motor and sensory skills for the value and pleasure these experiences provide in and of themselves. Many of us have strong positive memories related to exhilaration, freedom, and pride we felt as children when we mastered a motor skill or experienced delightful sensations. In addition to specific skill development, sensory and motor experiences for children can help them to develop heightened sensory awareness and perceptual-motor integration, positive attitudes toward their bodies, positive attitudes toward physical fitness, relaxation skills, and a general sense of well-being.

As we discussed in Chapter 6, young children often need help to release emotions. Motor and sensory experiences are beneficial in meeting this need. Many such sensory experiences as squeezing play dough; running hands through warm, bubbly water; or stroking a soft animal or blanket help children feel calm. Stroking children's backs, arms, or temples can also calm and relax them.

Many sensory activities and process-oriented art and movement activities have the added benefit of providing children with outlets for releasing tension. Kneading, squeezing, and pounding play dough, clay, and plasticine requires very little precision and can provide children with a relaxing tactile experience. Similarly, loosely structured movement and art activities such as finger painting or imitating how large animals walk can provide children with a constructive and safe outlet for their energy and frustration.

Some children are able to release feelings or excess energy through such physical activities as running or pounding with a hammer. A wise educator observes and works closely with each child to discover motor or sensory experiences that the child finds soothing. Helping the child to recognize and use these experiences to maintain a sense of calm pays off for everyone.

Specific techniques that enable children to relax can be useful for individuals as well as groups of children, particularly at rest time. Relaxation activities (see Box 12.2) that help children focus on their breathing and large-muscle groups help them gain increased insight into their own bodies and the physical sensations that accompany different activity states.

BOX 12.2 SAMPLE RELAXATION EXERCISE

HEART BREATHE NUMBER ONE

Have the children sit in comfortable places and then get them to focus on their breathing by giving them the following instructions:

While I count to three I want you to take a very deep breath, and really fill your lungs with air. Try to fill yourself up with air so your tummy is sticking way out. Then I am going to count backwards from three back to one again. While I count backward I want you to let the air out slowly. We will do this three times.

Afterwards, have the children close their eyes, listen to their breathing and their heartbeat, and imagine that they are floating. Or, try out one of the other imagery exercises listed in Claire Cherry's book.

Source: Claire Cherry. (1981). *Think of Something Quiet.* Belmont, CA: David S. Lake, p. 93.

Relaxation activities also give children practical skills to deal with stress that they can use throughout their lives to prevent injury and illness and promote their personal well-being.

LEARNING CENTRES

Many motor and sensory activities work well when you use learning centres that accommodate small groups of children. Choose a variety of centres that incorporate a range of activities from structured to unstructured and that accommodate a wide range of skills, interests, and abilities. A balance of large-muscle and small-muscle activities, process-oriented sensory activities and product-oriented activities, individual and group activities, and child-directed and teacher-led activities help to ensure that all children are challenged and engaged in the program. The list of small-equipment ideas in Box 12.3 will help you and the children to develop learning centres.

Large-Muscle Activities

Since preschoolers are developing fundamental movement skills, the curriculum should be designed to identify and enhance each child's balance, locomotor, and manipulation skills. In addition to providing children with opportunities to explore, practise, and refine their bending, twisting, walking, running, jumping, skipping, kicking, grasping, bouncing, throwing, catching, and climbing, the motor program should help children to develop body awareness, spatial awareness, and directional awareness. Games and activities that help children to identify body parts and their relative locations in space, such as "Simon Says" and "Head & Shoulders, Knees and Toes," and variations of tag games that require children to use a variety of body parts to "freeze" or "unfreeze" their classmates, are simple, fun, and easy to adapt to meet the unique needs of individual children. Similarly, games and activities that require children to experience the spatial concepts of under, over, beside, through, tall, short, narrow, and wide and such directional concepts as straight, forward, backward, sideways, around, diagonal, clockwise, right, and left help them understand these concepts in practical and concrete ways. Similarly, obstacle courses or games like "Slithery Snake" (pairs of children join other pairs to form a snakelike chain) or shadow games (children use their shadows to create animal and monster shapes) also provide opportunities to develop body, spatial, and directional awareness.

Concepts that are vague become clear with experience. For instance, children who ride their bikes down a hill understand the meaning of fast, straight, breezy, and glide because of their experience. The "Can You?" challenges listed in Box 12.4 provide ideas for integrating concepts into the large-muscle movement program.

Enhancing Physical Well-Being

In addition to providing opportunities to develop fundamental movement skills and body, spatial, and directional awareness, your large-muscle movement program can help to develop children's fitness and promote their well-being.

Like many members of our society, preschool children might not get enough physical activity to ensure health and wellness. Parents tend to drive the children to centres too far for walking, and parents' reluctance to allow children to play outdoors unsupervised means that many young children have limited opportunities for vigorous outdoor play. The early childhood curriculum must include adequate opportunities for intense physical workout. Even

BOX 12.3 SMALL-EQUIPMENT IDEAS

FOR BALANCING ACTIVITIES

Balance boards
Balance blocks
Coffee can stilts
Balancing wands/sticks
Balance ropes
Inner tubes and/or tires
Beanbags
Balance beam
Benches
Horizonal ladder

FOR LOCOMOTOR ACTIVITIES

Ropes
Hoops
Boxes and stairs

FOR LARGE-MUSCLE MANIPULATION ACTIVITIES

Balls
Beanbags
Hoops
Scoops

FOR SMALL-MUSCLE MANIPULATION ACTIVITIES

Puzzles
Beads and laces for threading straws
Sewing or threading cards
Paints and brushes
Crayons
Plasticine and play dough
Rolling pins and cookie cutters
Boards/dolls with buttons, zippers, knobs, dials, switches, keys, and locks
Screwdrivers, wrenches, and ratchets
Graters, measuring cups and spoons, pouring equipment (jugs, cups), and sieves

Eye droppers
Tape recorder
Flashlight
Flour sifter
Feather duster
Plant mister
Lettuce spinner

FOR SENSORY STIMULATION

Tactile Stimulation
(texture, temperature, weight)

Dirt
Sand
Leaves
Lychee nut skins
Seeds
Finger paint
Sandpaper
Cotton
Grass
Sponges
Gravel
Wallpaper
Liquid starch
Ice
Water
Snow
Clay
Flour
Corduroy
Eggshells
Velvet
Wood
Corn syrup
Brushes
Confetti
Marbles
Dandelions
Large feathers

(continued)

BOX 12.3 (continued)

Pineapple skin
Play dough
Pine-cones
Cornstarch and water
Soapflakes
Shaving cream
Silk
Tissue paper
Plastic bubble wrap
Waxed paper
Aluminum foil
Beads
Coconut shell
Artichokes

Visual Stimulation

Stained glass/sun catchers
Bubbles
Flashlight with coloured lenses
Fishbowl
Mirrors
Fluorescent paints
Student art
Kites
Candles
Pinwheels
Mobiles
Coloured sand/water
Streamers
Murals/wall hangings

Auditory Stimulation

Singing
Squeak toys
Records/tapes
Telephone
Instruments
Rattles
Tape-recorded or live sounds (e.g., weather: rain, wind; animal noises: farm animals, zoo animals; outdoor noises: birds, crickets, cicadas, traffic, machinery; household noises: broom, vacuum, beater, coffee grinder, running water)

Taste Stimulation

Sweet: flavoured yogurt, sugar cane, granola, ice cream, refined sugar, molasses, fresh fruits, dried fruits, beets
Sour: lemon, vinegar, cooking cherries, crabapples, pickles, lemon grass
Bitter: radicchio, bitter chocolate, baking powder, turmeric, cranberries
Salty: soya sauce, sardines, crackers, peanuts, cured meats

Olfactory Stimulation

Onions
Fruits
Mustard
Chocolate
Gingerroot
Pine needles
Powder
Plastic
Extracts (vanilla, peppermint)
Garlic
Spices
Herbs
Pickles
Coffee
Broccoli
Soap
Garbage
Vinegar
Tea
Flowers
Leather
Sour milk
Chalk

BOX 12.4 "CAN YOU?" CHALLENGES

Personal challenges can be used to promote development in each of the fundamental movement areas. The following are some basic ideas of challenges that can give you a starting point for your own ideas. The more imaginative the challenges, the more fun they will be. Often, using visual imagery such as "Can you be as tall as a smokestack, or as wide as a barn, or as small as an ant?" appeals to children more than the behavioural descriptions listed below. Images from children's daily experiences and interests will work best to engage their attention and motivate them to participate. Having children lead the challenges increases their interest and involvement and helps to develop important interpersonal skills.

STABILITY AND BALANCE CHALLENGES

Bending

1. How many ways can you bend your body?

2. Can you bend parts of your body down, up, like a pinwheel, a bucket, a wiggly worm?

3. Can you bend parts of your body when you are sitting down; lying on your front, back, side; kneeling; walking?

4. How many ways can you bend your arms, wrists, fingers, legs, ankles, toes?

5. Can you hook parts of your body together at the bends? Can you do that with a partner?

Stretching

1. How far up can you stretch? Can you stretch as tall as a tree, tower, chimney? How tall can you be?

2. How wide can you be? Can you stretch as wide as a school, barn, car, truck, blanket, whale?

3. How many different ways can you stretch your body at the same time? Pretend you are a piece of toffee/gum and let your partner pull and mould you.

4. How much floor can you cover by stretching? Can you be a rug?

5. Can you make two parts of your body touch by stretching?

Other balancing activities that you can challenge children with are twisting, swinging, dodging, landing, turning, stopping, and rolling.

LOCOMOTOR CHALLENGES

Walking

1. Try different animal walks, such as bunny hop, bear walk, elephant walk, ostrich walk, kangaroo jump, horse prance, crane dive, stork stand, crab walk, puppy run, horse gallop, worm inching, frog hop, seal walk, caterpillar walk.

2. Pretend you are walking up a steep hill, against the wind, on ice, through a jungle, like your partner.

3. Can you keep your hands up high, low, in front, behind, crossed while you are walking?

4. Can you walk fast, slow, medium, forwards, backwards, sideways, on different parts of your feet, turning your feet in different directions?

(continued)

BOX 12.4 (continued)

5. Can you walk like a giant, an elf, a dragon, a happy person, a sad person, an angry person, a silly person?

Running

1. Can you run and then stop when I clap once?

2. Can you choose a place in the room/yard and run to it and back without touching anyone?

3. Can you run very low to the ground, in slow motion, with a partner, like an animal, as though you are at the beach?

Jumping

1. Can you jump in different ways, directions, around the room?

2. Can you jump in place at different speeds?

3. Can you keep your legs crossed, move your legs in the air?

4. Can you jump lightly, heavily?

5. Can you jump with a partner and keep together?

MANIPULATION CHALLENGES

Rolling, Throwing, and Catching

1. Can you roll the ball from the following positions: on hands and knees like a dog, sitting cross-legged, squatting like a duck?

2. Can you bounce the ball from the following positions: sitting, kneeling, squatting, bending forward, on your tiptoes?

3. Can you bounce/roll the ball like a _____ _____ and catch the ball like a _____ _____ ?

duck	cat
horse	person on the moon
elephant	dinosaur
wind	baby
bowler	mail carrier
jumping bean	very tired teddy bear
forklift	boa constrictor
worm	steamroller

4. Can you throw the ball with one hand, with two hands, overhand, underhand, sideways, fast, slow, high, low, like a robot, like a person made of jelly?

5. Can you toss the ball and catch it with both hands, with one hand, from one hand to the other, and clap in-between, and touch the floor in-between, and jump in-between?

Kicking and Trapping

1. Can you kick the ball with your toe, heel, instep, top of your foot?

2. Can you kick the ball forwards, backwards, sideways, hard, soft, with one foot and then the other, to a partner?

3. Can you kick the ball like a (various animals, people, machines, etc.: crab, ballet dancer, bulldozer, etc.)?

4. Can you kick the ball and hit the wall, and hit a target, between two chairs, in a straight line, in a curly line, diagonally?

5. Can you stop (trap) the ball with your foot, toe, finger, chest, bottom, stomach, shins?

when time is planned for outdoor or gym play, the restrictions sometimes placed on running and other vigorous activities can limit the benefits to physical fitness. A planned exercise routine that is appropriate to the level of the children's skills, or a regular walk to an open area where children can run "full out" should be a feature of the motor curriculum.

By selecting activities that promote endurance, flexibility, and muscular strength, you can help children develop cardiovascular fitness and positive attitudes toward physical activity, and promote lifelong fitness. Games that involve extended periods of running or that require pushing, pulling, lifting (wagons, wheelbarrows, large blocks), stretching, and climbing are good choices for promoting cardiovascular fitness, flexibility, and muscular strength.

Small-Muscle Activities

Such small-muscle activities as sewing, using pegboards, doing puzzles, beading, using small blocks, cooking, woodworking, and many art

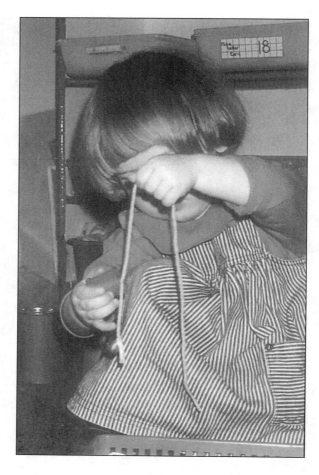

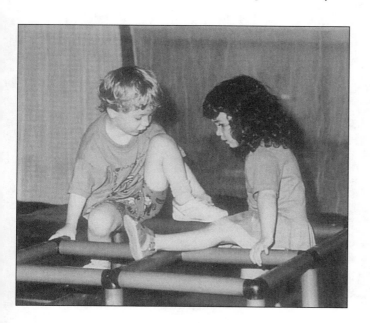

activities that require scissors, crayons, markers, brushes, and pencils demand considerable fine-motor control and eye–hand co-ordination. As we mentioned at the beginning of this chapter, children's small-muscle skills develop and are refined more slowly than their large-muscle skills. In addition, there is a wide range of ability in preschoolers' small-muscle skills. For these reasons, it is important to offer activities and materials that can accommodate a range of skills and provide all children with opportunities for success. For example, puzzles should include simple ones with only a few large pieces, intermediate ones with more large pieces, and more difficult ones with large numbers of smaller pieces.

Fine-motor activities require that the children sit in one spot and concentrate on the precise co-ordination of motor movements, which means they can easily become frustrated. Therefore, these activities should be of reasonably short duration. Children should be free to leave fine-motor activities when they have had enough.

Aside from developing skills, children need opportunities for exploration simply for the pleasure of the experiences. Smelling a lily, feeling a soft, warm breeze against their cheek, swinging high, running fast — this is how children experience life.

Sensory Experiences

The sensory curriculum should expand children's sensory awareness, develop their acuity, and help them combine and integrate information from a variety of sensory modalities. Sensory programming requires planning and preparation. Sandboxes and water tables need to be supplemented with a variety of sensory experiences. Rich sensory experiences are often messy, and they rarely result in a finished product — perhaps this is why educators sometimes avoid them.

Children can heighten their acuity by comparing stimuli in one sensory modality. For example, the mystery boxes mentioned earlier can be used to explore smell or taste. If you want to focus on smell, the substances in the bottles or boxes should be completely hidden from view (painted baby food jars with perforated lids work well). If you are having the children explore taste, they can use blindfolds. For hearing acuity, tape-recorded sounds work well.

Sensory experiences help children expand their understanding of an object and integrate what they learn. For example, when you introduce a new fruit or vegetable, you might consider playing a mystery bag game. Without seeing the object, the children reach into the bag and get tactile information about the fruit. Next, you might want to blindfold them and let them smell and taste the fruit or vegetable. After that, they get to see it, at first with the skin on and later without the skin.

Sensory activities such as this can be preceded and followed by information from books, trips, and discussions to extend the children's understanding of the concepts and materials presented and their personal sensory experiences. All the changes in weather, foliage, fruits, vegetables, birds, insects, wildlife, appropriate dress, celebrations, and everyday activities that accompany the changing seasons provide rich opportunities for increasing sensory awareness and expanding the children's understanding of themselves and their world. Sample games that can be used to enhance sensory awareness and integration are included in Box 12.5.

As children expand their sensory experiences, they also expand their vocabulary. Using words to describe their experiences helps them to remember them and to distinguish one from the other. A wide range of words is available to describe tastes, textures, smells, and sounds, and children enjoy interesting vocabulary. Use the adjectives listed in Box 12.6 as a vocabulary resource and an inspiration for creating your own exciting sensory activities.

SUMMARY

Motor development proceeds from head to foot and from the centre of the body outward. Therefore, preschoolers gain control of their large-muscle control before they master small-

BOX 12.5 GAMES FOR ENHANCING SENSORY AWARENESS AND INTEGRATION

MAKING BUTTER (TASTE)

You will need a glass jar with a firmly fitting top, cream, a pinch of salt, a knife, and some biscuits or crackers to spread the butter on. Put the cream in the jar, fasten the lid securely, and have the children take turns shaking the jar until the butter forms. (**Caution:** The glass jar will require careful supervision, but a transparent container is needed so that the butter can be seen forming.)

HANG OUT THE WASHING (SMELL)

Sprinkle small balls of cotton with liquids (such as vinegar) or powders (such as ground cinnamon) and then wrap them in small squares of cloth tied up with string. Hang these "smelly bags" at wide intervals on a low clothesline (about children's nose level). Children must then find whichever smell is asked for. (**Caution:** Be careful to hang the clothesline in a low-traffic area, preferably along a wall, to avoid children becoming tangled in it.)

RINGMASTER (HEARING)

One child stands blindfolded in the centre of a circle of children. They dance around her until she says, "Stop." Then she points to someone in the circle and says, "Make the noise of a lion (or mouse, bear, cat, dog, etc.)." If the blindfolded child can guess which child made the noise, then they trade places.

BEANBAG-EATING CREATURE (VISION)

Take a large cardboard box (from a grocery or liquor store) and paint a face or have the children paint a face on one side, then cut a large hole for a mouth. A bell can be hung inside the box like a giant epiglottis. Every time a beanbag is thrown into the mouth, the bell will ring to signal success.

TOUCH BINGO OR LOTTO (TOUCH — TACTILE DISCRIMINATION)

This game can be played like regular bingo or lotto using small cards that are matched to a master card. Instead of having pictures or numbers, the cards have different textures on them. The game is easy to make if you can gather up enough large pieces of cardboard for the master cards and some smaller pieces for the small cards. To create textures, glue pieces of sandpaper, velvet, fake fur, linoleum tile, wood chips, cotton, plastic bubble wrap, foam, and so on to the cards.

SNOW ANGELS (TOUCH — PROPRIOCEPTIVE AND KINESTHETIC AWARENESS)

Snow angels require a fresh patch of snow. The children fall into the snow on their backs, and move their arms up and down and their legs apart and back together. Making these angel imprints provides an opportunity to gain awareness of body parts in relation to one another (proprioceptive awareness) and how they move (kinesthesis). It also provides an opportunity to experience the unique tactile sensations of different types of snow (wet packing snow or dry fluffy snow) against clothes and skin. The children's clothes will make interesting noises as they rub against the snow, and often they will end up tasting a little snow in the process.

BOX 12.6 SENSORY VOCABULARY

TEXTURES

Smooth, rough, prickly, gritty, grainy, sharp, fuzzy, waxy, dry, wet, sharp, crunchy, slimy, sandy, hard, soft, hairy

SMELLS AND TASTES

Salty, sour, sweet, lemony, mouldy, bitter, spicy, hot, juicy, tart, fishy, burned, offensive

SOUNDS

Scary, melodic, loud, soft, low, high, light, heavy, noisy, quiet, sharp, piercing, whirring, buzzing, pulsing, monotone, dull, muted

muscle control. Preschoolers are developing stability and balance skills, locomotion skills, and manipulation skills. In addition, they are refining their sensory awareness, acuity, and integration skills. Children develop these skills at their own rate, but the sequence of motor-skill development appears to be similar all over the world.

There are numerous special conditions that can affect the rate and sequence of children's motor- and sensory-skill development, and careful and informed observation by early childhood educators can help in early identification of potential problems. Observation also helps educators to individualize their motor and sensory programs so that the activities they choose appeal to, challenge, and provide opportunities for success for each child. Preschoolers need a balance of free play and guidance from adults to expand their repertoire of movements and refine their sensory awareness and integration skills.

Motor and sensory skills are basic components of all learning. When creating environments and programs that promote motor- and sensory-skill development, educators can take advantage of opportunities to integrate skills into all curriculum areas.

REVIEW QUESTIONS

❶ What motor skills do children develop during the preschool years?

❷ What are the sensory capabilities and challenges of preschool children?

❸ How does the environment interact with biological processes in the development of motor and sensory abilities?

❹ Why are motor skills important to children's overall development?

❺ What roles does observation play in motor and sensory programming?

DISCUSSION QUESTIONS

❶ Discuss the relationship among motor-skill development, body image, and self-esteem in early childhood.

❷ Choose an activity that promotes some aspect of motor or sensory development during the preschool period. What practical changes would you need to make to this activity so that a child with a hearing impairment (or visual impairment, orthopedic impairment, or other specific special health condition) could participate?

❸ A child in your program seems to enjoy all areas of the curriculum and gets along well with the other children. However, you notice that he avoids the block area. When he does play there, he becomes extremely frustrated. His efforts at construction inevitably end with him throwing the blocks down and screaming with frustration. Discuss the course of action you would take to understand this problem.

❹ Discuss the influence of parental encouragement of boys versus girls in the acquisition of motor skills during early childhood.

❺ Debate the place of competitive (or co-operative) games in an early childhood curriculum.

ACTIVITIES

❶ Research your own motor development. Try to find out the approximate ages when you reached a variety of motor milestones (rolling over, sitting up, first step, riding a two-wheeled bike, learning to skip, swim, skate, etc.). If much of this information is unavailable, record the motor skills you now have. Compare your rates of skill development and your current variety of motor skills with other classmates. Summarize the age norms and number of people within the class who have particular skills. Compare your current attitudes toward physical activities, and discuss possible reasons for variations in rates of development and attitudes toward motor activities.

❷ Test two children (for example, a 3-year-old and a 6-year-old) in finger opposition (touch-ing each finger in order to the thumb of the same hand), and record and discuss observed differences.

❸ Compare children at different ages in their ability to identify and name body parts, distinguish between letters (for example, b and p) and shapes, and perceive differences in visual stimuli. Are there observable differences among children at different ages?

❹ To explore the idea that large-muscle development precedes small-muscle development, observe a group of children during outdoor play. Ask the early childhood educator which children work best with their hands. Are these the same children who move most efficiently during large-muscle activities? How can you account for your findings?

FURTHER READING

Beaty, J.J. (1994). *Observing the Development of the Young Child* **(3rd ed.). New York: Macmillan.**
This book provides concise summaries of developmental sequences, includes convenient checklists, and makes suggestions for activities that are appropriate to each developmental level. In addition, the book contains observation guidelines and helpful programming suggestions for children who have not yet achieved success with a particular skill.

Cherry, C. (1983). *Think of Something Quiet.* **Belmont, CA: David S. Lake.**
This book deals with stress and relaxation in the lives of young children and adults. The book includes a discussion of signs and causes of stress, strategies and techniques for reducing stress, and activities that promote relaxation.

Curtis, S. (1982). *The Joy of Movement in Early Childhood.* **New York: Teachers College Press.**

This is a valuable resource book specifically for motor-skill development. The book includes an overview of motor development during the preschool years, as well as a practical guide to motor activities. There are lots of activity ideas, sample curriculum plans, and observation checklists.

Gregson, B. (1984). *The Outrageous Outdoor Games Book.* **Belmont, CA: Fearon Teacher Aids.**
This book contains 133 group games, projects, and activities for the outdoors. The activities require very little equipment, and many are appropriate for preschoolers.

Kamii, C., and R. DeVries. (1980). *Group Games in Early Education: Implications of Piaget's Theory.* **Washington, DC: National Association for the Education of Young Children.**
This book focusses on all aspects of group games for young children. Familiar games are presented and modified to make them more appropriate for young children. This book links Piaget's theory directly with early childhood practices and demonstrates how children's play provides invaluable learning opportunities.

Lear, R. (1990). *Play Helps: Toys and Activities for Children with Special Needs.* **Oxford: Heinemann Medical Books.**
This was originally intended as a sourcebook of play ideas for handicapped or bedridden children, but the practical ideas regarding do-it-yourself toys, games, and activities are appropriate for all children.

Parry, C. (1984). *Let's Celebrate!* **Toronto: Kids Can Press.**
Organized seasonally, this book contains a wealth of information about celebrations and special events from across Canada. This is an invaluable information resource and provides inspiration for new and exciting sensory experiences, games, and crafts.

ADDITIONAL RESOURCES

Feeling Yes, Feeling No: A Family Program. **(1984). National Film Board.**
A three-part video series in which actors role-play situations of sexual assault and show children ways to prevent such assault. Each video is about fifteen minutes long. There is also an adult video that is intended as a user's guide.

New Brunswick Department of Education. (1984). *Basic Physical Education Kit — Levels 1 to 3.* **Toronto: Heath.**
Even though this kit was designed for children in Grades 1 to 3, it contains many excellent ideas for motor programming that can be used with preschoolers. The Beginning Skills, Simple Games, and Creative Movement sections are especially helpful. The format is clear, and the kit includes easy-to-follow activity cards that can be organized to meet your unique needs. Currently the kit costs less than $100.

FOR CHILDREN WITH SPECIAL NEEDS

The Canadian Hearing Society
271 Spadina Road
Toronto, Ontario
M5R 2V3
Phone: (416) 964-9595 TTY: (416) 964-0023
Serves children and adults with hearing problems across Canada.

Canadian National Institute for the Blind
1929 Bayview Ave.
North York, Ontario
M46 3E8
Phone: (416) 486-2500 Fax: (416) 480-7503
Provides information and services to adults and children with visual impairments. The head office can put you in touch with the district office nearest you.

Hugh MacMillan Rehabilitation Centre
350 Rumsey Road
Toronto, Ontario
M4G 1R8
Phone: (416) 425-6220 Toll-Free: 1-800-363-2440
Fax:(416) 425-6591
Serves children up to 19 years old with cerebral palsy, arthritis, spina bifida, muscular dystrophy, asthma, cleft lip and palate, head injuries, and amputations.

Lung Association
1900 City Park Drive, Suite 508
Gloucester, Ontario
K1J 1A3
Phone: (613) 747-6776
Educational programs and information regarding asthma and chronic respiratory disease for adults and children.

REFERENCES

Allen, K., and L. Marotz. (1994). *Developmental Profiles. Pre-Birth to Eight.* Albany, NY: Delmar.

Bowers, L. (1988). Children need playgrounds. *Journal of Physical Education, Recreation and Dance* 59 (7): 47–51.

Cherry, C. (1981). *Think of Something Quiet.* Belmont, CA: David S. Lake.

Cratty, B. (1979). *Perceptual and Motor Development in Infants and Children* (2nd ed.). Englewood Cliffs, NJ: Prentice-Hall.

Dennis, W. (1960). Causes of retardation among institutional children: Iran. *Journal of Genetic Psychology* 96: 47–59.

Dennis, W., and M.G. Dennis. (1940). The effects of cradling practices upon the onset of walking in Hopi children. *Journal of Genetic Psychology* 56: 77–86.

Gallahue, D. (1976). *Motor Development and Movement Experiences for Young Children.* Toronto: John Wiley & Sons.

Gallahue, D. (1982). *Understanding Motor Development in Children.* Toronto: John Wiley & Sons.

Goc Karp, G., and K. DePauw. (1989). Neurodevelopment bases of human movement. *The Physical Educator* 46 (2): 77–85.

Harlow, H.F., and M.K. Harlow. (1962). Social deprivation in monkeys. *Scientific American* 207: 136–46.

Harris, J.R., and R.M. Liebert. (1987). *The Child* (2nd ed.). Englewood Cliffs, NJ: Prentice-Hall.

Hendrick, J. (1992). *The Whole Child* (5th ed.). Toronto: Maxwell Macmillan.

Krogh, S. (1990). *The Integrated Early Childhood Curriculum.* Toronto: McGraw-Hill Ryerson.

Lahey, B. (1992). *Psychology. An Introduction* (4th ed.). Dubuque, IA: Wm. C. Brown.

Lewin, R. (1975). Starved brains. *Psychology Today* (September): 29–33.

Matthews, G.B. (1980). *Philosophy and the Young Child.* Cambridge, MA: Harvard University Press.

Plimpton, C.E., and C. Regimbal. (1992). Differences in motor proficiency according to gender and race. *Perceptual and Motor Skills* 74: 399–402.

Poest, C.A., J.R. Williams, D.D. Witt, and M.E. Atwood. (1990). Challenge me to move: Large muscle development in young children. *Young Children* (July): 4–10.

Rippee, N.E., R.P. Pangrazi, C.B. Corbin, L. Borsdorf, G. Peterson, and D. Pangrazi. (1991). Throwing profiles of first and fourth grade boys and girls. *The Physical Educator* 47 (4): 180–85.

Schmidt, R.A. (1988). *Motor Control and Learning: A Behavioural Emphasis.* Champaign, IL: Human Kinetics.

Shaffer, D.R. (1989). *Developmental Psychology. Childhood and Adolescence* (2nd ed.). Pacific Grove, CA: Brooks/Cole.

Wickstrom, R.L. (1983). *Fundamental Motor Patterns.* Philadelphia: Lea & Febiger.

Williams, H.G. (1983). *Perceptual and Motor Development.* Englewood Cliffs, NJ: Prentice-Hall.

CHAPTER 13
Enhancing Language and Literacy Development

✎ **Overview**

✎ **Communication and Language**

◆ Dimensions of Language

✎ **Development of Language**

◆ A Developmental Sequence for Language

◆ Influences on Language Development

✎ **Supporting Language Development**

◆ Conversations with Children

◆ Language in Social Interactions

✎ **Language throughout the Curriculum**

◆ Music

◆ Finger Plays

◆ Children's Literature

✎ **Emerging Literacy**

◆ Development of Reading

◆ Development of Writing

✎ **Setting the Stage for Literacy**

◆ Principles and Practice

◆ Linking Literature and Literacy

◆ The Benefits of Literature

- ◆ Sharing Literature with Children
- ◆ Linking Play and Literacy
- ◆ Encouraging Writing

✏ **Summary**

✏ **Review Questions**

✏ **Discussion Questions**

✏ **Activities**

✏ **Further Reading**

✏ **Additional Resources**

✏ **Children's Books Cited**

✏ **References**

OVERVIEW

Language development begins even before children can talk. The gurgling and babbling that draws parents' attention eventually become "dada" and "mama." After the babbling, words, phrases, and sentences develop.

Entering into conversations with young children is one of the delights of the early childhood professional. In the first three years of life, children learn to communicate — they develop as listeners and speakers through extensive use of language in play and other social interactions. Opportunities to discover the pleasure of books and reading set the stage for literacy and a lifelong interest in books.

The language and literacy curriculum is not a separate curriculum. It is part of all the activities of a young child. Language competence and literacy skills depend largely on the opportunities provided by children's families and early childhood educators. Today's early childhood programs offer an environment rich with language-learning activities and children's literature. Educators facilitate language development through their attentive and extensive conversations with children, and through support of play and social interactions that encourage communication.

This chapter explains the basic theoretical foundations and approaches that can help you understand and support children's speaking, listening, and emerging reading and writing skills. You will also become familiar with the nature of children's literature and discover the power of books for children's learning.

By the end of this chapter, you will be able to

❖ describe children's language and literacy development;

❖ identify the role of the early childhood educator in enhancing communication skills;

❖ describe interactions, approaches, curriculum strategies, and experiences that enhance communication and set the stage for literacy;

❖ appreciate and explain how children's literature plays a central role in the curriculum;

❖ recognize and describe characteristics of high-quality children's books.

COMMUNICATION AND LANGUAGE

Try to imagine going through a whole day without using your language or communicating with anyone. With no communication you would have no interchange with friends or your family, and you would make little progress in learning at school; certainly, nothing would happen in your classes. Furthermore, if you were to continue this experiment of not communicating with anyone, you would soon feel very insecure and isolated.

Learning to communicate with other people through language is an essential element of development. Children's ability to communicate affects their emotional security, their relationships with others, their cognitive development, and their literacy. They learn much of their communication during the first five years of life, and by that time most children are competent with language. Five-year-olds understand much of what they hear and express themselves effectively with a wide vocabulary. Their interest in and awareness of written language is emerging, and some children also have some reading and writing skills by age 5.

As you can see, the early years provide the foundation for effective communication and literacy. Effective educators are familiar with the developmental sequences of communication, language, and literacy, and encourage this development through a natural process that responds to the individual abilities and interests of the young child. Not every child is ready to read or write in the early years; for some, these interests and skills do not emerge until age 6 or 7.

As an early childhood educator, you play a major role in supporting language development through your daily interactions and conversations with children. As well, through the environment and experiences you provide, you are facilitating the practice and development of all aspects of communication. By exposing children to written language and a wide variety of children's literature, you are nurturing their interest and enthusiasm for reading and writing, interests that will develop naturally as their cognitive abilities allow.

Dimensions of Language

As we discussed in Chapter 4, language is made up of a number of communication skills. These include

❖ semantics (the meaning of words);

❖ syntax (the rules of grammar);

❖ phonology (speech sounds) and articulation (the ability to produce these sounds clearly); and

❖ pragmatics (the ability to follow communication rules, such as eye contact, taking turns, physical proximity, etc.).

You need to understand these four dimensions of language to understand children's language development.

The ability to convey meaning through spoken words is a highly complex feat of development that is found only in the human species. This significant skill emerges in young children before their first birthday as a result of the interaction of innate abilities and repeated exposure to communication experiences with other people. Children learn the social conventions of language even before they can speak. Babies play peek-a-boo and wave "bye-bye"; toddlers pause in their pretend conversations on the phone to allow the caller to respond, and sometimes they hang up on you!

After children have mastered basic vowel and consonant sounds, they learn to use sound patterns to create words by gaining greater control over their mouth and throat. Their articulation increases over the years. Eventually, children master different intonations for the same words (for example, "I *told* her" as opposed to "I told *her*"). Children begin to recognize the words for important people and events (mama, daddy, bottle, cracker, ball) very early, and by the end of their first year they begin to speak variations of these words.

Language comprehension grows incredibly quickly, so that by age 3 children have a vocabulary of about 1000 words and understand most simple sentences. By age 6 they have a vocabulary of about 3000 words and understand almost everything they hear. Children also become more competent not only in using basic grammar rules but in using longer sentences and more complex sentence structures.

In the following section, we'll look at this sequence of language development in more detail.

DEVELOPMENT OF LANGUAGE

A Developmental Sequence for Language

The process of developing oral language abilities, often called **language acquisition**, is primarily influenced by a "biological pre-wiring" that enables children to master the complexities of language (Chomsky 1957). It is also influenced by children's physical development (descent of the larynx) and cognitive development (connection of sounds and meaning, and the use of sounds to convey intent and understanding).

Pre-linguistic Speech

Unborn infants can hear sounds, and they react to loud noises. After their primal cry at birth, during their first month, babies use different cries and intonations. By the time they are 6 or 8 weeks old, they express their physical needs through squeals, gurgles, and coos.

At approximately 4 months, babies use **vocal play** to interact with others and as an expression of pleasure and contentment. In the following 3 to 6 months, babies experiment with pleasurable noises (babbling), blowing, and smacking sounds. They use most vowels and some consonants (ma, de, da) and different cries to communicate their need for food, attention, or comfort. Babies at this stage know how to initiate interactions with others through their vocalizations and have well-developed skills in "conversing," making and breaking eye contact to signal their intent to participate, taking their turn, and responding to others' words. They discriminate among and react to the familiar voices of family members, and their social smiling is more pronounced. They laugh, react to voice pitch, enjoy music, and use some body gestures, such as holding their arms out to be picked up. They also express a range of emotions through facial expressions and varying cries.

By their sixth to ninth month, babies babble more, repeat syllables, vocalize all vowel sounds, imitate motions and gestures, and better understand certain words. Kissing sounds, an understanding of key words and finger plays, waving bye-bye, and jargon-like sounds follow sometime between the ninth and eleventh month. Babies at this stage use an **expressive jargon**, which has speech-like characteristics and shows awareness of the rhythm and tone of the language of others. Already the infant has demonstrated many of the skills that will make him or her an effective communicator.

Meaningful Speech

At approximately 12 months, babies use **holophrases** (one-word utterances) to convey meaning. They can call others by name, express needs (bottle, "uppie"), and label familiar objects (doggie, ball, truck) with their versions of single words. They can understand as many as 40 or 50 words. For children, communication of meaning is crucial and occurs through both verbal and nonverbal means. Much of their language and communication at this stage is nonverbal, or combines verbalizations with gestures or symbolic signs (for example, head on shoulder for "night-night"). For the children, responding to nonverbal communication is as important as responding to verbal communication in these early stages of communication.

First Phrases

Around age 2, children begin to use 2-word and then 3-word utterances, called **telegraphic speech**, that are characterized by present-tense verbs and the absence of prepositions, articles, and most pronouns ("Emma milk," "Tanis cry"). Some of those telegraphic utterances become **anchor words** (all gone, bye-bye, more, eat).

The meaning of words in these first years is highly personal for each child. Mai refers to several varieties of fruit as "appo," and Harold calls anything with wheels a "kruck." Children gradually come to a more conventional use of words as their own vocabulary grows.

Children often misunderstand adults because the word for an object, such as cubbie or snack table, may be unfamiliar, or because children use a word or term differently at home. The use of gestures to point or to supplement new information is always helpful. Just as frequently, you can misunderstand a child's intent unless you take time to clarify his or her meaning — "My toy" may mean that the child owns the toy, wants the toy, or has one at home just the same. You will often need to use context and questions to determine the child's intent.

During the early years, children often simplify the pronunciation of words— "goggy" for doggie, or "toat" for coat. By repeating the consonant in the word, they simplify the complexity of quick shifts in mouth position that are needed for two different consonant sounds.

COMPLEX LANGUAGE

By the age of 4, children's pronunciation and grammar are more like those of adults, and their vocabulary reaches 1400 to 1600 words. During the following 2 years, children learn to master more complex and grammatically correct sentences (an average of 6-word sentences). They use past, present, and future verb tenses, use 2500 words, understand 6000, and respond to 25 000.

PRIVATE SPEECH

For decades, educators and parents have been puzzled by children talking to themselves. You probably do it, too, when you are preparing for a difficult test, trying to solve a difficult

problem, or rehearsing a conversation that is significant.

At the beginning of this century, Vygotsky (1962), a Russian researcher interested in children's cognitive development and language, recognized that private speech helps children think. Private speech is used to guide thinking and behaviour, at first aloud, but eventually internally. Private speech helps children in different ways:

❖ to monitor their work: "I need to find a block that is big and square to be a table";

❖ to answer questions: "Where is that car? Oh, here it is";

❖ to describe their actions: "I put water in the flowerpots. Now the flowers can grow."

SYMBOLIC LANGUAGE

Six- and seven-year-old children have a speaking vocabulary of about 3000 words and use longer and more complex sentences. After they have become effective listeners and oral communicators, their focus turns to written language. Having always been interested in listening to stories, children begin to associate language with printed symbols and show increased interest in reading and writing. When children reach this stage, literacy skills can be enhanced through more attention to written communication processes.

Influences on Language Development

FAMILY ATTITUDES AND PRACTICES

The most significant factor influencing the development of language (and later literacy) is the amount of language-based interaction the child experiences in the early years. The time and attention of adults who are genuinely interested sets the stage for language competence and literacy. Children need to hear language in many contexts and forms, such as conversations at their level, singing, reading aloud, and games with words to support their awareness of the value and processes of communicating. They need extensive opportunities to talk and to be listened to for the development of their communication skills and language acquisition. Many adults do this naturally, describing for young children what is happening and asking and answering questions, as you can see in the conversation between Daniel and his father.

Daniel: What are you doing?
Dad: I am making a sandwich. Would you like one?
Daniel: Yes. Can I help, too?

Dad: Sure. First we need the bread, two slices for me and two for you. Next the butter. Would you like to spread it?
Daniel: Yes, I can do it better.
Dad: Good job. Next, the meat. This meat is chicken. You like chicken, don't you Dan?
Daniel: Yes, I do. Put lots.
Dad: Next some lettuce and tomato. Do you want both?
Daniel: Lettuce, yes. Tomato, no. I don't like tomato.
Dad: Last, the mayo.
Daniel: What's mayo?
Dad: Mayonnaise — white, creamy stuff made of eggs.
Daniel: Oh, yeah, I like that. Can I put the lid on?
Dad: Sure, let's eat.

Not all families speak extensively with children or encourage and appreciate their chatter, sometimes as a result of cultural values and beliefs about the role and appropriate behaviour of children. In some cultures, talking is a highly valued skill, but not in others. Excessive talking may be considered a sign of rudeness, or a privilege to be earned with age, or associated with gender. In other families, adults have limited conversations with children because of outside pressures that distract parents, or because of deeper stresses that influence all communication patterns (such as depression, marital stress, or abusive practices). Children often learn to keep quiet to avoid unpleasant consequences.

The importance attached to literacy also varies in families. Some children are surrounded by books, experiences, and materials that enhance literacy; others have limited exposure to these. Children tend to imitate parents and other family members, so if they see no one reading or writing at home, they are less inclined to do so themselves. Sometimes family members have difficulties with reading and writing and are reluctant to have their children find out, so few stories are read.

These differences in language experiences lead to a wide diversity in language development and acquisition, which will be evident when children enter your program. Children who are not talked to and listened to and are not provided with rich language experiences often lag in their language development. They might not have the rich base of experience and vocabulary on which to build new knowledge. Early childhood programs can offer a language-rich environment and nurture the development of language and literacy, and can make a difference for children who have had limited language opportunities.

SENSORY AND PHYSICAL FACTORS

The natural process of language development is through hearing and responding to the speech of others. When hearing is severely limited, communication can also be delayed unless the impairment is recognized. Children who cannot adequately hear spoken language can still communicate nonverbally through gestures and, eventually, sign language. What is important is that they have some effective way of interacting with others and conveying their needs, ideas, and emotions. Although alternative communication bridges the language barrier, hearing impairment can result in isolation in a society that is so dependent on spoken language. Therefore, whenever possible, encourage children with hearing impairments to develop spoken language along with their nonverbal communication strategies.

Some children experience difficulty in speaking because of such physical characteristics as a cleft palate or such neurological conditions as cerebral palsy, which hinder the production of speech sounds. Articulation or voice quality can be affected, making it hard for others to understand what is being said. Language and communication skills can still develop, but they may take longer or may incorporate such alternative means as symbol boards or nonverbal language.

Because communication is vital to social interactions and emotional well-being, an inability to communicate can be unbearably isolating and frustrating. Early childhood educators working with children who have serious communication challenges need to collaborate with specialists to ensure that the children experience success in their communication.

LEARNING A SECOND LANGUAGE

When children's first language is different from that of the early childhood setting, they often feel insecure and vulnerable. Children who cannot understand English might feel isolated or on the fringe of what is happening. These children need a stress-free and supportive response.

For example, when Pablo came to the centre in his neighbourhood, he followed his mother closely, hanging onto her skirt. She spoke quietly, reassuring him in Spanish that his day would be fun. Pablo's father repeated her reassurances in German — Pablo understood and spoke Spanish, German, and French, but not English, so he was now immersed in a language he did not understand, and he was clearly anxious. Andrea welcomed Pablo and quickly noticed the airplane he was clutching, recognizing it as a source of security for him. She pointed to the airplane and asked, "¿Qué es eso?" ("What is that?"), one of the few Spanish phrases she knew. Pablo's father supplied the Spanish word, and Andrea repeated it. She invited Pablo and his parents to the book area where she found a book on transportation. They looked through it together, labelling pictures in Spanish, German, and English. Throughout that day and the next few days, Andrea incorporated many items related to transportation throughout the learning centres (airplane shapes to draw or to glue people onto). She taught the other children the Spanish words for car, truck, train, and boat with the help of Pablo's mother. The children also enjoyed the multilingual reading of the picture books. All the children enjoyed making loud sounds of planes, buses, and trains. Another child, Pierre, provided French labels and descriptions, to which Pablo responded with interest and relief. Andrea encouraged Pierre to translate into French whenever possible. As the days passed, Pablo relaxed more and became involved in play, first with Pierre and then with other children.

Children and their families should be able to use their own languages in the program. Encourage them to communicate in a variety of ways, including their own language or dialect and in gestures and pictures. Remember that the family's language is symbolic of their culture and deserves respect. When possible, translators can help parents to communicate with the staff and contribute to the program.

English is spoken all over the world, with the result that many dialects have developed. You will likely work with children who speak a dialect of English that might be different from yours. Their names for things are different and their pronunciations vary. Remember, however, that their dialect is as effective for communication for them as yours is for you.

Most children have already acquired several abilities in their first language. "The focus [should be] on what second language learners *have* rather than what they *lack*" (Ernst & Richard 1994). They are only disadvantaged by the limitations on your ability to understand them. Although children will need assistance to learn the vocabulary and grammar of English, they can do so quickly and with limited stress if they experience support from educators. Ultimately, children with more than one language will have an advantage over those who have only one.

Developing language and literacy skills is a highly complex task for children, and many factors influence the process by which children come to speak, understand, and, later, read and write. An enormous range of language proficiency exists in any group of children, even those of similar age. For the most part, this variability is still within the range considered "normal," and is not cause for concern or justification to work harder with children to catch them up. Where children are in the process of language and literacy development depends partly on the characteristics and learning style unique to each child, and also on the experiences they have had with language.

To enhance language and emerging literacy, you will need to know each child well so that you can provide experiences that encourage them in the next stages. Language and literacy curriculum in early childhood education cannot be provided effectively in an approach that is directed at a whole group of children.

SUPPORTING LANGUAGE DEVELOPMENT

Language is a social and communicative activity that bridges the distance between people. Language skills are a foundation for social interactions, cognitive development, and literacy.

How can the early childhood curriculum enhance language development?

Conversations with Children

Early childhood educators engage in talking with children throughout the day. When these conversations are open and two-way, you create an ideal experience for language development. The child leads the conversation, expressing her own ideas, observations, and feelings, while the educator listens attentively, responds, and expands with interested comments or further questions. These conversations provide a window into the child's world, telling you what is important to the child and how she perceives and understands her experiences. Language blossoms as the child organizes thoughts, expresses ideas verbally, and builds vocabulary.

Busy adults sometimes find that their conversations with children have become a one-way "dialogue," telling the children what to do or what they want them to think or learn. This kind of conversation does not help children develop communication skills, and may, in fact, may be perceived as intrusive or critical.

Children need to participate in interactions to derive the most benefit. They need to both talk and listen, and to experience the adult listening as well as talking. When talking with children, use strategies that prolong the conversation and involve children in continuous turn-taking. Ask the children to tell you more, or ask an open-ended question about what they think or feel about the topic at hand. Reinforce the child's ideas with supportive comments such as "I see what you mean," "That sounds like a special time," or "That sounds like it was quite a problem that you solved."

Let's listen in on a conversation between Dorothy, an educator, and Melanie, 4, at the creative table:

Dorothy: Melanie, I see you have been working here a long time. I'd like to see what you're working on.
Melanie: I'm making a dog. See, these are his long floppy ears.
Dorothy: You're right, his ears are long and I see he has a long tail, too.
Melanie: My dog at home has a long tail, and sometimes he chases it.
Dorothy: He chases his own tail?
Melanie: It's funny — he goes round and round in a circle. Once he banged right into the picnic table (she laughs as she remembers).
Dorothy: Poor dog. I hope he wasn't hurt.
Melanie: No. My mom says it's a wonder he doesn't get hurt more.
Dorothy: He sounds like a fun dog. What's his name?

The conversations you have with children are the most valuable ways of influencing language development. Box 13.1 provides some guidelines to assist you in enhancing your conversations with children.

Children enjoy conversation, and they develop ways of keeping adults and other children talking. For example, many preschoolers go through a stage when, no matter what is said to them, they respond with "Why?" because they genuinely want to know something, but they have also learned that this is one way of holding adults' attention and keeping them talking.

Children themselves expand their vocabulary through conversations. They sometimes use a word they know is not correct but is the closest they can come to what they mean. The adult then says the correct word and the child

BOX 13.1 GUIDELINES FOR CONVERSATIONS WITH CHILDREN

◆ Genuinely listen to what children are telling you. Avoid pretending to listen and then dismissing them with superficial responses such as "That's nice" or "That's interesting."

◆ If you feel too preoccupied or too busy when a child wants to tell you something, be honest and tell him or her so, and then say that you want to hear all about it later. Be sure to go back to the child when you are free.

◆ When children talk to you, show your interest by asking them to tell you more.

◆ When it is your turn to talk, elaborate on what the child has said and ask questions, which will lead to more talking.

◆ Use clear pronunciation and conventional grammar when you are with children.

◆ Enter children's play and model language that is appropriate to the situation.

◆ Enrich children's vocabulary at every opportunity you find.

◆ Read aloud from a wide variety of books. Besides reading stories, you might find ways to incorporate reading weather forecasts, shopping lists, recipes, brochures, and announcements.

◆ Provide children with opportunities to use many different kinds of talk: acting out stories, composing and telling original stories, composing and performing songs and poems, asking questions, explaining and reporting events, and recounting experiences.

remembers it. Many adults do this so automatically that they do not realize how much helpful information they are giving children.

Adults begin modelling language and conversation even before children can talk. For example, a parent often speaks to an infant, pauses as though expecting a response, and then articulates for the infant, and so goes on with the conversation until it is completed.

When children are just beginning to use language, adults often elaborate on what a child says. For example, this conversation occurred while a 2-year-old and her mother were waiting for a train.

Child: Goin' Gamma's.
Mother: Yes, we're going on the train to visit Gramma.
Child: Gamma tain?
Mother: No, Gramma won't be on the train.

Gramma will meet us when we get off the train. She'll take us in her car to her house.

As we already mentioned, adults also encourage language development by asking children for additional information. The children do not always answer, but the questions encourage them to give more elaborate statements.

Child: Goggy!
Adult: Do you like that doggy?
Child: Goggy.
Adult: Would you like to pet the doggy?
Child: Annie pet goggy.
Adult: I'll hold the doggy. Pet the doggy gently.

As you can see from these examples, conversations with young children provide essential opportunities for them to expand their language development.

Language in Social Interactions

The language curriculum is in many ways a spontaneous curriculum that occurs through play. Social play encourages the sharing of observations, ideas, and problem-solving strategies, while dramatic or sensory play can elicit discussions of feelings, relationships, and roles. While children manipulate, explore, and play, they share their own perceptions and hear the views of others. There is no need for the educator to structure communication; instead, the role of the educator is often one of listening, with occasional facilitating and interpreting as necessary.

Whenever you observe a group of children, you hear an abundance of language. Children share their opinions, knowledge, jokes, and observations; try to influence others, argue, and negotiate, all the while practising and fine-tuning their language and communication skills. Peer interactions provide an excellent opportunity for language development, no matter what their other activities are. For example, two children, Jamalie and Tony, who are best friends, are playing at the sand table, making roads for their trucks and cars.

Jamalie: Let's make our roads nice and smooth.

Tony: No, I don't want to.

Jamalie: Tony, the cars bump too much if the roads aren't smooth.

Tony: They aren't fun. (In a loud voice) Then you can't play with me in the sand.

Jamalie, with tears beginning to well up in her eyes, goes to get David, the educator, and brings him to the sand table.

Jamalie: Tony doesn't want to make the roads smooth and he said I can't play.

David: You must be feeling bad about that.

Jamalie: Tony, I don't like you to say I can't play.

David: It seems Jamalie wants to play with you. Do you want to work this out, Tony?

Tony: Yes.

David: How do you want the roads to be, Tony?

Tony: I want hills and going around corners.

David: Did you explain that to Jamalie?

Tony: No.

David: Why not tell Jamalie how you want to make the roads? Maybe if you talk about it you can work it out.

Tony: Jamalie, see, I want the roads to go up and down and around. I once went with my dad on a road like that and it was fun.

Jamalie: Well, we could make the roads hilly and with curves, but they still could be smooth. I just don't like bumpy roads.

Tony: Oh, sure. I didn't mean I wanted bumpy roads. I want hilly roads.

The two children motion to David to go away. As he walks away, he thinks about how crucial the use of language is for good communication, even among best friends.

Through social interactions, language becomes embedded in the experiences of children and offers extensive opportunities for practice and expansion of skills. Using language in peer interactions helps children to see the value of talking and listening.

You can facilitate conversations among children by withdrawing yourself from the centre of attention and by encouraging them to direct their observations, questions, and comments to the other children: "Why don't you tell the others about the castle you made in the sand?" "Ask Jack if he can tell you the way to put that puzzle together," "Can you invite Docia to have some cookies with us?"

LANGUAGE THROUGHOUT THE CURRICULUM

In addition to the social context of language, there are numerous opportunities to introduce a wide variety of language experiences such as music, finger plays, and stories that will appeal to and engage children. In the early childhood education setting, these opportunities occur throughout the day as children play, in small-group experiences, and in scheduled routines.

Ideally, these experiences should occur when group size is small (six or fewer children), so no child will feel overwhelmed and all will have opportunities to participate and to speak as often as they wish. For this reason, early childhood educators repeat language activities several times with one or more children rather than presenting an activity once to a larger group.

Music

Music is an excellent means of facilitating language. Nearly all of the children can sing such songs as "Wheels on the Bus" and "Mary Had a Little Lamb." Music offers a way for many children to use and expand language skills in comfortable, fun-filled activities. Songs often incorporate movement and games, such as "Farmer in the Dell" and "Going to Kentucky." Music is also an excellent way to introduce and facilitate other languages through songs from other cultures. Music and singing make play, routines, and transitions calm, all the while expanding language skills.

Finger Plays

Early childhood educators use songs and finger plays several times a day during play,

small-group time, and transitions. Songs and finger plays can be a part of conversations and interactions with individual children as well, serving to meet needs for closeness and individual attention. Through repeating songs and finger plays, children develop not only their speaking skills but also gain meaning of the words through the hand and finger actions (e.g., walking fingers for a spider). "This connection between actions and words is an essential precursor of literacy with print" (Jalongo 1992, p. 31).

At first, very young children join in through the finger movements, but progressively they use words and whole-body actions. Start collecting and memorizing children's favourite finger plays. Learn songs and finger plays in other languages; parents and children in your group can help you by sharing the ones they know.

Children's Literature

Reading aloud with children is another important contribution that adults make to the development of language in children. Children are never too young or too old to enjoy the pleasures of reading with a parent or an educator. In a relaxed and cozy setting, they enjoy the sound of the reader's voice and the rhythm of the words, along with experiencing comfort and pleasure in snuggling close to the reader. They feel warmth and caring, so this kind of experience in small groups of children enhances a sense of belonging.

Reading to children gives them an interest in books and the awareness that books are a source of pleasure and of information. Familiar stories create a sense of predictability and ease with new experiences. Books provide children with a rich base of background knowledge and exposure to a wide range of topics, giving them a sense of familiarity with things outside their personal experience.

Through books, children learn about feelings, relationships, their own and others' lifestyles, problems, and ways of solving problems. They learn about, and come to accept, others who are both similar to and different from themselves and their families. As you read, you play an important role as the mediator between the children and the story. You help children to find the parts in the stories that arouse feelings, excitement, happiness, wishes, and beliefs. Through this interaction, you help children to make sense of their own thoughts and their world.

With respect to literacy, exposure to books and literature provides experiences that are important to the processes of eventually learning to read and write. Books provide language patterns even before children start talking; they invite movements, finger plays, and sensorial experiences. Picture books introduce children to the reading process of turning pages and gaining information from the page.

READING WITH CHILDREN

Reading books with young children is an interactive experience. Do not feel that you must stick to the text, but draw the children into the experience by asking questions, modelling sounds, and commenting on the pictures. Let a child lead the interaction and experience the book in her own way. Never pressure a child to sit still and listen to a story, or to stay until a book is finished.

For young children, the following types of books are appropriate:

❖ **Stories:** fast-paced short-story line, humorous and rhythmic; favourite themes include food and body parts;

❖ **Concept books:** brisk, brief texts and bold illustrations;

❖ **Song and finger play books:** respond to the children's need to move and to make sense of new vocabulary;

❖ **Books that can be manipulated through moving parts:** for sensorial activities.

The maximum benefits of reading with children come when one adult and one child share a book together. Then you can focus on the child's personal experiences and perceptions, and help him to relate what is happening in the story to his own life. It is essential that early childhood educators find time to read to each child individually on a regular basis.

STORYTELLING

Many cultures, particularly Native ones, have an oral tradition of passing on their heritage and teaching children and adults through stories. In recent years, storytelling has gained popularity among many groups of people because of its benefits in developing imagination and for the simple pleasure and enchantment of telling and hearing a good story.

Storytelling has the same appeal for children. It encourages them to use their imagination and promotes oral expression and listening skills. To help children become familiar with stories that are told rather than read, use storytellers' traditional tools, such as a flannel board, dramatic props, puppets, or a story box. Choose stories initially that are familiar or based on repetition, so that the children will be able to follow without the familiar structure of pictures in a book.

How can you engage children in storytelling? By using voice pitch, pauses, faster or slower speech, facial expressions, emotional tone, vocal changes, eye contact, movement, and gestures to create and shape a story. Familiarity with storytelling experiences facilitates the children's use of props to dramatize their own stories.

DRAMATIZATION OF STORIES

A natural follow-up to storytelling is dramatizing familiar stories. Children often act out stories themselves or use puppets and flannel figures to re-create a story. "Through drama, they move from the particular experience of the story to a more general understanding of the nature of what is being explored, making explicit much of what is implied" (Booth 1988, pp. 27–28). When early childhood educators let children explore freely, provide them with a variety of environments, and encourage them to participate, children develop personal meanings from the story (Ishee & Goldhaber 1990; Booth 1988, 1991). *There's a Nightmare in My Closet, Teeny Tiny Woman, The Three Billy Goats Gruff*, and *Going on a Bear Hunt* are examples of stories that offer just the right actions, rhythms, and patterns for dramatizations.

FLANNEL BOARDS AND PUPPETS

Children who are familiar with books and excited by them spontaneously make up and present their own stories. Two ideal settings for this are the puppet theatre and the flannel board. In both of these centres, children use the props to create or act out stories — excellent language-enrichment opportunities.

The children or you can make puppets — you do not have to buy them. Through the puppets' conversations, children practise listening and speaking, take on roles, and express ideas and feelings indirectly. However, remember that the use of puppets by young children is for learning to communicate and play, not to perform in public. They enjoy puppets more when they can use them by themselves or in small groups.

Children enjoy telling stories with flannel boards because they can easily move the characters, mix them, and use props. Initially, children re-create stories you have told, but with experience they will soon be making up their own stories.

WORDLESS BOOKS

Wordless books, or books with few words such as those by David Wiesner, offer to children the possibility of making up their own stories either in private or in groups, and enhance their **visual literacy** (ability to infer meaning from pictures) (Read & Smith 1982).

Here are some ideas. Make up the dialogue that could have happened in *Mouse Around* by Pat Schories, or *Tuesday* by David Wiesner; make up the sounds that could be written in a wordless picture book such as *Oink*, by Arthur Geisert.

EMERGING LITERACY

Children's first exposure to and practice with reading and writing constitute the beginning

period of a lifelong literacy development, which experts refer to it as **emergent literacy**. Children learn to read and write similarly to the way in which they learn to talk (Cambourne 1987) — through experimenting, imitating, and active involvement in the processes of reading and writing. Providing they receive support and encouragement from their families and early childhood educators, they will go through the following stages naturally and spontaneously.

Development of Reading

There, perched on a cot, I pretended to read. My eyes followed the black signs without skipping a single one and I told myself a story aloud.
— *Jean-Paul Sartre*

From infancy, children are developing the foundations of their literacy education by becoming aware that print and pictures are different, and that meaning can be conveyed through written symbols. From simple picture and single-word books to the activity of putting one's name on possessions, drawings, and cards, children begin to grasp that certain patterns of lines and shapes have meanings. In the following example, you can observe evidence of the child's developing knowledge of literacy and how this has been influenced by members of his family.

Malcolm, a 3-year-old, is at a dinner party with his parents at Frances' house, a family friend. Now that Malcolm's stomach is full, he is restless because he has nothing to do. Realizing this, Frances retrieves a children's storybook from the shelf behind her and asks Malcolm, "Would you like me to read you this book?" "Yeah!" says the child. "Show me

where I should start reading the story," says Frances. Malcolm takes the book, places the cover in front of him, opens the book, turns the title page, scans the first page, points to the print, and says, "Here."

Somewhat amazed by his answer, Frances says, "How do you know this is where the story starts?" Moving his hands over the picture part of the page, Malcolm says, "Because this is the picture," and, showing the print, "This is the story."

How did Malcolm know? First, he knew that print conveys a message, for example, a favourite brand of cereal. Second, he knew that print and pictures are different. He had also acquired "book behaviours," such as finding the cover and turning pages — books are for reading, not playing. How did he learn this? By watching his parents and other adults reading, and weaving other literacy activities into their daily life, such as the television guide, cookbooks, road maps, notes on the refrigerator, sports scores in newspapers, and grocery lists. Malcolm also enjoyed "reading" logos, traffic signs, cereal boxes, signs on public washrooms and gas stations, and candy wrappers. When children begin to ask, "What does this say?" you know that they have taken an important step in recognizing that print conveys meaning. To become readers, children must have enormous amounts of experience with written language. What is a most important first step is that they associate written language symbols with meaning, an awareness that comes from an environment that is rich with print.

Learning to read develops through a series of stages (Cochrane, et al. 1984). Long before children read their first words, they are developing many related skills. An early awareness of and interest in books lays the foundation.

Children enjoy listening to stories and pointing out pictures that relate to the story being read. They "read" books themselves, either from memory or by paraphrasing a well-known story. They show knowledge of how stories work when they make up their own ("Once upon a time … ").

Before actually beginning to read, children must also recognize that those printed symbols (letters) have meaning. They begin to recognize their own name and letters of the alphabet, and include letter-like markings in their drawings.

Children are ready to make the transition to reading when they can read back their own stories, recognize a few words and letters, or read a few words in a familiar context. As children begin to read, they become excited and often want to read to everyone. Although a few children reach this stage by age 5, most children will be 6 or 7 before they become actual readers.

The characteristics listed in Box 13.2 are indicators of varying levels of readiness to read that you will observe in children ages 2 to 6 years. Although the majority of 6-year-olds will not yet be actually reading, you will see evidence of many of the foundation skills and knowledge in many young children. Observe children carefully to see which of these skills they demonstrate, and encourage involvement in literacy at the appropriate level.

Development of Writing

In the early stages, drawing and writing are not distinct. Young children begin their experimenting with paper and crayons, markers, and pencils by scribbling. Toddlers scribble randomly. Around 3 years of age, children's scribbling is more linear and shows some patterns. Most young children draw first and then write (Graves 1983; Calkins 1983). At the same time as children demonstrate more perceptual knowledge about print features, their writing becomes more complex to incorporate this awareness (Clay 1979).

Children who have developed awareness of print start to differentiate "writing" from drawing. The scribbling begins to mean something,

---

BOX 13.2 EVIDENCE OF EMERGENT LITERACY

Does the child
- show an interest in books?
- listen to stories for extended periods?
- notice examples of print in the environment?
- name items in picture books?
- include letter-like symbols in drawings?
- demonstrate an awareness of "book behaviours," such as starting at the front of the book?
- role-play the "reading" of familiar stories from memory?
- recognize her or his own name and common words in print?
- use pictures to construct the meaning of print in books and posters?
- have a beginning knowledge of the alphabet?
- have a beginning knowledge of phonetic qualities (rhymes, words that begin with the same sound)?
- show a sense of how stories work ("Once upon a time" or "What's going to happen?")?

for example, the child's name. Writing develops from scribbling and takes the form of wiggly horizontal lines that look like lines of print, or a series of vertical lines and shapes that resemble individual letters. The drawings also contain more recognizable objects. The children begin to combine their drawing and writing on the same page.

Some, but certainly not all, preschool children start to use mock letters and progress from letter-like graphics to actual letters. A small number try to write words using a strategy called "invented spelling" (for example, I LV YU). As with other skills of language and literacy, the range of development of writing is very broad, with many preschool children still scribbling or using mock letters. Children need to be encouraged to continue experimenting with writing, whatever their level, because it is vital that they not become discouraged at this crucial stage.

SETTING THE STAGE FOR LITERACY

When should literacy activities be presented to children? Some people say at 3 years, others say at 6; still others say "many children self-teach themselves," or "many children learn to read and write 'naturally' in print-oriented families." How should literacy activities — direct instruction versus child-centred learning — be presented? Literacy instruction for young children is still a controversial issue, although much has been learned about this topic in recent years.

Should children be literate in two languages? This is another controversial issue for many parents. In Toronto, many English-speaking children are enrolled in French immersion programs. In Montreal, children of immigrant parents must attend French schools.

In some Native communities, such as those of the Cree of James Bay, Quebec, children are taught the Cree language from kindergarten to Grade 3. Frequently, children of immigrants are expected to become literate in their parents' language through after-school programs.

Professionals are not alone in debating these and other issues of the early-literacy curriculum. Many Canadian parents are concerned, sometimes with good reason, about the literacy of their children. The media and parents often blame the education system for literacy problems, and occasionally educators argue that parents are too busy or stressed to support their children's literacy.

This is just a fragment of a very complex issue. Concerned organizations such as the International Reading Association (IRA), the National Association for the Education of Young Children (NAEYC), and the Canadian Association for Young Children (CAYC) offer guidelines for supporting the emergence of literacy. As early childhood educators, we attempt to answer these questions in the context of our philosophy of education, professional beliefs, knowledge of children's cognitive and language development, and principles of preferred practice for the education of young children.

Principles and Practice

The current debate about literacy and education has created a situation in which all educators need to reconsider their practice in light of their philosophy and current theory. There is excitement when practitioners and researchers come to similar findings regarding literacy, since it is from those findings that principles and practices can be generated. The following section presents current thinking with respect to children's early literacy. You will notice that it is more important to consider the children's stages of literacy development, the learning process, and the teaching strategies than the age of the children or the types of programs in which they are enrolled.

Regarding instructional methods, early childhood literacy programs should focus on the acquisition of knowledge about print through informal activities: recognizing print throughout the environment, engaging in pre-reading behaviours such as memorizing favourite stories, engaging in writing behaviours, and reciting finger plays. Only when children are competent oral communicators and environmental print readers and show an interest in learning to read and write should they be involved in word recognition, and then it should be through meaningful literacy events.

Repetitious drill and worksheets are not appropriate at this early stage (IRA 1986a, 1986b).

When designing a quality literacy program, early childhood educators should reflect on the principles articulated in Chapter 10 and consider their relevance for a curriculum that enhances literacy. As you implement a curriculum for literacy, consider the principles listed in Box 13.3. Remember, the principle of child-centred education provides us with clear direction. The best support for any learning comes from planning to enhance the skills the child is already beginning to demonstrate with experiences and activities that are interesting and meaningful to the child. The child sets the pace and determines through the choices offered how he or she will meet the learning challenges and acquire new knowledge and skills.

BOX 13.3 PRINCIPLES OF LITERACY DEVELOPMENT

- Children's literacy development is interrelated with their language development.
- Children learn to read at the same time that they learn to write.
- Children need meaningful learning opportunities as opposed to skill-development exercises.
- Children need a large number of self-directed experiences in which they can choose the level and area of involvement.
- Children need educators who model what is to be learned and present it at a level at which it can be grasped easily.
- Children have different learning styles and need a variety of experiences that match the way they learn most effectively.

- Children have diverse needs and need learning experiences that are meaningful and appropriate to their individual needs.
- Children learn best when they have the choice to participate and learn individually and in flexible small groups.
- Children learn through small-group and individual literacy explorations; large-group learning activities are less effective.
- Print-rich environments support child-centred **literacy events** (learning situations in which participants are involved with print material).
- A literature-based curriculum provides meaningful experiences that are integrated within a context that is relevant to children's interests.

Linking Literature and Literacy

Among all the strategies to enhance literacy described in this chapter, reading aloud is of utmost importance. Reading to preschool and kindergarten children increases their literacy prerequisites. They learn that printed words have sounds and that print contains meaning. They also learn how to handle a book and become familiar with its left-to-right and front-to-back format (Doake 1979; Holdaway 1979; IRA 1986a, 1986b; McGee & Richgels 1990; Morrow & Smith 1990). Reading aloud increases children's vocabulary (Karweit 1989), their awareness of story-like language (Sulzby 1985), and their meaning-making ability (Elley 1989).

The sense of warmth and contentment associated with reading establishes a lifelong source of pleasure (Sutherland & Arbuthnot 1991). Some children become passionate about certain books. When they are adults, they pass on their love of specific books to the next generation of readers.

Today, there is an abundance of excellent literature for children, which has attracted many talented authors and illustrators. Some of them write for babies and toddlers; others write for older children. The uniqueness of children's literature is its audience. It is common for early childhood students to have fond memories of their own childhood favourites. Did your parents save those books for you? How do you feel when you look through those old favourites?

Whatever the philosophical basis of the early childhood education program, children's literature is an integral part of it. A wise selection of children's literature provides a foundation for all other areas of the curriculum and provides excellent learning experiences that can be explored individually and in groups.

Every early childhood program should have a variety of literary genres, which can be classified as follows (see Children's Books Cited at the end of this chapter for further details on the examples):

❖ **Folk tales and fairy tales:** These kindle children's imagination, help them grow emotionally (Bettelheim 1976), and are part of their literary heritage. Many characters in such tales are supernatural (for example, witches, ogres, dragons) and stereotypical (good or evil). The numbers three and seven are common: three pigs, three bears, and seven ravens, for example. Example: *Lon Po Po: A Red-Riding Hood Story from China* by Ed Young.

❖ **Fantasies:** Fantasy stories are those about unreal objects, events, or people. Example: *Where the Wild Things Are* by Maurice Sendak.

❖ **Realistic fiction:** These stories contain realistic people and probable situations. They present adventures, drama, fears, and joys. Children tend to identify with such stories. Example: *Alexander and the Terrible, Horrible, No Good, Very Bad Day* by Judith Viorst.

❖ **Poetry:** The best poetry books for children are available either as one-poem books, with few lines on each page, or in anthologies. Some are available in "big book" form. Example: *Feathers for Lunch* by Lois Ehlert.

❖ **Biographies:** Only a few biographies are available for young children. Frequently they narrate an author or illustrator's own childhood. Example: *The Art Lesson* by Tomie dePaola.

The Benefits of Literature

As you learn more about child development and share books with young children, you will discover the numerous benefits of children's literature. Let's describe them briefly.

Books help children build up the foundations of their literature and literacy structures. From books, they borrow the language, stories, forms, styles, and moods for their own stories, and they learn about being an author (for a review of the research, see Galda & Cullinan 1991). Children also seem to learn complex concepts better through stories because they are placed in a meaningful context.

Perhaps most importantly, books provide enjoyment — they make children laugh, cry, giggle, scream, dance, dream, and fantasize. Literature develops children's imagination by helping them to think in new ways about people, events, and objects. Literature extends children's experience and insight about their self-image, feelings, and emotions. Good writing helps children deal with a wide range of emotions through story characters who experience, for example, the joy of gardening with a grandparent or the fear of being abandoned.

Literature immerses children in social conditions such as living in different families and cultures. For adults and children alike, the enticement of literature is that it takes us away from the reality of day-to-day routines and provides us with opportunities to enter the world of fantasy and mystery. There is a great deal of mutual pleasure and satisfaction in sharing with children the world that is alive in the imagination.

Sharing Literature with Children

Sabrina, an early childhood education student, asked her instructor if she could borrow some winter stories for her field placement. The instructor took some children's books from the shelves (*The Big Snow*, *The Snowy Day*, *The Mitten*) and commented on the educational value of each. Then, holding *Owl Moon* in her hand, she said, "Why don't you try this one with your children? The text is very poetic — it might be a different experience for you and the children. Let me know how they respond to it." When Sabrina returned the books a few weeks later, she left the following note for her instructor:

All the children enjoyed listening to *The Big Snow*, *The Snowy Day*, *The Mitten*, and *Owl Moon*. They seemed to be especially intrigued with the book *Owl Moon*. One afternoon, after the children came in and settled down in front of the reading chair, I began to read *Owl Moon* to them. This story was new to the children, and quickly captured their hearts. They listened attentively without interrupting as I read the story. All eyes were glued to the beautiful illustrations. Many children seemed to be in awe of the owl illustrated in the book. Just as I finished reading, the children broke out in wild applause. I believe *Owl Moon* is a story

BOX 13.4 SELECTING CHILDREN'S LITERATURE

Although "thousands and thousands" of readings are the best way to recognize quality in a picture book, beginning early childhood educators can use these suggestions:

- Select a book that has pictures and text that complement each other.
- Select imaginative stories — stay away from formulaic books, such as those that are monotonously repetitive and so predictable!
- Look for books in which illustrative devices are used to help children develop their story-prediction skills, such as *The Mitten*, *The Very Hungry Caterpillar*, *I Know an Old Lady Who Swallowed a Fly*, or *Where's My Teddy?* (See Children's Books Cited at the end of the chapter.)

- Choose books with pattern sentences to help children master the conventions of print.
- Choose books that use natural children's dialogue, rich vocabulary, and speech patterns.
- Stay away from books with choppy sentences.
- Select books that will springboard a multitude of learning experiences.
- Select books that are free from biases and stereotypes based on gender, ability, race, culture, and family practices in favour of books that convey acceptance and respect for diversity.
- Choose books that children enjoy. What better way to develop lifelong book lovers?

that will remain close to each child's heart and will not be easily forgotten.

This anecdote speaks eloquently about the impact of quality books on young children. It also illustrates one of the ways in which early childhood education students rediscover their own pleasure in children's books.

You can share children's literature by reading aloud to groups of children, especially if the children are at a similar stage in receptive language skills and have reasonable attending and listening skills. You can create and maintain an atmosphere of anticipation and excitement if you enjoy reading aloud and express your pleasure freely in telling the story — your pleasure in reading helps to engage and hold the interest of children. Four- and five-year-old children often look forward to story times with pleasure.

However, several factors can diminish the benefits of group story time. If the ages and developmental levels of the children are too varied, it is difficult to choose a story that will interest the older children and will not be too complex to keep the attention of the youngest. The attention span of children varies, so if you try reading to a large group, you might find yourself interrupting your reading often to remind children to sit quietly. Restless behaviour indicates that some of the children are not getting much out of the story, and chances are their behaviour is detracting from the experience of the others as well.

Sometimes stories are used to fill in time rather than as a planned and valid group experience. Pulling a book off the shelf to help in a transition time devalues the experience, as the environment has not been prepared for attentive listening. During transitions, when

BOX 13.5 STARTING YOUR OWN BOOK LISTS

As an early childhood student in a community college, Charlotte is educating herself on how to recognize high-quality children's books through different approaches. She enhances her literature background through a literature course and personal reading of books in all genres. She is learning to analyze children's books by consulting such magazines as *The Horn Book Magazine* and *School Library Journal* (available through the public library). Charlotte visits children's bookstores and asks for advice from the competent staff. Once a month she buys one softcover picture book, but mostly she borrows books from the library and reads them — many times. Then she enters her new references in her computerized bibliographies and cross-references them with other printed bibliographies, which she is collecting from libraries, courses, books, and early childhood educators. Recently Charlotte discovered several versions of her favourite fairy tale, "Cinderella." She read all of them and started to notice importance differences in the language, illustrations, plots, and character delineations. She also found several cultural variations of "Cinderella." Her latest finding is a First Nations version, *The Rough-Face Girl* by R. Martin, which initiated her into Aboriginal folk literature. Since then, she has read the books of Ann Cameron and C.J. Taylor, two Canadian folk-tale adaptors (Taylor is a talented First Nations author and illustrator). Charlotte is on a nonstop literary journey — fortunate are the children who will be in her program someday.

the staff expect children to enter or leave the group partway through the story, the children find the interruption frustrating and it renders the experience meaningless. During a transition time, the children are probably not focussed, and can be distracted by other things that are going on at the same time. It is usually better not to use a group story for a transition time unless you are able to give your reading a sincere and committed effort. If transitional routines are absolutely necessary, you can use music, poetry, and songs that are short, lively, and easier for keeping the children's attention. Another method is to encourage children to choose and look at books independently and at their own pace.

Overall, as we described in an earlier discussion of reading with children, there is more benefit for literacy development when children are read to individually or informally in small groups. Not all children have a similar attention span, listening skills, and interests, so it can be difficult to keep a large group of children all engaged in the book you are reading. If your goal is to enhance children's emerging reading skills, a one-to-one reading experience is best. You can observe the level of reading awareness, and support the child's active participation in the reading process. You can assess a child's level of comprehension, and through discussion expand and personalize the child's understanding of the story.

Sandro, an early childhood educator, is experienced in sharing literature with children. He reads to his children every day and, if possible, more than once a day. Sometimes he reads to a group of five children, sometimes to a pair of children, and other times to individual children. He makes sure that he reads a good balance of stories, poems, and informational books. Occasionally, one of the parents or the director of the child-care centre comes to read to the children. On those days, Sandro posts a special sign on the door that says "Today, _____ is our story reader."

Linking Play and Literacy

Similarities between pretend play and stories suggest that there is a relationship between play and the development of literacy. Children who play farming, going on a trip, or being a monster often build the components of stories into their play: characters, a specific situation or problem confronting the characters, and their efforts to solve the problem or achieve a goal. Children assign roles of "mother" or "father," and they specify a setting of "house" or "school." They also state the problem clearly: "There's a monster in the yard trying to go in my window." The play revolves around blocking the monster or diverting it to solve the dilemma.

Through pretend play, children expand their concept of stories, including dramatization, as mentioned earlier. You can expand this type of experience when children tell stories to an adult, and then dramatize their stories and act out the roles of the characters. Opportunities to dramatize result in increased

---

BOX 13.6 ACTIVITIES THAT ENCOURAGE EMERGENT LITERACY

Many experiences within the early childhood setting promote emergent literacy even though they do not directly require reading or writing skills. Some examples are as follows:

◆ Alexis becomes familiar with the letters of the alphabet through letter bingo, letter dominoes, letter puzzles, and magnetic letters.

◆ Christina is learning to match speech sounds with letter symbols (phonics) through sound-matching activities, such as identifying in a set of words those that start with a /d/ sound (for example, daddy, duck, deep), or by selecting pictures of familiar objects that begin with the /s/ sound (for example, snake, shoe, sun).

◆ Billy is working on recognition of whole words by matching pairs of words printed on a frog-like shape or by playing bingo with them. He also likes to match the two parts of word jigsaws.

◆ Fran, an advanced reader, has started using the sentence-reading strategy. She is able to read patterned sentences and colour-coded words on charts: Clifford is red, Clifford is cute, Clifford is nice.

From the above examples, you can see the wide diversity of reading readiness that is common in the early years. Although a minority of children, like Fran, may be able to read, the majority are like Alexis and Billy, still more comfortable with the pre-reading activities that are found in the language-rich environment. As long as they can set the pace and select from a range of experiences that are at their level, the process of getting ready to read will continue. We do children no favours by pushing them to memorize or learn letters, sounds, and words by rote.

sophistication in children's knowledge of the story-writing process.

When children enter into make-believe play, they practise language with their peers, language that is similar to what they hear in stories. For example, "This will be my very own wand, and this can be your magic sceptre." Children use explicit language in this kind of play because conveying meaning becomes crucial to the successful development of the play.

Encouraging Writing

Early childhood educators play a crucial role in setting up a learning environment in which each child develops her or his potential for becoming a writer. You can create a positive atmosphere for literacy learning by encouraging risk taking, sharing ideas and pleasures, and co-operating in completing tasks, and by offering a broad range of experiences.

Model writing as often as you can. For instance, point out to the children that you are writing a note to someone. Create a physical setting in which an abundance of children's works is posted everywhere. Provide children with learning centres where writing can be incorporated into dramatic play and other activities.

Children incorporate a range of literacy-related behaviours in their play. They handle all kinds of writing and pretend reading; they tell stories, take notes while on the phone, and reinvent stories (Roskos 1988, unpublished, quoted in Morrow & Rand 1991). Such behaviours occur often during play when literacy materials (papers, magazines, menus, cookbooks, pencils) are introduced. In the dramatic play area, a fast-food restaurant, supermarket, post office, airport, or gas station are all scenarios that encourage writing.

Children could write a restaurant menu or signs, set up props, and display literacy materials such as a *TV Guide*, pens, and pencils.

Kinesthetic experiences help children explore letter shapes. Children enjoy drawing/writing with finger paints, sand, cornmeal, and styrofoam chips. They also enjoy gluing things in the form of letters. Brian "writes" his name backwards on his painting (NAIRB), and glues popcorn on his name printed with glue. Once in a while Brian's early childhood educator shows Brian his name label and asks him, "Is it written the same way?"

Vanessa likes to make letters with snakes of plasticine. After she and her friends had read several ABC books and talked about them, they decided to make a big ABC book on Halloween. They chose the words, volunteered to do different tasks, and picked their letters. The group focussed on this project with intensity and carried it through to completion — an example of a spontaneous literacy curriculum. When you encourage young children to draw and write, keep in mind that they are meaning makers — makers of their own literacy learning (Wells 1986).

SUMMARY

In this chapter, we have described how children's language, reading, and writing abilities develop in the early years, and we discussed the factors that affect the development of language. In families who value and model rich language and print experiences, children develop a foundation for literacy.

Early childhood educators nourish language and literacy through the physical environment and curriculum experiences. Conversation and other literacy experiences, such as reading and storytelling, are an integral part of language development.

Children's literature is central to the literacy curriculum, and they benefit in many ways from listening to stories. Reading books provides comfort and offers children the foundation for a lifelong love of books and reading. Children imitate language in these rich experiences in pretend play, creating stories, and developing an interest in writing at their own pace.

REVIEW QUESTIONS

❶ Describe approaches that can be used to support children's oral language development.

❷ Explain why it is important that children become aware of print before they start to read and write.

❸ Describe briefly children's development in literacy.

❹ Explain the value of children's literature in the curriculum.

DISCUSSION QUESTIONS

❶ Discuss some of the issues associated with early literacy education.

❷ Save newspaper articles that relate to literacy education for young children or to children's literature. Highlight the main points and analyze them.

❸ Read three or four different versions of your favourite fairy tale. Are some versions more scary than others? Discuss which version you would use with 3-year-olds and 6-year-olds.

❹ Use the same book to discuss any stereotypes or biases that are perpetuated. How would you present these to children to increase their awareness of and acceptance of diversity?

ACTIVITIES

❶ Listen carefully to the oral language of young children and write down, as accurately as you can, what you hear. You might want to use a tape recorder to help you collect your examples. Identify the patterns of English that the child is using and the ways the child simplifies those patterns to communicate meaning. Share your examples and observations with others in your group.

❷ Find 2 or 3 children who are between 2¹/₂ and 5 years old. Work with one child at a time. Provide large paper for the children to write on, and a pencil or marker. Ask the children if they will write their names for you. Then ask if they will draw a picture. Follow this with a request to write something about the picture, and then ask if they will write their names somewhere else on the paper. You might also want to ask how old the children are and if they would write that down. Use the sample you collect as a basis for describing the understandings about written language that children have developed. Suggest activities you could provide to facilitate further literacy development.

❸ Observe 3-year-olds and 5-year-olds looking at books. Do you see a difference in their behaviours? Describe what you see.

❹ Obtain a copy of a children's book listed in this chapter and evaluate it using the criteria discussed earlier.

❺ List the favourite books of the children in a child-care centre.

❻ Go to the children's book section of a public library and ask the librarian to show you where to find and how to use *Children's Books in Print* and other bibliographies. Select a topic, such as bears, and look up all the listed titles for that topic. Check whether the books are available in different formats and in audiotape versions. How recent are these titles? Using the library computer, check whether these titles are available (older books may be very good, but they are not always easy to find). Start a list of children's books. If you have a computer, learn how to compile a database. Review the books to determine which are suitable for preschool children, and add this information to your file.

❼ Observe a group of children for half a day by focussing on the ratio of educator's talk versus children's talk. What are your findings?

FURTHER READING

BOOKS FOR EARLY CHILDHOOD EDUCATORS

Cullinan, B.E., ed. (1992). *Invitation to Read: More Children's Literature in the Reading Program.* Newark, DE: International Reading Association.

Donavin, D.P., ed. (1992). *American Library Association Best of the Best for Children.* New York: Random House.
An annotated bibliography of children's books and audiovisual materials.

Fox, M. (1987). *Teaching Drama to Young Children.* Portsmouth, NH: Heinemann.

Fox, M. (1993). *Radical Reflections: Passionate Opinions on Teaching, Learning and Living.* San Diego: Harcourt Brace & Company.

Gibson, L. (1989). *Literacy Learning in the Early Years: Through Children's Eyes.* New York: Teachers College Press.

Goodman, K. (1993). *Phonics Phacts.* Richmond Hill, ON: Scholastic.

Miller-Lachmann, L. (1992). *Our Family, Our Friends, Our World: An Annotated Guide to Significant Multicultural Books for Children and Teenagers.* New York: Bowker.

Morrow, L.M. (1989). *Literacy Development in the Early Years: Helping Children Read and Write.* Englewood Cliffs, NJ: Prentice-Hall.

Munroe, E.A. (1991). *Let Me Play*. Richmond Hill, ON: Scholastic-TAB.

A fine resource for parents and early childhood educators that describes play materials, environments, and activities for all learning strands, including literacy.

Norton, D. (1992). *The Impact of Literature-Based Reading*. New York: Macmillan.

Poulsson, E. (1971). *Finger Plays for Nursery and Kindergarten*. New York: Dover.

Rothlein, L. (1989). *Read It Again! Pre-K. A Guide to Teaching Reading through Literature*. Glenview, IL: Goodyear Books.

Rothlein, L. (1992). *Read It Again! Pre-K. Introducing Literature to Young Children*. Glenview, IL: Goodyear Books.

Rothlein, L. (1993). *Read It Again! Multicultural Books for the Primary Grades*. Glenview, IL: Goodyear Books.

Schickedanz, J.A. (1986). *More than the ABCs: The Early Stages of Reading and Writing*. Washington, DC: National Association for the Education of Young Children.

The author provides detailed suggestions for creating an early childhood program that is rich in language and literacy opportunities for young children. Her book also offers many helpful lists of books to read aloud and materials to include in learning centres.

Strickland, D., and L.M. Morrow, eds. (1989). *Emerging Literacy: Helping Young Children Learn to Read and Write*. Newark, DE: International Reading Association.

Temple, C., R. Nathan, F. Temple, and N.A. Burris. (1993). *The Beginnings of Writing* (3rd ed.). Boston, MA: Allyn & Bacon.

BOOKS FOR PARENTS

Fields, M. (1989). *Literacy Begins at Birth*. Tucson, AZ: Fisher Books.

Hill, M.W. (1989). *Home: Where Reading and Writing Begin*. Portsmouth, NH: Heinemann Educational Books.

ADDITIONAL RESOURCES

Literacy Development in the Preschool. Concord, ON: Irwin.

This is a helpful twenty-minute, full-colour filmstrip with cassette narration that demonstrates a wide variety of literacy activities in a preschool classroom.

Taking Off: Guided Reading at the Emergent Stage. Concord, ON: Irwin.

This 15-minute video shows a group of 5-year-olds in a literacy-rich environment learning to read from a predictable picture book.

Reading and Young Children. Washington, DC: NAEYC.

This is a fifteen-minute video described by its producers as the "perfect companion to the book *More than the ABCs*" and will help educators know what to say to parents who want their children to learn to read in preschool. Available from The National Association for the Education of Young Children, 1834 Connecticut Ave. NW, Washington, DC, 20009. Phone: 800-424-2460.

CHILDREN'S BOOKS CITED

Alborough, J. (1992). *Where's My Teddy?* Cambridge, MA: Candlewick Press.

Brett, J. (1990). *The Mitten. A Ukrainian Folktale.* New York: Putnam.

Carle, E. (1969). *The Very Hungry Caterpillar.* New York: Philomel.

dePaola, T. (1989). *The Art Lesson.* New York: Putnam.

Ehlert, L. (1990). *Feathers for Lunch.* New York: Harper & Row.

Galdone, P. (1981). *The Three Billy Goats Gruff.* Boston: Clarion Books.

Galdone, P. (1984). *Teeny Tiny Woman.* Boston: Clarion Books.

Geisert, A. (1991). *Oink.* Boston: Houghton-Mifflin.

Hader, B. (1949). *The Big Snow.* New York: Macmillan.

Hawkins, C., and J. Hawkins. (1987). *I Know an Old Lady Who Swallowed a Fly.* New York: Putnam.

Keats, E.J. (1976). *The Snowy Day.* New York: Puffin.

Martin, R. (1992). *The Rough-Face Girl.* New York: Putnam & Grosset.

Mayer, M. (1968). *There's a Nightmare in My Closet.* New York: Dial.

Rosen, M. (1989). *We're Going on a Bear Hunt.* New York: Macmillan.

Schories, P. (1991). *Mouse Around.* New York: Farrar, Straus & Giroux.

Sendak, M. (1963). *Where the Wild Things Are.* New York: Harper & Row.

Viorst, J. (1972). *Alexander and the Terrible, Horrible, No Good, Very Bad Day.* New York: Atheneum.

Wiesner, D. (1991). *Tuesday.* New York: Clarion.

Yolen, J. (1987). *Owl Moon.* New York: Putnam.

Young, E. (1989). *Lon Po Po. A Red-Riding Hood Story from China.* New York: Philomel.

REFERENCES

Adams, M.J. (1990). *Beginning to Read. Thinking and Learning about Print.* Cambridge, MA: MIT Press.

Bettelheim, B. (1976). *The Uses of Enchantment: The Meaning and Importance of Fairy Tales.* New York: Knopf.

Blazer, B. (1986). "I want to talk to you about writing": Five-year-old children speak. In B.B. Schieffelin and P. Gilmore, eds., *The Acquisition of Literacy: Ethnographic Perspectives,* pp. 75–109. Norwood, NJ: Ablex.

Booth, D. (1988). "Would you rather ... ": Looking at drama and story. In Ontario Ministry of Education, *Growing with Books.* Toronto: Ontario Ministry of Education.

Booth, D., and C. Thornley-Hall, eds. (1991). *Classroom Talk.* Markham, ON: Pembroke.

Calkins, L.M. (1983). *Lessons from a Child.* Portsmouth, NH: Heinemann.

Calkins, L.M., and S. Harwayne. (1991). *Living between the Lines.* Portsmouth, NH: Heinemann.

Cambourne, B. (1987). Language, learning and literacy. In A. Buttler and J. Turbill, eds., *Towards a Reading–Writing Classroom.* Portsmouth, NH: Heinemann.

Chomsky, N. (1957). *Syntactic Structures.* The Hague, Netherlands: Mouton.

Christie, J.F. (1990). Dramatic play: A context for meaningful engagements. *The Reading Teacher* 43: 542–45.

Clay, M.M. (1979). Reading: *The Patterning of Complex Behavior.* Auckland, NZ: Heinemann Educational Books.

Cochrane, O., D. Cochrane, S. Scalena, and E. Buchanan. (1984). *Reading, Writing and Caring.* Winnipeg: Whole Language Consultants.

Doake, D. (1979). Book experience and emergent reading behavior. Paper presented at the Preconvention Institute No. 24, Research on Written Language Development, International Reading Association annual convention. Atlanta, Georgia, April 1979.

Elley, W.B. (1989). Vocabulary acquisition from listening to stories. *Reading Research Quarterly* 24: 174–87.

Ernst, G., M. Castle, and L. Frostad. (1992). Teaching in multilingual/multicultural settings: Strategies for supporting second-language learners. *Curriculum in Context* 20 (2): 13–15.

Ernst, G., and K.J. Richard. (1994). Reading and writing pathways to conversation in the ESL classroom. *The Reading Teacher* 48 (4): 320–28.

Fields, M. (1988). Marbles lost, marbles found. *Language Arts* 64 (5): 474.

Galda, L., and B.E. Cullinan. (1991). Literature for literacy: What research says about the benefits of using books in the classroom. In J. Flood, J. Jensen, D. Lapp, and J.R. Squire, eds., *Handbook of Research on Teaching the English Language Arts*. New York: Macmillan.

Glazer, J.I., and L.L. Lamme. (1990). Poem picture books and their uses in the classroom. *The Reading Teacher* 44 (2): 102–10.

Graves, D. (1983). *Writing: Teachers and Children at Work*. Portsmouth, NH: Heinemann.

Hardt, U. (1983). *Teaching Reading with the Other Language Arts*. Newark, DE: International Reading Association.

Hickey, M.G. (1988). Developing critical reading readiness in primary grades. *The Reading Teacher* 42 (3): 258–93.

Hipple, M. (1985). Journal writing in kindergarten. *Language Arts* 62 (3): 255–61.

Holdaway, D. (1979). *The Foundations of Literacy*. Toronto: Ashton Scholastic.

Hough, R.A., J.R. Nurss, and D. Wood. (1987). Making opportunities for elaborated language in early childhood classrooms. *Young Children* (November): 6–12.

International Reading Association. (1986a). IRA position statement on reading and writing in early childhood. *The Reading Teacher* 39 (October): 822–24.

International Reading Association. (1986b). Literacy development and pre-first grade: A joint statement of concerns about present practices in pre-first grade reading instruction and recommendations for improvement. *Young Children* 41 (November): 10–13.

Ishee, N., and J. Goldhaber. (1990). Story reenactment. Let the play begin. *Young Children* (March): 70–76.

Jalongo, M.R. (1992). *Early Childhood Language Arts*. Boston: Allyn & Bacon.

Karweit, N. (1989). The effects of story-reading program on the vocabulary and story comprehension skills of disadvantaged prekindergarten and kindergarten students. *Early Education and Development* 1 (2): 105–15.

Katz, S. (1991). The role of personality in the acquisition of a second language. In D. Booth and C. Thornley-Hall, eds., *Classroom Talk*. Markham, ON: Pembroke.

Lehr, S. (1990). Literature and the construction of meaning: The preschool child's developing sense of theme. *Journal of Research in Childhood Education* 6 (1): 37–47.

Lehr, S. (1991). *The Child's Developing Sense of Theme. Responses to Literature*. New York: Teachers College Press.

McGee, L.E., and D.J. Richgels. (1990). *Literacy Beginnings: Supporting Young Readers and Writers*. Boston: Allyn & Bacon.

Miller, L., and L. Rothlein. (1994). *Read It Again! Pre-K Book 2*. New York: Goodyear Books.

Mills, H., T. O'Keefe, and D. Stephens. (1992). *Looking Closely: Exploring the Role of Phonics in One Whole Language Classroom*. Urbana, IL: National Council of Teachers of English.

Morrow, L. (1982). Relationships between literature programs, library corner designs and children's use of literature. *Journal of Educational Research* 78: 339–44.

Morrow, L., and C.S. Weinstein. (1982). Increasing children's use of literature through program and physical design changes. *Elementary School Journal* 83: 131–37.

Morrow, L.M., and M.K. Rand. (1991). Promoting literacy during play by designing early childhood classroom environments. *The Reading Teacher* 44 (6): 396–402.

Morrow, L.M., and J.K. Smith. (1990). *Assessment for Instruction in Early Literacy*. Englewood Cliffs, NJ: Prentice-Hall.

Platt, P. (1977). Grapho-linguistics: Children's drawings in relation to reading and writing skills. *The Reading Teacher* 31: 262–68.

Raines, S.C. (1994). *450 More Story S-t-r-e-t-c-h-e-r-s for the Primary Grades*. Mt. Rainier, MD: Gryphon.

Raines, S.C., and R.J. Canady. (1989). *Story S-t-r-e-t-c-h-e-r-s. Activities to Expand Children's Favorite Books*. Mt. Rainier, MD: Gryphon.

Raines, S.C., and R.J. Canady. (1991). *More Story*

S-t-r-e-t-c-h-e-r-s. Mt. Rainier, MD: Gryphon.

Read, D., and J. Smith. (1982). Teaching visual literacy through wordless picture books. *The Reading Teacher* 35: 928–33.

Roser, N.L., J.V. Hoffman, and C. Farest. (1990). Language, literature, and at-risk children. *The Reading Teacher* 43 (8) 554–60.

Roskos, K. (1988). Literacy at work in play. *The Reading Teacher* 41 (6): 562–66.

Strickland, D. (1994). Reinventing our literacy programs: Books, basics, balance. *The Reading Teacher* 48 (4): 294–304.

Sulzby, E. (1985). Children's emergent reading of favorite books. A developmental study. *Reading Research Quarterly* 20 (4): 458–82.

Sutherland, Z., and M.H. Arbuthnot. (1991). *Children and Books* (8th ed.). Glenview, IL: Scott Foresman.

Trachtenburg, P. (1990). Using children's literature to enhance phonics instruction. *The Reading Teacher* 43 (9): 648–54.

Valencia, S., E. Hiebert, and P. Afflerbach, eds. (1994). *Authentic Reading Assessment.* Newark, DE: International Reading Association.

Vygotsky, L. (1962). *Thought and Language.* Cambridge, MA: MIT Press.

Wells, G. (1986). *The Meaning Makers: Children Learning Language and Using Language to Learn.* Portsmouth, NH: Heinemann.

Williamson, P.A., and S.B. Silvern. (1988, April). The effects of play training on the story comprehension of upper primary children. *Journal of Research in Childhood Education* 4 (2): 130–34.

CHAPTER 14
Supporting Cognitive Development

✎ **Overview**

✎ **What Is Cognition?**

✎ **Theories of Cognitive Development**

◆ Jean Piaget

◆ Lev Vygotsky

✎ **Educational Perspectives**

◆ Maria Montessori

◆ Constructivist Theory

✎ **Influences on Cognitive Development**

◆ Culture

◆ Experiential Diversity

◆ Developmental Diversity

◆ Diversity of Learning Styles

◆ Gender

✎ **Observing Cognitive Development**

◆ Cognition and Play

◆ Cognition and Language

◢ **A Curriculum for Cognitive Development**

◆ The Importance of Play

◆ The Learning Environment

◆ The Role of the Educator

◢ **Components in the Cognitive Curriculum**

◆ Natural Science

◆ Mathematics

◆ Computer Skills

◢ **Summary**

◢ **Review Questions**

◢ **Discussion Questions**

◢ **Activities**

◢ **Further Reading**

◢ **References**

OVERUIEW

Wonder is the seed of Knowledge.
— *Francis Bacon*

To children, the world is a new and exciting place. They approach each day's events with natural curiosity and a sense of wonder, eager to experience all that life offers. If they had free rein, there is nothing young children would not explore even at the expense of their safety. This is the way they learn, and their drive for exploration seems to tell us that we are all born to learn.

This chapter traces the processes of learning and cognitive growth in children's development. We describe children's unique system of collecting information as they expand their knowledge and make sense of their world, and we discuss how children use discovery learning to understand relationships and physical causality and to build concepts.

We review the foundations of cognitive theory, beginning with the work of Jean Piaget (1896–1980) and Lev Vygotsky (1896–1934), and consider the educational perspectives of Maria Montessori (1870–1952) and others. Understanding these theories can give you a framework for understanding children's development and learning. It will become apparent that learning is a process that children actively initiate.

When you develop cognitive curriculum, you must take into account the interrelationship of play and development. Through play, children learn to build abstract thought — this is a natural process for them. One myth that we try to dispel in this chapter is that cognitive development occurs only within teacher-directed or formal academic activities. *Cognitive development is an integral part of all kinds of play and exploration.* The cognitive curriculum occurs spontaneously throughout the program, with the adult becoming a partner in the children's play as they learn at their own pace.

Early childhood educators must observe and listen carefully before developing and implementing cognitive curriculum, because it must match the ages, interests, learning styles, and developmental levels of the children. Children come with a wealth of learning they have already gained outside any structured environments. In fact, they learn a staggering amount in just the first few years of life. The early childhood education setting provides an environment where children can expand on what they have already begun. By being aware of the cognitive process and the individual cognitive achievements of the children, educators can provide experiences that are suitable for the children, whatever their background.

By the end of this chapter, you will be able to

❖ explain the process of learning and cognitive development;

❖ describe the contributions of theorists who influence our understanding of cognitive development;

❖ explain how culture, experience, gender, and learning style affect cognitive development;

❖ explain the role of the educator in facilitating cognitive development;

❖ describe the optimal environment for cognitive development;

❖ describe how the cognitive curriculum is implemented through natural science, mathematics, and computers.

WHAT IS COGNITION?

Cognition can be described as personal knowledge that develops from experiences and active participation in the environment. Through their openness to cultural and social experiences and sensory input, children begin to grasp patterns, relationships, and concepts, and to convert these bits of knowledge into abstract thoughts and ideas. Cognitive development is a natural process that is initiated by children and continues at a pace determined by their individual characteristics and experiences. Knowledge and understanding emerge as children ask questions, reason, and figure things out for themselves.

In this chapter, we make a distinction between children's learning of concepts and relationships within their experience, and the learning of specific, factual knowledge or skills. Cognition is much more than learning isolated concepts and such specific rote skills as number or letter concepts or vocabulary. In the cognitive curriculum, the children are their own educators, exploring, manipulating, discovering, and creating meaning and knowledge for themselves. They develop the ability to observe, predict, and make connections between events and outcomes. Through this process, children acquire a more global understanding of how the world works and how the pieces all fit together in predictable and understandable ways.

This view of cognition has implications for the early childhood curriculum — the focus is on the learning process, not on the teaching process. If we were to focus on what or how to teach, we would risk seeing learning in a way that is narrow, artificial, and limiting.

Cognitive development is the opposite of that — it is about coming to see the bigger picture, and seeing how the bits of new knowledge fit into this picture.

In designing the cognitive curriculum, our emphasis is on the natural events occurring in (and outside of) the early childhood setting that invite exploration, discovery, and learning. There is no specific content or skills to be taught or learned. All experiences result in learning, and all experiences are meaningful to those who participate in them actively. As early childhood educators, we believe this is the ideal way for children to learn, and that a less natural and spontaneous approach can be detrimental to children's attitudes and motivation for lifelong learning. You can see the process of cognitive development in the following example.

The children in Milo's day-care centre are painting a large mural. It all started in the spring when, after a storm, two 4-year-olds, Trevor and Nicholas, found a nest on the ground along with some broken robin's eggs. The two boys continued talking about the nest and the eggs, and they made several paintings about their experience.

One day Milo, the early childhood educator, brought in the book *Have You Seen Birds?* by Joanna Oppenheim (Scholastic-TAB, 1986) and read it during story time. Afterward, the two boys spent a long time looking at the book. Later, as the boys painted yet another picture of finding the robin's nest, Milo suggested they could paint a robin mural to cover the bottom half of one whole wall of the room. The boys, who were both usually quite shy, could not conceal their excitement, and talked about the idea with such enthusiasm that some of the other children became interested.

The next day, Trevor brought another book on birds that his father had checked out of a local library. Using the book, Trevor showed everyone the pictures and explained how robins make their nests and lay their eggs. He also said that sometimes robins do not fasten their nests to branches firmly enough to keep the wind from blowing them down. Trevor was impressed that the parents feed the young so long that sometimes the babies grow as big as the parents before they learn to get worms from the ground themselves.

The mural project mushroomed when Trevor said he wanted to glue some natural materials — sand and grass — onto the paper, so the children took expeditions outside to collect "stuff."

Making this mural — aside from giving the children a feeling of pride and accomplishment — led them through the process of cognitive development: perceiving (gathering information from the environment — finding the nest and broken egg), conceptualizing (putting together the parts of the information to form a concept — the robins' nests are not strong enough to withstand the wind sometimes), reasoning (figuring out what must have happened to make the nest fall out of the tree), and knowing, in this case, "all about robins."

This example is what is known as **discovery learning** — activities that evolve from the children's own interests and exploration. The two boys' repeated paintings of the robin's nest grew out of their need to organize and reorganize the information, and to find out more about what kind of creature a robin is and how it makes its nest. Their practice and repetition through related experiences gave them a wider and more elaborate view of the world.

THEORIES OF COGNITIVE DEVELOPMENT

In the early part of the twentieth century, Jean Piaget and Lev Vygotsky developed theories of cognition. Piaget concentrated on the cognition of the individual child, while Vygotsky researched cognition and the child in a social context. These theorists' work is still relevant to early childhood education.

Jean Piaget

Jean Piaget was a Swiss-born psychologist. His theories of the origins of cognition serve as a framework for all developmentally based programs. He had a remarkable empathy for young children, and was particularly gifted at interpreting and recording their natural development through observation of their spontaneous play. Piaget used his observations as a basis for describing both the process and the sequence of cognitive development.

HOW CHILDREN LEARN

Piaget began with observations of his own children and documented the process and changes in learning over their early years. Based on his observations, he concluded that children are naturally inclined to master logical thought in predictable, developmental stages, but that this development depends on energetic interaction with the environment. In other words, children are always active learners. Although there is a predictable sequence of cognitive development, children need a nurturing environment and freedom to explore in order to experience optimal learning. When offered opportunities for exploratory play and experiential learning, children construct their own perceptual and conceptual knowledge at an individual pace. The exploration and discovery of Nicholas and Trevor illustrate this process.

According to Piaget's theory, young children assimilate, or take in, new information. If this new information does not fit with what they already know and understand, they make accommodations and reorganize their old concepts to fit the new ones. Whenever children engage in play activities and free expression, they encounter challenges to their own perceptions, which results in new understanding and meaning. This is the essence of learning.

STAGES IN COGNITIVE DEVELOPMENT

Piaget believed that cognitive development occurs through a sequence of stages. He noticed that children of different ages have their own way of seeing, interpreting, and thinking. He concluded that young children think and develop cognitive understanding that is different from that of adults, not because they understand less, but because they interpret the initial images differently and respond with immature logic to make sense of what they perceive.

From Piaget's work, we have learned that in the early years children progress through two stages of development: the sensorimotor stage (birth to 2 years) and the pre-operational stage (2 to 5 years). Children in the first 2 years of their lives learn and understand by integrating sensory perceptions and initiating motor responses. Through motor and sensory activity, they explore and manipulate their environment and demonstrate knowledge. For example, an infant playing with a telephone is interested in pushing the buttons, fitting the receiver back onto the cradle, and stretching the cord. She shows us that she knows that buttons are for pushing and that some things fit into others.

By the end of the sensorimotor stage, children are developing language skills and are increasingly able to reproduce events symbolically, demonstrating readiness for the transition to the next stage. The child now begins to use the telephone in ways that show she has a mental concept of its purpose, such as jabbering into the receiver.

QUALITIES OF THE PRE-OPERATIONAL CHILD

In the years from 2 to 5, according to Piaget's theory, children begin to learn through mental representation and symbolic thought as they add language to sensory and concrete experiences. This is the time when children learn through imitating others, learn to think for themselves, and search for ideas. Because their mental skills are somewhat unsophisticated at this stage, it is called "pre-operational," which means that children have limitations on their interpretations of the relationships between objects and events.

During the pre-operational stage, children broaden their scope of learning through increasing exploration, which leads to greater understanding and expressive language. For example, young children who are learning to speak might initially call all animals "cat" if cat is the first animal they encountered. Later, children learn to discriminate and categorize. They learn, for example, the differences between cats, dogs, and rabbits, and that birds are not all the same, and they begin to use the concepts of colour, shape, and size to note differences.

The emergence of symbolic thought as a primary mental process is reflected in the extensive amount of children's pretend and dramatic play. By re-creating events in their play, they experience and master feelings, connections, and patterns. Acting things out provides the kind of concrete experiences that lead to personal and real understanding for children who are not yet in the stage where abstract thinking is meaningful.

Children acquire physical knowledge when they manipulate and handle real, concrete objects. As they discover qualities and attributes, they develop an awareness that exceeds sensory exploration — the qualities and attributes take on meaning. For example, the blocks are wooden, red, and square; the teddy is soft, yellow, and pliable. When children see how these objects are similar and different, and that the attributes and qualities are related to other toys and materials, this means they have physical knowledge. They discover that sand and water apart and combined have different qualities. The key ingredient in learning is the opportunity to vary play and create new ways of discovering attributes and observing changes.

As children develop, their logic and knowledge become more complex. They continue to discover the similarities and differences in objects, and learn to categorize. For example, Emily is playing with a farm set. She sorts pigs into the pen and the truck. At some point, she realizes that there are two different colours of pigs and she begins again, this time putting the pink pigs in the pen and the black and white pigs on the truck. This kind of conscious categorization is the beginning of more conventional cognition.

Sometimes children's high degree of confidence, interest, and general knowledge can mislead us into assuming they have a greater level of understanding than they actually do. For instance, they might use familiar words or phrases without a clear understanding of their meaning. This often occurs with more abstract concepts of number, colour, and time. For example, Leah calls her favourite white blanket blue, while also insisting that her yellow shirt is blue. It seems that she is aware of the idea that things have colour as a distinguishing characteristic, but she does not yet accurately discriminate among colours.

Similarly, Cole talks with great authority about going to bed at 40 o'clock on Friday, with no apparent idea of when Friday will arrive or whether 40 o'clock is in the morning or at night. Educators must remain aware that preschool children still live in the here and now and have little concept of time, past, and future. To make meaning of time, children count the number of sleeps, but they often confuse tomorrow with yesterday when relating stories or events. For example, after lunch, Hannah is telling a story about how she and her dad went "tobogganing tomorrow, a long time ago, and they went through a forest and wondered if bears would be there." In reality, this occurred on the morning of the same day, and Hannah's "forest" is five tall trees. Children develop the concept of time when they develop memory. An understanding of time is something they must develop gradually and internally by themselves — this notion cannot be taught.

Educational theorists today still have a high regard for Piaget's theories, because they provide a guide for understanding cognitive development and because the characteristics of development and the natural process of learning that he described can be observed in young children's behaviour and thinking. Although Piaget himself did not contribute a curriculum model, his theories provide the basis for others

to articulate educational and curriculum implications. A little later in this chapter, you will see the influence of Piaget in the discussion on constructivist theory.

Lev Vygotsky

Lev Vygotsky was a Russian psychologist whose work suggests that educators concerned about cognitive development should pay greater attention to interpersonal interactions and the social aspect of the curriculum. Play and social interactions enhance language, which contributes to thinking and learning. During play, children use speech, both in conversations with others and in the "self-talk" that directs their own activities. Children need to use spoken language to express ideas outwardly before they can focus on their internal mental processes.

As children gradually internalize their external or self-talk, they act without verbalizing their actions and enter the world of private thought. Vygotsky suggested that through this development of inner speech, children begin to control their own behaviour and guide themselves toward increasing cognitive competence.

When children engage in social activities, they use the higher mental processes of attention, memory, and reasoning. In our story at the beginning of the chapter, Trevor had to think to express his ideas, and Nicholas and the other children had to interpret and process the new information about birds. Social interactions create a need for thinking and communicating. When children say "I can show you," they not only gain pleasure and satisfaction themselves, along with self-affirmation, but they also are offering knowledge to their peers.

Whereas adults can take in new information and ideas through language, children do not change their thinking through conversation alone, but must have concrete experiences that demonstrate new perceptions (Santrock 1993). For example, Trevor's discovery of the robin's nest on the ground gave rise to new perceptions and understandings — these did not come from simply being told that robins sometimes do not fasten their nests securely on tree branches.

The theories of Piaget and Vygotsky form the basis of child-centred curriculums, which are more meaningful for children than are other types of programs. Programs that offer play-based learning with concrete sensorial experiences encourage young children to manipulate, identify, rearrange, sort, and classify freely. As a result, children think for themselves and extend their thinking through their exploratory play.

EDUCATIONAL PERSPECTIVES

Maria Montessori

Another person whose work has helped to clarify our understanding of the learning process is Maria Montessori, the first woman in Italy to earn a medical degree. Through her work at the Psychiatric Clinic at the University of Rome, she had contact with children in the asylums of the city. These children were herded into bare rooms with adults and had nothing to play with, no objects to manipulate or hold in their hands. She came to believe that their mental condition had more to do with the deprivations of their environment than their own abilities.

From these experiences early in her career, Montessori developed an interest in children's education. She saw first-hand what happens to children who have no tactile materials in their environment, and came to recognize that the process of active manipulation is the basis for abstract thought. In fact, Montessori theorized that the path to intelligence was through the hands. Further, she believed that all materials and equipment for children require an increasing level of complexity that matches their ability to see relationships in their own ideas. Concepts become fixed and permanent as young children begin to think and remember personal experiences.

Montessori designed educational materials that not only have tactile appeal in their colour, texture, and form, but are also self-correcting; that is, the objects fit together only one way so that children find out immediately whether they have achieved the goal of the activity. In the process, they also learn the correct steps in using the materials and comprehend the concepts for which the materials were designed.

For example, Julia is totally absorbed in building a pink tower. She is working with a self-correcting set of blocks designed to develop the concepts of weight and size, sensorially conveyed messages from the hand to the brain. As Julia selects the largest block, her small hand has to stretch to grasp it, and she physically feels the concepts of "large" and "heavy" and records them in her brain. As she continues to build in sequential steps, these physical sensations are integrated into conceptual patterns. By the time Julia places the smallest and last block, which requires only her pincer grasp, she has experienced the entire conceptual range. When she finishes, she exclaims, "Look what I did!" Through practice, Julia becomes aware of the concepts behind the design of the materials and successfully applies them to other areas of learning.

Montessori's theories focussed on individual learning through individual "work," the term she used for children's activities. If Julia's early childhood centre uses Montessori methods, her environment also uses child-sized furniture, including low shelves for the materials. Julia herself chooses the pink blocks and returns them to the shelf when she is finished. According to Montessori, these steps are also part of the learning process.

Constructivist Theory

Constructivism is the theory that has developed out of Piaget's work. It is based on the premise that children construct knowledge as they go about their daily activities. Learning occurs through children's interaction with both the physical environment (toys and materials) and with other people who provide the differing perspectives that challenge children's thinking. Input from new experiences causes children to rethink their understandings and expand their knowledge. Development is facilitated by activities that engage children's thinking; it is the result of children actively creating knowledge for themselves as they

BOX 14.1 PRINCIPLES OF CONSTRUCTIVIST–INTERACTIONIST LEARNING

◆ Intrinsic motivation is essential. Preschool children do not learn because it is important to someone else for them to learn something; preschool children learn best when they believe that the information or skill is meaningful and important.

◆ Child-initiated activity is essential. The child's curiosity is aroused and learning results from the child's active attempts to satisfy this thirst for knowledge. The child must be able to make choices of materials and experiences.

◆ Child-directed activities are essential. Children determine the way they will use the toy, material, or experience to satisfy their unique interests, to answer their own questions, and to add to their already existing knowledge.

◆ Children must feel free to take risks and make mistakes if they are to learn and develop new skills. Children who are confident, have positive self-esteem, and trust in their care-givers are much more likely to accept challenges and persist until they have mastered something new. All learning involves taking risks and venturing into an unknown area.

◆ Learning occurs as children are confronted with information or experiences that are novel and challenging, but that are within their ability to deal with and master. Children attempt to relate new information and experiences into already known and comfortable ways of thinking. Children deal with discrepancies and information that do not fit by changing their ways of thinking about their experiences. Adults can facilitate this process, but they should not attempt to control it.

◆ Learning in this model values the process more than the end result. Active involvement in the processes of experimenting, observing, thinking, problem solving, and creativity are more important factors in learning than being able to reproduce a specific product or repeat isolated facts and skills.

participate in and gain understanding of their world (Maxim 1993; Goffin 1994). Such educators as Constance Kamii (1985) and Rheta Devries (1984) have developed models for educational practice with young children that are based on constructivist theory.

According to the constructivist approach, the physical and mental processes of learning are carried out by children as they interact with their environment. Although a whole group of children may be offered similar experiences, each child will take out for him- or herself what is at his or her individual level of knowledge and experience. Thus, each child has a different level of learning and mastery of the concepts or tasks. However, each child can have a meaningful learning experience at a personal level.

You have an important role to play in this process. Involvement with the children and careful observation will enable you to see how each new experience fits with the children's current level of knowledge, and then you can expand or enhance the activity appropriately for individual children. You can assist them in the process of reflecting on their actions (and the results of those actions) by observing and asking questions about their perceptions, and by labelling or commenting on what you see happening. You do not tell children what to think, but rather encourage them to see for themselves. You will see this approach reflected in the later sections of this chapter in a discussion of the components of the cognitive curriculum.

INFLUENCES ON COGNITIVE DEVELOPMENT

Culture

Acceptance of all children has become the ground rule within early childhood education in Canada. The diversity that characterizes our country is something we claim to respect, treasure, and strive to protect. In the early childhood setting, educators need to be open to contemporary cultures and the mores of other societies, and recognize how this openness sets the stage for building respect among cultures. When you welcome diversity and include in your program and environment objects, dolls, hats, picture books, music, and food from diverse cultures, all children feel valued. Familiar objects from their culture make children feel at home, and make them better able to explore and respond to new experiences. When initial interactions among children of different cultures are meaningful and positive, children develop positive attitudes that hold for a lifetime.

Learning the social conventions of a culture, either our own or others', has implications for educators and children. We might not all share a language, customs, rules, and a his-

tory that give common shared meanings and knowledge of who we are and what we are. As educators, we must be aware of different ways of understanding and doing, and we must be careful not to confuse inexperience in the dominant language or practice with reduced cognitive competence.

Whether children are able to share a collective experience depends on how easy and comfortable they feel in any new environment (Kostelnik 1993). When they begin to understand these shared meanings, they are surprised by the associations and interconnections in language. For example, when Chadra first discovered that her peers understood what she meant when she used English words that represented her chair and the arms, legs, and back of the chair, her expression was one of amazement and she burst into giggles. At this point, cognitive development is fine-tuned as children become deeply immersed in discovering the conventions and meanings of the new world.

If you accept the principles of cognitive development — that from new experiences children make associations with what they already know — then learning cannot be postponed until they master a new language. The curriculum must provide opportunities for all children to construct thoughts and actions. Children do not express themselves freely until they are sure that adults understand them, even though the children might be able to comprehend what the adults say or want. Children communicate through gesture and expression, and they watch and wait for adults' responses. You can encourage children to think and communicate in their own language until they are comfortable with a new one. You can communicate and demonstrate shared meanings constantly through social behaviour in addition to language. When children see behaviours and actions that have meaning for them, they copy and imitate, which in turn increases a sense of belonging and community.

Regardless of children's origins, when they enter a social setting that is based on a language other than their own, they must eventually learn the language, social meanings, and conventions of the new culture at the same time that they are immersed in their own at home. When children begin to learn and use the inventions of the larger society, whether learning to eat with strange utensils or looking at a picture book from left to right, they need constructive support and reassurance as they attempt to integrate and balance traditions and values that are different at home and at the early childhood centre.

Experiential Diversity

Children's background experience affects their perceptions of the world, and where they live provides a key to understanding. Children who see the world from a fifteenth-floor apartment balcony become aware of height and distance long before these concepts become knowledge developed from learned principles. Children who travel by bus or car and those who walk might see the same images, but their different experiences result in a unique personal perspective.

When families move from one part of the country to another, children come to early childhood education centres with diversity of experience. They also have a variety of experiences of seasonal changes and settings — wilderness, rural, and urban lifestyles. A child who, say, at age 5 sees farm animals for the first time experiences them much differently from the one who lives with them every day.

Through the curriculum, you can broaden the experiences of individual children. For example, Blake, whose activity and experience are limited by living in a small apartment, will benefit from outdoor play and natural science activities. Sydney's family moves frequently, so he has less experience with books, art, and music and needs a range of creative experiences. The majority of children benefit from new experiences in science, technology, and computers.

As you get to know the children, you can create meaningful experiences that complement their diverse backgrounds. This way they will have an early start in appreciating the diversity that characterizes our country.

Developmental Diversity

In Canada, the move toward inclusive education means that children with a full range of special needs are now fully integrated in many early childhood programs. For this reason, you need to be knowledgeable about both typical and atypical patterns of development.

Because learning occurs best through active participation, it is up to you to ensure that the limitations created by delays or diversity in development are minimized. Children who are challenged by a disability or limitation in one developmental area learn to compensate by developing alternate ways of doing things. For example, Megan, who has reduced hearing, can effectively communicate with sign language. Shawn, who is limited in motor skills by cerebral palsy, nevertheless is a keen observer and eagerly participates in play with other children as he cruises on his scooter board or balances in his stander. Children with delayed development often learn more slowly than many of their peers, but they are learning nonetheless. Children with sensory or physical conditions may need to do things differently, but they, too, can develop skills and competence in alternate ways. No matter what the level of development of personal knowledge, children add new experience and knowledge constantly. All children need to feel competent and to experience many different successes each day. All children thrive if you build an individualized curriculum based on personal developmental readiness.

Diversity of Learning Styles

In the anecdote at the beginning of the chapter, what if Jerusa had found the nest? How would the outcome have been different? She was nearby when Trevor and Nicholas found it, and in fact, she told her mother about it and embellished the experience into quite a good story. After that, she did not mention it again.

Jerusa incorporates experiences in a different way than Trevor and Nicholas do. She is an auditory learner who uses language as her primary way of dealing with new experiences. It is common that children have different learning styles, and educators need to take into account this kind of diversity when they implement curricula and create an environment for young children.

In environments in which children are free to choose activities, you can observe their different approaches. For example, in an art centre where children freely choose the materials they want to work with, they express clearly their preferences as they explore and manipulate materials. A visual learner may focus intently on the details of her picture, a kinesthetic/tactile child may spread the glue dreamily with his fingers, and an auditory learner may talk or hum constantly to herself as she paints. Can you identify the styles of the children in the following examples?

Sarah concentrates intensely and becomes absorbed in the pattern of the paint. Her ideas and concepts become clearer as her painting develops and she recalls experiences. Her painting is a detailed representation that includes colour co-ordinates — the princess's crown has jewels in specific rows and colours, the shoes and purse match the dress. Sarah's facial expressions often reveal the mood or seriousness of her drawings. Have you guessed yet that Sarah is a visual learner? She is a child who can remember how things look and develops her own ideas by observing others and things around her. She is deeply affected by visual images, and she often daydreams. This child cannot be hurried into activities; she needs time and space to process her ideas.

BOX 14.2 TYPES OF LEARNERS

VISUAL LEARNERS	Predominantly react to and recall visual stimulation
AUDITORY LEARNERS	Talk and listen to internalize and express meaning
KINESTHETIC/TACTILE LEARNERS	Move and touch continuously to make sense of themselves and the environment

Ashoona's selections are quite different. She chooses the finger or sponge painting, box sculptures, or play dough. She needs to get "inside" and develop ideas because they "feel" right, and she quickly becomes engrossed in her activity. Although she is sometimes an impulsive and messy learner, she processes information in a kinesthetic and tactile manner. Ashoona is aware of textures, and finds words to aid her expressions. She expresses herself dramatically with expansive gestures and movement and physically demonstrates her thoughts. Ashoona literally jumps for joy when she is happy with her accomplishments.

Jared's interests reflect another style. He masters his activity and materials when he can talk about what or how he wants to develop them. He listens to what others say but enjoys talking and conversing as he works. Jared is a child who often hums and talks to himself. He recalls stories and uses sounds symbolically as he paints. He has acute hearing and is aware of unfamiliar sounds that occur in the surroundings. He enjoys all art expressions as long as he can express himself verbally. Painting murals to music would appeal to Jared because, as you guessed, he is an auditory learner.

Can you see from these examples of cognitive learning styles how they would relate to other areas of development in children? Each of us has our own learning style. How do you as an adult learn? What is your approach, for instance, when new equipment arrives? Do you read the instructions first, or manipulate the pieces to work out for yourself how it should look, or do you learn by watching others or actively participating with them? Do you play with a problem or idea, predicting the outcome, or let the idea float free and germinate? Through observation and engagement with children as they spontaneously play, educators can identify unique learning styles.

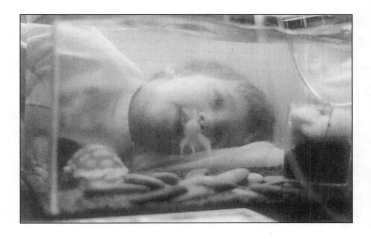

What they learn about children learning, educators can incorporate into their programs.

Gender

Early childhood educators need to think about this question: How does the predominance of female staff affect the cognitive development of young children? Further, is the supposed reluctance of women to implement new technologies a myth? Can early socialization patterns become continually reinforced? The following section is for debate and discussion, and it is up to you to draw your own conclusions.

Do children fare better in a program that fosters cognitive development through cross-gender play? Do adults unconsciously convey gender roles to children simply from their own conditioning? Do you change the focus of content to reflect and accommodate girls when your centre perhaps has a higher percentage of boys, or vice versa, or when there is an even number of both sexes? Do you offer strategies to girls to encourage them to be more assertive and effective communicators within this male group? Or when the circumstances in playroom numbers are reversed, do you accommodate the needs of boys? Are the learning centres gender-neutral play spaces?

According to Carole Beal (1994), a gender role is not only being established early, but is visible within specific behaviours such as play, independence, and mastery of skills. Very young children do not show preferences for toys that are based on gender. Yet during the second year, along with the development of speech, self-concept, and growing independence, toddlers demonstrate knowledge of gender roles in selecting gender-appropriate toys — girls choose dolls and soft "cuddlies," and boys choose solid trains and trucks.

Children's toy preferences and play behaviours are being shaped as they grow. By the age of 5 years, most children select gender-appropriate toys. The earlier cross-gender play decreases. On the surface, this might not seem to be a problem, but if you consider that this is the beginning of bias in attitude and learning, it does become an issue.

As you have learned from other chapters, preschool children are developing a broad and substantial amount of knowledge from adult expectations and unstated values, and from the environment adults provide. Effective role modelling contributes to the success or failure of children as they relate to and internalize these subtle messages.

Let's explore gender difference as it relates to development and learning. The expectations that girls will be passive, compliant, and co-operative become part of their socialization. Boys, on the other hand, are encouraged to explore, physically and mentally, and to take the accompanying risks. Adults give more attention to boys, which communicates a higher valuing of males. For girls the opposite occurs, with the result of lowered self-esteem.

These differences reflect educators' approach and have an impact on cognitive learning styles. Boys are afforded more autonomy, are given more time to actively work things out for themselves, and are granted wider access to resources and opportunities. Boys are accepted as being active and messy learners. The message often conveyed to girls is that watching, listening, and playing close by are positive traits. But these traits hinder any active and assertive explorations. Adults may work briefly with boys but then quickly leave them to their own devices, allowing them to become engrossed in deeper investigations. This freedom and discovery play develop the skills on which cognitive development is founded. The assistance to girls is focussed on the importance of relating and developing empathy for others, and girls become adept at compromise and care-giving skills very early. Educators read more to girls, so their language exploration and social communication is reinforced and rewarded.

The value of each of these groups of traits for *both sexes* cannot be overestimated. What strategies can you employ to balance them for gender-neutral learning? Educators must be aware that gender-biased messages inherent in our language are constantly voiced in stories, literature, and nursery rhymes. Traditionally, learning has been gender-specific and delivered for one learning style. In creating an environment that is not gender-biased, you can encourage girls to be investigative and to take initiative to make discoveries on their own. You can provide boys with opportunities to develop strategies for language and an awareness and responsiveness to others. Play spaces need to be created to facilitate exploration, experimentation, and problem solving that fosters confidence in all children to become actively involved with play materials, blocks, and science experiments and to use traditional tools and new technology.

In many learning environments, you can find gender-stereotyped play areas that are incompatible with cross-gender activities. The challenge is to create play and learning centres that provide opportunities to develop cognitive foundations naturally. What is our role as educators? We want to encourage children to be comfortable with who they are and to recognize the range of alternatives that are open to both sexes. We want children to feel positive about their own gender identity and to respect differences. Early childhood educators need to offer environments that do not present biased or traditional views of gender roles, but rather experiences that promote cross-gender learning. How can you plan or redesign a creative curriculum or play space that gives optimal and equal opportunities and experiences to both boys and girls?

OBSERVING COGNITIVE DEVELOPMENT

In the ECE curriculum, we strive to create a learning environment that responds to the different learning characteristics and preferences of children of different backgrounds, genders, and developmental levels. To do this effectively means we must first observe each child carefully, looking for indications of the children's thinking and understanding in their play and conversations.

Cognition and Play

As we discussed in Chapter 5, observing play opens a window onto various areas of children's development. The child's perceptions and understanding of many events and concepts can also be observed during play. When Ann labels the big spoons as "Daddy spoons," and the smaller ones as "baby spoons" she is demonstrating awareness of the relationship of size. When Dane carefully places one block in front of each of the animals, he is demonstrating knowledge of one-to-one correspondence in number relations.

The child's ability to create and act out a role in the dramatic play centre provides information on general knowledge and concepts: "I am the one who sells the flowers, and you have to give me money," "The doctor has to give you a needle to make you feel better," "I am going to fix this chair with my tools. This one is for hammering and this one is for putting in screws."

Observing play also provides you with information about the learning process and style of individual children. How a child completes a puzzle or approaches a creative experience gives you clues about organization skills, problem-solving processes, and attention to detail.

Cognition and Language

Young children are eager to share their observations and ideas with others. This makes conversation a highly valuable source of information about the child's thinking process and general level of understanding. Consider the following examples:

❖ Colton, upon seeing his mother with her hair in a pony tail: "You sound like Allison when you wear your hair like that." He is expressing in his own way his awareness of a perceived similarity.

❖ Blake, playing on the rug some distance from the cat, suddenly stands up and says, "Look, Grandma, the cat's sitting in the circle of her tail."

Throughout each day, children frequently come to educators to share perceptions and events and to show their accomplishments: "That looks like … ," "Guess what … ," "Look what I did." Each of these incidents offers a window to the child's cognitive development. "No, that's not a dog. A dog has pointy ears" tells you about general knowledge and misinformation. Careful listening provides many clues to the child's learning. Attention to the child's reasoning and connections gives you insight into the processes she or he is using to think and to solve problems.

A CURRICULUM FOR COGNITIVE DEVELOPMENT

The Importance of Play

From the very beginning of his education the child should experience the joy of discovery.
— *Alfred North Whitehead*

In Chapter 10, you read that the early childhood education curriculum emphasizes a play-based, experiential learning approach. The cognitive curriculum is best understood as an application of the constructivist process in which children are actively learning all the time. Take this opportunity to review the reasons why play is so pivotal to children's learning.

In all areas of the early childhood curriculum, cognitive development is quietly and effectively taking place. Thinking and learning are ongoing. Early childhood educators recognize that the cognitive component can be successfully integrated into all areas of age-appropriate curriculum. Educators value the teachable moment as the ideal opportunity to enhance children's understanding and build

abstract thought. When adults join children in the experience of exploration and discovery, they can see learning and cognitive development occurring naturally during play. The following scenario illustrates the process.

A group of children went to see a dinosaur exhibit. As they approached the large, darkened caves, they became apprehensive and somewhat frightened. They could not absorb the abundance of sensory stimulation and became overwhelmed. After a moment of hesitation, they quickly focussed on a computer. Through a picture program on dinosaurs, the children gradually found their bearings within some familiar, manageable information.

After the children felt at ease and comfortable with this known experience, they returned to the caves with much more confidence. Inside the caves, materials and equipment provided opportunities for exploration and extended understanding as the children manipulated dinosaur puzzles, dug for fossils, and sat on "dinosaur eggs." The children were able to integrate each new experience, cognitively and emotionally. Sometime later, when the same group of children returned to the dinosaur area, they did not hesitate to go inside the caves. They had grasped and internalized the experience successfully.

This kind of scenario occurs millions of times in millions of ways with millions of children around the world. This is the foundation of learning — taking in manageable pieces of information to make sense of the larger picture. If experiences are too unfamiliar, or conversely, too completely known, children fail to cognitively record and remember them long enough to make use of the new experience. In any new learning situation, they need to draw from previous knowledge and match their associations to this familiar understanding.

The Learning Environment

Let's wander through the doors of an early childhood centre and observe children at play in an environment that supports cognitive development.

In this centre, the children are working on making wings. From a wide variety of materials displayed on the shelf, they have cut out white paper triangles and are intently taping them to their arms. How the idea for this activity began or who thought of it is not apparent, but the ideas, conversation, and shared explorations are now complete. Four children ask if they can try their wings. This is how and when the flexibility of the adult can support the cognitive process.

Through the doors and into the playground, up the grassy slope to the top of the hill they go — these young explorers are discovering for themselves the idea of flight. Their attempts to increase speed, to jump, and to flap their arms rapidly demonstrate clearly the internal thinking and active problem-solving strategies. The adults observing this play resist the urge to state the dynamics of flight, the reasons why "it won't work." The children themselves discover the inadequacies of paper and tape, but that does not stop them from thinking about this experience, nor does it stop them from telling other people about it.

This example illustrates the optimal environment. It shows what this chapter is about — that children learn best through self-selection and self-evaluation within a program that is relevant to their world view and level of understanding. As we saw in Chapter 9, the early childhood environment offers children a wide range of connected experiences through the numerous learning centres that are available for active play and exploration. Within these centres, the educator provides a range of experiences that attract, respond to, and challenge the children's interests, such as the exploration of whales described in Box 10.6 in Chapter 10.

The Role of the Educator

SETTING THE STAGE FOR LEARNING

The curriculum must offer a wide variety of experiences from which children can construct their own cognitive awareness and discover patterns of relationships. The fundamental process of developing personal knowledge or cognition must be embedded in all activities and learning centres. By offering a curriculum that demonstrates an understanding of what is appropriate for cognitive development, educators are being resourceful. The program must include interesting and stimulating experiences through a selection of diverse materials that are not replicated at home. Ensure that curriculum content includes activities and topics to explore that are relevant and that reflect children's interests.

For example, in the block centre, a sense of control and "art" skills are experienced naturally. The children's spatial awareness — the relationship of size, shape, and weight — become constructively and consciously organized. The simple-to-complex progression is at work here. The structures begin as simple, random stacking and develop into buildings that include what children see and know as windows and doors. Adults can enhance this play by providing varying spaces and varying materials with which to build. In a large space, children build to cover it, but in a small space, children build up. The large wooden unit blocks may not be appropriate for more complex building because the children need

BOX 14.3 GROUP SIZE FOR OPTIMAL LEARNING EXPERIENCES

Auseful rule of thumb for early childhood educators is this: children can most comfortably interact with a group that numbers their present age minus 1. That is, 3-year-olds can interact successfully with 2 other children, 5-year-olds with 4 others. If we frequently require children to cope with much larger groups, we create unnecessary stress for them (and for ourselves, as anyone knows who has struggled to keep 20 3-year-olds quiet and orderly in a story circle!).

Of course, this does not mean that there can be only 3 or 4 children in a preschool centre. It simply means that when we group youngsters for snack, story circle, projects, learning centres, and so on, we should keep those subgroupings small, with each supervised to a greater or lesser degree by an adult (McCartney 1984). Then each child gets to have a say, can ask the questions important to him or her, has sufficient materials to enjoy, does not have to wait for excessive lengths of time, and is not required to interact with too many other people.

smaller, light units to make more intricate structures.

The dramatic play centre offers excellent opportunities for cognitive experiences. Let's eavesdrop on Lindsay's group of children after they visited the local market. They are discussing what they need to re-create their experience of the market.

"We need real money to go into the cash register," says David.

"We need boxes and baskets to show the vegetables, and bags to carry them," Sally adds.

"What kinds of vegetables?" asks Lindsay.

"Potatoes, carrots, broccoli, peas, pumpkins, celery, onions," the answers come quickly.

"We need fruit, too," someone says.

"Yes, apples, grapes, peaches, and bananas. I love bananas," says Juan.

"We need scales to weigh things," says David.

"Can we have red, blue, and yellow flowers in pots?" asks Fiona. "And tickets to say how much and the names of things?"

And so the children's enthusiastic planning continues. As you imagine listening to them, can you identify the concepts they are learning?

On a field trip to stables, children are bombarded with new experiences — the buildings, paddocks, the sunlight and contrasting shade of the cool stalls, and the horses. The look, feel, smell, and sound of everything on the field trip produce mental images to be stored and connected later through related follow-up activities. These experiences enable the children to see and comprehend the characteristics of "horse," which later becomes a category of animals, and provide opportunities to discover knowledge in context.

Educators need to take responsibility in providing a creative environment that values autonomy and self-direction in the learning process and in protecting children from curriculum that is not developmentally appropriate. David Elkind (1987) warns against a curriculum that places too much emphasis on isolated cognitive components, with the result that learning becomes defined as simply retaining facts. In this case, children begin to exhibit stress-related behaviours, their natural investigative power and risk taking decrease, and their learning is negatively affected. This pressure reduces positive self-concept and the natural excitement for learning. Early childhood educators must nurture, rather than structure, cognitive development and learning.

INVOLVEMENT IN THE LEARNING PROCESS

The intimate exchange in one-to-one conversations with small children is a joyful experience, especially if it is built on mutual respect and trust. R.D. Laing (1978) expresses this pleasure when he states that sharing language "is the free and open space between us where we can play with reality together, where we question and answer, and inquire into what is the case and what is not for the sheer heaven of it" (p. viii). The concept of "reinventing the wheel" applies to children's growth of knowledge, for from fresh insights the world of invention and discovery begins. By immersing themselves in the company of adults who value play, children become confident in their own abilities and begin to search for answers to other questions that puzzle them. Talking with children reveals to us the natural, unique mind of the child. By encouraging collaborative learning in small groups, children gain confidence in their own thoughts and ideas.

Similar to the process of enhancing emotional development through play (Chapter 6), the early childhood educator's responsive role in children's play best supports learning. Acting as a follower of the child's play, "wondering" what might happen next, and offering a range of possibilities to be considered all encourage the thinking process.

Shari, an educator, has collected a number of small appliances (clocks, a telephone, and a broken tape recorder) and placed them in the woodworking centre for "repairs." She has also provided a number of simple books that explain how things work. She is involved there as the children use screwdrivers and pliers to take apart the items and look at the workings inside. She casually observes that there seem to be a lot of different-coloured wires inside the phone and "wonders" why they are there. She expresses interest in the comments of the children, making sure to recognize the validity of each. "I think those are for the voices to travel through." "That's how you can hear people talking." She adds her own information, "That's right, the sound of our voices is changed inside the phone into a form that can travel along those wires." She shows the children pictures in a book and explains this in more detail. This approach is much more meaningful for children than presenting the same information through discussion and books alone.

COMPONENTS IN THE COGNITIVE CURRICULUM

Natural Science

One day in early summer, a group of preschool children discovered that the trees were covered with caterpillars. With enthusiasm

they collected the caterpillars in buckets, jars, and any other containers they could find. Even the sitting blanket became a moving mass. From the caterpillars the children gained first-hand experience as they watched and even retrieved escapees, all the while observing and discussing the movement, shape, and size of the creatures.

The children engaged the support of adults in this experience, who in turn adapted the curriculum to match this high level of interest. Charting, making pictures, counting, and then searching for chrysalises, the children discovered for themselves the life cycle of the butterfly in a context they could easily understand.

Ada Shermann (1990) suggests that "there is neither a season nor a special place for learning. Children will learn wherever and whenever new knowledge is available, or there is the opportunity to acquire or to practise a new skill" (p. 41). In Canada, our seasonal changes offer young children experiences of life cycles through natural events — the climatic changes of sunshine and shadows, cloud formation, rainbows, and snow, for example. Thus, the science table full of bulbs, pussy willows, and forsythia gives the children the images they can associate with spring. Lying in the shade of the tree for story time or sharing a restful hammock becomes a lasting sensory impression of summer. In autumn, raking coloured leaves, and in winter, measuring the depth of snow against tree trunks become images associated with the seasons in children's memories because of their activities. These natural experiences offer meaningful sequences, interpretations, personal memories, and basic principles of cognition.

LINKING SCIENCE AND COGNITION

Children's exploration is their introduction to the physical world. Physical principles that apply in scientific inquiry are duplicated in the natural way children develop cognition.

If you ask adults what science is, they often explain it as experimentation to increase knowledge and understanding. Yet this is precisely what young children do as they use some of the same strategies of investigative messing about while playing. As you can see from the children who found the caterpillars, when they spontaneously discover new things their curiosity and awareness heighten. They begin to understand that from this increased attention and sensory pleasure — experienced for themselves and not because someone wants to "teach" them something — they gain an understanding of the natural environment.

What is the link between science and cognition? Learning about the natural world engages children's curiosity, balancing the known and the unknown. Instinctively, children want to know and understand conceptually what they observe. Very young children are conscious of the tickle of grass, the soft rustle of leaves, and the buzzing and darting of insects long before they can name these things. Through scrutiny and inquiry into all things, they begin to understand their own relationship to the world. The natural process that children use in exploratory play is the very same process scientists engage in in research (see Box 14.4). If this inquisitiveness is nurtured in an environment in which they can share observations and conclusions and discuss findings, these active explorations assist them in seeing relationships not noticed before. For example, the seed-head hooks on the common burdock weed that renews itself by sticking to everything, including dogs, gave inventors the idea for the velcro strips found extensively on preschool clothing. That's discovery, and that's what makes science.

To facilitate discovery learning, educators must themselves be curious and retain their

---

BOX 14.4 EXPLORATORY PLAY, SCIENTIFIC PROCESS

OBSERVING	Absorbing information from the senses
COMPARING	Becoming aware of similarities and differences among things, events, and places
IDENTIFYING	Naming and making associations
CLASSIFYING	Grouping things
MEASURING	Quantifying, and seeing changes
COMMUNICATING	Explaining what you see, feel, or find
PREDICTING	Forecasting possible or probable outcomes
VERIFYING	Checking, confirming, and proving

own fascination with the mysteries of the natural world. Through their own broadly based knowledge, they can stimulate and sustain interest in science by being involved in children's play and explorations.

SCIENCE AND THE SPONTANEOUS CURRICULUM

Children are natural scientists because they are curious. You cannot "teach" them science, but they will learn it from their own discoveries and from your involvement with their investigations. Here are some examples of such investigations:

❖ Where does rain come from? Is it related to the bathtub, puddles, ditches, ponds, pools, streams, rivers, lakes, or oceans? Introducing a fish tank to your child-care centre stimulates investigation of frogs, crayfish, and water striders found outside the playroom.

❖ How fast do vegetables grow? What are the names of flowers? Can you help build miniature water gardens or bird feeders? Planting gardens gives children a basis for asking these questions. If adults know the names of plants and flowers and show interest in birds and insects found in the immediate outdoor play spaces, children are more inclined to explore. Educators can nurture inquiring minds and interest in all living things if they are also keen observers.

❖ Where does the material for our clothes come from? How are our shoes made? Children are curious about common, everyday things.

When all these motifs are interwoven throughout the curriculum, children are given real contextual information.

When children ask questions, experiences are naturally developmentally appropriate. For instance, when steam rises from the playground after that quick summer shower, or vapour streams from a jet plane, preschoolers need information about these images to answer their "Why?" and "How?" queries. They need adults who can interpret and define what they see. Although "needing to look it up" is sometimes the best response, overusing such a response is frustrating to a young child and may reduce the amount of wondering.

Adults need to be able to recall, talk about, and share accurate information. Can you as an adult comfortably explain shells, rainbows, thunderheads, lightning, and maple syrup in ways that young children can understand and "see" for themselves?

Time for dawdling is a must if children are to observe and experience the out-of-doors. Their discoveries need a place for further explorations and extensions. To be an effective learning experience, the natural event should be re-created or re-experienced so that children have sufficient exposure and opportunity to complete their learning.

Mathematics

Learning concepts in mathematics, like play itself, is spontaneous. New encounters result in new explorations and observations. Children can teach themselves math concepts and the use of symbolic technology when, through their daily experiences, they begin to understand how and why numbers are important. Dividing up the play dough or passing out one napkin to each child are examples of spontaneous math experiences.

Adults introduce children to math concepts very early. It is a part of speech from the beginning: the mother counts one, two, three as she dries the baby's toes after a bath; the toddler counts one, two, three, six, nine, "eleventy," as she excitedly peeks during hide-and-seek; the preschooler makes silent associations as he boards the number nine bus, or repeats goal scores, or counts geese as they fly overhead. For young children, math is a social experience, one in which they can share and still find answers for themselves.

Educators must understand that the basis of mathematical competence is the ability of the children to find patterns, relationships, and

structures for themselves — these cannot be found in rote learning. Rather, the learning occurs in the repetition of a process over and over in different ways, until the process forms a pattern and becomes fixed, regardless of the materials or events. Math learning occurs when children come to recognize and understand the predictable patterns and relationships of numbers and mathematical concepts. If they do not find a pattern or structure that makes sense to them, children experience doubts about their own competence that they carry into adult life, hindering their attempts at logical thinking, problem solving, or risk taking.

What are the prerequisite skills for math? Where are they found? Let us return to the playroom. Math concepts are at the core of most activities. For example, as children play in the housekeeping centre and place cups on saucers or lids on pots, or do up buttons on dolls' clothes, they are beginning to understand the basic principles of one-to-one correspondence. Once this correspondence is internalized and the connection is made — two shoes and two socks now make four things on your feet, and each is a separate concept of one within any number — it becomes a fixed pattern. Children not only verbalize the numbers, they understand them. The ingredients of play make math stimulating and absorbing.

Children's curiosity does not lead them to seek only one answer. They use new knowledge in every possible way, by counting the jumps down the steps, by counting nails, by sorting crayons or counters, by passing cookies, by measuring wood, and by mixing paint. All these activities are part of the enjoyment of mastering mathematical concepts. An imaginative, creative educator assists and supports young children in these discoveries, ensuring that they have opportunities to grasp concepts throughout all play experiences, interacting with the children, and teaching only to expand the context or meaning. The nuts, acorns, or fir cones children find outside and explore indoors become natural objects for counting and comparing sizes and weights.

How, then, in early childhood settings, do you set the stage for the acquisition of math concepts? As children progress in their cognitive skills, adult support becomes essential. If a child chooses an activity for which he is not quite ready, you can find a way to provide investigative clues that simplify understanding. Children benefit from repetitive practice if the same concepts are presented in various ways. By balancing and offering different activities from which children can reach the same conclusion, you expand their development and understanding of concepts. When this experience offers the opportunity for concentrated effort and the enjoyment of solving a problem, the children experience the pleasure of accomplishment and mastery.

Computer Skills

The processes and understanding that are used as children explore natural science lead them into the foundations of mathematical knowledge, which are reintroduced in such technological tools as computers. And yet, when you introduce technology, the natural cognitive process is now dependent on mastering specific skills. In the process of acquiring these skills, the child may be less focussed on acquiring the broader content and knowledge. This is one reason why early childhood educators are suspicious of technology. Another reason is that early childhood education is people-focussed, that is, we emphasize social aspects of children's development.

Educators must be sensitive to differences in the amount of previous exposure children have had to computers and ensure that all children have support in accessing any new technology that is introduced. It may be important to facilitate technological knowledge for children who do not have this opportunity at home.

Why introduce computers into early childhood education? In making any kind of change, most people feel some resistance. Television came with a set of instructions and legitimate concerns of how it should be used effectively. Similar questions arise again as science and technology become part of the preschool experience. So should we or should we not introduce computers? We will explore some of the reasons for and against them, but before we do, we need to clarify some absolutes. First, any learning centre should be enjoyable and integrated with all other learning centres. It will be used by all children as interest dictates.

In the book *The Computer as a Paintbrush*, Beaty and Tucker (1987) discuss some of the positive and negative aspects of using computers in education. In the computer, children have a personal, one-to-one, nonjudgemental tutor that presents information at their level and gives immediate feedback. It offers practice and additional instruction as the children choose. The computer requires active participation, is open-ended, and plays a role in experiential learning. It is intrinsically motivating because learning takes on a fun quality through the use of games and puzzles.

The opposing point of view — that computers are detrimental to education — forces us as educators to evaluate our own ideas and degree of comfort with new technology. Many educators see the computer as socially isolating, as shaping information, and as limiting learning experiences. We also see computers as meeting only one learning style, and question how computer play can be integrated into other areas of play. Do the computer, maths, and science become dominant aspects of the curriculum at the expense of art and literature? Do all children have access to computer experience? Educators must decide for themselves whether the learning advantages outweigh the disadvantages.

The dilemma you face is that of protecting the spontaneous playfulness of childhood and combining it with a technological tool that will lead children into another aspect of perceptual development for natural cognitive functioning. How do you address this dilemma? In the computer learning centre, you can provide not only the computer, but also a typewriter, a calculator, measuring instruments, paper, pencils, pictorial instructions, graphs, selected software, and individual notebooks. With all this it becomes a complete cognitive centre, which indicates that the computer is only one part of skill development.

Two chairs placed at the computer indicate participation and maybe complementary peer teaching. Using the computer becomes a natural social exchange because children cannot just sit and watch. When they control and interact with what is on the screen, they experience an exciting form of self-discovery play. "When the computer is first introduced there may be increased interest at the expense of other centre play. This phase passes quickly if the centre becomes part of the playroom" (Lipinski, cited in Beaty & Tucker 1987, p. 22). This is a good reason to avoid setting up a "taking-turns" policy — the children themselves will work out their own system if they have the opportunity.

As children work together, they talk about new perceptions and concepts as they occur. At the same time, they physically attune their

eye–hand co-ordination by finding and selecting keys or using a mouse to move images around the screen. This activity creates a high level of interest in the computer. The children increase their language and cognitive abilities, which enhance diverse thinking, and their skill development becomes interconnected as they engage in self-correcting explorations.

Studies have shown that all children, boys and girls alike, enjoy and participate in computer centres (Lipinski, cited in Beaty & Tucker 1987). However, you can influence the children with nonverbal messages if you are not comfortable with this technology. If you have a computer centre, offer encouragement for this new method of learning. If we become partners in this learning process, some of our adult apprehensions may disappear as we see the children use and extend their patterns of cognition.

SUMMARY

This chapter began with discussing how children develop thinking, and noted the different ways children relate to their world and make meaning of their experiences. We discussed the impact of culture, experience, learning styles, and gender on children's cognitive development.

When educators understand and apply theoretical approaches of cognitive development, the learning environment becomes child-centred. The ideal learning environment is a partnership between adults and children. The cognitive curriculum offers security and freedom for children to become confident explorers. Within this framework, early childhood educators promote and initiate experiences that are meaningful and sensitive to the natural curiosity and wonder of children.

REVIEW QUESTIONS

❶ What is discovery learning?

❷ What have you learned about cognitive development from Piaget's theories? Why are these theories important to early childhood education?

❸ Define constructivist theory in your own words.

❹ In what ways could gender affect children's cognitive development?

❺ As an early childhood educator, what is your role in enhancing cognitive development in children?

❻ Explain how children in an early childhood education program learn math spontaneously.

DISCUSSION QUESTIONS

❶ How do child-centred programs that are meaningful and relevant to the interests of young children support their cognitive development? Include in your discussion why personal knowledge and experience are crucial to cognitive development.

❷ What can you do to ensure that the diversity of children's individual needs is met through the curriculum in your program?

❸ How is the role of the educator in a child-centred early childhood education program different from a more formal teacher-directed program?

ACTIVITIES

❶ Observe young children at play in at least three programs that have learning centres. Compare the physical settings and the differences in the way cognitive curriculum is implemented.

❷ Choose one or two children in an early childhood program to observe for several hours every day for a week. Find out in what ways discovery learning is taking place. Compile your information and compare your findings with those of your classmates.

❸ In this chapter, we suggest that the socialization of children is an important factor in cognitive development. Many girls play in traditional ways — with dolls and other "girls' toys," for example. Is it myth or fact that child-care programs do not meet the needs of girls in math, science, and new technology? You might need to make observations in a playroom before you can answer this question. Give reasons for your answer.

FURTHER READING

Beal, Carole R. (1994). *Boys and Girls: The Development of Gender Roles.* **New York: McGraw-Hill.**
This book looks at the development of gender roles through socialization patterns, cultural distinctions, and biological diversity of boys and girls. A must-read for educators, it increases awareness of the ways in which our own behaviours contribute to gender identity.

Chattin McNichols, John. (1992). *Montessori Controversy.* **Albany, NY: Delmar.**
A balanced presentation of Montessori education and current practices in early childhood education.

Doxey, Isabel M. (1990). *Child Care and Education: Canadian Dimensions.* **Scarborough, ON: Nelson Canada.**
Doxey and 25 contributors have developed a comprehensive text that reflects the Canadian child's perspectives and experiences in play and learning and explores the historical and current influences on programs and curriculum content.

Goffin, Stacie G. (1994). *Curriculum Models and Early Childhood Education: Appraising the Relationship.* **New York: Merrill.**
Goffin presents the philosophies and practices of five curriculum models that demonstrate the historical beginnings and current principles of appropriate practice and education, and future directions of early childhood education.

Greenspan, Stanley, and Nancy Thorndike Greenspan. (1985). *First Feelings: Milestones in the Emotional Development of Your Baby and Child.* **New York: Penguin Books.**
The emphasis of this text is on the emotional development of children from infancy to preschool as a foundation of all learning. Insightful reading for parents and teachers.

Greenspan, Stanley, and Nancy Thorndike Greenspan. (1989). *The Essential Partnership: How Parents and Children Can Meet the Emotional Challenges of Infancy and Childhood.* **New York: Penguin Books.**
Discusses the relationship between adults and children working and playing together in partnership, and includes practical explorations of real-life situations for parents and educators.

Hughes, Fergus P. (1995). *Children Play and Development* (2nd ed.). **Needham Heights, MA: Allyn & Bacon.**
Extensive look at play as the essential ingredient for facilitating intellectual and social development, considering differences in gender and background.

Kostelnik, M.J., A.K. Soderman, and A.P. Whiren. (1993). *Developmentally Appropriate Programs in Early Childhood Education.* **New York: Merrill.**
Describes the connection between early education and child care. The links are highlighted by responding to the developmental needs of children and creating appropriate environments.

Laing, R.D. (1978). *Conversations with Children.* **New York: Penguin Books.**
This text offers insight into the world of the child through conversation and dialogue. The emotional and intellectual development of the child is revealed.

Lillard, Paula Polk. (1972). *Montessori: A Modern Approach.* **New York: Schocken Books.**

An introduction to Montessori methods, principles, and techniques used in Montessori education in the United States. The text addresses the nature of the child, construction of the child's own power, and the importance of observation.

Lind, Karen K. (1991). *Exploring Science in Early Childhood: A Developmental Approach.* **Albany, NY: Delmar.**

A practical introduction to science for preschool and primary-age children. The emphasis is on three types of learning — naturalistic, informal, and structured — with exploratory constructivist principles and strategies for conceptual learning.

Samples, Bob. (1976). *The Metaphoric Mind.* **Reading, MA: Addison-Wesley.**

The text discusses the impact of a technological world on present and future generations, and asks how we can blend the sciences and the humanities so that a creative process endures.

Samples, Bob. (1987). *Open Mind, Whole Mind: Parenting and Teaching Tomorrow's Children Today.* **Rolling Hills Estates, CA: Jalmar Press.**

An exploration of thinking, learning, and knowing in a holistic approach. The author integrates a broad social view of the challenges and joys of nurturing and empowering young children.

Shipley, Dale. (1993). *Empowering Children: Play-Based Curriculum for Life Long Learning.* **Scarborough, ON: Nelson Canada.**

An in-depth study and a step-by-step approach to child-centred, self-directed play that demonstrates the interrelationship of theory and practice for planning, implementing, and evaluating early childhood curriculum.

Smilansky, Sara. (1990). *Facilitating Play: A Medium for Promoting Cognitive, Socio-Emotional and Academic Development in Young Children.* **Gaithersburg, MD: Psychosocial and Educational Publications.**

A detailed description of the essence of sociodramatic play. Children's self-expressive play, combined with adult intervention methods, can enhance growth in cognitive, social, and emotional development in the preschool child. Includes international research and theories.

Taylor, Barbara J. (1993). *Science Everywhere: Opportunities for Very Young Children.* **New York: Holt, Rinehart & Winston.**

A text that illustrates that science can be meaningful even for very young children. Environments are created with multifaceted sensory experiences that engage children in exploring individual interests.

Williams, Robert A., Robert E. Rockwell, and Elizabeth A. Sherwood. (1987). *Mudpies to Magnets: A Pre-school Science Curriculum.* **Mount Rainier, MD: Gryphon House.**

A hands-on text with a wealth of ideas for everyday experiences from which children find answers for themselves. Adults find the children's starting point and build on this interest, creating an informal transition into the scientific world that will last a lifetime. The child-directed approach provides meaningful experiences that excite children's interest in the magic of science.

REFERENCES

Baratta-Lorton, M. (1979). *Work Jobs.* Reading, MA: Addison-Wesley.

Baroody, A. (1987). *Child Mathematical Thinking.* New York: Teachers College Press.

Beal, C. (1994). *Boys and Girls: Development of Gender Roles.* New York: McGraw-Hill.

Beaty, J.J., and W.H. Tucker. (1987). *The Computer as a Paintbrush: Creative Uses for the Personal Computer in the Preschool Classroom.* Columbus, OH: Merrill.

DeVries, R. (1984). Developmental stages in Piagetian theory and educational practice. *Teacher Educational Quarterly* 11: 78–94.

DeVries, R., and L. Kolberg. (1987). *Programs of Early Education: The Constructionist View.* New York: Longman.

Doxey, I.M. (1990). The Canadian child. In I.M. Doxey, ed., *Child Care and Education: Canadian Dimensions,* pp. 3–12. Scarborough, ON: Nelson Canada.

Eisenburg, N. (1985). Parental socialization of young child's play. Short term longitudinal study. *Child Development* 56: 1506–13.

Elkind, D. (1987). *Mis-Education: Pre-Schooler at Risk.* New York: Alfred Knopf.

Goffin, S. (1994). *Curriculum Models and Early Childhood Education: Appraising the Relationship.* New York: Merrill.

Greenspan, S. (1989). *The Essential Partnership.* New York: Viking Press.

Hendrick, J. (1993). *The Whole Child* (2nd Canadian ed.). Toronto: Maxwell Macmillan.

Kamii, C. (1985). Leading primary education towards excellence. *Young Children* 40 (6): 3–9.

Katz, L. (1989). *Engaging Children's Minds, Project Approach.* Norwood, NJ: Ablex.

Kostelnik, M.J., A.K. Soderman, and A.P. Whiren. (1993). *Developmentally Appropriate Programs in Early Childhood Education.* New York: Merrill.

Laing, R.D. (1978). *Conversations with Children.* New York: Penguin Books.

Maxim, G.W. (1993). *The Very Young: Guiding Children from Infancy through the Early Years.* New York: Merrill.

Montessori, M. (1964). *Montessori Method.* New York: Schocken Books.

Nash, C. (1979). *The Learning Environment.* Don Mills, ON: Collier Macmillan.

Santrock, J. (1993). *Children* (3rd ed.). Dubuque, IA: Brown and Benchmark.

Shermann, A. (1990). The learning child. In I.M. Doxey, ed., *Child Care and Education: Canadian Dimensions.* Scarborough, ON: Nelson Canada.

Smilansky, S., and L. Shefatya. (1990). *Facilitating Play: A Medium for Promoting Cognitive, Socio-Emotional and Academic Development in Young Children.* Gaithersberg, MD: Psychosocial and Educational Publications.

Vygotsky, L. (1962). *Thought and Language.* Cambridge, MA: Institute of Technology Press.

PART 5
History and Visions

For the past 200 years, various individuals and agencies have supported families by providing care and educational experiences for young children. In Canada, the traditions of child care and early education are strong and have emerged as a clear voice of advocacy and leadership in articulating the needs of young children and their families.

As numerous social and economic influences create a variety of pressures on Canadian families, early childhood educators will serve as a valuable resource for families and young children. Our heritage of caring, our commitment to the rights and needs of children, and our acceptance of this responsibility as we face the challenges of the future contribute to the vision of a Canada that cares for all of our children.

CHAPTER 15
Early Childhood Education: Heritage and Vision

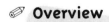

✐ **Overview**

✐ **The Evolution of Child Care and Early Childhood Education**

◆ The European Beginnings

◆ Day Care in Canada, 1850 to 1950

◆ Increasing Interest in Child Development and Educational Practices

◆ Early Childhood Care and Education in Canada, 1960s to 1980s

✐ **Early Childhood Care and Education in Canada in the 1990s**

◆ What Is the Legislation?

◆ Who Provides Funding?

◆ What Is the Administrative Structure?

◆ What Are the Types of Care?

◆ Who Provides the Care, and Where?

✐ **Current Issues**

✏ **Into the Twenty-First Century**

◆ Families and Children at Risk

✏ **Visions for Early Childhood**

Education

◆ Supporting Children

◆ Supporting Families

◆ Ensuring Quality Educational

Experiences

◆ Beliefs in Action

✏ **Summary**

✏ **Discussion Questions**

✏ **Activities**

✏ **Notes**

✏ **Further Reading**

✏ **References**

OVERVIEW

Have you ever noticed that when a parent with young children travels on a bus or subway, all the other people — most likely including yourself — cannot take their eyes off them? Babies and very young children always attract attention. Ask yourself why you are drawn to watching children. There may be a number of reasons, but is it not partly their vulnerability, innocence, and dependency that draw you to them?

The interest that young children generate on a bus or subway is only a minor example of our society's more serious interest in children. No matter in what context you raise the subject, how to care for children and how to educate them are topics that elicit strong opinions.

In children's early years, how should care and education be provided? This chapter gives an overview of Canada's responses to this question over the years. Policies on child care are changing radically, accompanied with considerable debate. The increased acknowledgement that governments should support child care is reflected in the United Nations Convention on the Rights of the Child, signed by 80 countries in 1990 (including Canada), which states that quality child care is a children's rights issue.

One of the best ways to gain clarity on this debate is to look at how the responsibility for children's care and education has changed over time, and how this responsibility is evolving in Canada to reflect an integration of care and education. In this final chapter, we discuss a vision of early childhood education for the coming century.

By the end of this chapter, you should be able to

❖ identify key periods in the historical development of child-care policy and programs in Canada;

❖ identify the issues linking and separating the provision of care and education for young children;

❖ describe current provincial legislation regarding child-care provision and early education;

❖ describe the funding basis for child care and education;

❖ identify the range of programs for the care and education of young children;

❖ discuss the current issues in early care and education.

THE EVOLUTION OF CHILD CARE AND EARLY CHILDHOOD EDUCATION

Any early childhood program you might choose to visit in Canada today is the product of a history that crosses continents and encompasses the traditions of early child care and early childhood education. In practice, the two traditions have been almost indistinguishable. In the past, infant schools, orphanages, poorhouses, day nurseries, and charity kindergartens were all sincere attempts to rescue children from what the rescuers thought were impoverished moral and material conditions.

At the beginning of the nineteenth century, early education for poor children was usually aimed at protecting them and developing their spiritual lives. Memorizing Bible verses was combined with a variety of activities designed to help children form good habits. Caring for young children also included attending to their physical needs. By the end of the nineteenth century, institutional child care and education began to assume a form that would be familiar to you. Many of the child-care practices people now take for granted have their origins in the traditions of the infant asylum, crèche, kindergarten, and nursery school of the nineteenth and early twentieth centuries.

The European Beginnings

In the nineteenth century, an approach to social welfare called "child saving" or "rescue" developed out of John Locke's (an English philosopher of the 1600s) optimistic belief in progress and the human capacity for improvement. The Protestant pastor Jean-Frédéric Oberlin's belief in bettering the life of the poor led him to hire a day-care teacher, Sarah Banzet, in 1770. She is known as the first day-care teacher in Europe. The day-care centres started by Oberlin and the several women who worked with him in the Alsace region of France were called "knitting schools" because the teachers taught the children to knit as part of the program.

In Switzerland, in the late 1700s, Heinrich Pestalozzi's life work represented the beginning of early childhood education. At a time when society was in transition from an agrarian to an industrial economy, the industrialized factory system resulted in family disintegration and child neglect. Pestalozzi opened an industrial school for destitute children on his farm near Zurich in 1774.

In 1805, the Pestalozzi Institute opened with the support of the Swiss government. It was based on enhancing natural childhood and human relationships. Children learned in a "love circle" environment and atmosphere that Pestalozzi believed to be the origin of all

education. Pestalozzi was to become famous as an innovator in elementary education in the early 1800s.

Friedrich Froebel, a student of Pestalozzi, was the founder of the first kindergartens and introduced the concept of play as learning. He considered the image of a child wholly absorbed in play to be the most beautiful expression of a child's life. Froebel's influence spread, and in 1883, a kindergarten based on Froebel's beliefs was opened in Toronto. These programs spread throughout Canada and formed the basis for today's kindergarten programs.

From the examples of Oberlin, Pestalozzi, and Froebel, the idea of caring for the child, as well as educating the child, has remained a part of early childhood education to the present day. The knowledge of Oberlin's pioneering work in the Alsace region led to Madame de Pastoret opening an *asile*, or refuge, for infants under age 3 of working mothers in Paris in 1801. News of Pastoret's centre spread to England, and the first infant "asylum," known as the Sunshine Day Care Program, was opened in London for slum children.

De Pastoret's centre also could have been the inspiration for Robert Owen's work with children of industrial workers in Scotland. Owen's original centre, established in 1816 at his factory in Lanark, was a pioneering example of workplace child care. He expanded his child-care experiment throughout England, Scotland, and Ireland, and in the utopian community he subsequently established at New Harmony, Indiana, where his goal continued to be both education and social reform.

As the child-rescue movement grew throughout the nineteenth century, child care was gradually associated with such institutions as the crèche, the orphanage, and the charity kindergarten. The infant schools that were started throughout Great Britain and Europe provided basic care and education for children older than 2 years. In contrast, the French crèche was specifically designed to care for the infant children of working mothers in relatively small groups. The first crèche was established in Paris in 1844 by Jean-Baptiste-Firmin Marbeau, a charitably minded municipal counsellor. He chose the name to invoke images of the manger in Bethlehem. With the help of Marbeau's numerous publications, word of this new charitable institution soon spread. By the 1850s, there were similar institutions in Vienna, Milan, Brussels, and Dresden. In Great Britain, the crèche was called a day nursery, and did not develop until after the compulsory school law of 1870 was passed.

Day Care in Canada, 1850 to 1950

FORERUNNERS OF CONTEMPORARY DAY CARE

The first crèche in Canada was established in Montreal in 1850. It provided care for impoverished and working mothers who served as domestics or wet-nurses (women employed to breastfeed the children of other women) for wealthier families. Because wet-nurses generally lived in the home of their employer, their own infants were often neglected. Caring for the children of wet-nurses was also the goal of a group of wealthy women in Toronto who established Upper Canada's first day-care centre. Called the Public Nursery, it was established in a house on Victoria Street in Toronto in 1857. Until 1875, when it became an orphan home, the Public Nursery was the only child-care centre in English Canada.

Because there was no assistance available for the poor or destitute in nineteenth-century Canada, many parents used orphanages in times of crisis. Orphanage staff cared for children on a temporary basis while their mothers were working as wet-nurses or domestics, recovering from an illness, or confined to a lying-in hospital (a childbirth facility for poor women). Understandably, at the end of the nineteenth century children in day nurseries were sometimes called "day orphans." Children were also cared for by the day in poorhouses alongside the sick, the infirm, and the aged. Charity, or free, kindergartens also provided care for children of working mothers, while ostensibly aiming to offer a spiritual and moral boost to children and their families. The development of charity kindergartens marked the beginning of the incorporation of educational goals into the day nursery.

DAY NURSERIES

The number of day-care centres in Canada did not grow until the 1890s. Compulsory school laws, increasing industrialization, the beginning of mass immigration, and a bias against such institutions as the orphanage contributed to the creation of a handful of day nurseries by 1900, such as the one in Vancouver's Infants' Hospital in 1910, the Ottawa Day Nursery in 1911, and Halifax's Jost Missions Day Care in 1914. Most day nurseries were organized by private charitable or religious organizations. Typically, a group of church women organized a day nursery as part of their mission work with the urban poor. The women raised funds in door-to-door campaigns, sewed uniforms for the children, visited sick "crèche women" and children, and even on occasion substituted for ailing or absent staff. The staff consisted of a matron, who was usually a mature woman with training as a practical nurse; one or two untrained "baby nurses," who were usually teenage girls; a cook; a maid; and a laundress. The staff lived in the crèche, a practice that persisted in some institutions until the 1950s. Crèches were generally located in former private residences that had been modified to include an office and a playground.

Early crèches offered a wide variety of services to children and their families. Most combined an employment service for day workers with temporary care for their children. Some offered training for women in domestic service, or employed them in the institution itself. Doctors and public-health nurses operated weekly well-baby clinics at crèches, and some offered their facilities as free milk depots. Mothers' clubs were formed to provide women with modern child-rearing information. A few agencies during this period experimented with supervised home day care, referred to as foster care at the time.

For a number of reasons, most working mothers did not use day nurseries. Some mothers were reluctant to use an institution they recognized as a form of welfare. Some day nurseries were also located a great distance from the mothers' homes and workplaces. The day nurseries limited their services in some ways, such as by having policies of not admitting children of single mothers or children younger than 2 years old. As day nurseries became part of the Charity Organization Movement in the 1910s (the forerunner of the United Way), they were pressured to restrict care to families on the basis of "genuine" need.

Other options for working mothers were similar to those of today. Some made arrangements with neighbours, landladies, or relatives, while older children, the original latchkey children, were often supplied with a door key and left to care for themselves. The availability of public kindergartens in some cities relieved the need for child care for 5-year-olds, and

even for many children who were 4 or even younger who were unofficially permitted to attend.

Increasing Interest in Child Development and Educational Practices

In the early 1900s, interest in child study was growing. The University of Manitoba included a child development component in its Home Economics Faculty, and many institutions underwent a reorganization in line with contemporary principles. McGill University Day Care in Montreal and St. George's School for Child Study in Toronto became centres of extensive research into the personality development of children. The research contributed a foundation for early education. St. George's School was directed by William Blatz, who is known as the founder of Canada's early childhood education movement. Blatz was influential in early childhood education through his role as consultant on child-welfare issues to provincial and federal governments. The work at St. George's led to the development of training programs for teachers and social workers. Matrons were replaced by trained social workers or graduates from the masters program at the newly established St. George's Nursery School in Toronto. Nursery school programs were established in many day nurseries for children as young as 2 years of age. As day nurseries began to regard their primary clients as the individual children, rather than the mothers, they began to question their role as employment bureaus.

In the 1930s, the Depression created a crisis in many charitable organizations. Some day nurseries were forced to close, while others offered direct relief to families in the form of money, food, and clothing. However, the need for women workers during World War II stimulated a new demand for day care. By 1942, the West End Crèche in Toronto had a waiting list of 500 children. A cost-sharing agreement between the federal government and the two provinces with large war industries, Ontario and Quebec, resulted in the establishment of a number of wartime day nurseries to supplement the private centres.

Although the governments of both Ontario and Quebec considered the nurseries to be a wartime measure and attempted to close them following the war, their legacy was significant. In Ontario, there was such an outcry due to the closures that the government responded with the Day Nurseries Act in 1945. First, Ontario temporarily changed the status of day care from a welfare to a normative service. Second, regulations to govern day care and a bureaucracy to administer it were established.

Third, the closing of the nurseries stimulated a well-organized parent protest in Ontario that foreshadowed the day-care activism of the 1960s and 1970s.

Early Childhood Care and Education in Canada, 1960s to 1980s

The number of local and provincial advocacy groups grew during the 1960s and 1970s. At the same time, the demand from working mothers for child day care increased, the provinces and territories initiated legislation to create minimal standards for child care, the federal government started in 1966 to provide some funding for child care through the Canada Assistance Plan, community colleges developed training programs for child-care workers and teachers, and local and provincial professional early childhood education associations formed.

Even though these groups were addressing somewhat different issues, the interconnections were apparent. Care for young children was needed to support women in the work force. The need for quality of care resulted in standards and education for the providers, while funding was needed to make child care accessible and to sustain quality. At the same time, advocates for the children and the profession were needed.

These trends grew into a national agenda in the 1980s. In 1982, a Canadian Conference on Daycare in Winnipeg passed resolutions calling for the enactment of national legislation to create a universally accessible, high-quality, nonprofit child-care system, and a mandate to form a broad-based national child-care advocacy organization. As a result, the Canadian Day Care Advocacy Association was established in 1983.

TABLE 15.1 PROVINCIAL AND TERRITORIAL CHILD DAY CARE LEGISLATION

PROVINCE OR TERRITORY	NAME OF LEGISLATION (ACT AND REGULATIONS)
British Government Legislative Assembly	Community Care Facilities Act. Chapter 57. 1988. British Columbia Child Care Regulation 319/89. As amended to O.C. 1476/89. Guaranteed Available Income for Need (GAIN) Act. 1979.
Alberta Legislative Assembly	Social Care Facilities Licensing Act. Chapter S-14, 1980. As amended. Alberta Day Care Regulations 333/90. As amended to Chapter S-14, 1980.
Saskatchewan Legislative Assembly	The Care Act. Bill 8, 1990. Child Care Regulations. 1990.
Manitoba Legislative Assembly	The Community Child Day Care Standards Act. 1983 as amended in 1986. Manitoba Child Day Care Regulations 23/87, 62/86, and 148/83. As amended to Chapter C-158. 1986.
Ontario Legislative Assembly	The Day Nurseries Act. Revised Statutes of Ontario, 1990. Ontario Regulations 262. 1990.
Québec Assemblée Nationale	An Act Respecting Child Day Care. R.S.Q., Chapter S-4.1, as amended June 1992. Regulation Respecting Child Day Care Centres, S-4.1, R.2
New Brunswick Legislative Assembly	Family Services Act. 1980. Family Services Act Regulations, 1983, as amended, 1992.
Nova Scotia Legislative Assembly	Day Care Act and Regulations. Chapter 6. 1980. As amended.
Prince Edward Island Legislative Assembly	The Child Care Facilities Act. 1988. Child Care Facilities Regulations. 1988. The Welfare Assistance Act. 1988.
Newfoundland House of Assembly	The Day Care and Homemaker Services Act. RSN 1990, CD-2 and Newfoundland Regulation 219/82 as amended to O.C. 979/82. Day Care and Preschool Licensing Requirements, Newfoundland and Labrador. 1991–92.

(continued)

TABLE 15.1 (continued)

PROVINCE OR TERRITORY	NAME OF LEGISLATION (ACT AND REGULATIONS)
Northwest Territories Legislative Assembly	The Northwest Territories Child Day Care Act and the Child Day Care Standards and Regulations. 1988.
Yukon Legislative Assembly	Child Care Act. Bill 77. 1990. Family Day-Home Regulations and Day Care Centre Regulations. O.C. 1986/29.

Source: Based on Child Care Resource and Research Unit. (1993). *Child Care in Canada: Provinces and Territories.* Toronto: CRRU, University of Toronto.

Task forces such as the Task Force on Child Care (1984) were established to report to the federal Ministry Responsible for the Status of Women "concerning the federal government's role in the development of a system of quality child care in Canada." In 1986, the report of the Task Force on Child Care was released, which called for a fully publicly funded, comprehensive, high-quality, not-for-profit system of child care and paid parental leave. At the same time, the federal government established the Special Committee on Child Care to study child-care needs. In 1987, the Special Committee made its report, which called for increased tax credits for families, continuation of subsidies for low-income families through the Canada Assistance Plan, small operating grants for profit and nonprofit programs, enhancement of maternity leave to six months, and small capital grants for profit and nonprofit child care. The report was greeted with an unfavourable response from child-care advocates, the women's movement, and trade unions.

At the end of 1987, the federal government announced its National Child Care Strategy, which included new tax deductions and credits for parents, a federal fund for special projects and research, and an intention to introduce a national Child Care Act. The act would allow $3.2 billion in federal funds to be matched by the provinces over 7 years. Decisions about how the funds would be spent were to be made by the provinces, including allocating the funds for subsidies to low-income families previously guaranteed by the federal government to the provinces under the Canada Assistance Plan. Funding could also be made available to commercial programs. Response to the National Child Care Strategy from child-care advocates was unanimously negative.

In 1988, the Canada Child Care Act was introduced, moved through the House of Commons to committee stage, and went on to the Senate for approval. The act was vigorously opposed by the opposition parties and was allowed to die on the eve of the federal election.

EARLY CHILDHOOD CARE AND EDUCATION IN CANADA IN THE 1990S

What Is the Legislation?

At present there is no federal legislation directly related to child care in Canada. The legislation that spells out administrative structures, standards, and enforcement procedures operates at the provincial or territorial government level. Every provincial and territorial government in Canada has such legislation, which is listed in Table 15.1.

The child-care centre standards that are regulated through these acts and regulations include those related to health and safety, numbers of children permitted in care without regulation, size of centres, size of groups of children, staff–child ratios, staff training, and parental involvement. They can also include conditions for the involvement of municipal governments, and monitoring and enforcement procedures. Table 15.2 gives an overview of the variations in these standards among provinces. There are also regulated standards for home-based care. However, these standards affect only a few operators who receive government subsidies, because the majority operate privately outside the regulations (see the explanation on page 371).

Who Provides Funding?

The majority of child-care costs are paid by parents. According to the National Child Care Survey[1] carried out in 1988, four out of five children in child care received no government subsidy.

Government funding for child care comes from three government levels. The federal government, through the Canada Assistance Plan, pays 50 percent of the cost of child-care subsidies for eligible parents through a cost-sharing agreement with provincial and municipal governments. There was no ceiling to this funding until 1990, when the federal government limited the amount it would cost-share with British Columbia, Alberta, and Ontario (the largest child-care budgets). The federal government also provides a child-care expense deduction whereby the lower income earner in a family can deduct child-care expenses of up to $4000 per child up to the age of 7.

The provincial government sets the eligibility levels, initiates the requests for funding, administers the funds, and matches the federal government's 50 percent share. There is a great deal of variation in eligibility levels across the country. In one province, a 2-parent family with 2 children might not be eligible for a subsidy with an annual income of $13 000, but in another province, such a family with an annual income of $35 000 might receive a partial subsidy. Most provinces also provide some form of operating, maintenance, or salary grants to child-care centres or programs.

In two provinces, municipal governments also share in the funding of child care. Participating municipalities in Ontario contribute 20 percent of funding for subsidies, lowering the province's share to 30 percent. In Alberta, municipalities provide funding for school-age child care.

What Is the Administrative Structure?

Who is responsible for the management and operation of child-care programs? Table 15.3 presents the government administrative structures for child care in each of the provinces and territories, as well as indicates municipal involvement where appropriate. Responsibility for the management and operation of individual child-care centres or agencies may be taken by municipal governments, nonprofit community organizations (with a voluntary community board), or private commercial organizations.

What Are the Types of Care?

Child-care arrangements can be divided into two general categories: public or near-public, and private. Centre-based programs usually provide education as well as care.

TABLE 15.2 PROVINCIAL AND TERRITORIAL CHILD-CARE CENTRE REGULATIONS

Province	Max. Allowed without Licence	Max. Centre Size	Max. Group Size	Ratios	Training
British Columbia	2	not spec.	0-3 — 12 3+ — 25	0-1 — 1:4 3-6 — 1:8 6-7 — 1:10 7+ — 1:15	Supervisor — 1 yr. ECE; 1 staff with each group — 1 yr. ECE; all staff — enrolled in training; 1 staff with infant/toddlers — additional training
Alberta	3	80	0-18 m — 6 19-35 m — 10 3-5 y — 16 5-6 y — 20	1:3 1:5 1:8 1:10	1 in 6 staff in centre: 1 yr. ECE cert.; by 1995 — all directors — 2 yr. ECE; 1 in 4 workers with ECE; all others 50-hr. course
Saskatchewan	8	80	0-12 m — 6 13-18 m — 8 19-35 m — 12 3-5 y — 16 5-6 y — 20	1:3 1:4 1:10 1:8 1:10	All directors — equiv. to 2 yr. ECE; 1 in 6 staff equiv. to 1 yr. ECE; all others 50 hr. orientation
Manitoba	4 under 12; 2 under 2	70	*Mixed* 12 w-2 y — 8 2-6 y — 16 6-12 y — 30 *Separate* 12 w-1 y — 6 1-2 y — 8 2-3 y — 12 3-4 y — 16 4-5 y — 18 5-6 y — 20 6-12 y — 30	 1:4 1:8 1:15 1:3 1:4 1:6 1:8 1:9 1:10 1:15	Supervisor — CCW III (app. degree, adv. certificate diploma) + 1 yr. exp.; 2/3 staff — CCW II (certif. or equiv.) or III; all other CCW I
Ontario	5	not spec.	0-18 m — 10 18-30 m — 15 31 m-5 y — 16 5-6 y — 24 6-9 y — 30	3:10 1:5 1:8 1:12 1:15	Supervisors — 2 yr. ECE dip. or equiv.; 1 staff with each group with ECE diploma

(continued)

TABLE 15.2 (continued)

Province	Max. Allowed without Licence	Max. Centre Size	Max. Group Size	Ratios	Training
Quebec	6	60	0-18 m — 15 per room 18 m+ — 30 per room	0-17 m — 1:5 18 m-5 y — 1:8 5-12 y — 1:15	1/3 of staff must have CEGEP or univ. degree in ECE or 3 yr. experience + college degree or univ. cert. in ECE
New Brunswick	4 inc. operator's own (2 under 2)	60	0-2 — 9 2 — 10 3 — 14 4 — 20 5 — 24 6-12 — 30	1:3 1:5 1:7 1:10 1:12 1:15	16 yr. old and supervised; no ECE required; willingness to take training; understands needs of children and community
Nova Scotia	6 preschool, 8 school-age	60	not spec.	0-2 — 1:4 0-5 — 1:7 (full day) 1:12 (pt. day) 5-12 — 1:15	Director + 2/3 staff — trained in ECE (ECE or Gr. 12 + 2 yr. exp. + course and 25 hr. workshop)
Prince Edward Island	3 (if all under 2; 5 if no more than 2 under 2; 6 of mixed up to 10 if no more than 2 under 2 — not including operator's own)	50	*Mixed* 0-3 — 12 3+ — 33 *Separate* 0-2 — 6 2-3 — 10 3-4 — 30 5-7 — 36 7+ —	 1:3 1:5 1:10 1:12 1:15	1 staff with ECE; 30 hrs. continued education every year
Newfoundland and Labrador	4	50	not spec.	2-3 — 1:6 3-6 — 1:8 7-12 — 1:15	Directors — 1 yr. ECE + 1 yr. exp. or 2 yr. ECE or related degree + 1 yr. exp.

(continued)

TABLE 15.2 (continued)

Province	Max. Allowed Without Licence	Max. Centre Size	Max. Group Size	Ratios	Training
Northwest Territories	4	no max.	0-12 m — 6 13-24 m — 8 25-35 m — 12 3-16 y 4-15 y 5-10 y — 20	1:3 1:4 1:6 1:8 1:9 1:10	No training required; ECE encouraged; 19 yrs.; cultural background of children reflected
Yukon	3	not spec.	not spec.	0-18 m — 1:4 18m-2 y — 1:6 3-6 y — 1:8 6-12 y — 1:12	Min. age — 18 yr., no training required

Source: Based on Child Care Resource and Research Unit. (1993). *Child Care in Canada: Provinces and Territories.* Toronto: CRRU, University of Toronto.

1. **Public or Near-Public:** Child-care arrangements that are regulated and receive some public funding (referred to as public, regulated, or formal). These include

   ❖ child-care centres;

   ❖ part-day programs — nursery schools;

   ❖ regulated, home-based care, called family day care or family day-care homes — care of small groups in the home of a child-care provider, either under the supervision of an agency or a municipal government, or supervised directly by provincial or territorial government officials;

   ❖ school-aged care — outside school hours, before or after school, during school holidays, or during professional activity days.

2. **Private:** Child-care arrangements that are unregulated and receive no public government funding (referred to as private, unregulated, or informal). These include

   ❖ care in an unrelated care-giver's or relative's home, not regulated by the government;

   ❖ care in a child's own home — baby-sitter, nanny, relative, or friend.

Commercial child-care centres or agencies, operated as private businesses, sometimes fall into the private category when they are regulated, but receive no public funds. When they receive public funds, they fit into the near-public category.

In addition, the government provides some funding and monitoring of programs that support parents and private care-givers. These

TABLE 15.3 PROVINCIAL CHILD-CARE ADMINISTRATION STRUCTURES

PROVINCES AND TERRITORIES	MINISTRY (IES)	MUNICIPAL INVOLVEMENT
British Columbia	Ministry for Women's Equality	Vancouver provides some funding of new centres and special programs
Alberta	Alberta Family and Social Services — Day Care Programmes	Until 1980, paid 20% of subsidized care; now responsible for all school-age care
Saskatchewan	Dept. of Social Services, Child Care Branch	Legislation provides for municipal child-care centres, but there are none
Manitoba	Dept. of Family Services, Child Care	No involvement
Ontario	Ministry of Community and Social Services, Child Care Branch — developing partnership with Ministry of Education (full day sr. kindergartens, plans for day care in all schools)	The Act allows municipalities and Indian bands to directly operate child-care services. In March 1990, Ontario municipalities operated 204 child-care centres, also regulated private home day care; administer and pay 20% of cost of subsidies
Quebec	L'Office des Services de Garde à l'Enfance — a semiautonomous body, sets standards and regulations and is appointed by the provincial government	2 municipalities operate child care; many provide space, land, and/or services to parent-operated child-care centres
New Brunswick	Office for Childhood Services in Dept. of Health and Community Services	No involvement
Nova Scotia	Daycare Services, Department of Community Services	Legislation allows municipalities to operate child care but none has done so
Prince Edward Island	Early Childhood Services, Division of Special Services, Department of Health and Social Services	No involvement

(continued)

TABLE 15.3 (continued)

Provinces and Territories	Ministry (ies)	Municipal Involvement
Newfoundland and Labrador	Day Care and Homemaker Services, Department of Social Services	No involvement
Northwest Territories	Department of Social Services	No involvement
Yukon	Child Services Unit, Department of Health and Human Resources	No involvement

Source: Based on Child Care Resource and Research Unit. (1993). *Child Care in Canada: Provinces and Territories.* Toronto: CRRU, University of Toronto.

include resource or drop-in centres, which provide information, parenting and care-giving resources, toy lending, networking, socialization and respite care, and emergency-care programs when children are mildly ill or when regular care-givers are not available.

Who Provides the Care, and Where?

Providers of early childhood care and education who work in child-care centres are variously referred to as early childhood educators, child-care workers, infant teachers, and preschool teachers. Data from an eighteen-month nationwide study[2] gives us the following picture of their wages and working conditions:

1. Sixty-eight percent have a postsecondary certificate, diploma, or degree, compared with 41 percent of the nationally employed labour force.

2. Ninety-eight percent are women.

3. Many have incomes close to, or below, the Statistics Canada poverty line. The average yearly wage of someone in charge of a group, often with supervisory duties, is $18 498. The hourly rate for unionized staff is 33 percent higher than for non-unionized staff. Municipal centres pay the highest average wage; commercial centres pay the lowest.

Providers of early childhood care and education in home-based care, whether regulated or private and unregulated, provide the majority of child care in Canada and are much more difficult to study as a group. Some provide care as a way of staying at home with their own small children and earning some income, some are older care-givers whose children are all in school or grown, some give care to supplement social-welfare payments but do not consider themselves full-time care-givers, while others are experienced early childhood educators who stay at home to be care-givers when they become mothers. Income from home-based care tends to be lower than from centre-based care, but varies considerably: some care-givers see themselves as business-women running a private business, while others see themselves as providing informal support to neighbours or extended family.

It is interesting to compare the status of home-based care-givers in Canada to that in Sweden, where all home-based care-givers are unionized employees of the local governments, with negotiated salaries and benefits and required training.

Table 15.4 gives a picture of how many children are being cared for in home-based care as opposed to centres, nursery schools/kindergartens, and after-school programs.

CURRENT ISSUES

Who shares in the care and education of young children? The family, centres for early childhood care and education within the child-care system, and kindergarten settings within the school system. The care parents choose for their children does not depend only on their own values; it also depends on the political, social, cultural, and economic beliefs and conditions in our country. These beliefs and conditions have varied at different times in Canada, and they vary from country to country. In Canada, education is the responsibility of the family until a child is 4 or 5, and then

education becomes the responsibility of the school. The government is responsible for the care of children only if the family is unable to take this responsibility. Some people in Canada believe that care is the primary responsibility of the family throughout the child's dependency years. However, many Canadians, including early childhood educators, believe that society has an obligation to support families in providing care and education for young children, as we do for older children.

As we stated at the beginning of this chapter, children's needs and how they should be met stirs up a great deal of strong opinion in most people. This is no less true for groups of people who have come together to work on community problems, groups of parents, women's groups, or political parties. Almost any group could formulate a policy on child care, and each one would likely be different. However, probably they would all include discussion on the issues we outline here.

1. What should be the relationship between child care and early education?

2. For whom is public child care intended? Should public/government funding be

TABLE 15.4 DISTRIBUTION OF CHILDREN IN NONPARENTAL CHILD-CARE ARRANGEMENTS, 1988

Arrangement	Total Number of Children in Care	Children in Care While Mother Is Working
Home-Based Care	1 814 000	1 042 000
Kindergarten/Nursery School	578 000	189 000
Day-Care Centre	202 000	141 000
Before/After-School Program	83 000	64 000

Source: National Child Care Survey. (1991). In Statistics Canada, *Perspectives.* Reproduced by authority of the Minister of Industry, 1996.

used to pay for child care only for parents who cannot afford it, or should it be provided universally, like health care or education?

3. Who benefits from early childhood education? Who should fund and provide early education? When should early education begin?

4. Who should run child care? Should all public child care be provided by the government (as schools are, and as is the case in Sweden)? If not, what other structures should receive government funding to provide child care — nonprofit community organizations, commercial organizations, school boards, parent co-operatives?

5. Should early childhood education and child care be co-ordinated? If so, how?

6. Should all publicly funded child care be centre-based, or is there a role for home-based child care in a public provision?

7. Under what jurisdiction should child care be included — the Ministry of Education (as in New Zealand), the Ministry of Health (as in France for children under age 2½), Social Services (as in Canada), or the Ministry of Labour (as in Israel)?

8. Who should pay for child care — parents or government? How should public funds be distributed, through direct child-care provision or through tax deductions to parents?

9. What role should the federal government take in providing a national child-care system?

These debates are ongoing throughout Canada. Many groups and organizations influence child-care policy and have different perspectives on these issues. Some examples are

❖ **Professional associations:** They stress the need for quality of care, and the training, education, and professional status of care-givers.

❖ **Advocacy associations:** They focus on the working conditions of staff, universality of provision, and the government's responsibility for effective intervention.

❖ **National Action Committee on the Status of Women:** They have two concerns: child care as essential to women's equality in the labour force, and women's status as public care-givers as a currently undervalued occupation.

❖ **Organized labour:** They also have two concerns: employee rights to child care, and child-care workers as currently part of the labour force that is underpaid and exploited.

As you prepare to enter the profession of early childhood education, you will also enter into this debate. The final sections of this book address some of the issues that you will face as we move into the next century. We have drawn together some of the values and principles that will likely guide the direction early childhood educators will take in the debate.

INTO THE TWENTY-FIRST CENTURY

Families and Children at Risk

Throughout this textbook, we have often assumed and presented a positive and idealistic view of the overall experiences of children. However, we must admit that a realistic look at children and families reminds us that there are many factors that threaten the well-being of far too many of our children. As professionals who will have significant influence in

the lives of hundreds of children and their families over the years, early childhood educators have an obligation to consider some of the factors that place our children at risk, and to do all that is in our power to reduce — and try to eliminate — the impact of such negative stressors.

TECHNOLOGY

Many people have mixed feelings about the increased use of technology. High-tech development in the areas of medical equipment and techniques is an obvious example of the potential of this expansion. The benefits resulting from technological developments in other areas as well cannot be denied. However, the rapid developments in technology have been partly responsible for two disturbing trends in our society: the pressure to become more competitive as a society, and the increasing feelings of depersonalization as we deal with machines more often and with other people less frequently.

With regard to increasing demands for competitive levels of performance and output, our society is experiencing rising levels of personal and communal stress to do everything faster and better. We hear these attitudes filtering down through the education system when people argue for higher standards of performance and earlier acquisition of skills. Continual pressure and high demands for performance take their toll on such important areas of development as self-esteem, sense of calm, sense of security, sense of competence, and general well-being, for both children and adults.

There is validity to the argument that technology has resulted in the replacement of human relationships with mechanical ones. Consider television, video games, automated bank machines, and telephone answering machines, and it is easy to see where this argument comes from. Although these technologies are convenient in many cases, and informative and entertaining in others, all of us need a balance in our lives. Machines cannot nurture, support, or build self-esteem. Our children need meaningful interpersonal relationships and interactions with a range of members of our society, in many different situations, if they are to develop as well-rounded individuals.

ECONOMIC AND TIME STRESSORS

As a result of pressures and economic factors within Canada and internationally, our society is increasingly experiencing economic insecurity and financial pressures. The majority of Canadian families experience the same pressures and economic insecurity (Glossop, interviewed in Statistics Canada 1994). Jobs are being eliminated or transformed into less secure positions. Most families now require two incomes to meet their needs. This situation places growing demands on the family, demands that originate outside the home and reduce time for tending to family and children's needs. These factors result in ongoing and sometimes intolerably high levels of stress for families, which are clearly experienced by the children as well.

POVERTY

Closely related to the economic pressures arising from demands outside the family is the distressingly high level of poverty experienced by families with young children. As you read in Chapter 2, recent statistics tell us that more than 1 million Canadian children live in poverty (Vanier Institute of the Family n.d.). This intolerable situation not only limits the range of experiences and options for families, but it influences children adversely for their entire lives unless adequate supports for them and their families are available.

VIOLENCE

Our children are exposed to alarming amounts of violent behaviour in various forms. For some children, this exposure is primarily through the media (television, movies), and toys that re-create this violence in play. For far too many children, violence is also a way of life that is experienced or observed within their own families. Violence, and the fear of violence, erodes the sense of security and trust, and the resulting anxiety interferes with relationships and development. Even within settings for young children, highly aggressive or out-of-control behaviour creates difficulty and distress for children and adults alike.

Although some segments of our society are taking leadership in moving toward zero tolerance of violent behaviour of any kind, we still have far to go in ensuring a safe and secure environment for all children, within and outside the family. We have much to do to heal the hurt resulting from childhood experiences with violence, both for the children and for the parents who may have been victims in the past.

VISIONS FOR EARLY CHILDHOOD EDUCATION

Early childhood education, as a profession, takes its direction from the commitment to support the well-being and development of children and their families in the face of these individual and societal pressures. In meeting these important challenges, we draw on many areas of knowledge, strength, and expertise.

Supporting Children

Our first, and most effective, way to protect children from some of these stresses is through warm, caring relationships with them. These relationships form the foundation of quality care and education in the early years, and nourish a strong sense of self as well as high self-esteem. Through our relationships with children, we can ensure that they feel valued. We can ensure a supportive human environment where all children are respected by others and experience the satisfaction of meaningful and intimate relationships, both with their peers and with adults.

We can also support children by providing a quality early childhood program, ensuring that the learning experiences are meaningful and at an appropriate level. We can resist pressure to rush development or to pressure children to perform, advocating instead a natural and meaningful process of learning.

Although we cannot directly influence the economic situation of individual families, we can provide sufficiently for children's needs during the time they are in our care. We can work to ensure that we minimize stress while the children are in the centre, and even teach coping strategies so that they will be more able to deal with stresses in the home.

To counteract the images and experience of violence in families and society, we can create and maintain an atmosphere in which aggressive behaviour is not acceptable, while working continuously to support children who are trying to resolve personal issues and feelings. We can teach more appropriate strategies to assert individual needs and rights and to resolve interpersonal conflict. We can work with all children to help them become more empathic and caring of others.

Supporting Families

Children thrive in families that are thriving. In Chapter 2, and earlier in this chapter, you read about some of the challenges and stresses faced by today's families. All of us have a role to play in supporting families in the important work of caring for and raising children. Our acceptance of and respect for families, regardless of different beliefs, backgrounds, or practices, is the foundation for a meaningful partnership in caring for young children. Although each family has its own beliefs and goals for children, which may differ somewhat from yours, rest assured that we all share in a desire to do what is best for the children. Families have in-depth knowledge of their own children, and you, as an early childhood educator, have expertise in many areas of child development and practical child-rearing practices. Together, with trust and communication, we can achieve our common goals for children.

When circumstances make it difficult for families to provide all that the children need, either temporarily or for the long term, you take on a crucial role as support for both the family and the children. Because you are available to the child on a daily basis, you can share the responsibility of ensuring the child's well-being and in turn reduce some of the worries and stresses for the family. When you provide this caring support, you enable the family to grow and you ensure that the child's needs are supplied in the process. All of us fare much better knowing there are people who care and stand behind us as we struggle to do the best we can.

Ensuring Quality Educational Experiences

As it becomes more common for 4-year-olds, and even 3-year-olds, to enter the formal education system, early childhood educators will be drawn into the debate over the content and quality of education. Our profession has a comprehensive and clearly articulated perspective about preferred practices for early education.

We believe that quality education is determined by considering the overall experiences of children and the process of learning, more so than by the actual outcomes in defined knowledge and skills. We value meaningful learning activities that provide understanding at a level that can be integrated with previous knowledge and experience, and we understand the importance of mastery and a sense of competence in new areas of knowledge and skills. Experiencing success more often than failure in meeting new challenges is crucial to a positive self-concept and ongoing learning.

The early childhood education philosophy values children as the centre of our work and the most important focus of everything we do. We provide experiences that reflect children's interests and needs, balancing this with our own views of what is important for each child's well-being and long-term development and learning. This child-centred approach helps to ensure the acknowledgement of the whole child, as it reflects wide variation in children's preferences, strengths, and interests. To accomplish these goals, we recognize and advocate that education must be based on a clear understanding of general patterns of development, as well as on observations of individual styles, paces, and levels of learning. We recognize that we cannot truly benefit children unless we plan for all areas of development and learning, making the early childhood curriculum a curriculum for the whole child.

Beliefs in Action

In the process of becoming an early childhood educator, you are developing your own philosophy, knowledge base, and wide repertoire of skills. As you have completed your study of this book, we hope that you have discovered the foundations for your personal belief system and the knowledge to carry out your most important role: providing quality care and education for some of the youngest members of our society.

Far too often, the voices of children and families are not heard when policies are developed and decisions are made. There will be times when you will need to articulate the value of early childhood principles and practice. As well, you will often face the need to advocate for the needs and rights of children and families. We urge you to become informed about issues in your community that affect children and their families, join organizations that work to support children and families, get involved in the debates that take place, and be a voice for the children. As we enter the next century, your beliefs and expertise can make a difference in the lives of children.

SUMMARY

Several themes arise from our review of the history of child care and early childhood education in Canada:

❖ the shift from private to public sponsorship;

❖ the eclectic range of child-care services;

❖ the roots of child care as a welfare service;

❖ the increasing professionalization of care;

❖ the influence of psychological and educational theory on child care;

❖ the coming together of early care and education.

History should not be seen only as a story of progress. It can also be used to help us pose questions that make us more reflective practitioners. Being aware of the history of our profession is critical to the continued growth and relevance of the services that we offer to children and their families. Our vision for the future clarifies our responsibilities to support children and families, to provide high-quality educational programs, and to advocate on behalf of children and their families.

DISCUSSION QUESTIONS

❶ Considering the involvement of family members, the school system, and the child-care system, discuss how your parents were cared for and educated in their early years, how you were, and how you think your children will be. What has caused the changes? What effect does ethnicity and immigration status have on the choices?

❷ Given the history of care and education in Canada, what do you think our child-care system will look like in 50 years? in 100 years?

❸ What is included in the act of caring for children? What is included in the act of educating children? What are the differences? How would you describe your philosophy of caring? of education?

❹ Are early childhood educators who are working in child-care centres professionals? What does that mean? Are home-based care-givers professionals?

ACTIVITIES

❶ Discover the history of early education in your own area by identifying and interviewing pioneers in child-care work. Create a local child-care archive consisting of taped interviews and transcripts, photographs, and other artifacts.

❷ Find out what your local federal or provincial member of parliament's political party thinks about the issues listed on pages 374–75.

❸ Contact a member of the professional child-care workers or advocacy association in your area and find out her or his views on these issues.

❹ Contact a National Action Committee on the Status of Women representative in your area and find out her views on these issues.

❺ Contact a local union and find out their views on these issues.

❻ Compare the child-care policies and programs of Canada or your province with those of another country.

❼ Find a parent who is searching for child care and follow his or her search over several weeks. What is the parent looking for? Does the parent find it? If not, why not?

NOTES

❶ The National Child Care Survey (NCCS) is the most comprehensive survey on child-care arrangements ever carried out in Canada. Conducted in September and October 1988, the NCCS was administered as a supplement to the monthly Labour Force Survey in all households with at least one child under the age of 13. In conjunction with Statistics Canada, the survey was designed and developed by the National Daycare Research Network, a consortium of researchers from 4 universities sponsored by Health and Welfare Canada. See the References list for reports of this study.

❷ The nationwide study was jointly carried out by Health and Welfare through a CCIF grant, the Canadian Child Care Advocacy Association, and the Canadian Child Care Federation. The study surveyed 969 centres and more than 7200 staff.

FURTHER READING

Arnup, K., A. Levesque, and R.R. Pierson. (1990). *Delivering Motherhood: Maternal Ideologies and Practices in the 19th and 20th Century.* New York: Routledge.
A collection of essays that examine the ideologies of motherhood in a variety of contexts.

Beer, E. (1957). *Working Mothers and the Day Nursery.* New York: Whiteside and Morrow.
A classic in the history of day-care literature, written by a former board member of a New York City day nursery. First published in 1938.

Braun, S., and E. Edwards. (1972). *History and Theory of Early Childhood Education.* Belmont, CA: Wadsworth.
A valuable collection of original sources related to the history of early education.

Child Care Resource and Research Unit. (1991). *Child Care in Canada: Selected Child Care Topics. An Annotated Bibliography.* Toronto: CRRU.

Child Care Resource and Research Unit. (1993). *Child Care in Canada: Provinces and Territories.* Toronto: CRRU.
Provides information on the variations among provincial and territorial legislation and regulations governing child care in Canada.

Corbett, B.E. (1989). *A Century of Kindergarten Education in Ontario.* Mississauga, ON: The Froebel Foundation.
Corbett describes the incorporation of the kindergarten ideal into the public schools of Ontario.

Crompton, S. (1991). Who's looking after the kids? Child care arrangements of working mothers. *Perspectives* (Summer). Ottawa: Statistics Canada.
Report on the Statistics Canada National Child Care Survey.

Doherty, G. (1991). *Quality Matters in Child Care.* Huntsville, ON: Jesmond.
A review of the research on effects on child development of quality characteristics of child-care programs.

Friendly, M. (1994). *Child Care Policy in Canada: Putting the Pieces Together.* Toronto: Addison-Wesley.

This book gives an in-depth look at the development of child care in Canada, including discussion of political, social, and funding issues as they relate to child-care policy for early childhood education students. Uses Canadian and other country case examples effectively.

Friendly, M., L. Rothman, and M. Oloman. (1991). Child care for Canadian children and families: A discussion paper. Conference paper for Canada's Children: The Priority for the 90s. Ottawa, October 27–29.
A background paper for discussion at the conference, leading to policy recommendations to the federal government.

Gould, M.S. (1933). The day nursery in the programme of child care. Ottawa: The Canadian Council on Child and Family Welfare.
An important historical source that describes the day nursery in the context of child care, the contemporary term for child welfare.

Marbeau, J.B.F. (1843). *Des Crèches: Ou, Moyen de Diminuer la Misére Enaugmentant la Population.* Paris: Comptoir des Imprimeurs-Unis.
Marbeau's original manual for the operation of crèches is available in microform in major university libraries.

Melhuish, E., and P. Moss, eds. (1991). *Day Care for Young Children: International Perspectives.* London: Tavistock/Routledge.
The editors use their experience with the European Community Child Care Network to bring together papers on child care in Sweden, the United States, the United Kingdom, former East Germany, and France.

National Child Care Conference and Lobby. (1992). A child care agenda for the 90s: Putting the pieces together. Ottawa, October 15–19.

Papers
Beach, Jane. A comprehensive system of child care.
Bertram, Jane. Human resources in child care.
Cameron, Barbara. Structure and management.
Friendly, Martha. Child care in a public policy context.
Oloman, Mab. Child care funding.

These were prepared as background papers for discussion at the National Child Care Conference, leading to policy recommendations. The papers are available from the Child Care Resource and Research Unit, University of Toronto (Phone: (416) 978-6895) or the Ontario Coalition for Better Child Care, 297 St. George St., Toronto, Ontario M5R 2P8 (Phone: (416) 324-9080, Fax: (416) 929-5485).

Smandych, R., G. Dodds, and A. Esau, eds. (1991). *Dimensions of Childhood: Essays on the History of Children and Youth in Canada.* Winnipeg: Legal Research Institute.
A good example of current work in child and youth history in Canada. Of particular interest is John Bullen's article on the Children's Aid movement.

REFERENCES

Barman, J. (1989). Constructing the historical ethnography of childhood through oral history. Paper presented at the Annual Meeting of the American Educational Research Association. San Francisco, CA, 27 March–1 April. ERIC, ED307022.

Burke, M.A., S. Crompton, A. Jones, and K. Nessner. (1991). Caring for children. *Canadian Social Trends*, Catalogue no. 11-008E. Ottawa: Statistics Canada.

Cahan, E. (1989). *Past Caring: A History of U.S. Preschool Care and Education for the Poor, 1820–1965.* New York: National Center for Children in Poverty, Columbia University.

Child Care Resource and Research Unit. (1993). *Child Care in Canada: Provinces and Territories.* Toronto: CRRU.

Deasey, D. (1978). *Education under Six*. London, UK: Croom Helm.

Friendly, M. (1994). *Child Care Policy in Canada: Putting the Pieces Together*. Toronto: Addison-Wesley.

Gallagher-Ross, K. (1990). *Child Care — Your Choice*. TVO videotape.

Gluck, S., ed. (1991). *Women's Words: The Feminist Practice of Oral History*. New York: Routledge.

Hendrick, J. (1993). *The Whole Child* (2nd Canadian ed). Don Mills, ON: Maxwell Macmillan.

Kaiser, B., and J.S. Rasminsky. (1991). *The Daycare Handbook*. Toronto: Little, Brown & Co.

Lind, L., and S. Prentice. (1992). *Their Rightful Place — An Essay on Children, Families and Childcare in Canada*. Toronto: Our Schools/Ourselves Education Foundation.

Lummis, T. (1987). *Listening to History*. London, UK: Hutchinson.

Peters, D., and A. Pence, eds. (1992). *Family Day Care: Current Research for Informed Public Policy*. New York: Teachers College Press.

Rooke, P., and R. Schnell. (1983). *Discarding the Asylum: From Child Rescue to the Welfare State in English Canada, 1800–1950*. Lanham, MD: University Press of America.

Sissons, B., and B. McDowell. (1992). *Choosing with Care*. Toronto: Addison-Wesley.

Statistics Canada. (1991). National child care survey. *Perspectives*.

Statistics Canada. (1992a). *Canadian Child Care in Context: Perspectives of the Provinces and Territories*. (2 vols). Ottawa: Health and Welfare Canada.

Statistics Canada. (1992b). *Canadian Families and Their Child Care Arrangements: The Canadian National Child Care Study*. Ottawa: Statistics Canada and the National Day Care Research Network.

Statistics Canada. (1994). Robert Glossop on the Canadian family. Interview in *Canadian Social Trends*, Catalogue No. 11-008E. Ottawa: Supply and Services Canada.

Status of Women, Canada. (1986). *Report of the Task Force on Child Care*. Ottawa: Minister of Supply and Services.

Vanier Institute of the Family. (n.d.). *Canadian Families in Transition: The Implications and Challenges of Change*. Ottawa: Vanier Institute of the Family.

Woodill, G. (1986). The international roots of North American early childhood education. *International Journal of Early Childhood* 18 (1): 6–21.

APPENDIX
Bibliographies of High-Quality Children's Books

The following bibliographies are presented to help you build your own collection of books. Most of them have been used by early childhood educators for many years and count among children's favourites.

BOOKS FOR PRE-READERS

Barton, B.H. (1987). *Machines at Work.* New York: Harper-Collins.

Brown, M. (1980). *Finger Rhymes.* New York: Dutton.

Butterworth, N. (1989). *Just Like Jasper!* Boston: Little, Brown & Co.

Calmenson, S. (1989). *What Am I? Very First Riddles.* HarperCollins.

Christelow, E. (1990). *Five Little Monkeys Jumping on the Bed.* New York: Clarion.

Demarest, C. (1988). *No Peas for Nellie.* New York: Macmillan.

Ehlert, L. (1988). *Planting a Rainbow.* New York: Harcourt Brace Jovanovich.

Ehlert, L. (1989). *Color Farm.* New York: Harper & Row/ HarperCollins.

Ehlert, L. (1989). *Color Zoo.* New York: Harper & Row/ HarperCollins.

Goennel, H. (1990). *Colors.* Boston, MA: Little, Brown & Co.

Guarino, D. (1989). *Is Your Mama a Llama?* New York: Scholastic.

Hill, E. (1987). *Spot Goes to the Farm.* New York: Putnam.

Kasza, K. (1988). *The Pig's Picnic.* New York: Putnam.

Landstrom, O., and L. Landstorm. (1992). *Will's New Cap.* New York: R & S Books.

McMillan, B. (1988). *Growing Colors.* New York: Lothrop.

Miller, M. (1988). *Whose Hat?* New York: Greenwillow.

Oxenbury, H. (1989). *Tom and Pippo and the Dog.* New York: Aladdin.

Reid, B. (1991). *Zoe's Rainy Day.* Toronto: HarperCollins. (Series.)

Stock, C. (1990). *Christmas Time.* New York: Bradburry.

Stock, C. (1990). *Halloween Monster.* New York: Bradburry.

Tafuri, N. (1988). *Spots, Feathers and Curly Tails.* New York: Greenwillow.

Wells, R. (1992). *Voyage to the Bunny Planet.* New York: Dial.

Westcott, N. (1987). *Peanut Butter and Jelly.* New York: Dutton.

BOOKS FOR EMERGENT READERS

The following books can be used as basic classroom materials. Some have large print, others have pattern sentences, and others have cumulative elements.

Barton, B. (1991). *The Three Bears.* New York: HarperCollins.

Bogart, J.E. (1991). *Sarah Saw a Blue Macaw.* Toronto: Scholastic.

Brown, M.W. (1947). *Goodnight Moon.* New York: Harper & Row.

Carle, E. (1987). *Have You Seen My Cat?* New York: Scholastic.

Carlson, N. (1990). *I Like Me!* New York: Puffin.

Domanska, J. (1969). *The Turnip.* New York: Macmillan.

Emberley, B. (1974). *Drummer Hoff.* New York: Simon & Schuster.

Fox, M. (1989). *Shoes from Grandpa.* New York: Orchard Books.

Geisert, A. (1991). *Oink.* Boston, MA: Houghton Mifflin.

Hutchins, P. (1968). *Rosie's Walk.* New York: Macmillan.

Hutchins, P. (1989). *The Doorbell Rang.* New York: Morrow.

Inkpen, M. (1990). *The Blue Balloon.* Boston, MA: Little, Brown & Co.

Kraus, R. (1972). *Whose Mouse Are You?* New York: Macmillan.

Noble, T.H. (1986). *The Day Jimmy's Boa Ate the Wash.* New York: Dial.

Numeroff, L.J. (1985). *If You Give a Mouse a Cookie.* New York: Harcourt Brace Jovanovich.

Rice, E. (1983). *Goodnight, Goodnight.* New York: Puffin.

Sendak, M. (1962). *Chicken Soup with Rice.* New York: Harcourt Brace Jovanovich.

Tafuri, N. (1989). *The Ball Bounced.* New York: Greenwillow.

Waddell, M. (1992). *Owl Babies.* Boston, MA: Candlewick.

Walsh, E.S. (1989). *Mouse Paint.* New York: Harcourt Brace Jovanovich.

Wiesner, D. (1991). *Tuesday.* New York: Clarion.

Williams, S. (1990). *I Went Walking.* New York: Delacorte.

Wood, A. (1984). *The Napping House.* New York: Harcourt Brace Jovanovich.

Zolotow, C. (1985). *William's Doll.* New York: Harper-Collins.

BIG BOOKS

Barbour, K. (1990). *Little Nino's Pizzeria.* New York: Harcourt Brace Jovanovich.

Brown, R. (1981). *A Dark, Dark Tale.* New York: Dial.

Cole, J. (1986). *The Magic School Bus at the Waterworks.* New York: Scholastic.

Dodds, D.A. (1989). *Wheel Away!* New York: Scholastic.

Dunbar, J. (1990). *Ten Little Mice.* New York: Harcourt Brace Jovanovich.

Ehlert, L. (1988). *Planting a Rainbow.* New York: Harcourt Brace Jovanovich.

Fox, M. (1989). *Night Noises.* New York: Harcourt Brace Jovanovich/Gulliver.

Kraus, R. (1970). *Whose Mouse Are You?* New York: Scholastic.

Martin, B. (1991). *The Happy Hippopotami.* New York: Harcourt Brace Jovanovich.

Most, B. (1990). *The Cow That Went Oink.* New York: Harcourt Brace Jovanovich.

Walsh, E.S. (1989). *Mouse Paint.* New York: Harcourt Brace Jovanovich.

ABC BOOKS

Aylsworth, J. (1992). *Old Black Fly.* New York: Henry Holt.

Blades, A. (1985). *The Sea Alphabet Book.* Toronto: Kids Can Press.

Ehlert, L. (1989). *Eating the Alphabet: Fruits and Vegetables from A to Z.* San Diego: Harcourt Brace Jovanovich.

Harrison, T. (1982). *A Northern Alphabet.* Montreal: Tundra Books.

Lobel, A. (1990). *Alison's Zinnia.* New York: Greenwillow.

Martin, B., Jr., and J. Archambault. (1989). *Chicka Chicka Boom Boom.* New York: Simon & Schuster.

Merriam, E. (1987). *Halloween ABC.* New York: Macmillan.

Van Allsburg, C. (1987). *The Z Was Zapped.* Boston: Houghton Mifflin.

BOOKS ABOUT FAMILY LIFE

Galloway, Priscilla. (1985). *Jennifer Has Two Daddies.* Toronto: Women's Press.

Hogan, Paula Z. (1993). *Will Dad Ever Move Back Home?* Chatham, NJ: Raintree Steck-Vaughn.

Paris, Susan. (1986). *Mommy and Daddy Are Fighting.* Toronto: Seal Books.

Schein, J. (1988). *Forget Me Not.* Toronto: Annick Press.

Stinson, Kathy. (1984). *Mom and Dad Don't Live Together Anymore.* Toronto: Annick Press.

Stinson, Kathy. (1992). *Steven's Baseball Mitt.* Toronto: Annick Press.

BOOKS ABOUT FEELINGS

Boynton, Sandra. (1983). *A Is for Angry.* New York: Workman.

Brisson Murphy, Joanne. (1985). *Feelings.* Windsor, ON: Black Moss Press.

Crary, Elizabeth. (1992). *I'm Frustrated.* Seattle, WA: Parenting Press.

Munsch, Robert. (1979). *The Dark.* Toronto: Annick Press.

Simon, Norma. (1991). *I Am Not a Crybaby.* New York: Puffin Books.

Vecere, Joel. (1992). *A Story about Courage.* Chatham, NJ: Raintree Steck-Vaughn.

Wilhelm, Hans. (1985). *I'll Always Love You.* New York: Crown.

Zolotow, Charlotte. (1969). *The Hating Book.* New York: Harper & Row.

Photo Credits

Brittany Ber, age 3 — pages 259, 378
Janet Blaxall — pages 5, 10, 61, 73, 77, 80, 102, 137, 161, 164, 205, 213, 230, 290, 311, 347, 376
First Light/Niigata Photo Library — page 28
Brett Lamb — pages 36, 55, 107, 177, 223, 236, 249, 341
Jessica Lute, age 5 — pages 13, 364

Masterfile/Nick White — page 23
Jenayr Radojkovic, age 3 — page 155
Paul Till — pages 3, 9, 44, 49, 69, 75, 84, 96, 111, 122, 127, 132, 141, 149, 193, 196, 201, 216, 242, 255, 263, 265, 271, 274, 279, 297, 317, 328, 335, 352
Paul Williams — pages 15, 27, 40, 167, 170, 182, 187, 290, 302, 321, 359, 379

Readers wishing further information on data provided through the co-operation of Statistics Canada may obtain copies of related publications by mail from Publications Sales, Statistics Canada, Ottawa, Ontario K1A 0T6, by phone at 1-613-951-7277 or toll-free 1-800-267-6677. You may also fax your order to 1-613-951-1584.

Name Index

A.B.C. Task Force, 120
Adams, H.B., 12
Ainsworth, M.D.S., 119
Allen, K.E., 73, 102, 103, 282
Alward, K., 231
Anderson, Z., 47, 93
Arbuthnot, M.H., 316
Atwood, M.E., 279

Bagnoto, S.J., 76
Banzet, S., 362
Beal, C., 342
Bear, S.A., 94
Beaty, J.J., 89, 90, 91, 92, 97, 103, 351, 352
Bettelheim, B., 316
Blatz, W., 364–65
Booth, D., 311
Bowers, L., 283
Bredekamp, S., 65, 227, 228, 229, 231
Brewer, J., 199–200
Brice, P., 29
Bronfenbrenner, U., 41, 42
Browne, K.W., 175–76, 227, 231, 235, 237
Buchanan, E., 312

Calkins, L.M., 313
Cambourne, B., 312
Canadian Association for Young Children (CAYC), 54, 314
Canadian Child Care Federation (CCCF), 54, 220
Carlsson-Paige, N., 159
Chandler, K., 236
Cherry, C., 284
Chess, S., 65, 66, 117, 119

Child Care Advocacy Association of Canada (CCAAC), 54
Chomsky, N., 301
Chud, G., 118, 131, 224
Clay, M.M., 313
Clewett, A., 185–86
Clifford, R.M., 240
Cochrane, D., 312
Cochrane, O., 312
Crain, W., 227, 229
Cullinan, B.E., 317
Curry, N.E., 145, 149, 156

Davis, M.D., 235
Dennis, M.G., 278
Dennis, W., 273, 278
dePaola, T., 316
DePauw, K., 275
Derman-Sparks, L., 120, 153, 224
Devries, R., 337
Dewey, J., 41
Doake, D., 316
Doherty-Derkowski, G., 11–12, 24

Ehlert, L., 316
Elkind, D., 65, 137, 227, 230–31, 346
Elley, W.B., 316
Erikson, E.H., 63, 69, 119, 145–48, 149
Ernst, G., 305
Eron, L.D., 29
Esbensen, S.B., 204

Fahlman, R., 118, 131
Fischer, P., 29
Froebel, F., 362

Galda, L., 317
Galdone, P., 311

Gallahue, D.L., 265, 282
Garcia, E.E., 71
Gartrell, D., 117
Geisert, A., 311
Ginsburg, H., 72, 229
Glossop, R., 25, 376
Goc Karp, G., 275
Goffin, S.G., 227, 238, 337
Goldhaber, J., 311
Gonzalez-Mena, J., 71, 77
Gordon, A., 175–76, 227, 231, 235, 237
Graves, D., 313
Greenspan, N.T., 63, 67, 114, 116, 120, 127–28
Greenspan, S., 63, 67, 113, 114–15, 116, 120, 127–28
Gruen, G., 197
Guralnick, M.J., 99, 130, 131

Harlow, H., 277
Harms, T., 240
Harris, J.R., 275, 276
Hayden, A.H., 94
Hendrick, J., 225, 227, 231
Heusman, L.R., 29
Hildebrand, V., 173
Hodgins, D., 161
Hoffman, L.W., 24
Holdaway, D., 316

International Reading Association (IRA), 314, 315
Ishee, N., 311

Johnson, C.N., 145, 149, 156
Jones, E., 224
Jost Missions Day Care, 363

Kagan, J., 154
Kamii, C., 41, 337
Karweit, N., 316
Klein, R., 29
Kohlberg, L., 41
Kontos, S., 42
Kostelnik, M.J., 197, 225, 338
Kritchevsky, S., 197, 201

Lahey, B., 275, 276
Laing, R.D., 347
Lee, D., 264
Lero, D.S., 23, 25
LeShan, E.J., 4, 5
Levin, D.E., 159
Lewin, R., 273
Lewis, H.P., 261
Lieberman, A.F., 113–14, 117
Liebert, R.M., 29, 275, 276
Locke, J., 362

Marbeau, J.-B.-F., 363
Margolin, E., 258
Marion, M., 185–86
Marotz, L., 73, 102, 103, 282
Martin, R., 319
Maslow, A., 113, 225
Matthews, G.B., 275
Mayer, M., 311
McGee, L.E., 316
McGill University Day Care, 364
McKenna, D., 236
Mead, M., 4
Metraux, R., 4
Mills, L., 260
Milner, D., 153
Mock, K.R., 221
Montessori, M., 330, 335–36
Morrow, L.M., 316, 321

National Action Committee on the
    Status of Women, 375
National Association for the
    Education of Young Children
    (NAEYC), 314
National Film Board of Canada, 277

Neisworth, J.T., 76
Newman, B.M., 158
Newman, P.R., 158
Nourot, P., 231

Oberlin, J.-F., 362
Oppenheim, J., 331
Opper, S., 72, 229
Ottawa Day Nursery, 363
Owen, R., 362

Parten, M.B., 75
Pastoret, Mme de, 362
Pearce, J.C., 4–5
Pestalozzi, H., 362
Peters, D., 42
Piaget, J., 41, 63, 72, 229–30,
    332–35
Pierce, K., 241–42
Plato, 10
Plimpton, C.E., 278
Poest, C.A., 279
Prescott, E., 197, 201
Public Nursery, Toronto, 363

Rand, M.K., 321
Regimal, C., 278
Richard, K.J., 305
Richgels, D.J., 316
Rimer, P., 84
Rogers, C., 145
Rosen, M., 311
Roskos, K., 321
Rousseau, J.J., 4

Santrock, J.W., 70, 71, 72, 119, 335
Saracho, O.N., 235
Scalena, S., 312
Scales, B., 231
Schmidt, R.A., 278
Schories, P., 311
Schurch, P., 222
Sendak, M., 316
Shaffer, D.R., 276, 277
Shermann, A., 348
Singer, D.G., 28

Singer, J.L., 28
Smith, J.K., 316
Smith, R.K., 94
Special Committee on Child Care,
    367
Spitz, R., 277
Spodek, B., 235
Sprafkin, J., 29
St. George's Nursery School, 365
St. George's School for Child Study,
    364
Statistics Canada, 24, 25
Sulzby, E., 316
Sunshine Day Care Program, 362
Sutherland, Z., 316

Task Force on Child Care, 367
Thomas, A., 65, 66, 117, 119
Tucker, W.H., 351, 352

United Way, 364

Van Hoorn, J., 231
Vanier Institute of the Family, 17,
    24, 25, 377
Viorst, J., 316
Von Hippel, C.S., 94
Vygotsky, L., 302, 330, 335

Wach, T.D., 197
Walling, L., 197, 201
Warberg, C., 236
Wells, G., 321
West End Crèche, Toronto, 365
Wiesner, D., 311
Williams, J.R., 279
Williams, T.M., 30
Witt, D.D., 279

Yeates, M.D., 236
Yolen, J., 317–18
Young, E., 316

Zolotow, C., 153
Zuckerman, D.M., 28

SUBJECT INDEX

Acceptance, of children, 150, 156–57
Activities, *see also* Transitions
    behaviour guidance and, 180
    free-play, 73–75
    gender roles in, 255
    peer interactions and, 132
    rest, 211
    space arrangement for, 131–32,
        198
Admiration, 157–58
Adult–child relationship, 67–68,
        101, 114, *see also* Child–edu-
        cator relationship
    behaviour and, 101
    child development and, 64–65,
        67–68
    communication in, 123–24
    dependency in, 114, 118–19
    emotional well-being and, 114,
        169
    predictability in, 149
Adults, *see also* Early childhood edu-
        cators; Parents
    dependency upon, 118–19
    playground design and, 205–206
    relationship with children, *see*
        Adult–child relationship
Advertising, on television, 29
Advocate, early childhood educator
        as, 105
Aesthetics, 253, *see also* Creativity
Affection, self-esteem and, 150
Affirmation, self-esteem and, 156–57
Aggression, *see also* Violence
    in behaviour, 164
    in society, 27
Alexander and the Terrible, Horrible,
    No Good, Very Bad Day
    (Viorst), 316
Allergies, to food, 213
Alligator Pie (Lee), 264

Anchor words, 301
Anecdotal records, 87–89, 103
Animals, 136
Approval, self-esteem and, 150
Art
    cognition and, 261–63
    creative, 260–64
    experiences, 263–64
    language and, 261
    movement and, 267
    music and, 267
Articulation, 71
The Art Lesson (dePaola), 316
Assessments, of children, 104–107
Asylums, for infants, 362
Audiotapes, in observation, 96
Auditory discrimination, *see* Hearing
Autonomy, in child development,
        146, 149–50

Balancing, 274, 280, 288
    equipment for, 286
Behaviour
    aggressive, 164
    changes in, 162–64
    consequences of, 178–79
    coping with, 173–74
    destructive, 69
    developmental diversity and, 76,
        83
    emotional development and, 67
    guidance of, 168–88
    inappropriate, 169–70, 185
    limits on, 174, 176–77
    mistaken, 169–70, 172
    observation of, 84, 100–101, 182
    peer acceptance and, 159
    recording of, 87–93
    redirection of, 184
    rules for, 174, 176–77
    self-esteem and, 158

Behaviourist theories, 41
Biases
    anti-bias curriculum, 223–24
    of educators, 119–20
Bilingualism, 314
Biographies, in children's literature,
        316
Body awareness, 265
Body language
    as creative expression, 261
    cultural differences in, 180
    in guidance, 179–80
Books, *see* Children's literature

Calming, of children, 118
Canadian Children (periodical), 54
Care-givers, *see also* Early childhood
        educators; Parents
    attitudes of, 170–71
    children's relationship with, 119
    early childhood educators as,
        44–45
    influence on emotional well-
        being, 113–14
    values of, 170–71
Caring, definition of, 44–45
Categorization
    development of, 334
    identity and, 152
Challenges
    mastery vs., 282–83
    physical, 288–89
Charity kindergartens, 363
Charity Organization Movement,
        364
Charter of Rights and Freedoms, 220
Checklists
    health and safety, 207, 208–210
    in observation, 93–94, 97
Child abuse, 26–28, *see also* Violence
    confidentiality and, 104

observation and, 84, 95
Child–adult relationship, *see* Adult–child relationship
Child care, 367–74
    administration of, 368, 372–73
    arrangements, 368, 372–73
    current issues in, 374–75
    effect on children, 24–25
    environment, *see* Learning environment
    funding of, 368
    history of, 361–67, 365–67
    home-based, 373
    legislation regarding, 366–68, 369–71
    non-parental, 23–25, 374
    providers of, 373–74
    quality of, 24
    societal attitudes toward, 374–75
    standards of, 368
    stress and, 9
    types of, 368, 372–73
    workplace, 362
Child Care Act, 1988, 367
Child care environment, *see* Learning environment
Child development, 62–78
    cognitive, 72–73
    culture and, 7–8
    curriculum and, 227–28
    effect of child care on, 12–13, 24
    family and, 7–8
    guidance relationship and, 172
    individual profiles of, 102
    interconnections in, 101, 121, 123–24
    language and, *see* Language development
    milestones of, 101–102, 103
    motor skills programs, *see* Motor skills
    norms of, 101–102, 103
    observation of, 96, 101–104
    physical, *see* Physical development
    social, *see* Social development
    study of, 364–65
    theories of, 64–65
    through play, *see* Play

Child–educator relationship, *see* Educator–child relationship
Childhood
    qualities of, 227
    views of, 4–5
Child–parent relationship, *see* Adult–child relationship; Families; Parents
Children
    acceptance of, 150, 156–57
    appreciation of, 85
    communication with, 45–46
    control of, 27, *see also under* Behaviour
    conversation with, 46
    custody of, 25
    diversity of, *see* Diversity
    dressing themselves, 7–8
    employed mothers and, 23–25, 364
    family breakup and, 25–26
    as individuals, *see* Individual children
    needs of, *see* Needs of children
    observation of, 84, 106–107
    pre-operational, 333
    profiles of, 102
    relationship with adults, *see* Adult–child relationship
    at risk, 8–9, 375–77
    society and, 26–27
    stress in, *see under* Stress
    television and, 28–31
    temperament of, 65–66
    viewpoint of, 6
Children's literature, 309–11, 317–20
    books about families, 134
    books about feelings, 135
    dramatizations of, 320–21
    literacy and, 316
    making lists of, 319
    wordless books, 311
Child-rescue movement, 362–63
Climbing structures, 205
Cognition, 331–32
    art and, 261–63
    definition of, 331
    language and, 343–44

play and, 343
Cognitive curriculum, 331, 344–47
    computer skills in, 351–52
    mathematics in, 350–51
    natural science in, 347–50
Cognitive development, 72–73
    culture and, 338–39
    curriculum for, *see* Cognitive curriculum
    developmental diversity and, 339–40
    experiential diversity and, 339
    gender and, 152, 341–43
    learning environment and, 345
    observation of, 95, 99, 343–44
    theories of, 332–35
    through creativity, 254
    through play, 233
Colleagues, consultation with, 104–105
Communication, 70–72, 120–22
    with children, 45–46, 177–80
    difficulty with, 121–22
    emotions and, 121, 123–24
    of ideas, 234
    language development and, 70–72, 121, 299–300
    nonverbal, 121, 179–80
    observation of, 99
    with parents, 48
    as a social skill, 129–30, 234
    stress in, 53
    temperament and, 121
    through play, 234
Community
    child and, 135–36
    curriculum and, 135–36, 236
    early childhood education and, 49–50
    services, 50
Competence, *see* Mastery
Computer as a Paintbrush, The, (Beaty and Tucker), 351
Computer skills, in cognitive curriculum, 351–52
Confidentiality, 104
Conflict, 53, 130
    cultural, 67

Consequences, sense of self and, 122–23
Constructive play, 74
Constructivist-interactionist learning, principles of, 337
Constructivist theory, of child development, 41, 231, 336–38
Consultation
  with colleagues, 104–105
  with specialists, 105
Consumerism, 29
Control
  of behaviour, 168
  by children, 149–50, *see als* Mastery; Success
  creativity and, 259
  loss of, 124–25, 186
  sense of self and, 122
  of children, 27
  self-, 172–73, 186
Conversations, *see also* Communication; Listening
  with children, 46, 95, 306–307
  observation of, 99
Co-operation
  guidance in, 170
  in play, 75, 130
  self-concept and, 157
Creativity, 251–68
  body language and, 261
  cognitive development through, 254
  control and, 259
  culture and, 255–56
  definition of, 252
  development of, 252–55
  divergent thinking and, 254
  emotional development through, 253–54
  environment of, 258–59
  language and, 267–68
  movement and, 265–66, 267
  nurturing of, 257–60
  observation of, 256–57
  outdoor space and, 266
  physical development and, 254–55
  play and, 233, 258
  process approach to, 259–60

  programming and, 258
  self-esteem through, 254
  visualization and, 265–66
Crèches, 363–64
Cultural diversity, 18–21, 255
  in body language, 180
  child-care environment and, 131
  in the curriculum, 220–22
  dramatic play centre and, 134
  in food, 213
  relationships and, 119–20
  self-awareness and, 133
Culture
  child development and, 7–8
  cognitive development and, 338–39
  creativity and, 255–56
  diversity in, 338
  identity and, 153–54
  language development and, 303
  motor development and, 278
Curriculum, *see also* Scheduling
  anti-bias, 223–24, *see also* Biases
  child-centred, 85
  cognitive, *see* Cognitive curriculum
  community and, 236
  cultural diversity in, 220–22
  decision making about, 235–37
  design, 47–49
  developmental diversity and, 224–25
  developmentally appropriate, 227–31
  educators' role in, 241–42
  emergent, 237–39
  evaluation of, 239–41
  family in, 133–34
  gender differences and, 223
  for individuals, 228–29
  integrated, 226
  interaction skills for, 132
  language development and, 306–11
  languages in, 221–22
  legislation regarding, 236–37
  literacy, 315
  multiculturalism and, 221–22

  observation and, 85, 239–40, 242
  parents and, 236
  planning, 65
  play-based, 48, 231–35
  self-awareness and, 65, 132
  space arrangement and, 198
  spontaneity in, 239, 349–50

Day care, *see* Child care
Day nurseries, 363–64
Day Nurseries Act, 1945, 365
Day orphans, 363
Density, of creative environment, 258–59
Developmental diversity, 6–7, 75–76, 83–84, 224–25
  cognitive development and, 339–40
  curriculum and, 224–25
  in language, 304
  in motor development, 278–79
  in motor skills, 274
  observation of, 83–84
  in reading readiness, 319, 320
  in sensory development, 278–79
  socioemotional development and, 130–31
Developmentally challenged
  initiative and, 150–51
  self-concept of, 156
Development of children, *see* Child development
Digging areas, in playground, 205
Directions, to children, 100–101, 177, 178
Disadvantaged children, *see* Special needs children
Discipline
  of children, 27, 174
Discovery learning, 332
Distraction, in behaviour guidance, 184
Divergent thinking, 258, 260
  creativity and, 254
Diversity, 133
  of children, 6–8
  cultural, 255, *see* Cultural diversity
  in development, *see* Developmental diversity

experiential, *see* Experiential
    diversity
of individuals, 223–24
of learning styles, 340–41
programs and, 8
Divorce, *see* Marriage breakup
Dolls, race and, 153, 154
Dramatic play, 160–61, 334
    language in, 308
Dramatic play centres, 133–34, 199,
    346
Dramatization, of stories, 320–21
Drawing
    observation of, 95
    writing and, 313–14

Early childhood education, 10–13
    community and, 49–50
    history of, 361–67
    inclusive, 224–25
    influence on children's lives, 9–10
    legislation regarding, 367–68
    philosophy of, 40–43, 379
    principles of, 219
    as a profession, 50–55, 377–79
    programs in, 11
    quality in, 11–12
    reflective practice in, 43–44
    theories of, 40–43
Early childhood educators, 38–55,
    see also Adults; Care-givers
    attitudes of, 38–39, 170–71, 221
    as care-givers, 44–45
    children's identification with, 154
    education of, 43
    ethical responsibilities of, 52
    influence on emotional
        well-being, 113–14
    life-histories of, 38–39
    relationships with children, *see*
        Educator–child relationship
    relationships with families, 46–47,
        378
    rights of, 52–53
    role in cognitive development,
        345–47
    role in curriculum, 241–42
    roles of, 44–50

self-evaluation of, 242
self-knowledge of, 38–39
self-nurturing of, 39–40
stress in, 53–54
television and, 31
values of, 170–71
Ecological theory, of child develop-
    ment, 41–43
Economic insecurity, 20–22, *see also*
    Poverty
    the family and, 376
Educator–child relationship, 45–46,
    171–72, 377–78, *see also*
        Adult–child relationship
    socioeconomic differences in,
        119–20
Educators, *see* Early childhood edu-
    cators
Emergent curriculum, 237–39
Emergent literacy, 311–14
Emotional development, 66–69
    ideas and, 123–25
    milestones of, 114–25
    observation of, 96, 97
    social development and, 128–31
    tasks in, 67–68
    thinking and, 125
    through creativity, 253–54
Emotional well-being, 113–14,
    125–27
    adult–child relationship and, 169
    guidance relationship and, 172
    motor and sensory skills and, 284,
        285
Emotions
    control of, 186–87
    development diversity and, 76
    expression of, 69, 232
    play and, 74, 232
    smell and, 276
Employment
    changes in, 20–22
    of mothers, *see under* Mothers
    rights in, 52–53
Encouragement, in self-esteem,
    157–58
English as a second language, 20,
    118, 121–22

Environment
    of creativity, 258–59
    early childhood, 194–213
Environmental issues, 137
Environment Rating Scale, 240
Equipment, 286–87
    arrangement of, 131–32
    for the disabled, 133
    familiarity with, 198, 201
    in learning centres, 198, 201
    for motor skills programs, 283
    outdoor, 205–206
    safety of, 204
    for social play, 196–97
Evaluation
    of curriculum, 239–41
    of early childhood environment,
        206–207
    self-evaluation of educators, 242
Event sampling, 91–92
Exosystem, 42
Experiential development, curricu-
    lum and, 221–22
Experiential diversity
    cognitive development and, 72,
        339
    cultural, 76–77
    new situations and, 117–19
Exploration
    motor and sensory, 283
    sensory, 334
Expressive jargon, 301

Fairy tales, 316
Families
    books about, 134
    breakup of, *see* Marriage breakup
    child development and, 7–8
    composition of, 16–18
    conferences with, 105–106
    culture, creativity, and, 255
    in curriculum, 133–34
    dangers to children in, 23
    economic status of, 20–22
    emergent curriculum and, 237–38
    emotional development and,
        117–19
    employment and, 20–22

financial pressure on, 376–77
language development and,
    303–304
lifestyle of, 23, see also Culture
at risk, 375–77
stress in, 9, 22, 376–77
support of, 46–47
technology and, 23
violence within, 26–28, 377
Fantasy stories, 316
Farms, effect of technological change
    on, 21
Fathers
    as care-givers, 17
    effect of divorce on, 25
    effect of mother's employment
        on, 24
Feathers for Lunch (Ehlert), 316
Feelings, curriculum planning and,
    135
Feeling Yes, Feeling No (National Film
    Board of Canada), 277
Finger plays, language development
    and, 309
Flannel boards, 311
Floor time, 127–28
Folk tales, 316
Food, 212–13
    allergies, 213
    cultural differences in, 213
    on television, 29
Free kindergartens, 363
Free-play activities, 73–75
Friendships, 128–29, 131
    in the curriculum, 134–35
Functional play, 74
Furnishings, for social play, 196–97

Games, cultural identity and, 154
Gender differences, 133
    cognitive development and,
        341–43
    curriculum and, 223
    learning environment and, 197
    in motor experiences, 278
    roles in activities, 255
    on television, 29
    toys and, 342

in treatment of child, 119
Gender identity, 152–53
    cognitive growth and, 152
    occupations and, 153
    parents and, 152–53
    possessions and, 152
Global concerns, 136–37
"Goodness of fit," 119, 120
Groups
    individuals vs., 168
    space for activities, 198
Guidance
    body language in, 179–80
    distraction in, 184
    language of, 177–80
    nonverbal, 179–80
    physical, 184–85
    process, 173–77
    punishment vs., 175–76
    relationship, 168–73
    techniques, 180–87
        direct, 182, 184–87
        indirect, 180–82
    verbal, 177–79
Guided imagery, 266
Guilt, 146–48, 151
Gustation, see Taste

Have You Seen Birds? (Oppenheim),
    331
Health, see Emotional well-being;
    Physical well-being
Hearing, 275–76
    activities, 287, 292
    impairments and language devel-
        opment, 304
Heroes, see Superheroes
Holophrases, 301
Home, see Culture; Families; Parents
Housekeeping play area, 154

Ideas
    emotional, 123–25
    through play, 234
Identity, 151–55
    culture and, 153–54
    gender, 152–53
    possessions and, 152

race and, 153–54
Imagery, guided, 266
Immigrants, see also Culture
    children of, 18–19, 118
    English-speaking, 19
    non-English-speaking, 20
Immigration, changes in, 19–21
Incidents, recording of, 87–93
Inclusive education, 224–25
    curriculum in, 225
Individual children, 49
    in constructivist theory, 337
    curriculum planning and,
        132–33, 228–29
    diversity of, 223–24
    groups vs., 168
    language curriculum and, 305
    needs of, 182
Infants
    asylums, 362
    motor development of, 273
    schools, 363
    sensory development of, 252–53,
        274–75
    speech of, 301
Infants' Hospital, Vancouver, 363
Inferences, in observation, 86
Initiative, 146–48, 150–51
Insecurity
    economic, 20–22
    self-concept and, 162–64
Interactionist theories, of child
    development, 41
Interaction (periodical), 54
Interactive play, 127–28
Interpretations, of observations, 86,
    101
Interviews
    with children, 94–95
    with parents, 95
    play, 94–95, 103
Isolation, 186

Jobs, see Employment

Kindergartens, 362, 363
Kinesthesis, 265, 276
    activities, 292

writing and, 321
Knitting schools, 362
Knowledge
  development through play, 233
  physical, 334

Language
  acquisition of, 300–303
  art and, 261
  cognition and, 343–44
  communication difficulties and, 121
  creativity and, 267–68
  emotional ideas and, 123–24
  of guidance, 177–80
  observation of, 99, 256–57
  play and, 234, 335
  social interactions and, 308, 335
  symbolic, 303
Language development, 70–72, 300–308
  communication and, 299–300
  curriculum and, 306–11
  diversity in, 304
Languages
  in the curriculum, 221–22
  curriculum for individual children, 305
  dialects of, 305
  first, 71–72
  of immigrants, 19–20
  second, 118, 121–22, 304–305
Learners, types of, 340
Learning
  child development and, 104
  creative, 257–58
  curriculum and, 227–28
  discovery, 332
  diversity of styles in, 83, 340–41
  observation of, 99
  process-oriented, 234
  scheduling of, 207
  through play, 233–34
Learning centres, 197–201
  for motor and sensory skills, 285, 290, 291
Learning environment
  atmosphere of, 196

cognitive development and, 345
gender stereotyping in, 197
for motor development, 279, 282–87
multicultural influences in, 222
needs and, 195–96
observation of the, 206–207
planning of, 194–213
self-concept and, 148
socioemotional development and, 131–37
Learning theories, 41
Legislation
  child day care, 366–67, 369–70
  curriculum and, 236–37
  safety, 207
  of space arrangement, 202
Listening, 46, 180, see also Conversations
Literacy
  children's literature and, 316
  curriculum, 315
  development of, 315
  emergent, 311–14
  family and, 303–304
  instruction, 314–21
  play and, 320–21
  television and, 31
Locomotor challenges, 288–89
Locomotor skills, 273–74, 280–81
  equipment for, 286
Lon Po Po (Young), 316
Love circles, 362

Macrosystem, 42–43
Mainstreaming, 224
Manipulation, 336
  challenges, 289
  equipment for, 286
  skills, 274, 281–82
Marriage breakup, 9, 22–23, 25–26
Mastery, see also Control; Success
  challenges vs., 282–83
  computers and, 351
  self-concept and, 155–56
Mathematics, in cognitive curriculum, 350–51
Maturation

motor development and, 277
theories regarding, 41
Memory, in observation, 89
Mental activity, definition of, 231
Mesosystem, 42
Microsystem, 41–42
"Mine" syndrome, 157
Miseducation, 230–31
Mistakes, 169–70, 172, see also Behaviour
Models, see Role models
Mothers
  as care-givers, 17
  effect of divorce on, 25
  employed, 21, 22, 23–25, 364, 365
Motor development, 73, 273–74, 280–82
  concerns about, 279
  diversity in, 274, 278–79
  gender differences in, 278
  impairments and, 277
  large, 73
  learning environment for, 279, 282–87
  observation of, 278–79
  play and, 74
Motor skills, 73, 95
  large, 100, 273, 281
    equipment for, 286
    learning centres for, 285–89
  learning centres for, 285, 290, 291
  small, 73, 100, 273, 282, 286, 290, 291
Mouse Around (Schories), 311
Movement
  art and, 267
  creative, 265–66
  music and, 267
  space for, 132, 266
Multiculturalism, 196, 220–21
  curriculum and, 221–22
Multilingualism, 19, 20, 304–305, see also Languages
Music, 264–65
  art and, 267
  creative movement and, 267

language development and, 309
Names, self-esteem and, 156–57
National Child Care Strategy, 367
Natural science, *see* Science
Needs of children, 77, 102, *see also*
    Special needs children
    emotional, 113
    learning environment and, 195–96
    peers and, 128
    response to, 182
    scheduling and, 207, 210–12
    social, 131
    stress and, 53
Nonverbal communication, 121
Normality, 6–7
"Notel," 30
Nutrition, 212–13

Objectivity, in observation, 86
Observation, 82–107
    audiotapes used in, 96
    of behaviour, 162–63, 182
    of characteristics, 92–93
    children's attitudes toward,
        106–107
    of cognitive development, 99–100,
        343–44
    communicating findings of,
        104–107
    of communication, 99
    of conversation, 99
    of creativity, 256–57
    of the curriculum, 239–40, 242
    of development, 101–104
    drawings and, 95
    of the early childhood environ-
        ment, 206–207
    inferences in, 86
    interpretations of, 86, 101
    interviews used in, 95
    of language, 99, 256–57
    of learning, 99–100
    memory in, 89
    methods of, 86–96
    of motor development, 278–79
    objectivity in, 86
    of problems, 84
    purposes of, 85–86

records of, 104, 257
of self-concept development,
    160–64
of sensory development, 278–79
subjectivity in, 86
of temperament, 96
use of data, 103–104
videotapes used in, 96
writing stories and, 95
Occupations, gender identity and,
    153
Oink (Geisert), 311
Olfaction, *see* Smell
Open space, 197
Orphanages, 363
Orthopedic impairment, motor
    development and, 277
Outdoor space, 203–206, *see also*
    Playgrounds
    creativity and, 266
    equipment for, 205–206
    zones of, 204–205
Owl Moon (Yolen), 317–18

Parallel play, 75, 253
Paraphrasing, 46
Parent–child relationship, 119, *see*
    also Adult–child relationship;
    Families
Parents, *see also* Adults; Care-givers;
    Fathers; Mothers
    children's identification with, 154
    children's separation from, 115–16
    communication with, 48
    conferences with, 105–106
    curriculum and, 236
    effect of divorce on, 25
    gender identity and, 152–53
    interviews with, 95
    relationship of ECE with, 47
Pathways, 201–202
Peers
    acceptance by, 158–60
    emotional needs and, 128
    interactions with, 132
    language development and, 308
    relationships with, 69–70
Phonology, 71

Physical activity, definition of, 231
Physical development, 73
    creativity and, 254–55
Physically challenged, initiative and,
    150–51
Physical well-being
    learning centres and, 285, 290
    observation of, 100
Platforms, 205
Play, 11
    child development through, 232
    child-directed, 235
    cognition and, 233, 343
    communication of ideas through,
        234
    constructive, 74
    co-operative, 75, 130
    creativity and, 233, 258
    curriculum based on, 48, 231–35
    dramatic, 334
    emotions and, 74, 131, 232
    environment for, 196–97
    functional, 74
    indoor space for, 197–203
    interactive, 127–28
    interviews, 94–95, 103
    language and, 234, 335
    learning through, 233–34
    literacy and, 320–21
    motor, 74
    outdoor space for, 203–206
    parallel, 75, 253
    patterns of, 73–75
    pretend, 320, 334
    problem solving through, 233
    self-concept and, 160–61
    self-knowledge through, 232
    sensory, 74
    skills development through, 232,
        234
    social, 75, 98, 196–97, 232
    social skills and, 96, 98–99
    sociodramatic, 74
    solitary, 75, 98
    superheroes in, 204–205
    units, 201–202
Playgrounds
    design of, 203–206

equipment for, 283
Poetry, 316
Poor children, education of, 362
Positioning, in behaviour guidance, 181–82
Possessions, self-identity and, 157
Poverty, 20, *see also* Economic insecurity
  the family and, 377
  of single-parent families, 25
  stress of, 9
Power struggles, 149–50, 185
Pragmatics, 70
Praise, *see* Admiration
Pre-operational children, 333
Pre-operational thinking, 72, 99
Pressuring, of children, 230–31
Pretend play, 320, 334
Problem solving
  in behaviour guidance, 182, 184
  through play, 233
Process approach, to creativity, 259–60
Process-oriented learning, 234
Programming for Friendship (Guralnick), 131
Programs, *see* Curriculum; Scheduling
Proprioception, 276
  activities, 292
Punishment, 174
  guidance vs., 175-76
Puppets, 311

Quality Matters (Doherty-Derkowski), 11–12

Race, *see* Culture
Racism, 21
Rating scales, 92–93
Reading
  to children, 309–10, 318
  development of, 312–13
  readiness, 319, 320
Realistic fiction, 316
Reception areas, 203
Records, *see also* Checklists; Samples
  anecdotal, 87–89, 103
  confidentiality of, 104

of observations, 104, 257
  running, 89–91, 103
Redirection, of behaviour, 184
Reflective practice, 43–44
Regulations, *see* Legislation
Relationships, *see also* Adult–child relationships; Educator–child relationships; Parents; Peers
  formation of, 119–20
  social, 129–31
Relaxation
  exercises, 284
  techniques, 118
Responsibilities, observing responses to, 100
Rest activities, 211
Risk, children at, 8–9, 375–77
Risk taking, 150–51
Role models, *see also* Superheroes
  children's identification with, 154
  educators as, 130
Role-playing, 160–61, 232, 257
The Rough-Face Girl (Martin), 319
Routines, planning of, 207, 211
Running records, 89–91, 103
Rural communities, effect of technological change on, 21

Safety
  of children, 23
  of community, 50
  of equipment, 204, 283
  physical, 207
Salary scale, 52
Sandboxes, 205
Scheduling, 207, 210–12, *see also* Curriculum
  observation of children and, 100
Science
  cognition and, 348–49
  in cognitive curriculum, 347–50
  spontaneous curriculum and, 349–50
Security, sense of, 115–19
Self, sense of, 122–23
Self-awareness, curriculum planning and, 132
Self-concept, 67, 114, 143–65

definition of, 144
  negative, 162
  observation of, 160–64
  play and, 160–61
  positive, 161–62
  theories of, 144–48
Self-confidence, 150–51, 161–62
Self-control, *see under* Control
Self-doubt, 123
Self-esteem, 156–58
  definition of, 144
  through creativity, 254
Self-knowledge, through play, 232
Semantic aspects, of children's language, 71
Senses
  activities for, 292
  in creative learning, 259
  development of, 253, 274–77, 334
  observation of, 278–79
  equipment for development of, 286–87
  exploration of, 263–64
  of infants, 252–53
  information through, 275
  language in, 308
  learning centres for development of, 285, 290, 291
  use in play, 74
Sensory experiences, 291, 292
  curriculum for, 291
  vocabulary for, 291, 293
Separation anxiety, 115–16
Shyness, 159–60
Single-parent families, poverty of, 25
Smell, 276
  activities, 292
  equipment for, 287
Social development, 69–70, 158–60
  emotional development and, 128–31
  observation of, 96, 98–99
  play and, 96, 98–99
Social interactions, language in, 308, 335
Social play, 75, 98, 232
  equipment and furnishings for, 196–97

language in, 308
Social skills, 129–31
Society, *see also* Community
  attitudes toward children, 26–27
  curriculum planning and, 136
  threats to children in, 23
Socioemotional development,
    128–31
  child-care environment and,
    131–37
Songs, 264
  language development and, 309
Sorry, saying of, 185
Space
  arrangement of, 131–32, 202–203
    behaviour guidance and, 180
    legislation regarding, 202
    supervision and, 202
  in creative links, 268
  for movement, 266
  open, 197
  play, 197–206
    indoor, 197–203
    outdoor, 204–206
  private, 197
Specialists, consultation with, 105
Special needs children, *see also* Hear-
    ing; Orthopedic impairment;
    Speech
  curriculum planning for, 224–25
  self-concept of, 155–56
Speech impairments, language
    development and, 304
  pre-linguistic, 301
  private, 302
  telegraphic, 301
Spontaneous curriculum, 239
  language and, 308
  science and, 349–50
Sports-related movement, 274
Stability
  challenges, 288
  skills, 274, 280
Staff meetings, 105
Standards, of child care, 368
Stereotypes, 223–24, *see also* Culture;
    Diversity; Gender differences
  on television, 29

Stories, *see also* Children's literature
  children's, observation and, 95
  dramatization of, 311, 320–21
Storytelling, 310–11
Stress
  in children, 8–9, 375–77
  in early childhood educators,
    53–54
  from economic change, 22
  in families, 375–77
  from family breakup, 25–26
  language development and, 303
  reduction of, 182, 183
  time and, 25
Subjectivity, in observation, 86
Subsidies, for child care, 368
Success, *see also* Control; Mastery
  sense of self and, 122
Superheroes, 160, *see also* Role models
  identification with, 154–55
  in play, 204–205
Symbolic language, 303
Symbolic thinking, 334
Syntax, 71

Tactile skills, *see* Touch
Taste, 276
  activities, 292
  equipment for, 287
Teachers, *see* Early childhood educa-
    tors
"Teacher talk," 177
Technological change
  effect on economy, 21–22
  effect on family, 23
Technology, 264
  in early childhood education,
    351–52
  society and, 376
Teeny Tiny Woman (Galdone), 311
Telegraphic speech, 301
Television
  early childhood education and, 31
  impact on family, 28–31
Temperament, 65–66
  communication and, 121
  development diversity and, 76
  differences in, 66

new situations and, 117
  observation of, 96
There's a Nightmare in My Closet
    (Mayer), 311
Thinking
  creativity and, 254
  divergent, 258, 260
  emotional, 125
  pre-operational, 72, 99
  symbolic, 334
The Three Billy Goats Gruff (Galdone),
    311
Time
  in creative links, 268
  "crunch," 25
  pressure on families, 377
  sampling, 91
  understanding of, 334
"Time-out" strategy, 186
Toddlers, 146
  creativity in, 253
  emotional ideas of, 123
Touch, 276–77
  activities, 292
  equipment for, 286–87
  materials for, 336
  sensitivity development, 276–77
Toys, 196, *see also* Dolls
  gender and, 342
Transfer of learning, to outdoors, 203
Transitions
  planning of, 207, 211
  reading during, 319
Traumas, 117–18
Trust, self-concept and, 149
Tuesday (Wiesner), 311

United Nations Convention on the
    Rights of the Child, 361
Units, play, 201–202

Values, of early childhood educators,
    38–39
Vestibular apparatus, 276
Videotapes, in observation, 96
Violence
  the family and, 26–28, 377
  on television, 29

Visible minorities, 20, 21, *see also* Cultural diversity
Vision, 275
   activities, 292
   equipment for, 287
   impairment and motor development, 277
   materials, cultural identity and, 154
Vision (periodical), 54
Visualization, creative, 265–66

Vocabulary, development of, 306–307

Well-being
   emotional, *see* Emotional well-being
   physical, *see* Physical well-being
We're Going on a Bear Hunt (Rosen), 311
Where the Wild Things Are (Sendak), 316
"Whole child" philosophy, 225–26

William's Doll (Zolotow), 153
Withdrawal, 162–64
   in behaviour guidance, 185–87
Words, *see also* Language
   anchor, 301
Working mothers, *see under* Mothers
Writing, 321
   development of, 313–14
   observation of, 95

Zones, outdoor, 204–205

Reader Reply Card

We are interested in your reaction to *Children at the Centre: Principles of Early Childhood Education in Canada,* by Janet Blaxall, Kenise Murphy Kilbride, Donna McKenna, Carolyn Warberg, and Marilynn Yeates. You can help us to improve this book in future editions by completing this questionnaire.

1. What was your reason for using this book?

   ❏ university course   ❏ continuing education course   ❏ personal interest

   ❏ college course   ❏ professional development   ❏ other _____

2. If you are a student, please identify your school and the course in which you used this book.

3. Which chapters or parts of this book did you use? Which did you omit?

4. What did you like best about this book?

5. What did you like least about this book?

6. Please identify any topics you think should be added to future editions.

7. Please add any comments or suggestions.

8. May we contact you for further information?

   Name: _____

   Address: _____

   _____

   Phone: _____

(fold here and tape shut)

Heather McWhinney
Publisher, College Division
HARCOURT BRACE & COMPANY, CANADA
55 HORNER AVENUE
TORONTO, ONTARIO
M8Z 9Z9